GREATER DUBLIN
Streetfinder Atlas

Contents

Tourist & travel information 2
Key to map symbols 3
Key to map pages 4-5
Distance chart 4
Route planner (8 miles to 1 inch) 6-7
Dublin approaches (4 miles to 1 inch) 8-9
Main Dublin maps (4 inches to 1 mile) 10-143
Central Dublin map (6.6 inches to 1 mile) 144-145
Guide to central Dublin 146-165
Index to place names 166
Index to street names 166-200

Published by Collins
An imprint of HarperCollins Publishers
77-85 Fulham Palace Road, Hammersmith, London W6 8JB

www.collins.co.uk

Copyright © HarperCollins Publishers Ltd 2007

Collins® is a registered trademark of HarperCollins Publishers Limited

Mapping generated from Collins Bartholomew digital databases

Based on Ordnance Survey Ireland by permission of the Government of Ireland. Ordnance Survey Ireland Permit No. 8045
© Ordnance Survey Ireland/Government of Ireland

Printed in Hong Kong   ISBN 978 0 00 725825 3   Imp 001   UI12273 / CDL
e-mail: roadcheck@harpercollins.co.uk

Tourist and travel information

Air

Dublin Airport
☎ 01 814 1111.
www.dublinairport.com

The airport is 12km (8 miles) north of the city centre with Dublin Bus operating many services to and from the airport including the **'Airlink'** express coach service operating between the airport, the central bus station in Store Street (Bus Áras) and the two mainline rail stations, Connolly and Heuston. It runs every 10-15 mins (15-20 mins on Sundays) between 05.45 (07.15 on Sundays) and 23.30 from the airport and between 05.15 (07.35 on Sundays) and 22.50 from O'Connell Street in the centre of Dublin. ☎ 01 873 4222
www.dublinbus.ie.

'Aircoach' runs between the airport and Dublin City and South Dublin City stopping at major hotels. The 24 hour service operates every 10-20 minutes except from 24.00 and 05.00 when an hourly service operates.
☎ 01 844 7118 www.aircoach.ie.

Services at Dublin airport include Travel Information, Tourist Information and Bureau de Change.

Frequent direct flights operate between Dublin and many airports in Britain, Europe and North America. Internal flights are available to Cork, Donegal, Galway, Kerry, Knock, Shannon & Sligo and are operated by

Aer Arann	☎ 0818 210210 (R of I)
	☎ 0800 587 2324 (UK)
	www.aerarann.com
Aer Lingus	☎ 0818 365 044 (R of I)
	☎ 0870 876 2020 (UK)
	www.aerlingus.com

Other operators flying into Dublin are:

British Airways	☎ 1890 626 747 (R of I)
	☎ 0870 850 9850 (UK)
	www.britishairways.com
Flybe	☎ 00 44 1392 268529 (R of I)
	☎ 0871 522 6100 (UK)
	www.flybe.com
BMI	☎ 01 407 3036 (R of I)
	☎ 0870 6070 555 (UK)
	www.flybmi.com
Ryanair	☎ 0818 30 30 30 (R of I),
	☎ 0871 246 0000 (UK)
	www.ryanair.com

Passenger and vehicle ferries

Numerous modern ferries and high-speed services with drive-on drive-off facilities cross the Irish Sea from Dublin to Britain (Liverpool, Birkenhead, Holyhead), and the Isle of Man (Douglas).

Irish Ferries (Dublin–Holyhead).
☎ 01 855 2222 / 0818 300 400 (R of I)
☎ 08705 17 17 17 (UK)
www.irishferries.com

Norfolk Line Ferries (Dublin–Birkenhead).
☎ 01 819 2999 (R of I) ☎ 0870 600 4321 (UK)
www.norfolkline-ferries.co.uk

P & O Irish Sea (Dublin–Liverpool).
☎ 01 407 3434 (R of I) ☎ 0870 24 24 777 (UK)
www.poirishsea.com

Isle of Man Steam Packet Company (Dublin–Douglas).
☎ 1800 80 50 55 (R of I) ☎ 0871 222 1333 (UK)
www.steam–packet.com

Stena Line (Dún Laoghaire–Holyhead, Dublin–Holyhead).
☎ 01 204 7777 (R of I) ☎ 08705 70 70 70 (UK)
www.stenaline.co.uk

Dublin Port and Dún Laoghaire have bus and taxi services to the city centre although on busy sailings it may be prudent to pre-book a taxi. The ferry terminal at Dún Laoghaire is also linked to the city by the DART rail service with a 20 minute journey time.

Tourist information

Dublin Tourism Centre, Suffolk Street.
☎ 01 605 7700.
Open: (July & August) Mon–Sat 09.00–20.00, (Sept & June) Mon–Sat 09.00–19.00, (Oct–May) Mon–Sat 09.00–17.30. Open Sun & bank holidays 10.30–15.00; closed 25 & 26 Dec & 1 Jan.

Formerly St. Andrew's Church, the centre provides details of visitor attractions and events in the city as well as acting as a ticket and accommodation bureau. Transport and tour information, exchange facilities and a café are also on hand.

Other tourist information and reservation centres in Dublin (walk-in only) are located at:
Dublin Airport. Open: Mon–Sun 08.00–22.00.
Open bank holidays except 25 & 26 Dec & 1 Jan.
Dún Laoghaire Ferry Terminal.
Open: Mon–Sat 10.00–18.00, closed 13.00–14.00.
Open bank holidays except 25 & 26 Dec & 1 Jan.

Baggott Street Bridge. Open: Mon–Fri 09.30–17.00, closed 12.00-12.30. Closed bank holidays.

For accommodation reservations in Dublin and Ireland contact Ireland Reservations.
☎ 1800 363 626 (R of I) ☎ 008 002 580 2580 (UK)

Official tourism website for Dublin:
www.visitdublin.com
Email: information@dublintourism.ie
or reservations@dublintourism.ie

Irish Tourist Board Website:
www.ireland.ie

The Dublin Pass allows fast-track entry to many visitor attractions for a 1, 2, 3 or 6 day period. It can also be used on public transport and to obtain discount in some shops and restaurants. www.dublinpass.ie

Key to map symbols ③

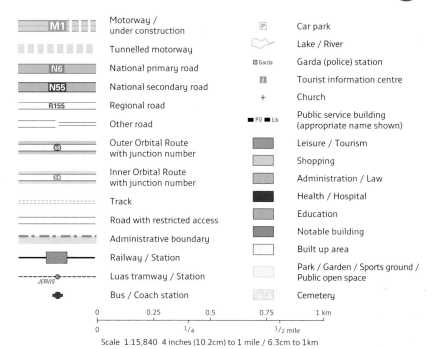

M1	Motorway / under construction
	Tunnelled motorway
N6	National primary road
N55	National secondary road
R155	Regional road
	Other road
68	Outer Orbital Route with junction number
14	Inner Orbital Route with junction number
	Track
	Road with restricted access
	Administrative boundary
	Railway / Station
JERVIS	Luas tramway / Station
	Bus / Coach station

P	Car park
	Lake / River
Garda	Garda (police) station
i	Tourist information centre
+	Church
PO Lib	Public service building (appropriate name shown)
	Leisure / Tourism
	Shopping
	Administration / Law
	Health / Hospital
	Education
	Notable building
	Built up area
	Park / Garden / Sports ground / Public open space
	Cemetery

Scale 1:15,840 4 inches (10.2cm) to 1 mile / 6.3cm to 1km

| 0 | 0.25 | 0.5 | 0.75 | 1 km |
| 0 | 1/4 | | 1/2 mile | |

Key to map symbols (pages 6-9)

M2	Motorway
M1 Toll	Toll motorway
5 8	Motorway junction with full / restricted access
i i	Tourist information centre (open all year / seasonally)
m	Ancient monument
✗	Battlefield
⛫	Castle
∩	Cave
⛲	Country park
†	Ecclesiastical building
❋	Garden
⚑	Golf course

⚎	Historic house
£	Major shopping centre / Outlet village
⚡	Major sports venue
⚑	Motor racing circuit
🏛	Museum / Art gallery
↳	Nature reserve
⛟	Preserved railway
🏇	Racecourse
🎡	Theme park
🎓	University
🐾	Wildlife park or Zoo
★	Other interesting feature

water	0	100	200	300	400	500	700	1000 metres
	0	330	650	980	1310	1640	2295	3280 feet

Dunshaughlin
Ashbourne
10 - 11
Ratoath
Drumree
Batterstown
Rathmolyon Summerhill
Moynalvy
Kilmore
Agher Mullagh Kilbride
Garadice
Ballynare
28 - 29
Dunboyne
Clonee **30 - 31** **32 - 33**
Toll
Newtown Kilcock Rathleek **44 - 45** **46 - 47**
Blanchardstow
Clonsilla Castlekr
Maynooth
64 - 65 **67** **68 - 69** **70 - 71** **72 - 73**
Leixlip
Lucan Palmer
66 **82 - 83** **84 - 85**
Celbridge
Donadea
94 - 95 **96 - 97**
Clondalki
Mainham Straffan **106 - 107** **108 - 10**
TALLAGH
120 - 121 **122 - 12**
Saggart
Rathcoole

DISTANCE CHART

The distance between two selected towns will be found at the intersection of the respective vertical and horizontal rows, e.g. distance between Belfast and Dublin is 104 miles/166 kilometres. In general, distances are based on the shortest routes by classified roads.

DISTANCE IN KILOMETRES

Athlone	Belfast	Castlebar	Cork	Donegal	DUBLIN	Dundalk	Galway	Kilkenny	Killarney	Larne	Limerick	Londonderry	Roscrea	Rosslare	Sligo	Tralee	Waterford
	266	130	214	182	125	144	93	125	230	261	120	208	64	208	117	187	173
		291	422	179	166	83	304	283	434	35	322	117	267	328	205	426	331
			283	150	242	251	80	248	293	326	182	221	189	349	86	285	296
				400	256	323	208	147	86	459	104	426	152	206	334	118	125
141					221	157	203	307	405	189	294	69	245	389	66	408	355
81	182					85	218	117	307	202	197	235	123	162	216	301	157
134	264	177					237	197	350	118	240	155	186	245	166	344	242
114	112	94	250					155	192	339	104	270	109	272	138	162	219
78	104	151	160	138					197	318	112	333	50	99	243	213	48
90	52	157	202	98	53					469	110	438	182	274	341	32	192
58	190	50	130	127	136	148					358	115	301	363	240	462	366
78	177	155	92	192	73	123	97					346	74	210	230	104	128
144	271	183	54	253	192	219	120	123					290	395	134	430	381
163	22	204	287	118	126	74	212	199	293					160	181	176	109
75	201	114	65	184	123	150	65	70	69	224					325	290	82
130	73	138	266	43	147	97	169	208	274	72	216					285	291
40	167	118	95	153	77	116	68	31	114	188	46	181					208
130	205	218	129	243	101	153	170	62	171	227	131	247	100				
73	128	54	209	41	135	104	86	152	213	150	144	84	113	203			
117	266	178	74	255	188	215	101	133	20	289	65	269	110	181	178		
108	207	185	78	222	98	151	137	30	120	229	80	238	68	51	182	130	

DISTANCE IN MILES

Londonderry Larne
Donegal Belfast
Sligo Dundalk
Castlebar
Galway DUBLIN
Athlone Roscrea
Limerick Kilkenny
Tralee Waterford Rosslare
Killarney
Cork

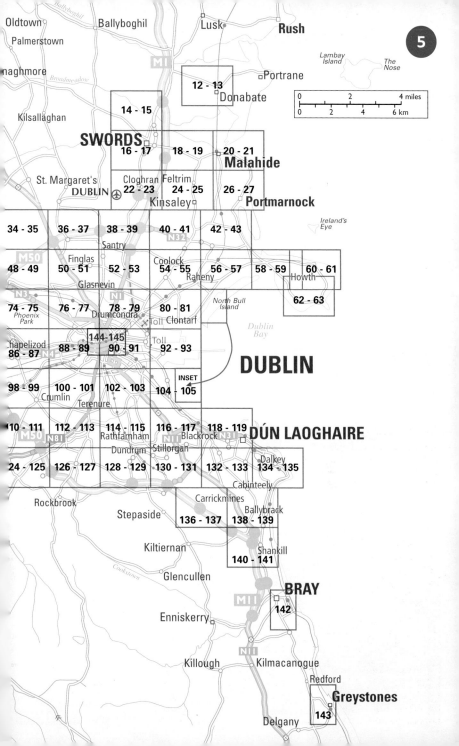

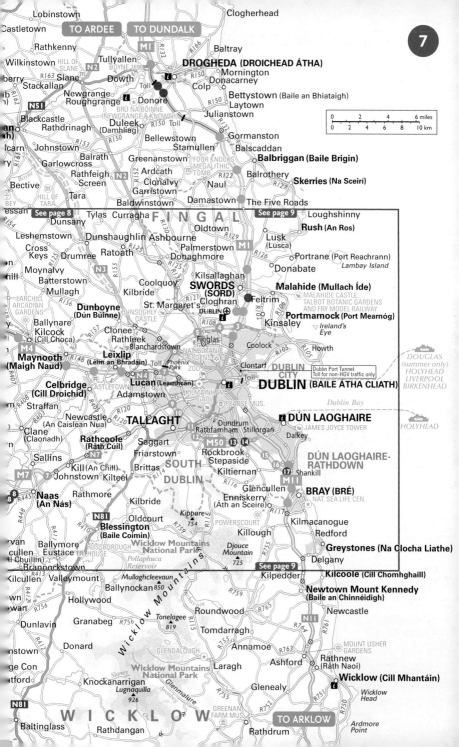

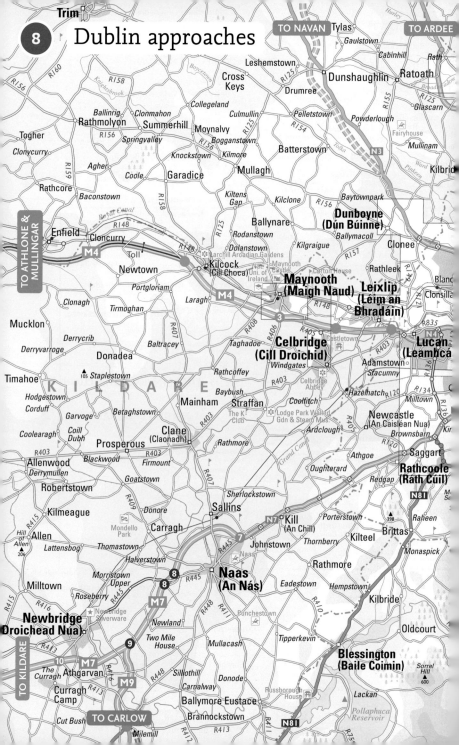

A

B

R135

N2

1916 Rebellion Mon.

Cookstown

Rath Cross
Roads

1

ASHBOURNE
INDUSTRIAL
PARK

RATH
LODGE

RACE
LODG

RACE HILL LANE

THE ASHES

WEST
GRN

TUDOR

GROVE

WEST
WD.

WD. CT.

TUDOR CRES

RAC

BRINDLEY PK GDN

ST JOHNS

BR.
PK.
SQ.

DERRY HA.

BRI. PK. CRES

ST. JOHNS
WD. PK.

RISE

Health
Centre

2

ST. JOHNS WD. DR.

CLUAIN

KILLEGLAND PARK

KILL.
CT.

Lib

BALLYBIN ROAD

COOKSTOWN
BRIDGE

ASHBOURNE

Ballybin

CAST

CRES

CRESTWOOD
GREEN

3

CEM

CRESTWOOD
PARK

Killegland

So

BROAD MEADOW RIVER

WESTV

BOURNE VIEW

THE BAILEY

BOURN

N2

BROADMEADOW
GREEN

A

B

Dunreagh

RACE HILL
MANOR

Sch

Shopping
Centre

PO

CEM

Garda

Milltown

Ashbourne Rugby
Football Club

HUNTERS LANE

BROOKVILLE

MAPLE GRO

MILLTOWN ESTATE

ASH DALE CRES

THE HAWTHORNS

PINE CL

Sports
Ground

ARCHERSTOWN ROAD

Archerstown

BROAD MEADOW

BACHELORS WK

BRIDGE ST

MEAD BR. CT

DUBLIN ROAD

DEERPARK

DEERPARK

MILLTOWN ROAD

MILLTOWN
BRIDGE

ASHBOURNE
GOLF COURSE

CASTLE

D ROAD

CASTLE WAY

CASTLE CL

ALDERBROOK GLEN

ALD VALE

DEERPARK

Sch

CASTLE
THE GREEN
PARK

KILLEGLAND RD

BROADMEADOW RD

GREEN GRO

ALDERBROOK RISE

ALDERBROOK DOWN

ALD PK
RD

CHERRY
LANE

Sports
Ground

Pitch and
Putt Course

Ashbourne
Golf Club

BROAD MEADOW RIVER

TARA PL

TARA CL

R135

BALDARA COURT

THE BRIARS

1

2

3

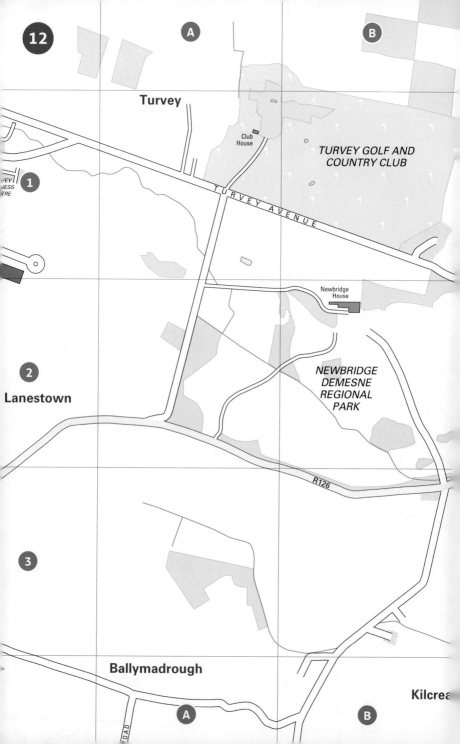

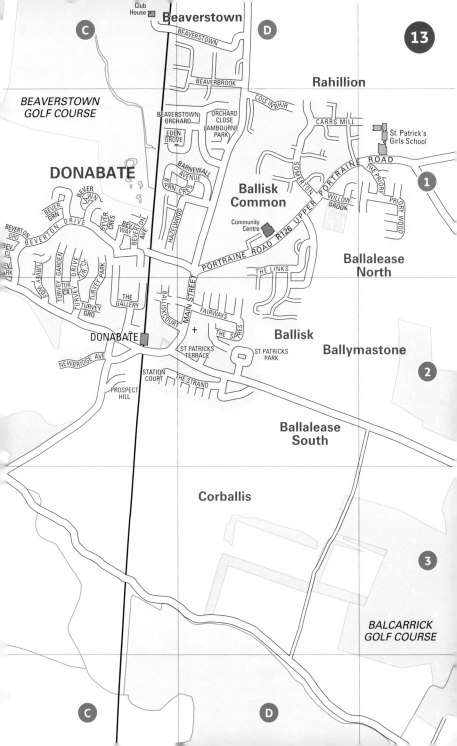

A

B

Balh

MEADOW RIVER

Saucertown

1

Oldtown

CASTHOWN
CASTHOWN GRN
CASTHOWN GROVE
CASTLE CT
RIS 3
AST. LAWNS
AST. DR
CASTLEVIEW HTS
CASTLEVIEW RISE

CASTLEVIEW

CAS. HEATH
CAS. CL
CAS. GRO
CASTLE GREEN
CASTLE WAY
CASTLEVIEW AVENUE
CASTLEVIEW PARK
CAS. PL
CAS. MEADOWS
C.V. WK
CAS. CT
CASTLE LAWNS
CASTLEVIEW CRES
CAS. ROW
CAS. CRES

BUNBURY GATE AVE
BUNBURY GATE CRES
BRIDE'S GLEN AVE
GLEN AVE
BRI. GLEN PK

2

Outlands

RATHBEALE

LAURELTON
GLEN ELLA
ST. ANDRE
PINE GRO V
GLEN ELLAN GDNS
ELLAN WK

CIANLEA

Mooretown

BRODAN PK
ARDCIAN PARK
DALE VIEW
ELMWOOD DRIVE
ABBEYLEA GRO
ELMWOOD PARK
ELMWOOD ROA
GLASMO
GLASMORE

R123

AVENUE
CRONAN'S
LIOS CIAN

3

ABBEY GRO
BERWICK GROVE
ORMOND CRESCENT
ABBEY CT
ABBEY CRES
ABBEY DR
BERWICK DR
BERWICK CRES
ORMOND CRES
ORMOND GRO
SW. MANOR CRESCENT
ABBEYVALE
ABBEY CLO
BERWICK WAY
ORMOND DR
COURT
ABBEY PL
BERWICK CT
ORM DR
SWORD MANOR DR
VALLEY VIEW
ST. CRO LAWN
ST. CRO GRO
ABBEY RISE
AB. RISE
ABBEY LAWN
BERWICK LAWN
ORMOND PL
VW
VW
WAY
ST. CRONAN'S
ST. CRO GRO
GLASMORE
ABBEY AVENUE
BERWICK AVENUE
ORM CLO
VW
GRO 3
AVENUE
ABBEY VW
BER VW
BER RI
ORM WAY
SWORD
ST. CRONAN'S
Schools
ABBEY GRN
ABBEY WAY
Shopping Centre
BRACKENSTOWN

PARKVIEW

Windmill Lands

BRACKENSTOWN ROAD

FORT RD
TIAN
WOOD

PARK AVENUE

WAR RIVER

A

16

B

WARD RIVER VALLEY PARK

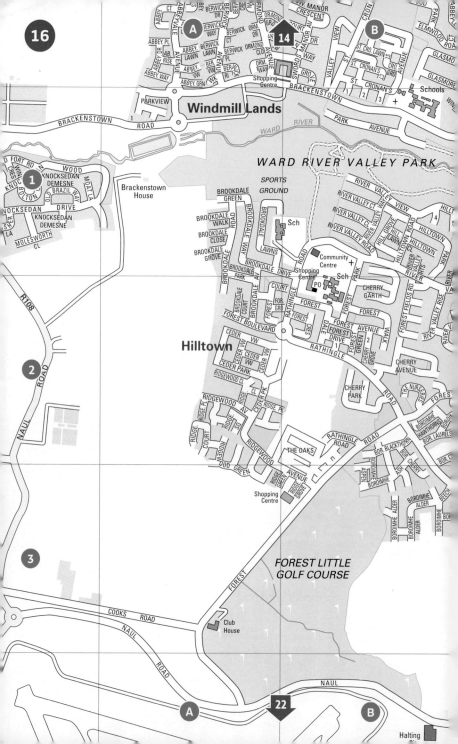

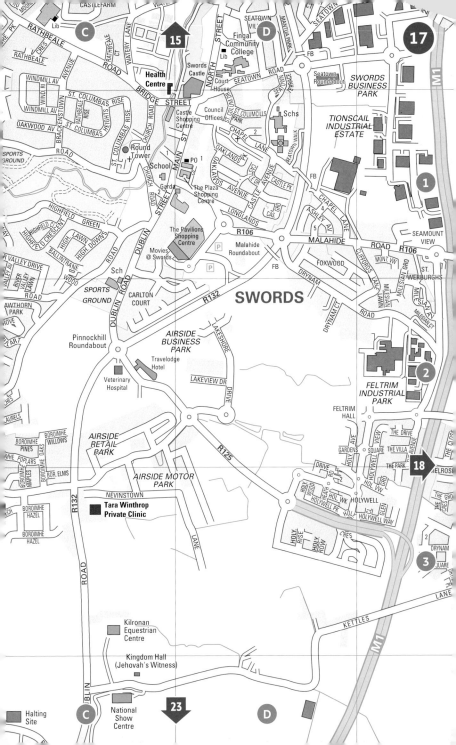

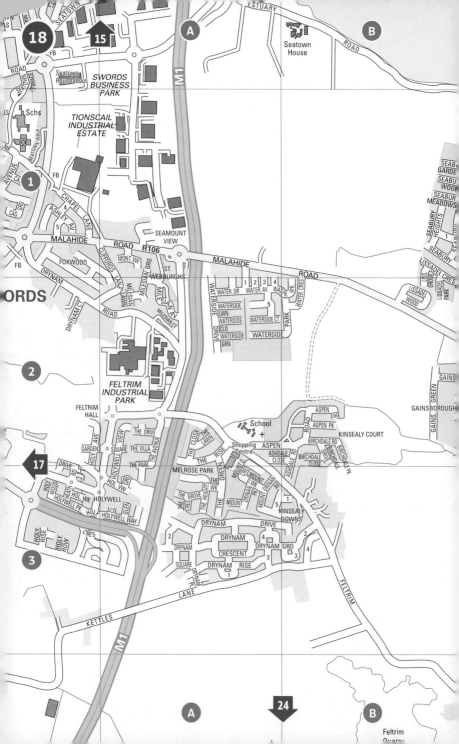

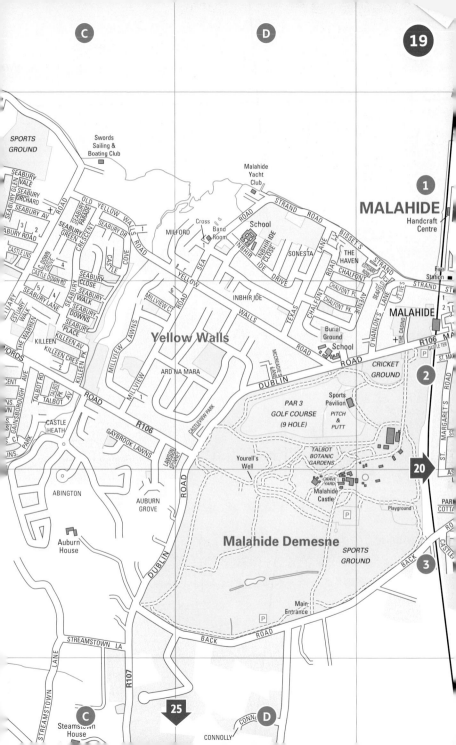

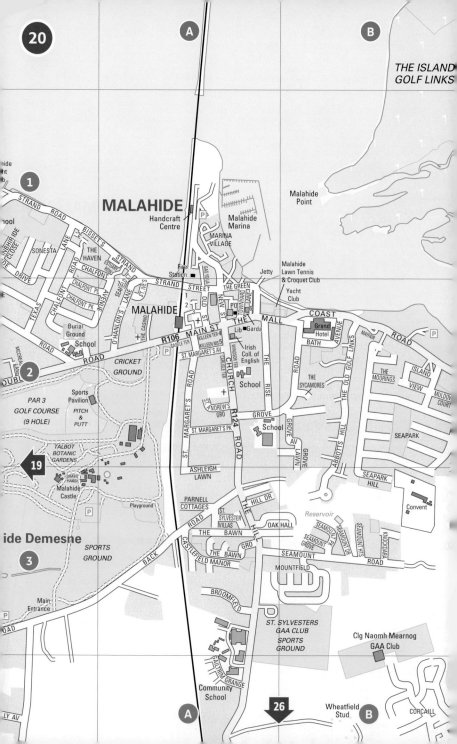

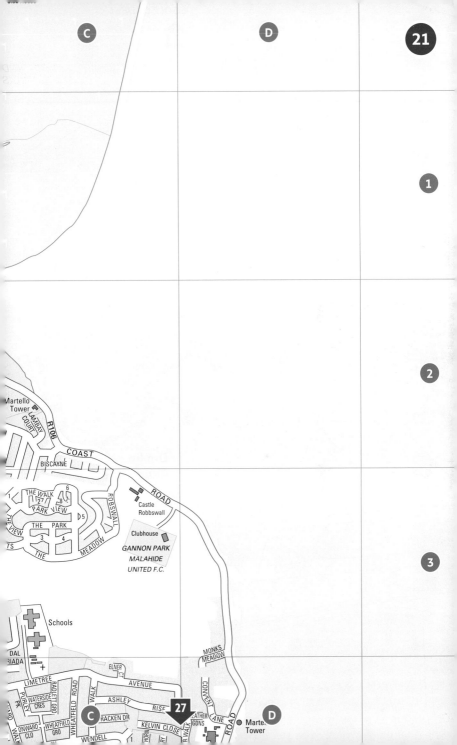

1

2

Martello
Tower
LAMBAY COURT
R106
COAST
BISCAYNE
ROAD
THE WALK
6
27
8
7
PARK VIEW
5
Castle
Robbswall
ROBBSWALL
THE VIEW
THE PARK
3
4
Clubhouse
TS
THE
THE MEADOW
GANNON PARK
MALAHIDE
UNITED F.C.

3

Schools

DAL
RIADA

ELNER CT
AVENUE
MONKS
MEADOW
LIMETREE
PURLEY
WATERSIDE CRES
RADLETT GRO
WHEATFIELD ROAD
WALK
ASHLEY
RISE
CONVENT LANE
WHEATFIELD
GRO
WENDELL
BRACKEN DR
KELVIN CLOSE
HORN
R WALK
HEATHER
GDNS
ROAD
Martel.
Tower
ONWARD
CLO
C
27
D

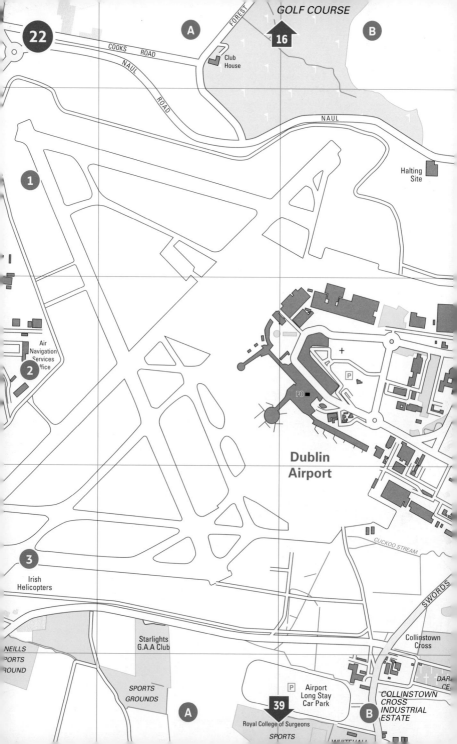

22

GOLF COURSE

A

B

COOKS ROAD

NAUL ROAD

Club House

16

NAUL

Halting Site

1

Air Navigation Services Office

2

Dublin Airport

PO
P

+
P

CUCKOO STREAM

3

SWORDS

Irish Helicopters

Collinstown Cross

NEILLS SPORTS GROUND

Starlights G.A.A Club

SPORTS GROUNDS

P Airport Long Stay Car Park

39

Royal College of Surgeons

SPORTS

DAR CE

COLLINSTOWN CROSS INDUSTRIAL ESTATE

A

B

WHITEHALL

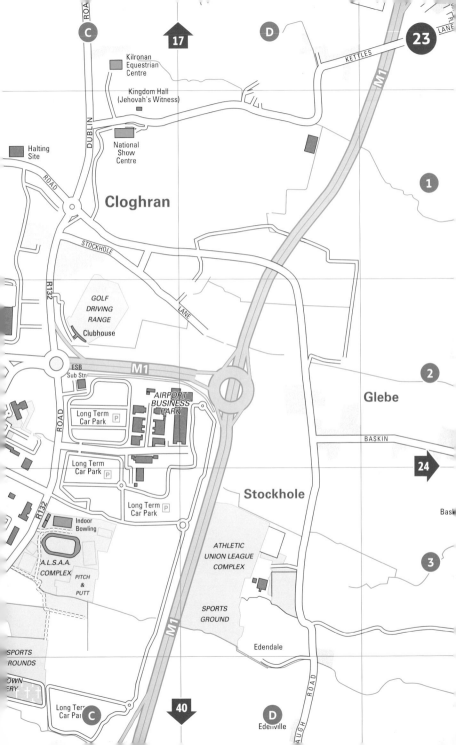

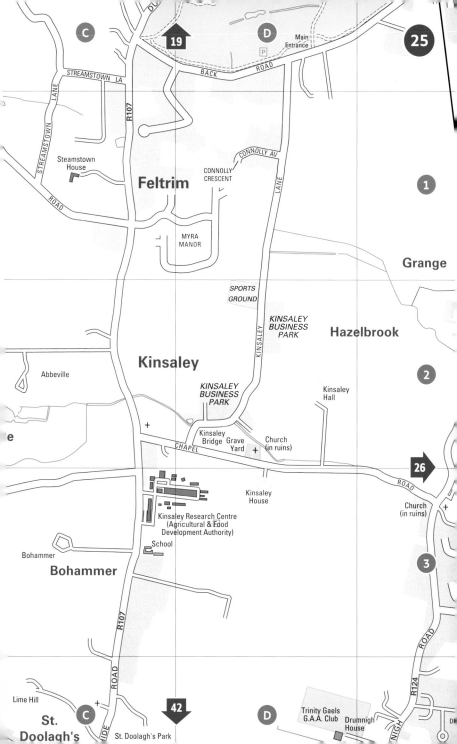

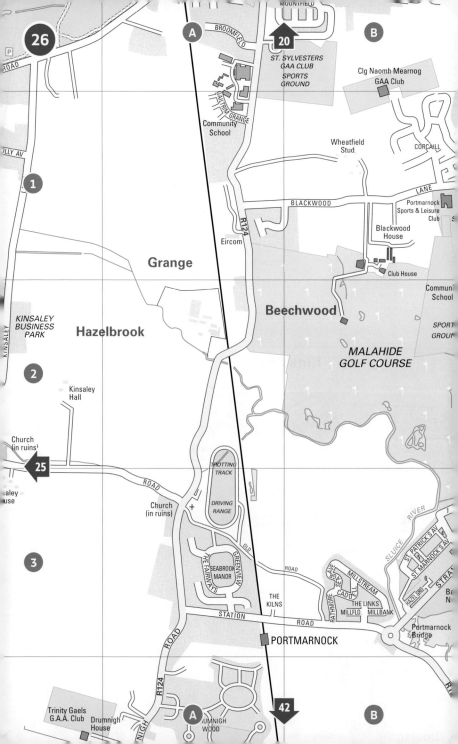

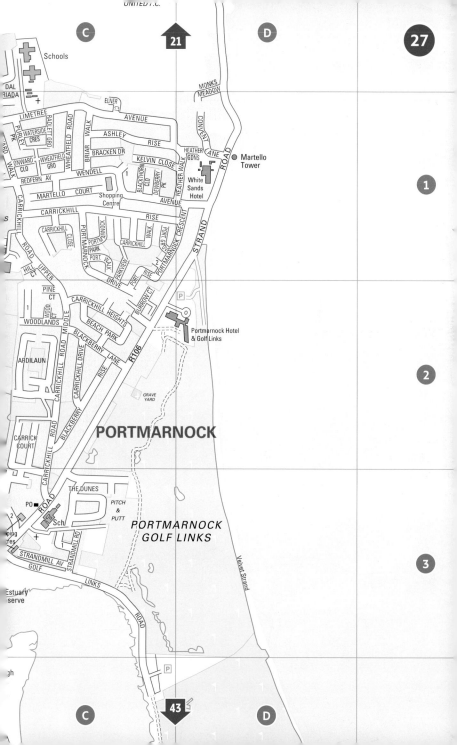

UNITED F.C.

Schools

DAL
RIADA

MONKS
MEADOW

LIMETREE

PURLEY
PK

WATERSIDE
CRES

RADLET GRO

ELNER
CT

AVENUE

WHEATFIELD ROAD

BRIAR WALK

ASHLEY

RISE

BRACKEN DR

CONVENT LANE

HEATHER
GDNS

Martello
Tower

1

ONWARD
CLO

WHEATFIELD
GRO

WENDELL

KELVIN CLOSE

BLACKTHORN CLO

HEATHER WALK

White
Sands
Hotel

REDFERN AV

1

DEWBERRY
PK

STRAND ROAD

MARTELLO COURT

Shopping
Centre

AVENUE

CARRICKHILL

CARRICKHILL

RISE

CARRICKHILL
CLOSE

PORTMARNOCK

PORTMARNOCK
PARK

CARRICKHILL
WALK

PORT CLO

PORT WALK

PORTMARNOCK CRESCENT

HILL
CT

UPPER

PORT
WALK

PARKVIEW

DRIVE

PORT
RISE

PINE
CT

WOOD
CT

CARRICKHILL HEIGHTS

BURROW CT

P

WOODLANDS

BEACH PARK

BLACKBERRY LANE

R106

O

Portmarnock Hotel
& Golf Links

ARDILAUN

CARRICKHILL ROAD MIDDLE

CARRICKHILL DRIVE

RISE

GRAVE
YARD

2

CARRICK
COURT

CARRICKHILL ROAD

BLACKBERRY

PORTMARNOCK

THE DUNES

PO

ROAD

PITCH
&
PUTT

**PORTMARNOCK
GOLF LINKS**

Sch

2

ping
res

STRANDMILL AV

STRANDMILL RD

GOLF

LINKS

Velvet Strand

3

Estuary
serve

ROAD

gh

P

A
B

Brookville
Stud Farm

1

PLUNKETT
HALL

THE COURT
THE AVENUE
THE CLOSE
THE GROVE
THE CRES
THE
THE GROVE

THE GREEN
THE AVENUE
THE DRIVE
THE DALE

DUNBOYNE
BUSINESS
PARK

LUTTERELL
HALL

THE PADDOCKS
KILBRINA
THE PADDOCKS

Newtown
Bridge

R156

THE PARK
THE LAWN
SUMMERHILL

THE PARK
THE CRES
THE AVENUE
THE CLOSE
ROAD

ST. PETER'S
PARK

OLD FAIR GREEN
NAVAN

GARNETT
HALL

THE DRIVE
THE
COURT

THE COURT
COURTHILL
DRIVE

ST. PATRICK'S PARK

SPORTS
GROUND

THE GROVE
SADLEIR
HALL

MEADOW VIEW

Garda

Garda

AVONDALE
SQ

DU

2

PO

Hall

GRAVE
YARD

Hall

MAIN ST

NEWTOWN

ROAD

CASTLEVIEW
ESTATE

Lib
Community
Service
Centre

Hotel

THE HEIGHTS
THE
COURT
THE DRIVE

ROUSKE

R157 MAYNOOTH

THE
CLOSE
THE WALK
THE PLACE
THE
THE AVENUE
THE
CRES

THE GRN
THE DRIVE
THE DRIVE

CONGR
PARK

3

THE
DOWNS
THE GROVE

THE WAY
THE PARK

THE VIEW

DUNBOYNE
CASTLE

Castlefarm House

Dunboyne
Athletic
Club

St. Peter's
Dunboyne

A
B

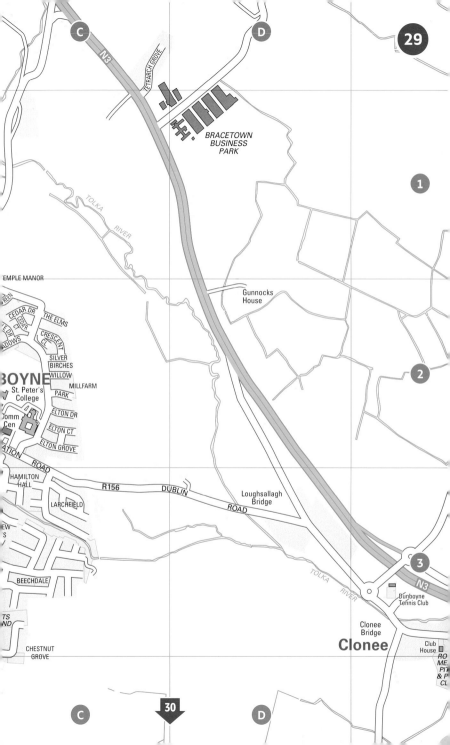

N3

PETRIARCH GROVE

BRACETOWN
BUSINESS
PARK

1

TOLKA

RIVER

EMPLE MANOR

Gunnocks
House

CEDAR DR

THE ELMS

CRESCENT
CL

SILVER
BIRCHES

WILLOW

BOYNE

St. Peter's
College

MILLFARM

PARK

2

ELTON DR

Comm
Cen

ELTON CT

ELTON GROVE

ATION ROAD

HAMILTON
HALL

R156

DUBLIN

Loughsallagh
Bridge

LARCHFIELD

ROAD

EWS
S

BEECHDALE

TOLKA

RIVER

3

N3

Dunboyne
Tennis Club

Clonee
Bridge

TS
ND

Clonee

Club
House

RO
ME
PI'
& P
CL

CHESTNUT
GROVE

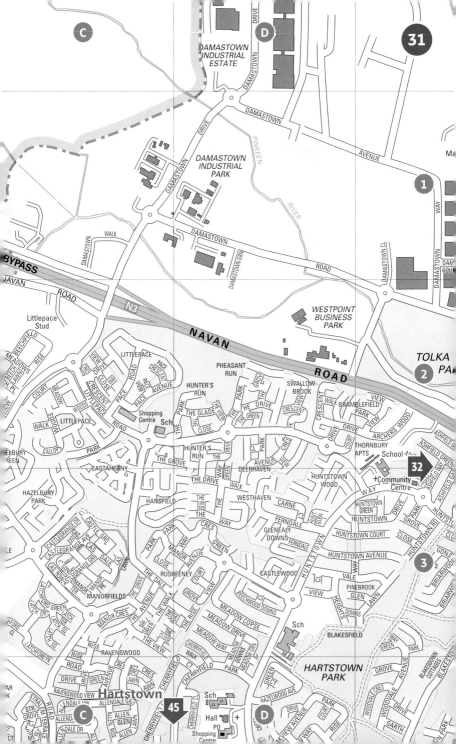

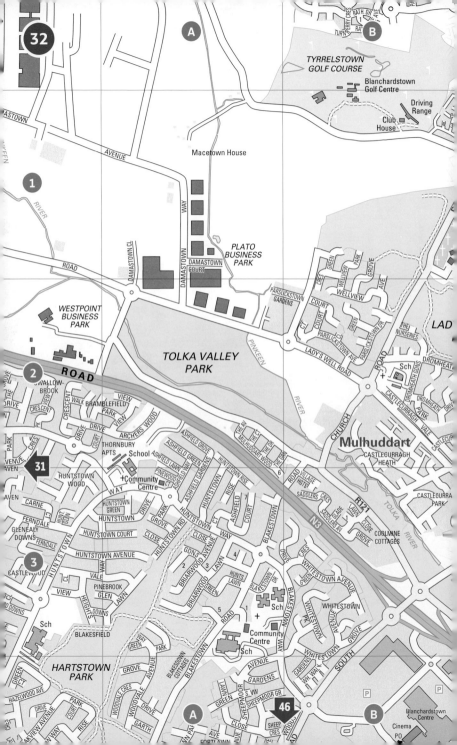

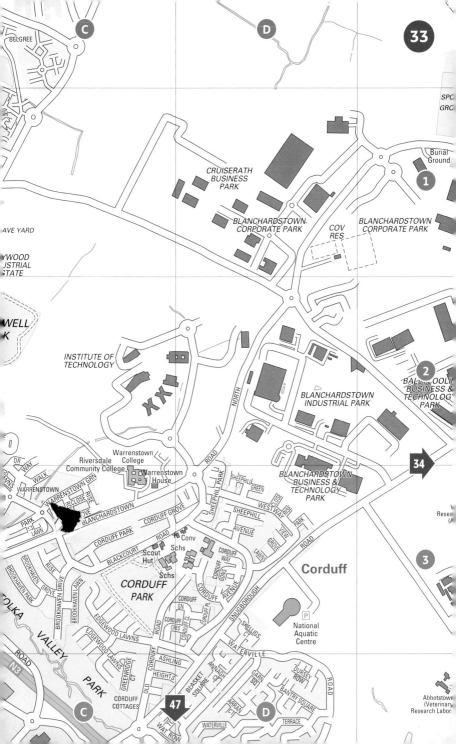

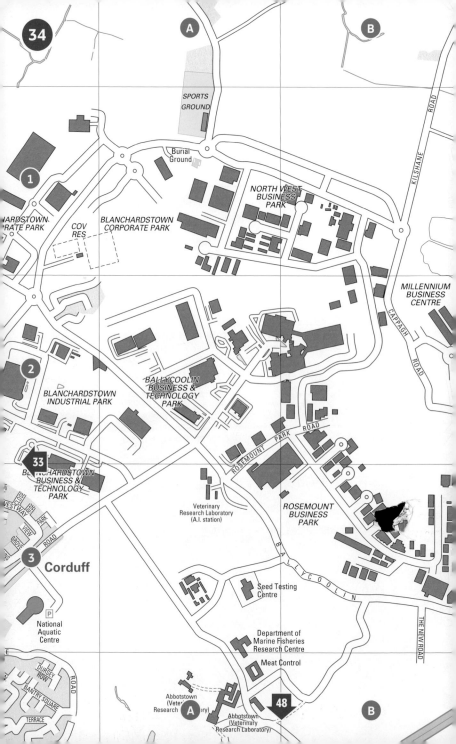

A

B

SPORTS GROUND

Burial Ground

1

NORTH WEST BUSINESS PARK

KILSHANE ROAD

...ARDSTOWN ...RATE PARK

COV RES

BLANCHARDSTOWN CORPORATE PARK

MILLENNIUM BUSINESS CENTRE

CAPPAGH ROAD

2

BLANCHARDSTOWN INDUSTRIAL PARK

BALLYCOOLIN BUSINESS & TECHNOLOGY PARK

ROSEMOUNT PARK ROAD

33

BLANCHARDSTOWN BUSINESS & TECHNOLOGY PARK

...WESTWAY

VIEW

...PARK

...GROVE

...ROAD

3 Corduff

Veterinary Research Laboratory (A.I. station)

ROSEMOUNT BUSINESS PARK

BALLYCOOLIN

THE NEW ROAD

P

National Aquatic Centre

Seed Testing Centre

DURSEY ROW

...ROAD

BANTRY SQUARE

Department of Marine Fisheries Research Centre

Meat Control

...TERRACE

Abbotstown (Veter... Research ...ory)

A

Abbotstown (Veterinary Research Laboratory)

48

B

Sand &
Gravel Quarry

NORTH ROAD

R135

N2

1

2

Electricity
Station

Ju

Grange House

Kildonan
House

36

NORTH PARK
BUSINESS
& OFFICE
PARK

NOR
ES

CAPPAGH ROAD

STADIUM
BUSINESS
PARK

CAPPOGE
COTTAGES

3

NORTH
ESTA

PLUNKET

PLUNKETT
AVENUE

PLUNKETT
DRIVE

BARRY

PLUNKETT GRN

PLUNKETT RD

ROAD

BARRY PK
DR

BARRY

BARRY PARK
GRN

CAPPAGH ROAD

BARRY ROAD

K

M50

CAPPAGH ROAD

C Cappagh National
Orthopaedic Hospital

49

D

Sch

Sch

Sch

AVILA PK

AVILA PK

KILDONAN ROAD

KILDONAN
PARK

MELIO

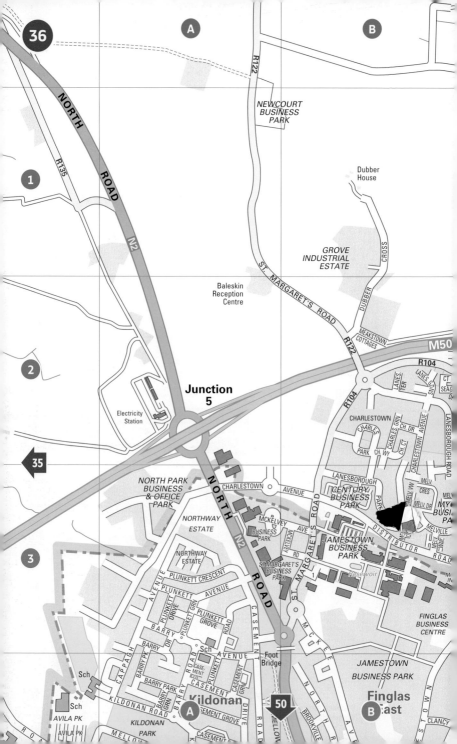

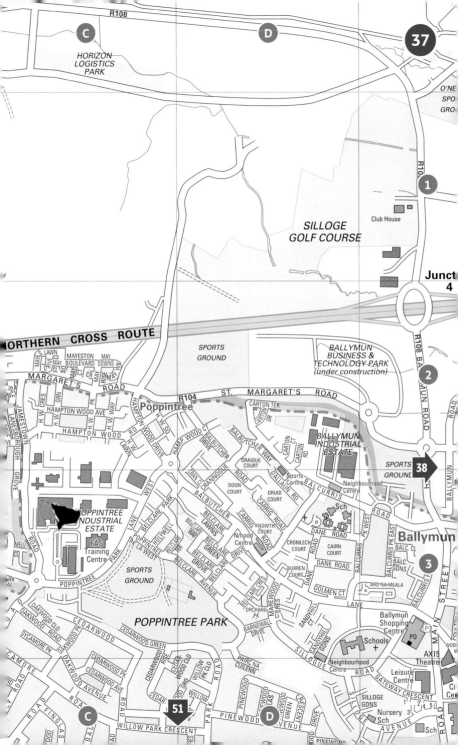

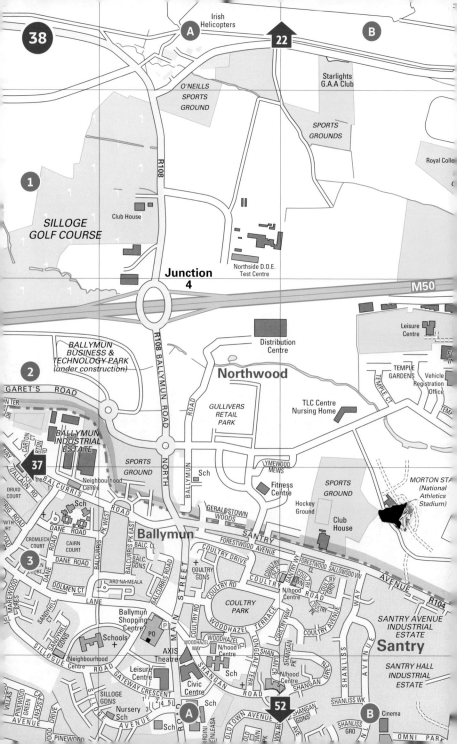

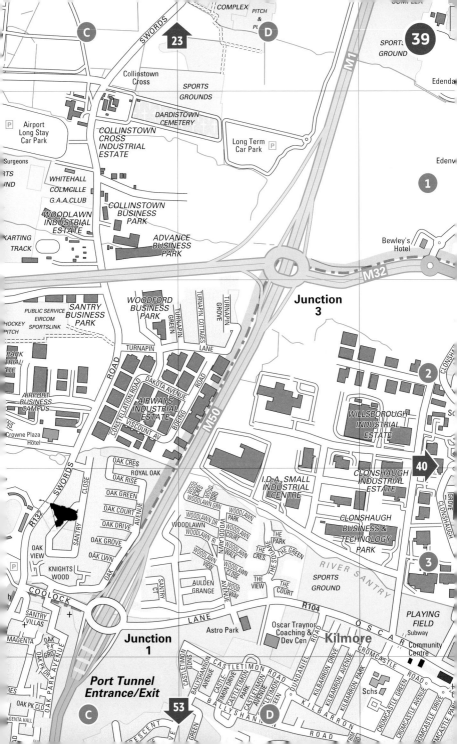

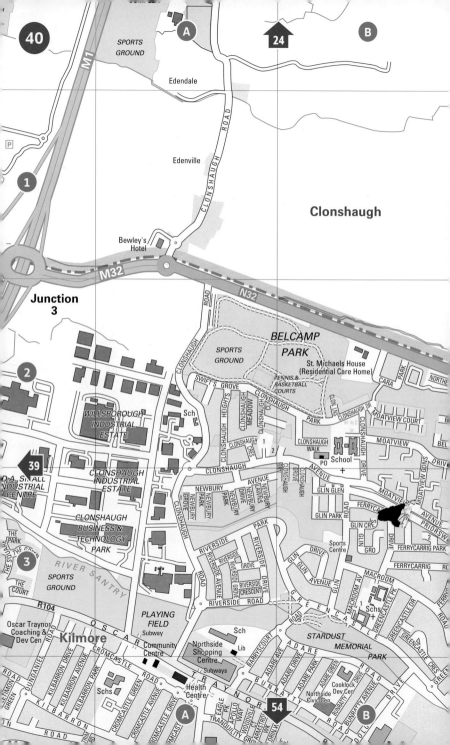

Spring Hill

Lime Hill

St. Doolagh's Park

St. Doolagh's

Burgage

PITCH & PUTT

CEMETERY

SPORTS GROUND

Balgriffin

Belcamp Hutchinson

FINGAL BURIAL GROUND

SPORTS GROUND

BALGRIFFIN

ST. SAMSON CT   CASTLEMOYNE

ST. SAMSON SQ

BALGRIFFIN COTTAGES

Belcamp College

Bal

1

2

R107

R107

ROAD

MALAHIDE

ROAD

GARDENS

CRESCEN

DARNDALE PARK

Darndale

N32

CITY JUNCTION BUSINESS PARK

MAYNE RIV AVE

Hilton Dublin Airport

Leisure Centre

R841   **CLARE HALL AVENUE**

42

TEMPLEVIEW

TULIP COURT

Sch

Community Centre

PRIMROSE GROVE

SNOWDROP WALK

MARIGOLD AVE

Clare Hall Shopping Centre

CLARE VILLAGE

GROVE LANE   GROVE PK

TEMPLEVIEW

TEMP. CT   TEMP CRES   VAT WAY   TEMP WALK

PARK   GREEN

TEMP GRO

TEMP DOWNS   TEMPLEVIEW   TEMP PL

TEMP LAWN   TEMP SQ

TEMP ROW   TEMP COPSE

ELM RISE   EMFIELD WAY

ELM FIELD GROVE   ELMFIELD WALK

ELMFIELD AVENUE   ELMFIELD

NURNEY LAWN

TEMPLEVIEW   GREENWOOD   GREEN

AVENUE

WHYTELEAF DR

MANOR

ARDARA   GRANGEMORE CRESCENT

GRANGE

GRANGEM

BELCAMP LANE

BELCAMP GROVE

AVENUE

ROAD

SPORTS GROUND

Clare Hall

BLUNDEN   DRIVE

Ayrfield Community Sports & Leisure Centre

GREENWOOD GRN

GREENWOOD DR

GREENWOOD GREEN

GREENWOOD CT

GREENWOOD AVENUE

FOXHILL PARK

FOXHILL GRN

FOXHILL CLO   FOXHILL GRO

FOX- HILL LWN

FOXHILL CRES   FOXHILL CT

FOXHILL DRIVE

FOXHILL AVE

LENTISK LAWN

CEDAR PARK

STREAMVILLE RD

ROSAP

ALLY LAWN

TARA LAWN

NEWTOWN ROAD

NEWTOWN INDUSTRIAL ESTATE

SLADEMORE

SLADE   MORE CT   SLADE DR

NEWTOWN DRIVE

GLENTWORTH PARK

ELTON DR   ELTON PK

Sch

+

3

NURSORA DRIVE

WOODVIEW

THE BEECHES

KARAGH CLO   CARRAGE AVENUE

COOLOCK INDUSTRIAL ESTATE

C

55

GREENCASTLE PARADE

NEWTOWN AVENUE

AYREFIELD DRIVE

AYREFIELD AVE

AYREFIELD

AYRFIELD

CLONROSSE

MILLBROOK GRO

MILLBROO

D

R107

ROAD

44

Athdara

A

Williamstown

30

B

HANSFIELD

BLACKWOOD

ONGAR CHASE

Hilltown House

1

R149

ONGAR VILLAGE

WILLANS DRIVE

WILLANS WAY

WILLANS AV

ONGAR GREEN

BARRY LANE

HAYWORTH

DELHURST

2

Barnhill

Pakenham Bridge

LC

Barb Hous

ROYAL CANAL

Westmanstown Park

P

TENNIS COURTS

Westmanstown Sports Centre

SPORTS PITCHES

3

Allenswood House

WESTMANSTOWN GOLF COURSE

R121

Marymount Care Centre

Collins Bridge

ROYAL CANAL

A

70

B

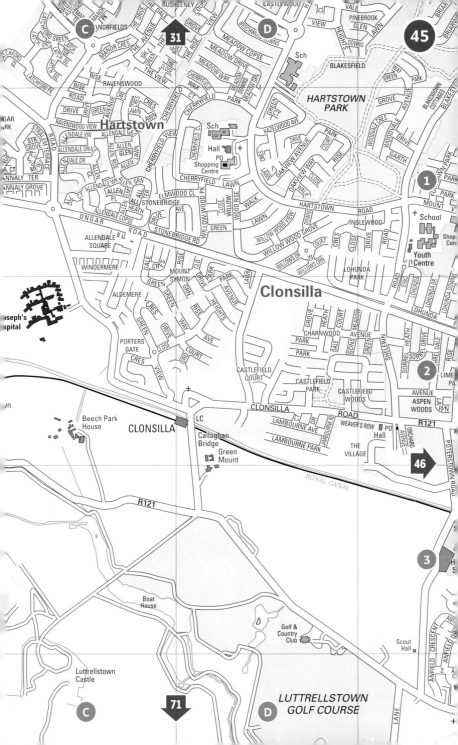

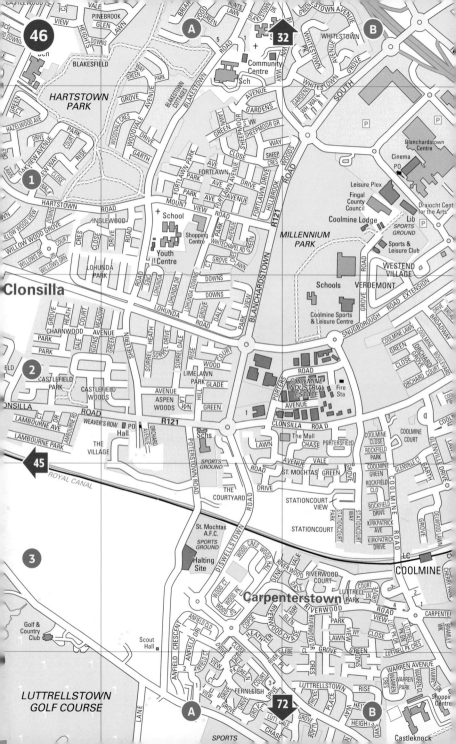

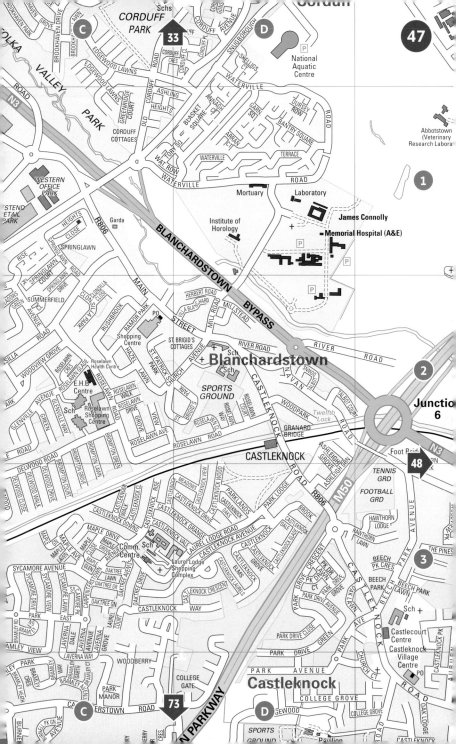

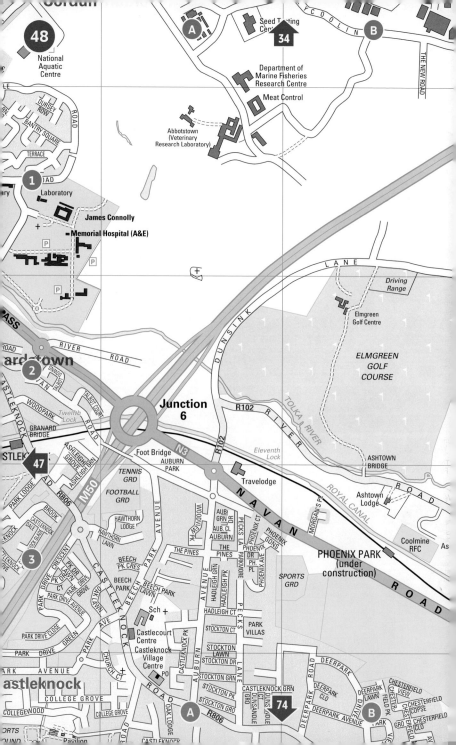

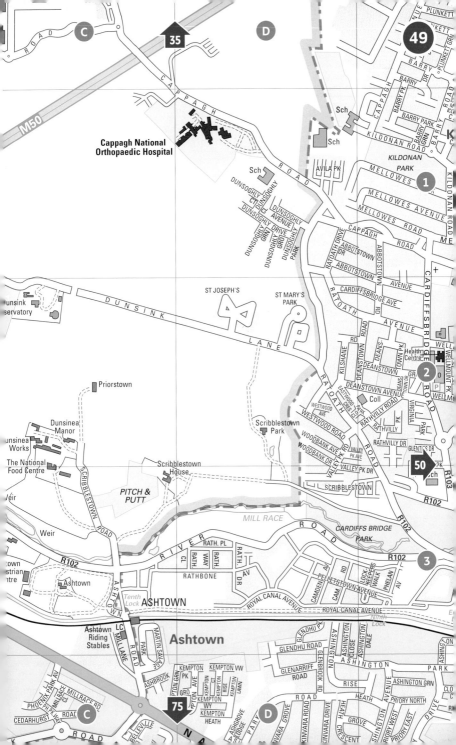

35

M50

Cappagh National
Orthopaedic Hospital

Sch

Sch

Sch

CAPPAGH   ROAD

DUNSOGHLY CT
DUNSOGHLY
DUNSOGHLY AVENUE
DUNSOGHLY DRIVE
DUNSOGHLY GRN
DUNSOGHLY GRO
DUNSOGHLY
DUNSOGHLY PARK

AVILA PK

KILDONAN ROAD

KILDONAN
PARK

MELLOWES

MELLOWES   AVENUE

MELLOWES   ROAD

ME

BARRY

BARRY PK
BARRY DR
BARRY PARK
BARRY GRN
BARRY

CAPPAGH

KILDONAN ROAD

K

1

CAPPAGH

RATOATH DRIVE
ABBOTSTOWN
DR
ABBOTSTOWN
ABBOTSTOWN
AVENUE

CAPPAGH
ROAD

CARDIFFSBRIDGE AVE

RATOATH   ROAD

CARDIFFSBRIDGE   AVENUE

ROAD

St JOSEPH'S

St MARY'S
PARK

DUNSINK   LANE

Dunsink
servatory

Priorstown

Dunsinea
Manor

unsinea
Works

The National
Food Centre

eir

SCRIBBLESTOWN   ROAD

PITCH &
PUTT

Scribblestown
Park

Scribblestown
House

KILSHANE
RD

DEANSTOWN

DEANSTOWN

DEANSTOWN AVENUE

DEANS
PK

EASTWOOD
CRES

WESTWOOD
AVE

WESTWOOD ROAD

WOODBANK AVE

WOODBANK DR

SCRIBBLESTOWN

MILL RACE

Coll

RATHVILLY ROAD

RATHVILLY
PK

RATHVILLY DR

VALLEY PK RD

VALLEY
PK AVE

VALLEY PK DR

VIRGINIA
PARK

GLENTIES DR

Health
Centre

2

WELL
WELLMOUNT
WELLMOUNT
P
ROAD
Wellm

GR

R103

50

Sch

R102

Weir

RIVER   ASHTOWN

R102

ASHTOWN   ROAD

RATH. PL
RATH.
WAY
RATH.
CL
RATH.
DR
RATH.
AV
RATHBONE

CARDIFFS BRIDGE
PARK

ROAD

R102

CAMDEN   AV
CAM   RD

PELLETSTOWN AVENUE

PHELAN   AV

LOCK
KEEPERS
WALK

R102

3

Ashtown

Tenth
Lock

ASHTOWN

Ninth
Lock

ROYAL CANAL AVENUE

ROYAL CANAL AVENUE

Ashtown
Riding
Stables

Ashtown

LC

MILL LANE

MARTIN SAVAGE
PARK

ASHBROOK

PTON GRN
PTON GRO

KEMPTON
PK

KEMPTON VW

KEMPTON
CT
KEMPTON
RISE

KEMPTON
WY

KEMPTON
LAWN

KEMPTON
HEATH

ASHGROVE

PARY   ROAD

GLENDHU ROAD

GLENDHU ROAD

GLENBROOK RD

GLENARRIFF
ROAD

GLENAVARA   GROVE

KINVARA DRIVE

KINVARA GROVE

ASHINGTON
CLOSE

ASHINGTON
DALE

ASHINGTON

ROAD

ASHINGTON

PARK

ASHINGTON GRN

RISE

HEATH

PRIORY WEST

PRIORY NORTH

PRIORY EAST

ASHINGTON AVENUE

GROVE
CRESCENT

DRIVE

75

N 3

C   D

PHOENIX PARK AV
MILLRACE AV
MILLRACE RD

PH. PK. VW

CEDARHURST

BELLEVILLE   ROAD

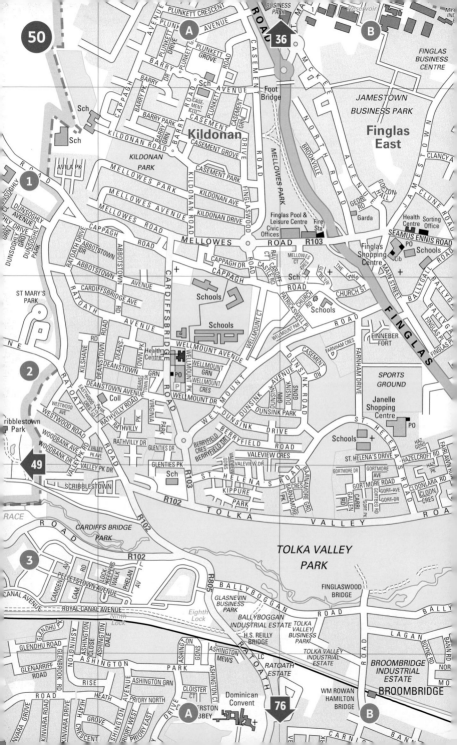

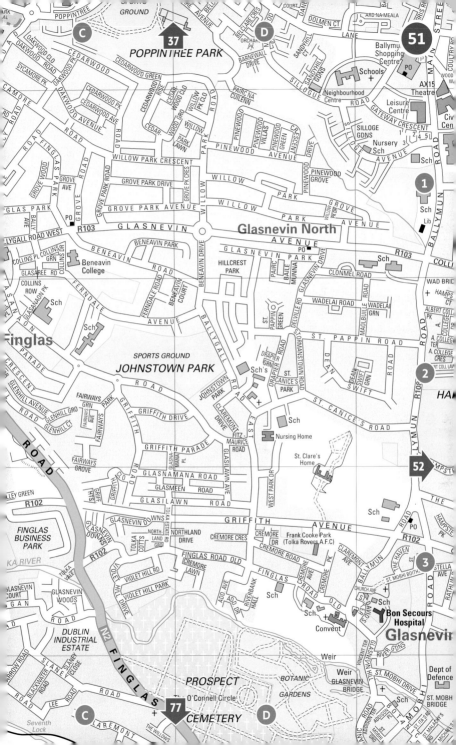

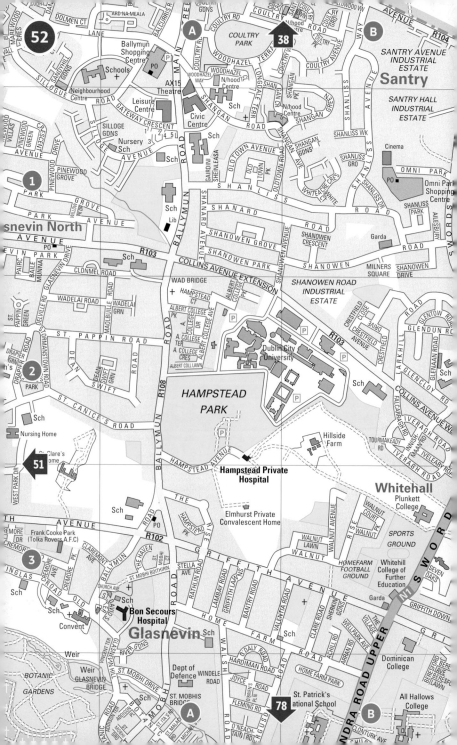

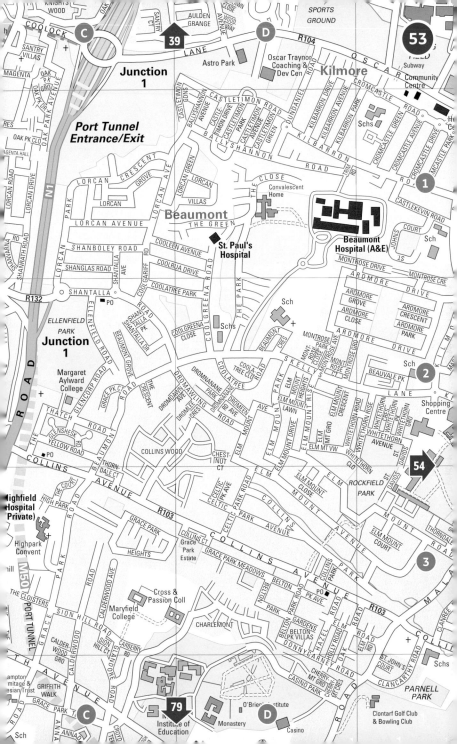

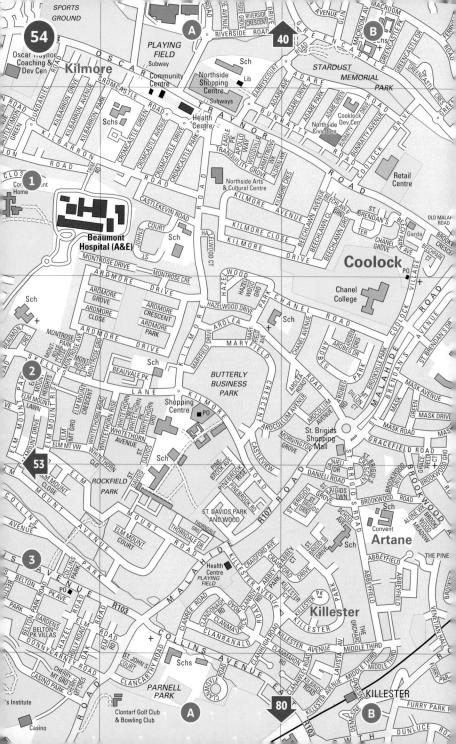

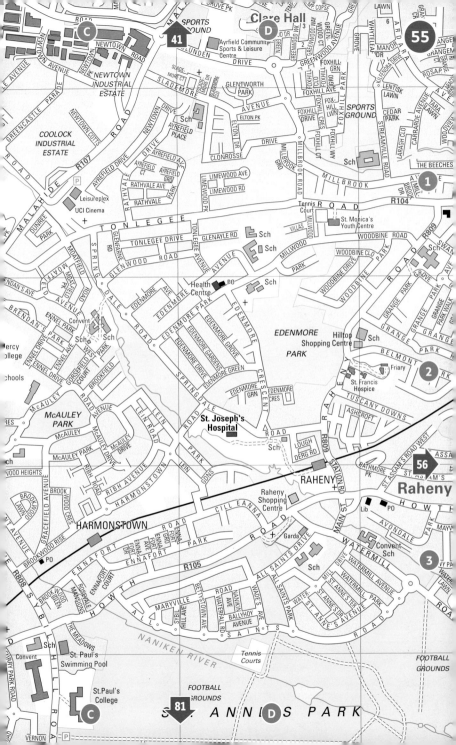

Clare Hall

41

SPORTS GROUND

D

Ayrfield Community Sports & Leisure Centre

CLUNDEN DRIVE

GREENWOOD COPSE

GREENWOOD DR

GREENWOOD GREEN

LAWN

GRAND CR

WHYTELAF

6

ARDARA

MANOR

WHYTELAF ROAD

GRANGEM

RANGE

C

NEWTOWN

NEWTOWN AVENUE

NEWTOWN ROAD

SLADE MORE CT

GLENTWORTH PARK

GREENWOOD CT

FOXHILL GRN

FOXHILL WOOD CT

LENTISK LAWN

CARRAROE AVENUE

TARA LAWN

ROSAPT.

WOODIEL

NEWTOWN INDUSTRIAL ESTATE

SLADEMORE AVENUE

ELTON PK

FOXHILL AVE

FOX-HILL LWN

SPORTS GROUND

CEDAR PARK

LARAGH CLO

STREAMVILLE ROAD

GREENCASTLE PARADE

NEWTOWN COTTS

NEWTOWN DRIVE

Sch

AYRFIELD PLACE

CLONROSSE

FOXHILL DRIVE

FOXHILL CRES

FOXHILL VWY

FOXHILL FT

Sch

THE BEECHES

COOLOCK INDUSTRIAL ESTATE

R107

AYREFIELD DRIVE

AYREFIELD AVE

AYREFIELD CT

AYREFIELD GROV

LIMEWOOD AVE

MILLBROOK GRO

MILLBROOK ROAD

1

MALAHIDE ROAD

P

Leisureplex

UCI Cinema

RATHVALE

RATHVALE AVE

LIMEWOOD PK

LIMEWOOD RD

R104

TONLEGEE

DUNREE PARK

MOATFIELD ROAD

SPRING DALE ROAD

GLENAYRE RD

TONLEGEE DRIVE

TONLEGEE AVENUE

GLENWOOD ROAD

GLENAYLE RD

Sch

Sch

Tennis Court

MILLWOOD VILLAS

St. Monica's Youth Centre

WOODBINE ROAD

WOODBINE CLO

R809

SWAN

BRENDAN'S AVE

MOATFIELD AVENUE

GLENWOOD

EDENMORE AVE

EDENMORE PARK

Health Centre

PO

Sch

MILLWOOD PARK

WOODBINE DRIVE

WOODBINE

GRANGE PARK

GRANGE GROVE

GRANGE

BRENDAN'S PK

ENNEL PARK

Convent

Sch

EDENMORE

EDENMORE GROVE

EDENMORE GREEN

EDENMORE

Sch

EDENMORE PARK

Hilltop Shopping Centre

Sch

GRANGE PARK WAY

GRANGE PARK

Mercy College

ENNEL DRIVE

GORSEFIELD COURT

BROOKFIELD

EDENMORE DRIVE

EDENMORE GARDENS

SPRINGDALE ROAD

EDENMORE GRN

EDENMORE CRES

Friary

BELMONT

St. Francis Hospice

2

RK

Schools

ENNEL DRIVE

McAULEY PARK

McAULEY

LEIN ROAD

EDENMORE

St. Joseph's Hospital

RAHENY ROAD

TUSCANY DOWNS

ASHCROFT

WOOD HEIGHTS

McAULEY PARK

McAULEY DRIVE

RIBH AVENUE

HARMONSTOWN ROAD

LEIN GDNS

LEIN ROAD

LOUGH DERG RD

R809

Sch

RAHENY

STATION RD

RATHMORE PK

ST. ASSAM'S ROAD WEST

56

ASSA

ST. ASSAM'S

Raheny

BROOKFIELD LAWN

GRACEFIELD AVENUE

BROOK

WOOD CRES

CILLEANNA ROAD

Raheny Shopping Centre

Garda

MAIN ST.

Lib

PO

AVONDALE PARK

HOWTH

MAYW

HARMONSTOWN

R105

BROOKWOOD RISE

PO

R808 SYB

ENNAFORT AVENUE

ENNAFORT COURT

ROSSDALE MANSIONS

HOWTH ROAD

ENNAFORT ROAD

ENNAFORT DR

ENNA FORT PK

ALL SAINTS DRIVE

Sch

ALL SAINTS PARK

WADE'S DR

ST. ANNE'S TER

WATER

WATERMILL

Convent Sch

WATERMILL AVENUE

WATERMILL PARK

ST. ANNE'S AVENUE

3

VY PK

WATER

ROA

THE MEADOWS

Sch

MARYVILLE

SYBIL HILL AVE

BETTYSTOWN AVE

NANIKEN RD

ALL SAINTS ROAD

WATERFALL RD

BALLYHOY AVENUE

MILL DRIVE

ST. ANNE'S DR

ST. ANNE'S

ST. ANNE'S AVENUE

HOWTH ROAD

Convent

St. Paul's Swimming Pool

ALL

SAINTS

NANIKEN RIVER

Tennis Courts

FOOTBALL GROUNDS

THE PARK ROAD

St. Paul's College

C

FOOTBALL GROUNDS

81

S T.   A N N S   P A R K

D

VERNON

P

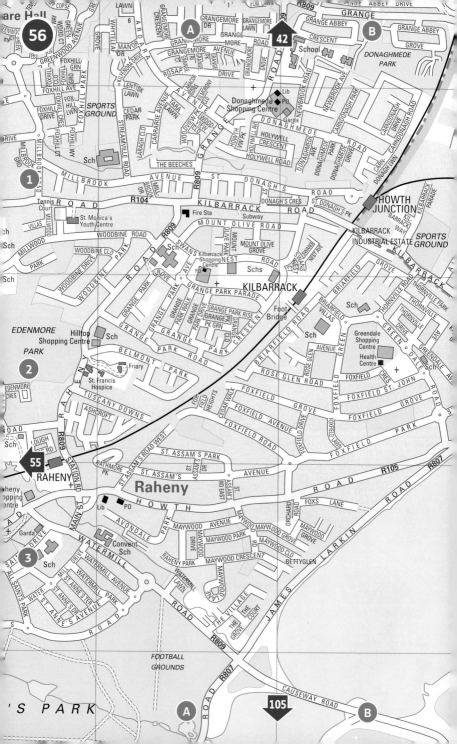

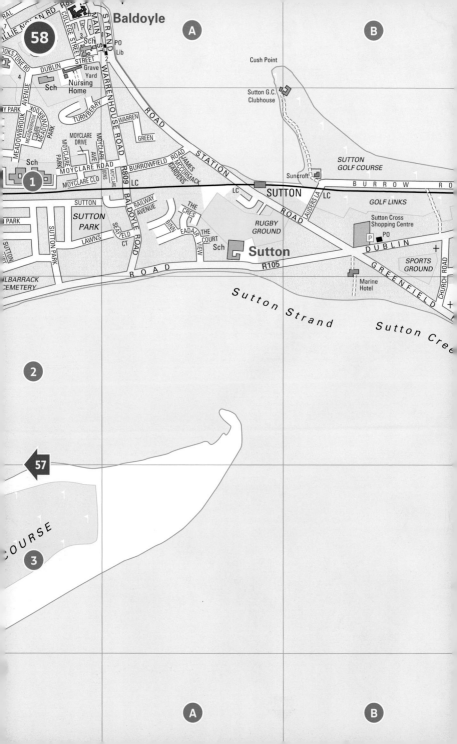

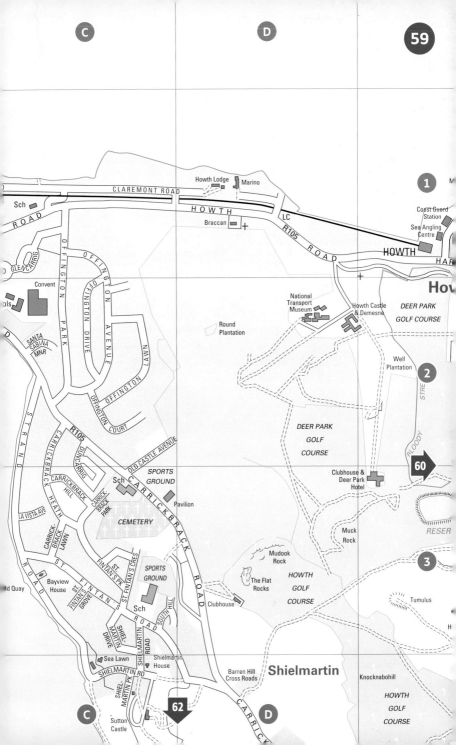

CLAREMONT ROAD

Howth Lodge Marino

Sch

HOWTH

ROAD

GLEN CARRIG

ols

Convent

OFFINGTON

OFFINGTON PARK

OFFINGTON DRIVE

OFFINGTON AVENUE

OFFINGTON LAWN

OFFINGTON COURT

SANTA SABINA MNR

Braccan

LC

R105 ROAD

HOWTH

HAR

Coast Guard Station

Sea Angling Centre

M

Hov

DEER PARK

GOLF COURSE

National Transport Museum

Howth Castle & Demesne

Round Plantation

Well Plantation

STRE

BLOODY

DEER PARK GOLF COURSE

Clubhouse & Deer Park Hotel

RESER

R105

CARRICKBRACK

CARRICKBRACK HILL

DUNCARRIG

LA VISTA AVE

CARRICK-BRACK HEATH

CARRICK-BRACK PARK

CARRICK-BRACK LAWN

STRAND

OLD CASTLE AVENUE

CARRICKBRACK ROAD

SPORTS GROUND

Sch

Pavilion

CEMETERY

Muck Rock

Mudook Rock

The Flat Rocks

HOWTH GOLF COURSE

Tumulus

H

ROAD

ld Quay

Bayview House

ST. FINTAN'S ROAD

ST. FINTAN'S PK

ST. FINTAN'S GROVE

ST. FINTAN'S CRES

SOUTH HILL

SPORTS GROUND

Sch

Clubhouse

SHIEL-MARTIN DRIVE

SHIELMARTIN ROAD

Sea Lawn

Shielmartin House

SHIELMARTIN RD

SHIEL-MARTIN PK

Barren Hill Cross Roads

Shielmartin

Knocknabohill

HOWTH GOLF COURSE

Sutton Castle

CARRICK

A

B

1

CLAREMONT ROAD

Howth Lodge Marino

Mariners
Hall

West Pier

H O W T H

LC

Coast Guard
Station

Braccan

Sea Angling
Centre

R105 ROAD

HOWTH

P

HOWTH HARBOUR ROAD

Promenade

Howth

OFFINGTON DRIVE

OFFINGTON

AVENUE

OFFINGTON LAWN

National
Transport
Museum

Round
Plantation

Howth Castle
& Demesne

DEER PARK
GOLF COURSE

Garda CHU

ST LAWREN

EVORA PARK

EVORA CRES

GRACE O'MALLEY ROAD

Sch

TUCKE
ST PETERS

2

OFFINGTON COURT

Well
Plantation

BLOODY STREAM

GRACE
O'MALLEY
DRIVE

BALGLA
ESTAT

DEER PARK

GOLF

COURSE

BALGLASS ESTATE

BALKILL PK

59

OLD CASTLE AVENUE

SPORTS
GROUND

Clubhouse &
Deer Park
Hotel

BEA
G

CARRICK
BRACK
PARK

Sch

CARRICKBRACK

Pavilion

CEMETERY

ROAD

RESERVOIR

Old
Plantation

Muck
Rock

3

ST FINTAN'S CRES

SPORTS
GROUND

Mudook
Rock

The Flat
Rocks

HOWTH

GOLF

COURSE

Tumulus

Ben
of
Howth

Lough

ST FINTAN'S

ROAD

Sch

Clubhouse

SOUTH HILL

Blac
Linn

SHIEL-
MARTIN
DRIVE

Sea Lawn

SHIELMARTIN
ROAD

Shielmartin
House

SHIELMARTIN RD

Barren Hill
Cross Roads

Shielmartin

Knocknabohill

SHIEL
MARTIN PK

CARRICK

A

62

HOWTH

GOLF

Blac

Sutton
Castle

B

COURSE

1

Lighthouse

HOWTH
HARBOUR

East Pier

P

Martello
Tower

BALSCADDEN BAY

Puck's Rocks

Health
Centre

B A L S C A D D E N   R O A D

P

Kilrock

Nose
of
Howth

2

ABBEY STREET

MAIN STREET

ST.

Lib

ASGARD PK.

KILROCK ROAD

NASHVILLE PARK

NASHVILLE RD

Kilrock

CROSSTREES

T H O R M A N B Y

ASGARD
ROAD

CANNON ROCK VIEW

COWBOOTER LANE

C L I F F   W A L K   (fingal   Way)

THORMANBY
LAWNS

UPPER
CLIFF RD

Cannon Rock
Cottage

DUNGRIFFAN   ROAD

BALKILL

MARINERS
COVE

WOODCLIFF
HEIGHTS

R O A D

CASANA VIEW

3

GREYS
L'NE

THORMANBY WOODS

THORMANBY
LODGE

Rookstown

Green
Ivy

Hills

WINDGATE

ROAD

Ashville

Highfield

Bearna

Piper's
Gut

KITESTOWN ROAD

R105

Oakley Park

NEW ROAD
R'SE

WINDGATE

R O A D

ROAD

KE CK

BAILEY GRN RD

C L I F F   W A L K

The
Haven

Fox Hole

White
Water

Old Baily
Cottage

60

A

B

C

1

2

3

OFFINGTON
OFFINGTON COURT

R105

DUNARRIG

CARRICKBRACK HILL

LA VISTA AVE

CARRICKBRACK HEATH

OLD CASTLE AVENUE

Sch

CARRICKBRACK
CARRICK-
BRACK
PARK

CARRICK-
BRACK
LAWN

CARRICKBRACK ROAD

SPORTS
GROUND

Pavilion

CEMETERY

Old Quay

ST. FINTAN'S ROAD

Bayview
House

ST. FINTAN'S PK

ST. FINTAN'S CRES

ST FINTAN'S GROVE

SPORTS
GROUND

Sch

SOUTH HILL

Clubhouse

SHEL-
MARTIN
DRIVE

SHELMARTIN ROAD

Sea Lawn

SHELMARTIN RD

SHELMARTIN PK

Shielmartin
House

SHEL-
MARTIN

Sutton
Castle

Martello
Tower

DEER PARK

GOLF

COURSE

Clubhouse &
Deer Park
Hotel

Muck
Rock

Mudook
Rock

The Flat
Rocks

HOWTH

GOLF

COURSE

Barren Hill
Cross Roads

Shielmartin

Knocknabohill

HOWTH

GOLF

COURSE

Pumping
House

CARRICKBRACK ROAD

Somali

Shielmartin
Cottage

CARRICKE

R105

CEANNCHOR ROAD

BALSAGGART STREAM

Pumping
House

Shearwater

CLIFF WALK

The
Cliffs

The
Tansey

CEANNCHOR RD

The
Needles

Cean
Hous

Drumleck

Sheep Hole

Worn
Hole

Drumle

Tumulus

RES

BLOODY
STREA

A

B

C

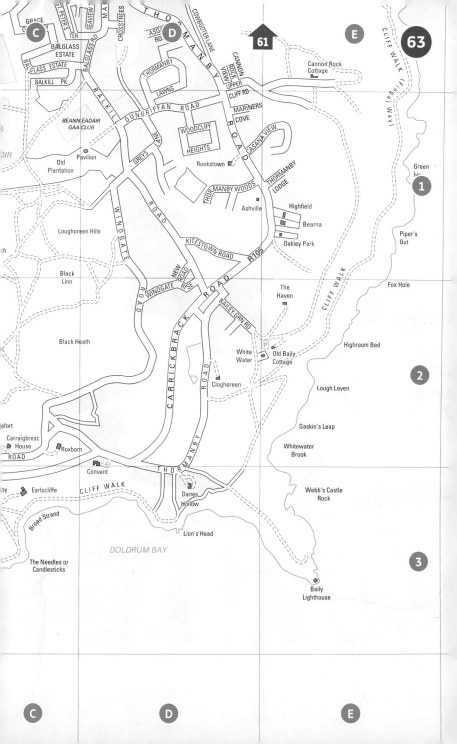

GRACE

ST PETER'S

SEAVIEW

CROSSTREES

C

BALGLASS ESTATE

BALGLASS ESTATE

BALKILL PK

ASGA ROAD

D

THORMANBY

COWBOOTER LANE

E

CLIFF WALK (Fingal Way)

Cannon Rock Cottage

BALKILL RD

THORMANBY LAWNS

CANNON ROCK VIEW

UPPER CLIFF RD

MARINERS COVE

DUNGRIFFAN ROAD

CASANA VIEW

Green Ivy

1

BEANN EADAIR GAA CLUB

GREYS LANE

WOODCLIFF HEIGHTS

Rookstown

THORMANBY WOODS

THORMANBY LODGE

Piper's Gut

Old Plantation

Pavilion

Ashville

Highfield

Bearna

Oakley Park

Loughoreen Hills

WINDGATE ROAD

KITESTOWN ROAD

R105

Fox Hole

Black Linn

NEW ROAD

WINDGATE ROAD

RISE

The Haven

CLIFF WALK

Highroom Bed

2

Black Heath

CARRICKBRACK ROAD

BAILEY GRN RD

White Water

P

Old Baily Cottage

Lough Leven

Cloghereen

sfort

Carraigbreac House

Roxborn

ROAD

Convent

THORMANBY ROAD

Gaskin's Leap

Whitewater Brook

Earlscliffe

CLIFF WALK

Danes Hollow

Webb's Castle Rock

3

Broad Strand

Lion's Head

The Needles or Candlesticks

DOLDRUM BAY

Baily Lighthouse

C

D

E

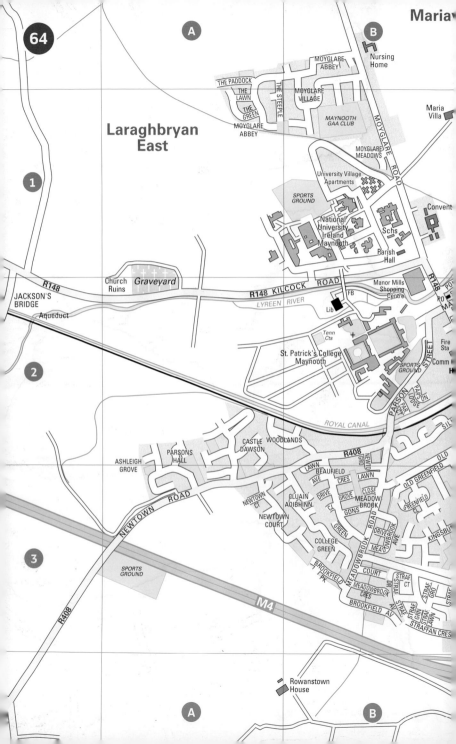

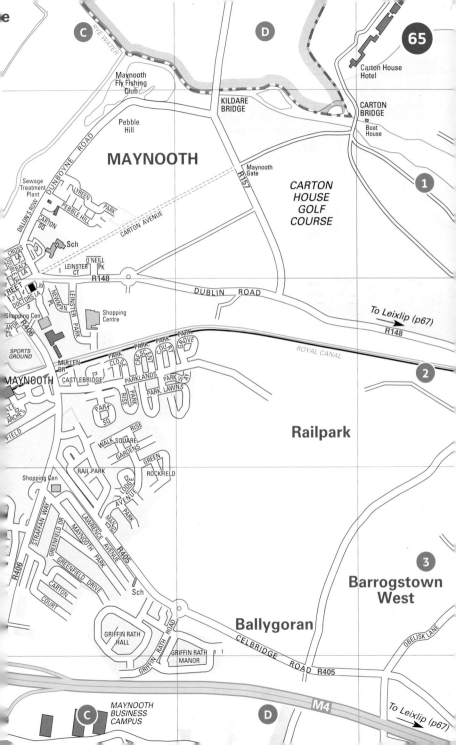

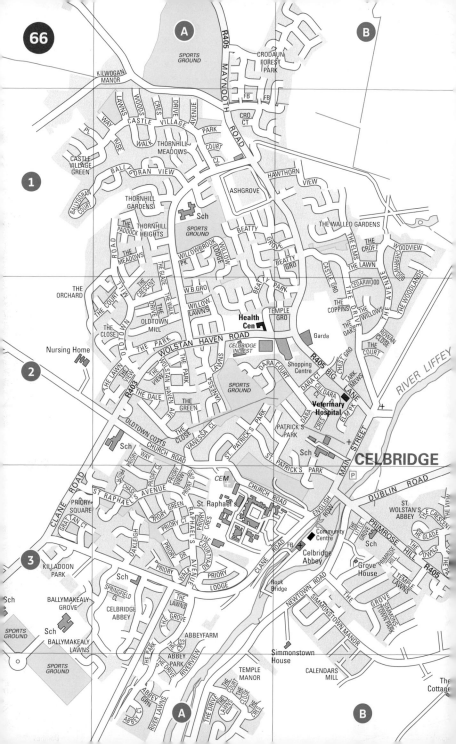

To Maynooth (p65)

DUBLIN ROAD

ROYAL CANAL

C

D

COLLINSTOWN
INDUSTRIAL
PARK

INTEL
INDUSTRIAL
ESTATE

DEEY
BRIDGE
R148

LC

Am...s
Centre

1

ROYAL CANAL

SPOR...
GROU...

WOODS
WAY
VIEW
MANOR
GREEN
GLEN EASTON
SQUARE
GARDENS
RISE

PARK
GROVE
DRIVE
CLOSE
AVE
AVE
CRES

LOUGH
MON...
CRE...

Shopping
Centre

EASTON
ROAD

CL

2

Kilmacredock
Stud

Kilmacredock
House

EASTON
ROAD

R449

R449

LEIXLIP GATE

VIEW
VIEW
VIEW
VIEW
VIEW
LAWNS
RINAWADE
RISE
RINAWADE AVENUE
DOWNS
SQUARE
CRES
RINAWADE GROVE
GRO...

68

To Maynooth (p65)

R449

To Celbridge (p66)

M4

3

C

D

THORN

Barnhall

HEWLE...
IND...

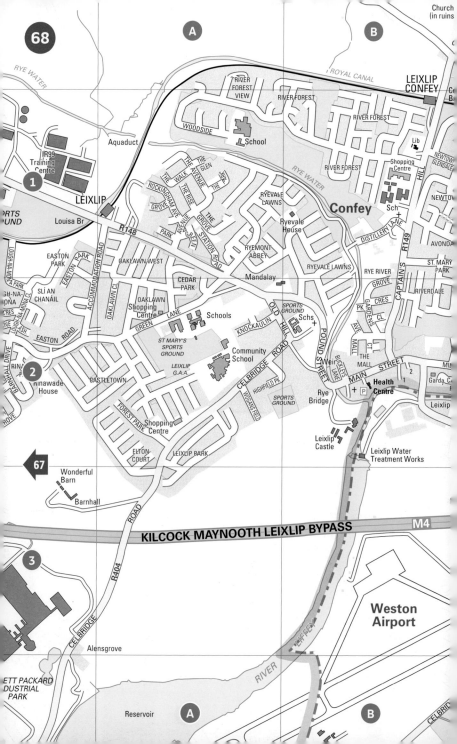

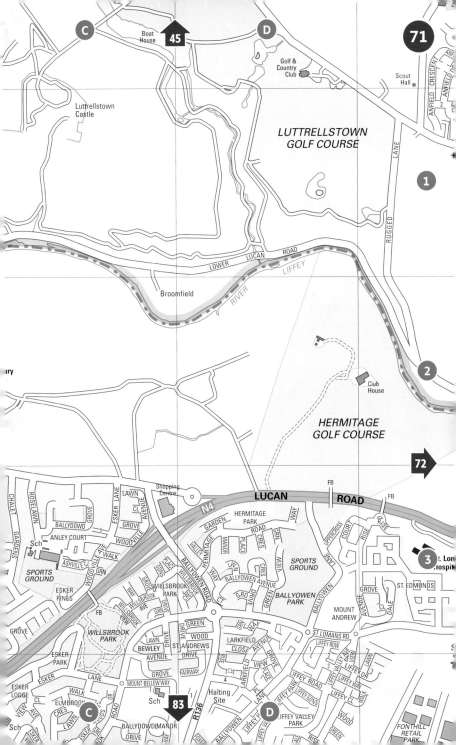

Boat House

45

Golf & Country Club

Scout Hall

ANFIELD CRESCENT
ANFIELD
ANFIELD

Luttrellstown Castle

LUTTRELLSTOWN GOLF COURSE

1

RUGGED LANE

LOWER LUCAN ROAD

LIFFEY

Broomfield

RIVER

2

ury

Club House

HERMITAGE GOLF COURSE

72

Shopping Centre

LUCAN **ROAD**

FB
FB

N4

CHALET GARDENS
ROSELAWN GROVE
ESKER LANE
LAWN
CL
AVENUE
GROVE

HERMITAGE PARK

WAY

UPPERCROSS LANE

COURT
RISE
RISE

BALLYDOWD
GROVE

GARDEN

HERMITAGE

ROAD

PLACE

CRES

GRN

t. Lom
tospi

3

ANLEY COURT
WOODVILLE

MANOR

VALLEY
WAY

GROVE

ST. EDMUNDS

Sch
ASHVILLE CL
WOODVILLE AVE
WALK
WOODVILLE GRN

BALLYOWEN ROAD
PLACE
GDNS

CRES
LAWN

SPORTS GROUND

MOUNT ANDREW

AVENUE
GROVE
DALE

SPORTS GROUND

ESKER PINES

GROVE
GRV

WILLSBROOK PARK
CRES

BALLYOWEN AVENUE

BALLYOWEN PARK

BALLYOWEN

GROVE

GROVE

WILLSBROOK AVE
WILLSBROOK DRV

DRIVE

GROVE
CT

ST LOMANS RD
LIFFEY ROW

FB

WILLSBROOK PARK

GREEN
WOOD

LAWN

LAWN GRN
VIEW

LIFFEY VALLEY AVE
LIFFEY DR

ESKER PARK

LAWN
BEWLEY AVENUE
ST. ANDREWS DRIVE

LARKFIELD
CLOSE

AVENUE

LIFFEY VALLEY WAY
LIFFEY ROAD

GROVE
FAIRWAY

LARKFIELD
PL
VIEW

LIFFEY GDNS
LIFFEY

ESKER LANE

GROVE

ESKER WALK

LANE

MOUNT BELLEW WAY

Sch

83

R136

Halting Site
4

LIFFEY
LANE

LIFFEY VALLEY PARK

WOOD

FONTHILL RETAIL PARK

ESKER LODGE
VIEW
AVE
CL
ELMBROOK CRES
LAWN

C

GRV
ROAD

D

LIFFEY VALLEY
AVE
RISE

Sch

BALLYDOWD MANOR DRIVE

BALLYOWEN

GREEN

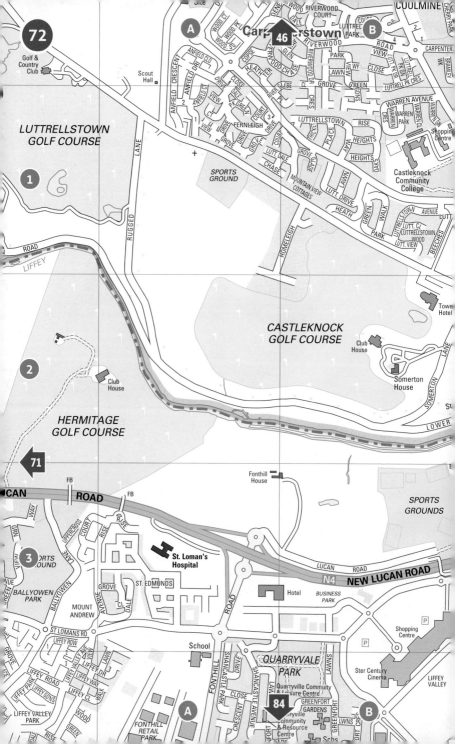

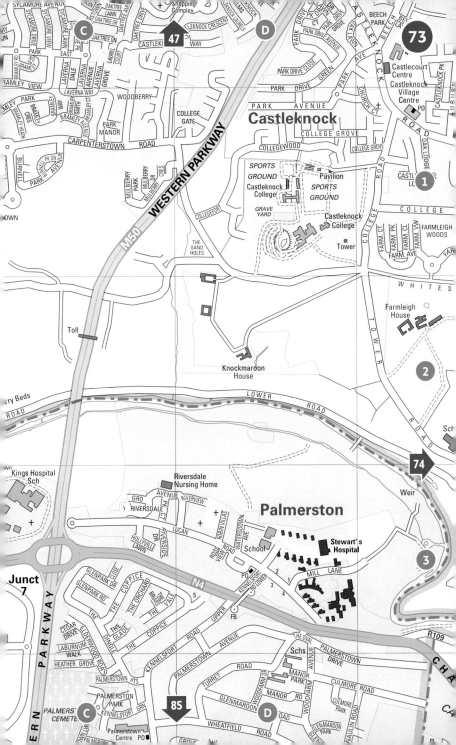

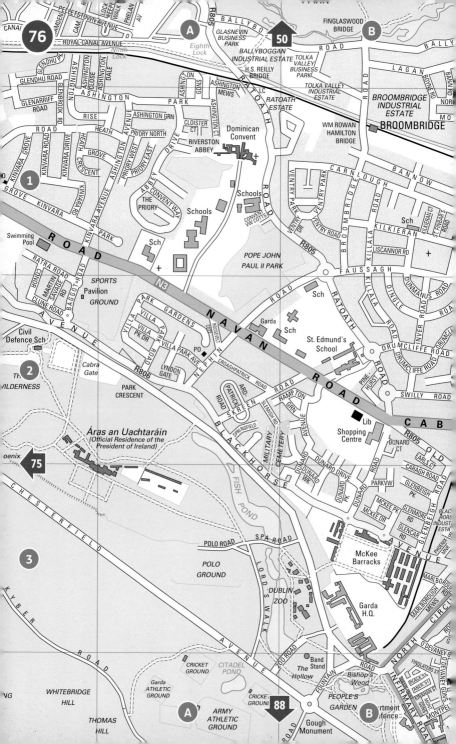

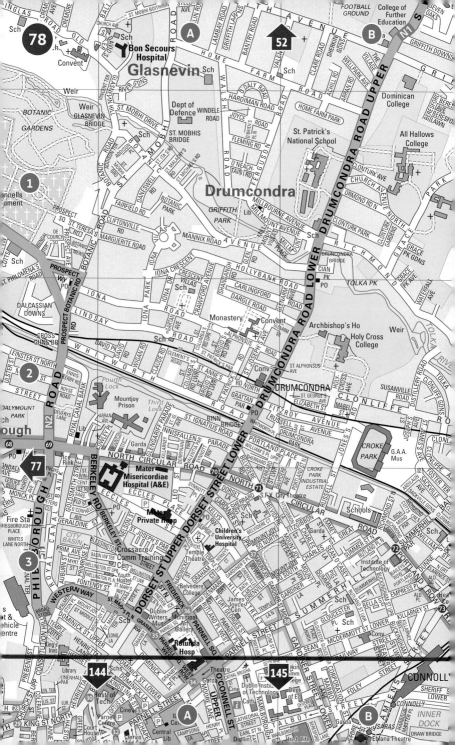

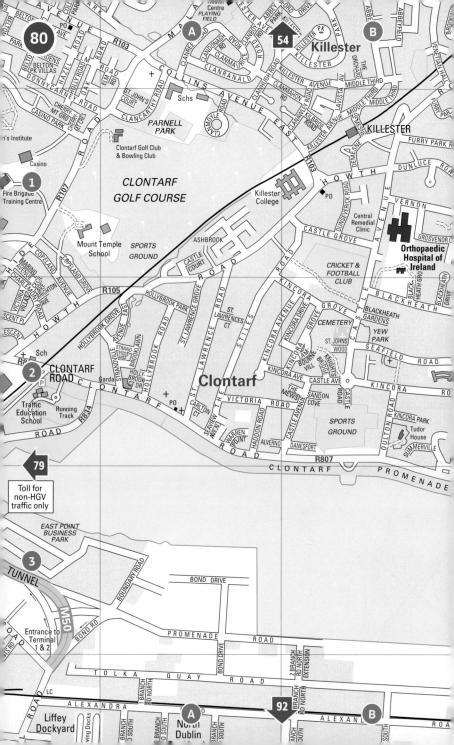

C
55
D

Sch
Convent
St. Paul's
Swimming Pool
The MEADOWS
St.Paul's
College

NANIKEN RIVER

Tennis
Courts

FOOTBALL
GROUNDS

FOOTBALL
GROUNDS

ST. ANNE'S PARK

1

VERNON
RISE

VERNON DR

VERNON
HEATH

VERNON

WOODSIDE

MOUNT PROSPECT DRIVE

FOOTBALL
GROUNDS

Rose
Garden

PARK LAWN

AVENUE

St. Anne's
(Ruins)

JAMES

LARKIN

HAMPTON

COURT

OAKLEY PK

BLACKHEATH
COURT

CASTILLA
PARK

VERNON
PARK

VERNON

SEAPARK
AVENUE

SEAFIELD AVENUE

Sch

MOUNT
PROSPECT
LAWNS

MOUNT
PROSPECT
PARK

MOUNT

PROSPECT

MOUNT
PROSPECT GROVE

SEAFIELD
GRO

Convent

Dollymount

BAYMOUNT
PARK

Manresa
Retreat House

THE OAKS

THE
MEWS

DOLLYMOUNT AVENUE

R807

MERCHAMP

KINCORA

SEAFIELD

VERNON GDN

VERNON GRO

CHELSEA
GARDENS

SEAPARK ROAD

SEACOURT

DOLLYMOUNT
GROVE

PO

ST. GABRIELS CT

DOLLYMOUNT

ST. GABRIELS ROAD

DOLLYMOUNT
RISE

DOYLE'S
LANE

DOLLYMOUNT

PARK

2

R808

Sch

SEAPARK DRIVE

KINCORA GRO

KINCORA COURT

SEAFIELD
ROAD

EAST

REDCOURT
OAKS

DANES
COURT

KINCORA RD

SEAFIELD
DOWN

BULL BRIDGE
(WOODEN BRIDGE)

105

CLONTARF
PARK

FORTVIEW
AVENUE

VERNON COURT

CONQUER
HILL ROAD

BRIAN
BORU ST

TRAM
TERRACE

BRIAN
BORU AVE

CLONTARF

GATE
AVE

Yacht Club Slipway

Royal Dublin
Golf Club

3

BULL

WALL

P

TERMINAL
ROAD
NORTH

C
93
D

ALEXANDRA ROAD
EXTENSION

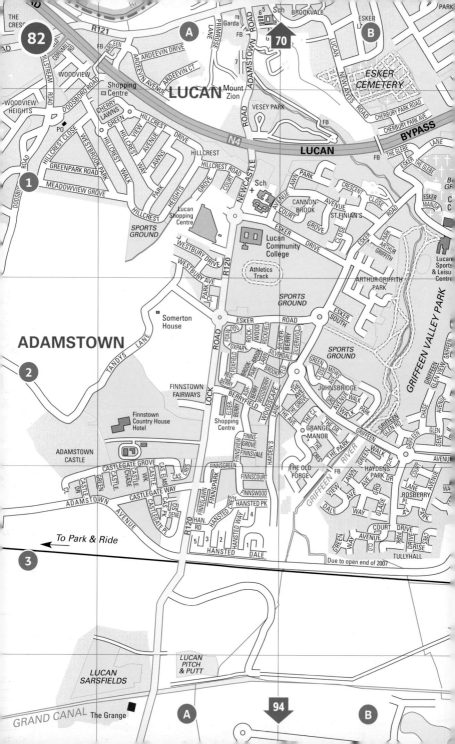

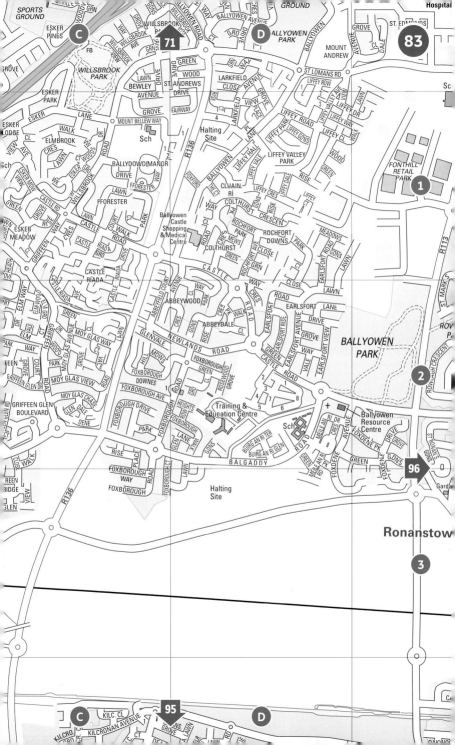

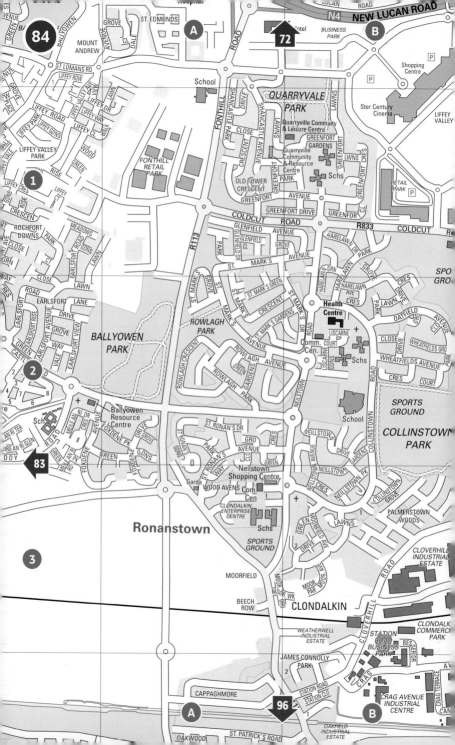

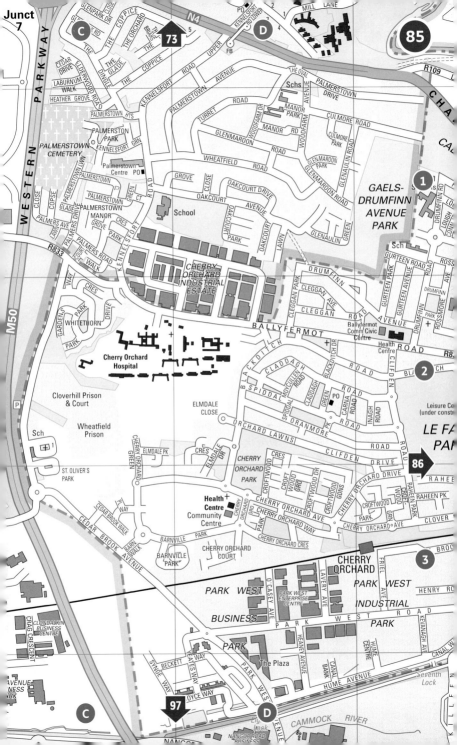

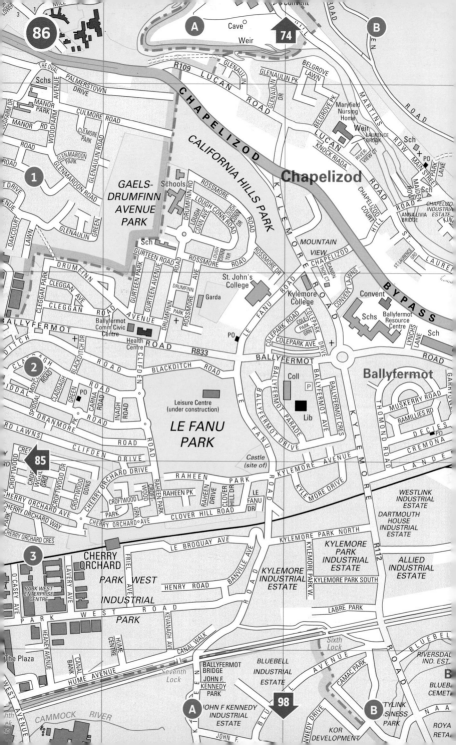

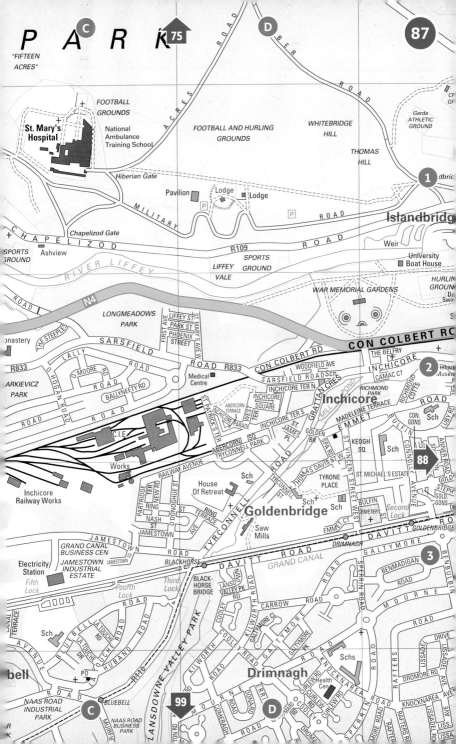

P A R K

C A R K 75

"FIFTEEN ACRES"

FOOTBALL GROUNDS

St. Mary's Hospital

National Ambulance Training School

FOOTBALL AND HURLING GROUNDS

WHITEBRIDGE HILL

Garda ATHLETIC GROUND

THOMAS HILL

Hiberian Gate

1

dbrid

Pavilion

Lodge Lodge

P

MILITARY ROAD

Islandbridge

CHAPELIZOD

Chapelizod Gate

R109

SPORTS GROUND

R O A D

Weir

SPORTS GROUND

Ashview

LIFFEY VALE

University Boat House

RIVER LIFFEY

WAR MEMORIAL GARDENS

HURLIN GROUN Sw

N4

ROAD

Monastery

THE STEEPLES

LONGMEADOWS PARK

LIFFEY ST

FIRST AVE

ST. MARY'S AVE

PARK ST

PHOENIX STREET

CON COLBERT RO

THE BELFRY

INCHICORE

inhal Muse

SARSFIELD

ROAD R833

CON COLBERT RD

WOODFIELD AVE

CAMAC CT

2

R833

LALLY ROAD

HOGAN ROAD

MOORE RD

ROAD

BALLYNEETY RD

ROAD

Medical Centre

SARSFIELD ROAD Sch

INCHICORE TER N.

Richmond Park

MILL POND

RICHMOND COTTS

INCHICORE

GRATTAN CRES

Inchicore

ROAD

MARKIEVICZ PARK

ROAD

ST. PATRICK'S TER

ABERCORN TERRACE

INCHICORE PARADE

WEST TER

INCHICORE SQUARE

INCHICORE TER S.

ST JAMES PL

GOLDEN BR

BULFIN

CON. GDNS

Sch

EMMET

MADELEINE TERRACE

Sch

KEOGH SQ

ANNER ROAD

88

C.I.E.

ABERCORN SQ TYRCONNELL PARK

THOMAS DAVIS ST W

ST. VINCENT STREET WEST

ST. MICHAEL'S ESTATE

STEPH

GOLD.

GDNS

Works

Inchicore Railway Works

RAILWAY AVENUE

House Of Retreat

Sch

ROAD

TYRONE PLACE

BULFIN CEMETERY

Second Lock

CONNELL AVENUE

PARTRIDGE TER

RING TER

NEW RD

NASH ST

O'DONOGHUE ST

Ring Terrace

JAMESTOWN

TYRCONNELL

Sch

Sch

EMMET CT

Goldenbridge

DAVITT

Goldenbridge

JAMESTOWN

GRAND CANAL BUSINESS CEN

JAMESTOWN INDUSTRIAL ESTATE

JAMESTOWN RD

ROAD

BLACKHORSE

Saw Mills

DRIMNAGH

ROAD

GALTYMORE

3

Electricity Station

Fifth Lock

Fourth Lock

Third Lock

BLACK-HORSE BRIDGE

LANSDO

VALLEY PK

DAVITT

GRAND CANAL

ROAD

SPERRIN ROAD

BENMADIGAN ROAD

MOURNE

BENBULBIN

CANAL TERRACE

AVENUE

Sch

BLUEBELL

LA TOUCHE RD

LA TOUCHE DR

HUBANO

ROAD

R810

LANSDOWNE VALLEY PARK

LANSDOWN VALLEY PK

KILWORTH ROAD

CARROW

COOLEY ROAD

COOLEY ROAD

GALTYMORE ROAD

GALTYMORE RD

ROAD

ROAD

RAFTERS

LISSADEL DRIVE

LISSADEL RD

DROMORE RD

bell

ROAD

NAAS ROAD INDUSTRIAL PARK

MUIRIE

PO

C

BLUEBELL

NAAS ROAD BUSINESS PARK

99

KILWORTH ROAD

NE RD

DONARD

COMERAGH

MOU

COOLEY RD

CURLEW RD

CURLEW

Drimnagh

Health Cen

Schs

KNOCKNAREA ROAD

CURLEW RD

KNOCKNAREA AVE

LISSADEL AV

RAFTERS

D

DROM

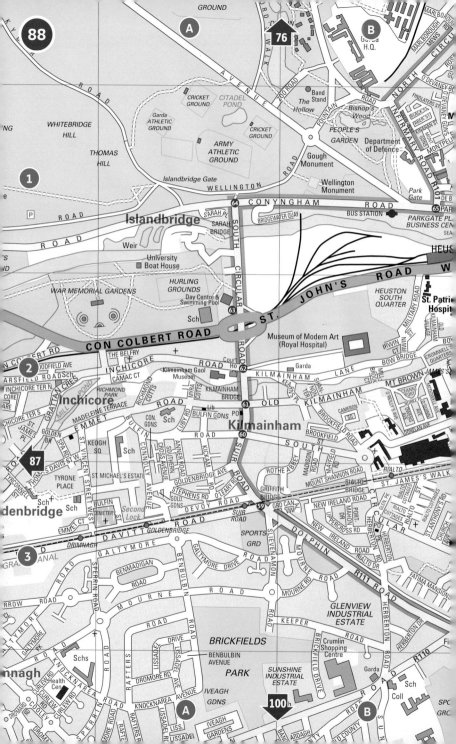

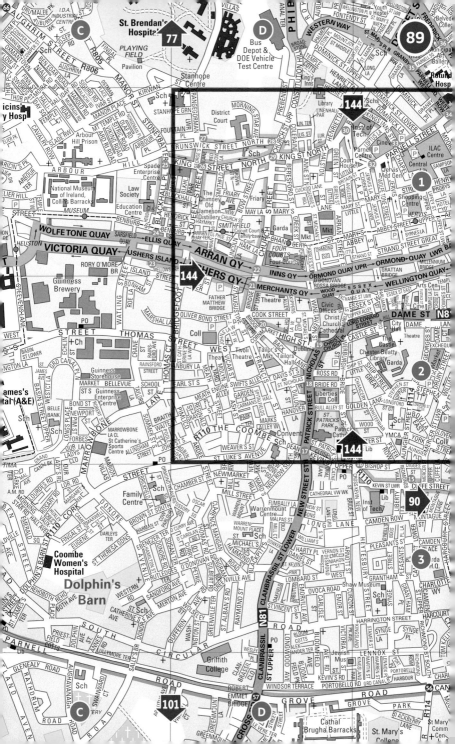

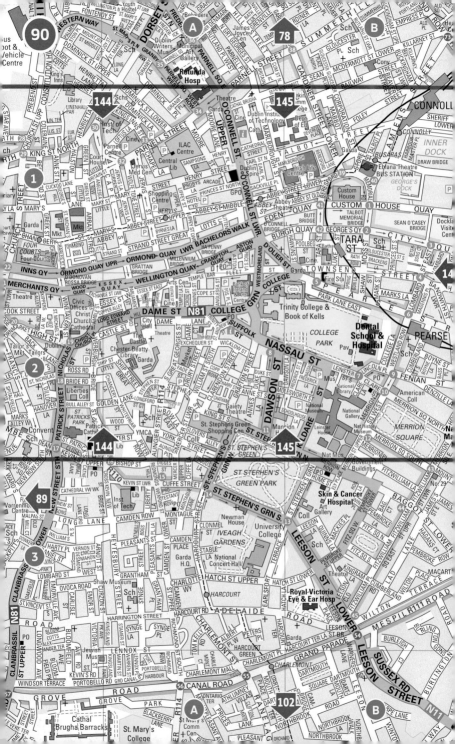

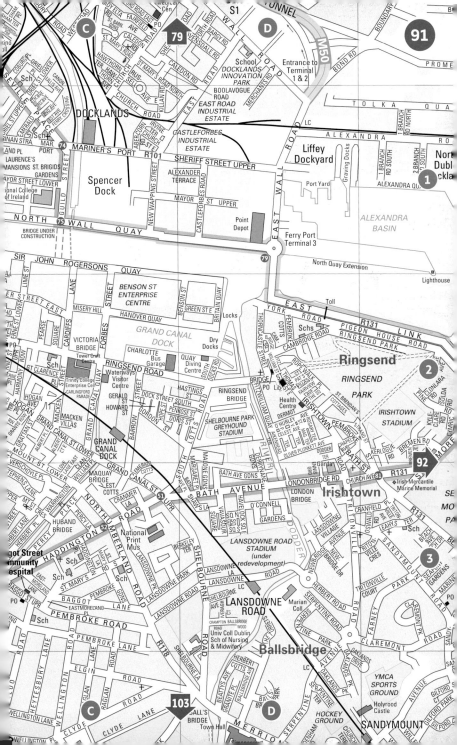

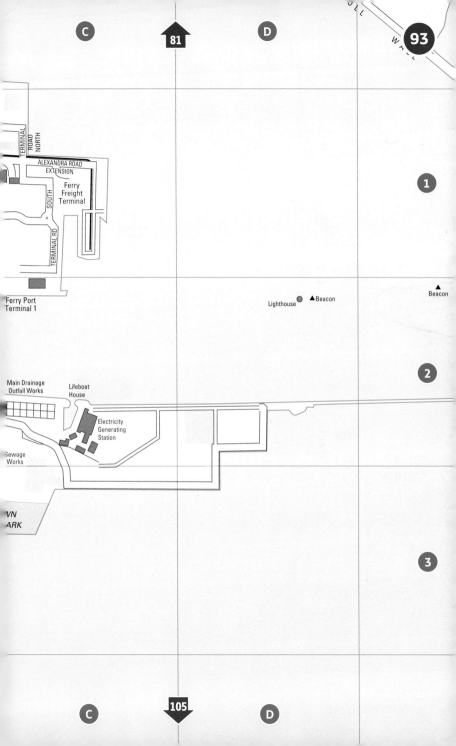

1

TERMINAL ROAD NORTH

ALEXANDRA ROAD EXTENSION

TERMINAL RD SOUTH

Ferry
Freight
Terminal

Ferry Port
Terminal 1

Lighthouse ● ▲Beacon

▲
Beacon

2

Main Drainage
Outfall Works

Lifeboat
House

Electricity
Generating
Station

Sewage
Works

VN
ARK

3

A   82   B

LUCAN
PITCH
& PUTT

LUCAN
SARSFIELDS

GRAND CANAL   The Grange

R120

1

Clutterland

GRANGE C
INTERNAT
BUSINE
PARK

Ballybane
Pitch & Putt

2

KILCARBERRY
INDUSTRIAL
ESTATE

THE COURTYARD
BUSINESS
PARK

R120   R134

NANGOR   ROAD   R134

Milltown

3

GR
GO

Castle
Bagot
House

Burial
Ground

Kilmactalway   A   106   B

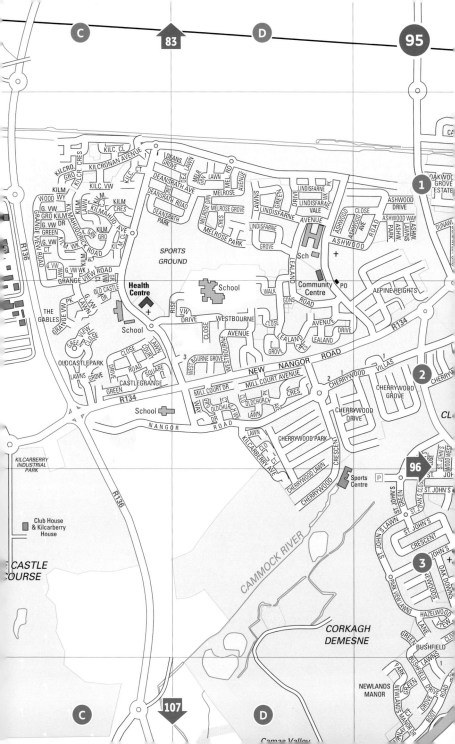

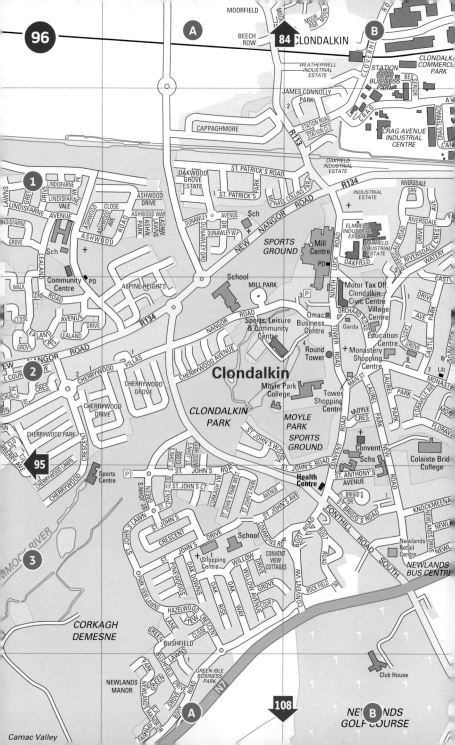

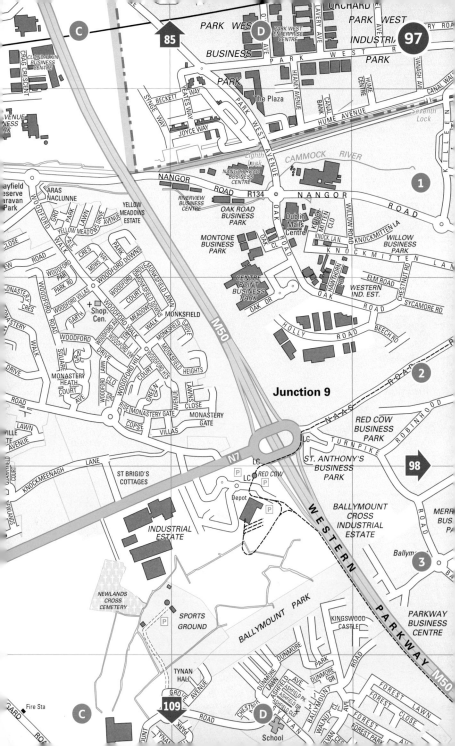

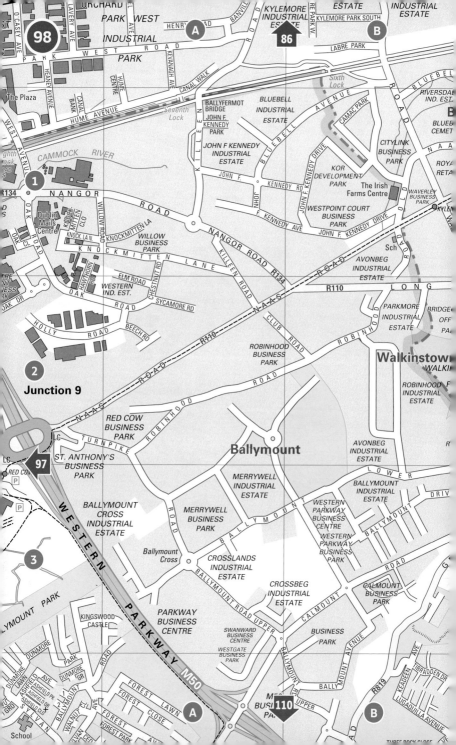

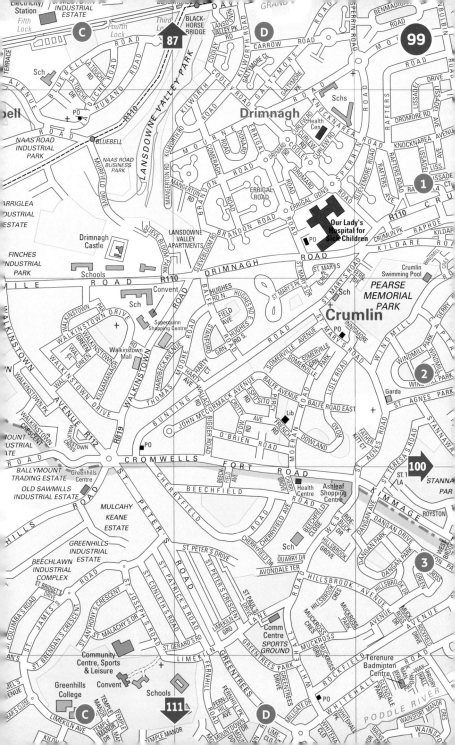

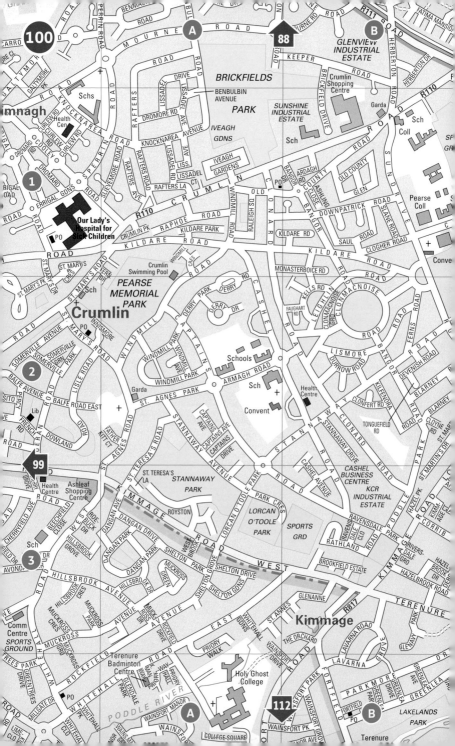

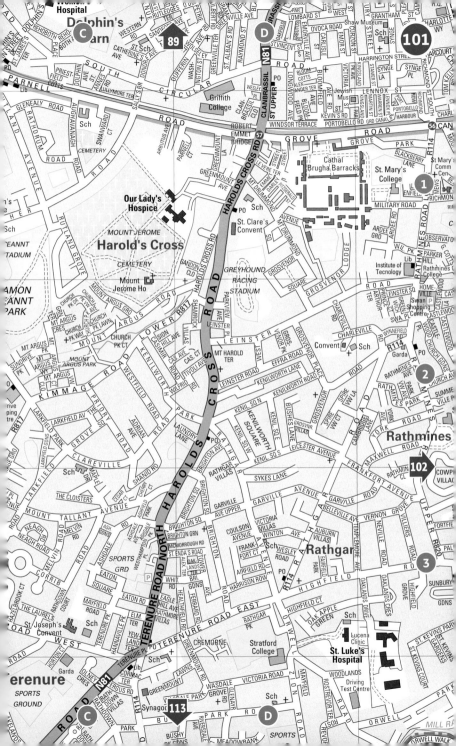

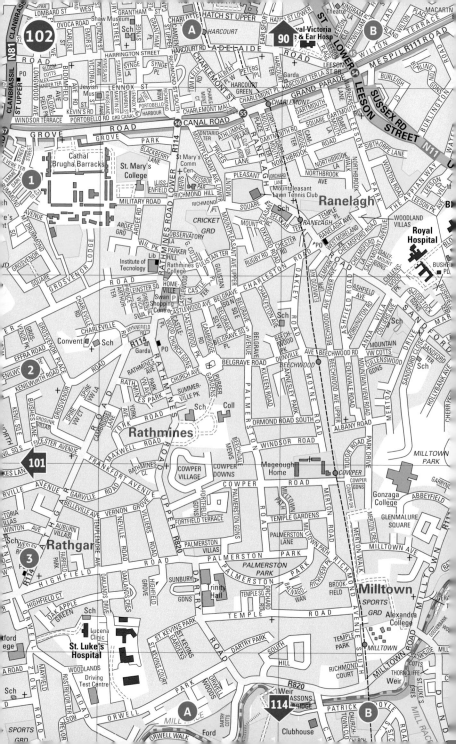

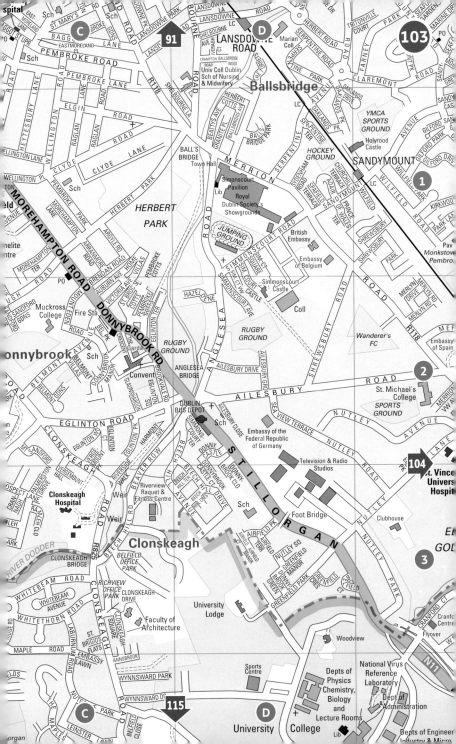

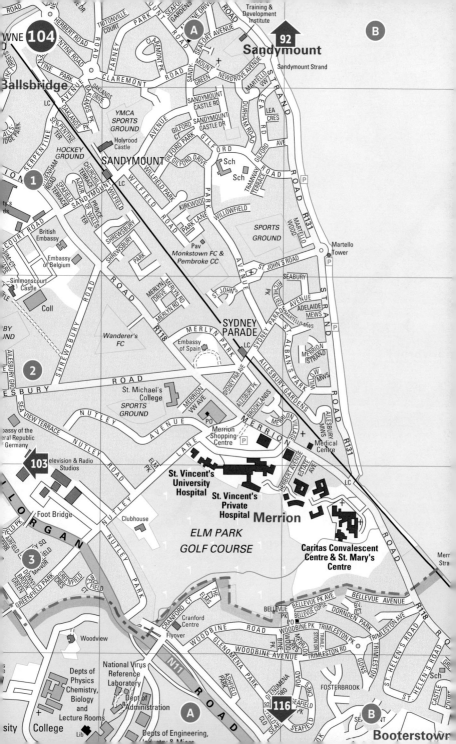

MILL AVENUE

PARK ROAD

MILL AVENUE

MAYWOOD LANE

THE VILLAGE

THE GROVE

THE COURT

JAMES

R809

R807

JAMES LARKIN ROAD

FOOTBALL GROUNDS

CAUSEWAY ROAD

North

St. Anne's (Ruins)

81

Interpretive & Visitors Centre

P

1

R O Y A L   D U B L I N   G O L F   C O U R S E

2

3

Royal Dublin

)TERSTOWN

P

AVENUE

School

Martello Tower

ROAD

Castle
Bagot
House

A

94

B

GO

Burial
Ground

Kilmactalway

1

ROCK
ENTERPRISE
CENTRE

Casement Military Aerodrome
(Baldonnell)

2

Jordanstown

Collegeland

3

CLONLARA ROAD

BALDONNELL
BUSINESS
PARK

CLONLARA AVENUE

N7

CLONLARA

GARTER LANE

CITYWEST
GOLF COURSE

120

A

B

108

CORKAGH DEMESNE

NEWLANDS BUS CENTRE

A

96

B

Club House

NEWLANDS GOLF COURSE

BUSHFIELD

GREEN ISLE BUSINESS PARK

NEWLANDS MANOR

NAAS ROAD

BOOT ROAD

Camac Valley Camping & Caravan Park

1

Kingswood Interchange

2

QUARRY

Sports Club

Kingswood

Club H

Walkin Rugby Club

2

PITCH & PUTT

SPORTS FIELD

107

KINGSWOOD DRIVE

KINGSWOOD ROAD

3

Re (co

ALPINE RISE

BELGARD GREEN

Fettercairn Youth Horse Project

Community Centre

FETTERCAIRN ROAD

KILCARRIG AVENUE

KILCARRIG CRES

KILCARRIG CLOSE

KILCARRIG

Schs

School

McGEE PARK

St. Mark's G.A.A. Club

KILMARTIN PK

KILMARTIN GDNS

KILMARTIN DRIVE

KILMARTIN AVENUE

DRUMCAIRN DRIVE

PARK AVENUE

COOKSTOWN ROAD

St Aiden's Halting Site

BROOKFIELD COURT

BROOKVIEW GDNS

BROOKFIELD ROAD

ROSSFIELD DRIVE

ROSSFIELD GROVE

ROSSFIELD PARK

ROSSFIELD AVENUE

ROSSFIELD GARDENS

CHEEVERSTOWN AVENUE

DRUMCAIRN AVENUE

SPORTS GROUND

Sch

Health Centre

Sch

Community Centre

BROOKVIEW

BROOKFIELD GROVE

ROSSFIELD CRESCENT

ROSSFIELD GRN

A

SWIFTBROOK AVE

GLENSHANE GRO

GLENSHANE

122

B

BROOK PARK

Shopping Centre

PO

MAPLE

CRES

RAHEEN

School

Shopping

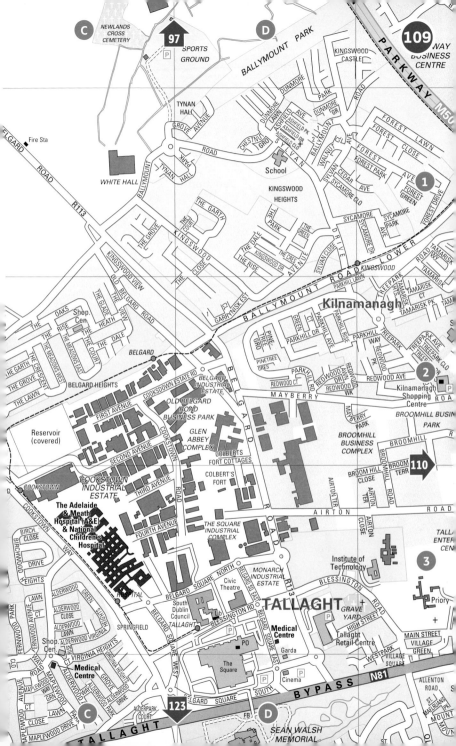

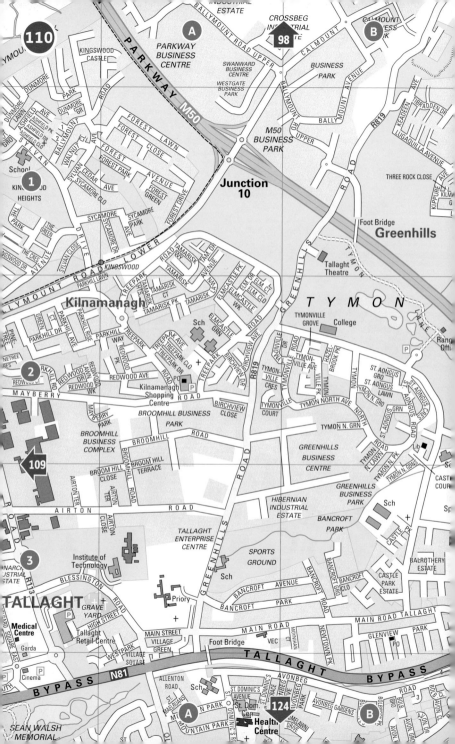

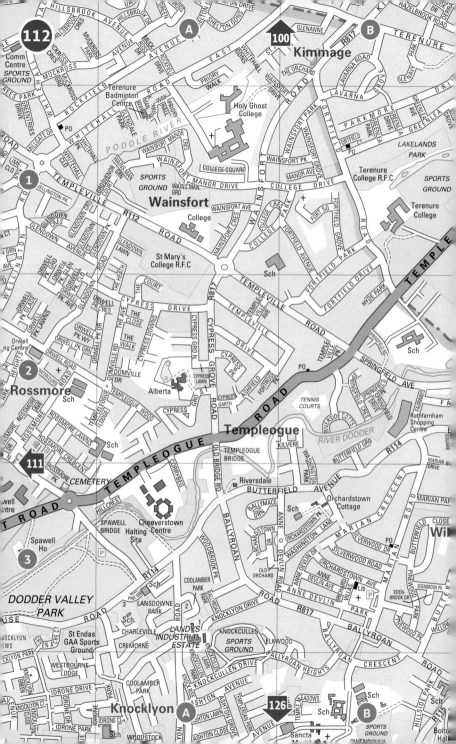

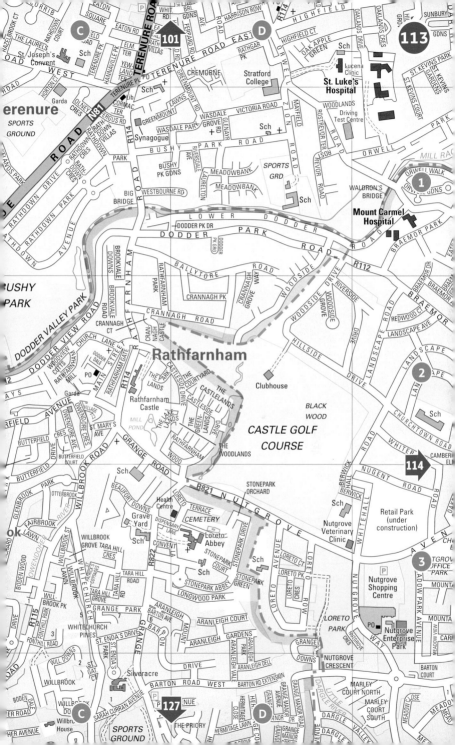

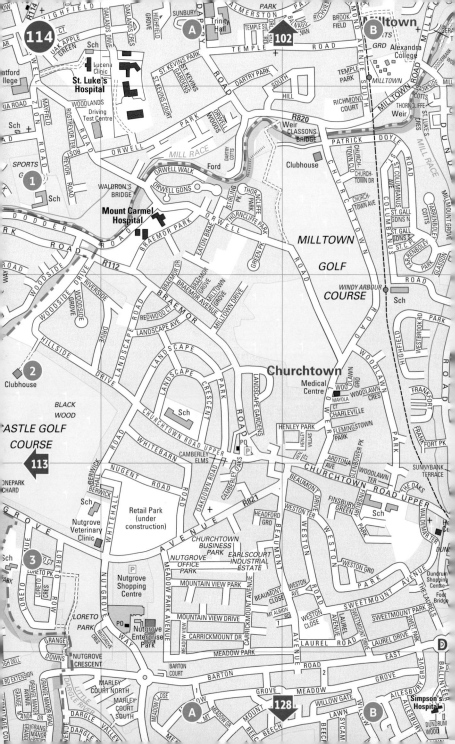

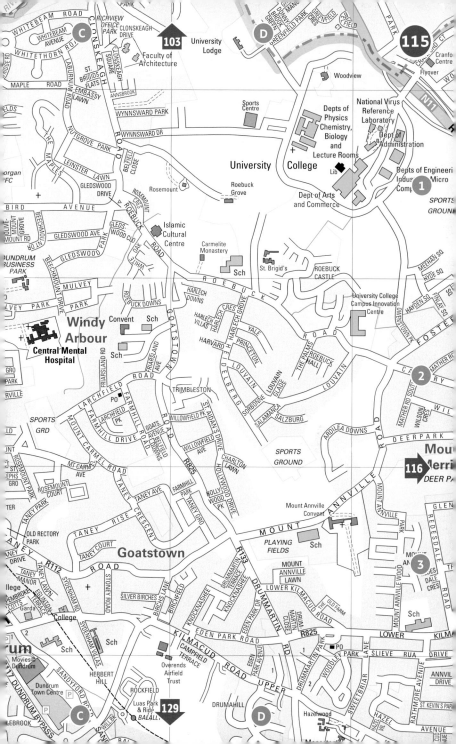

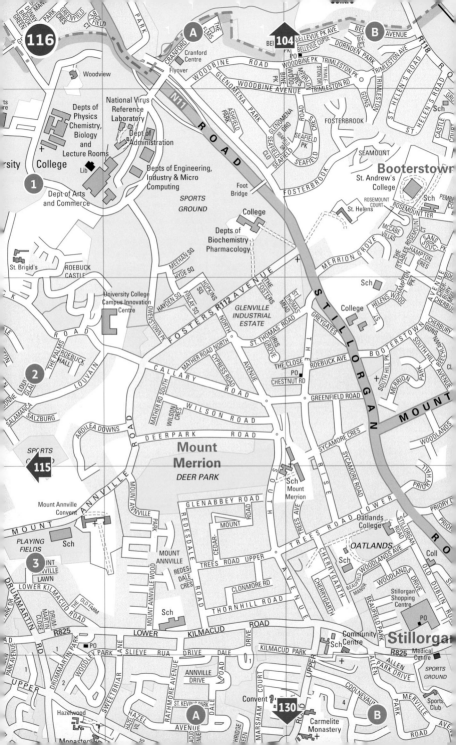

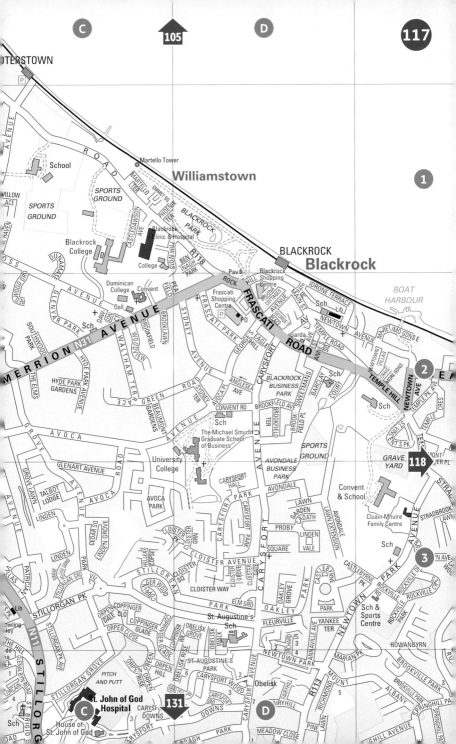

OTERSTOWN

P

School

SPORTS
GROUND

Martello Tower

Williamstown

SPORTS
GROUND

WILLOW
ACE

SPORTS
GROUND

Blackrock
College

College

Blackrock
Clinic & Hospital

BLACKROCK
PARK

Dominican
College

Convent

Coll

DAW

Frascati
Shopping
Centre

P

Rock
Hill

Pav

Blackrock
Shopping
Centre

BLACKROCK

Blackrock

IDRONE TERRACE

BOAT
HARBOUR

Sch

Lib

PO

Garda

NEWTOWN

TEMPLE ROAD

Temple Road

2

E

MERRION AVENUE N31

HYDE PARK
GARDENS

THE ELMS

GLENVAR PARK

SOUTHWOOD
PARK

DUNAMASE

BROOKLAWN

SYDNEY AVENUE

WALTHAM TERRACE

GREEN

BEAUMONT GARDENS

FRASCATI PARK

FRASCATI ROAD

GEORGE'S AVENUE

CARYSFORT AVENUE

EAGLE HILL

ANGLESEA
AVE

CONVENT RD

BLACKROCK
BUSINESS
PARK

SWEETMANS AVE

BROOKFIELD AVE

BROOKFIELD PL

BARCLAY
COURT

Sch

Sch

NEWTOWN AVENUE

NEWTOWN
VILLAS

CRAIG-
MORE GDNS

MARETIMO GDNS E

NEWTOWN PK

TEMPLE HILL

NEWTOWN AVE

TEMPLE PK AVE

TEMPLE CRES

STRA

MONT PIER PL

TEMPLE PL

AVOCA

GLENART AVENUE

TALBOT
LODGE

LINDEN

AVOCA ROAD

GROVE LAWN

GROVE AVENUE

The Michael Smurfit
Graduate School
of Business

University
College

AVOCA
PARK

CARYSFORT
HALL

CARYSFORT PARK

SPORTS
GROUND

AVONDALE
BUSINESS
PARK

AVONDALE

GARDEN
LAWN

COATH

LINDEN
VALE

AVONDALE
LAWN EXTENSION

Convent &
School

Cluain-Mhuire
Family Centre

Sch

GRAVE
YARD

118

STRADBROOK
LAWN

3

'N AVE

LINDEN

PATRICIAN

CEDAR SQ

LINDEN GROVE

STILLORGAN GRO

VIL

CLOISTER
GRN

CLOISTER

SHELLERS
COPSE

CLOISTER AVENUE

CLOISTER
GROVE

CLOISTER
GATE

CARYSFORT AVENUE

PROBY
SQUARE

OAKLEY
GROVE

CASTLE-
BYRNE
PK

CASTLEBYRNE
PK

ROCKVILLE RD

Sch &
Sports
Centre

ROCKVILLE PARK

ROCKVILLE CRE

NEWTOWN PARK AVENUE

THE HILL

Lib

owling
een

STILLORGAN PK N11

GER WOOD

STILLORGAN

PARK

ELM GRO

CLOISTER WAY

COPPINGER
DALE

COPPINGER
CLO

COPPINGER
GLADE

COPPINGER
CLOSE

COPPINGER GLADE

COPPINGER GREEN

OBELISK
GROVE

OBELISK
RISE

OBELISK
WALK

St. Augustine's
Sch

ST. AUGUSTINE'S
Park

FLEURVILLE

ANNAVILLE AVE

YANKEE
TER

ORCHARD

MARIAN PK

ROWANBYRN

BROOKVILLE PARK

STILLORGAN

N11

THE
HILL

ea

PITCH
AND PUTT

St. John of God
Hospital

C

House of
St. John of God

OAD

Sch

STILLORGAN GROVE

ORPEN
HILL

ORPEN RISE

ST. AUGUSTINE'S
Park

CARYSFORT WOOD

CARYSFORT
DOWNS

CARYSF

131

Obelisk

NEWTOWN PARK

CARYSFORT
GRO

OBELISK

RICHMOND

MOUNT

FAIRHILL

FAIRHILL

R113

D

MEADOW CLOSE

RAGH

PINE LAWN

PARK

ALBANY

BROOKVILLE PARK

SPRINGHILL AVENUE

SPRINGHILL PA

1

Lighthouse

Lighthouse

MARINA WEST BREAKWATER

WEST PIER

Automatic
Weather
Station

Captain Boyds
Memorial

DÚN LAOGHAIRE HARBOUR

MARINA EAST BREAKWATER

2

EAST PIER

Traders
Wharf

Old
Pier

Jetties

OLD
HARBOUR

Marine
Activity
Centre

Old
Coastguard
Station

HARBOUR
ROAD

HARBOUR ROAD

Yacht
Club

DÚN
LAOGHAIRE

Car Ferry
Terminal

Mail Boat or
Carlisle Pier

Band
Stand

OLD DUNLEARY RD

DUNLEARY RD

CROFTON ROAD

RNLI

Geographical
Pointer

RT18 QUEENS ROAD

CROFTON
TER

DUNLEARY HILL

CUMBERLAND
ST

LONGFORD
PLACE

DUNLEARY PLACE

DE VESCI
GARDENS

OPERTON

SPACKENHAM

MONKSTOWN
GATE

HILL

BARRETT
ST

DE VESCI
TER

SMITHS
VILLAS

THE SLOPES

WILLOW
BANK

VESEY GARDENS

VESEY PLACE

VESEY
MEWS

GEORGE'S PLACE

CLARENCE ST

GEORGE'S KELLYS AVE

GEORGE'S
STREET
LOWER

YORK
TERRACE

ROSARY
GDNS E

ROSARY
GDNS S

ROSARY
GDNS W

CHARLEMONT AVE

CROFTON AVE

LIBRARY

York Lib

PO

County Hall

Coll

St. Michael's
Hospital

IMC Cinema

Shopping
Centre

Pavilion
Theatre

Yacht
Club

Lifeboat
Station

RESERVOIR

MORAN
PARK

MARINE ROAD

NORTHCOTE
AVE

DOMINICK ST

CROSS AVE

DÚN
LAOGHAIRE

KNAPTON
LAWN

YORK ROAD

TIVOLI

Community
Training
Workshop

CROSS
AVE

DESMOND AVE

TERRACE NORTH

WOLFE TONE AVE

MULGRAVE STREET

PATRICK STREET

NORTHUMBERLAND AVE

CONVENT ROAD

GEORGE'S STREET UPPER

MELLIFONT AVE

STONEHAM

Garda

District
Court

Shopping
Centre

PO

Sch & Coll

ARCADE AVE

SUSSEX ST

SUSSEX PARADE

KNAPTON
RD

EGLINTON
PK

TIVOLI TERRACE SOUTH

TIVOLI TERRACE EAST

Nursing
Home

TIVOLI
ROAD

MULGRAVE
TERRACE

CORRIG
PK

CLARINDA
PARK WEST

CLARINDA
PARK NORTH

CLARINDA
PARK EAST

CLARINDA
MANOR

UMBERLAND
PARK

CROSTHWAITE
PK NORTH

ROSMEEN
GDNS

PARK
AVE

PEOPLES
PARK

SUMMERHILL ROAD

WINDSOR
TER

NEWTOWNSMITH

SCOTSMAN
BAY

3

TURKISH
Consulate

Clubhouse

Sch

TIVOLI
ROAD

CORRIG
ROAD

ROYAL
TERRACE WEST

ROYAL
TERRACE
EAST

CROSTHWAITE PARK WEST

CROSTHWAITE PARK EAST

CROSTHWAITE
PARK SOUTH

EDEN ROAD UPPER

EDEN ROAD LOWER

EDEN TER

MAGENTA

LOWER RT18

GLENGEARY
PK

SANDYCOVE
GLASTULE

Sch

College

Nursing
Home

Consulate
of Malta

GLASTHULE

LINK ROAD

MARINE ROAD

SEA RD

Sch

Pav

SPORTS

HUDSON
ROAD

BEAU

HUDSON
ROA

PO

COLDWELL

CATHERINE

133   **134**

DÚN LAOGHAIRE
GOLF COURSE

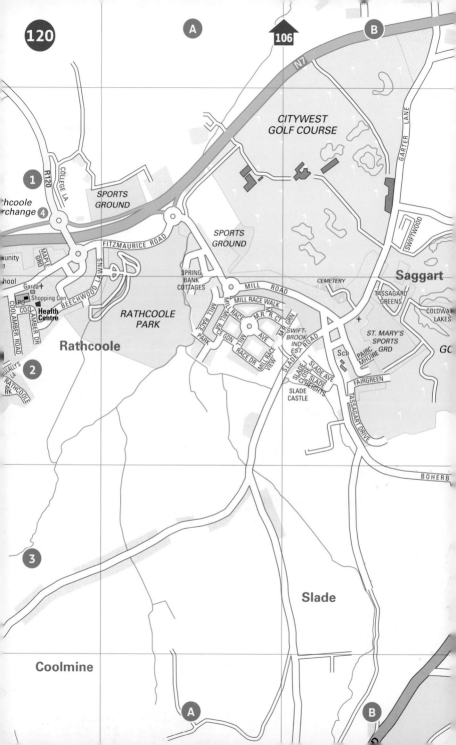

A

106

B

N7

CITYWEST
GOLF COURSE

GARTER LANE

1

R120

COLLEGE LA

SPORTS
GROUND

SWIFTWOOD

Rathcoole
Exchange **4**

MAPLE GRO

FITZMAURICE ROAD

SPORTS
GROUND

MILL   ROAD

CEMETERY

Saggart

unity

School

Garda +
PO
Shopping Cen

**Health
Centre**

COOLAMBER DR

BEECHWOOD LAWNS

SPRING
BANK
COTTAGES

MILL RACE WALK

M.R. R. CT. GRN

SWIFT-
BROOK
IND
EST

TASSAGARD
GREENS

COLDWAT
LAKES

COOLAMBER ROAD

Rathcoole

RATHCOOLE
PARK

MILL RACE PARK

MILL RACE GDN

MILL RACE DR

MILL RACE AVE

MILL RACE VIEW

SLADE AVE

SLADE
CLOSE

SLADE
HEIGHTS

+

Sch

PAIRC
MHUIRE

ST. MARY'S
SPORTS
GRD

GC

NUALLY'S LA

RATHCOOLE PARK

2

SLADE
CASTLE

SLADE ROAD

FAIRGREEN

TASSAGART DRIVE

BOHERB

3

Slade

Coolmine

A

B

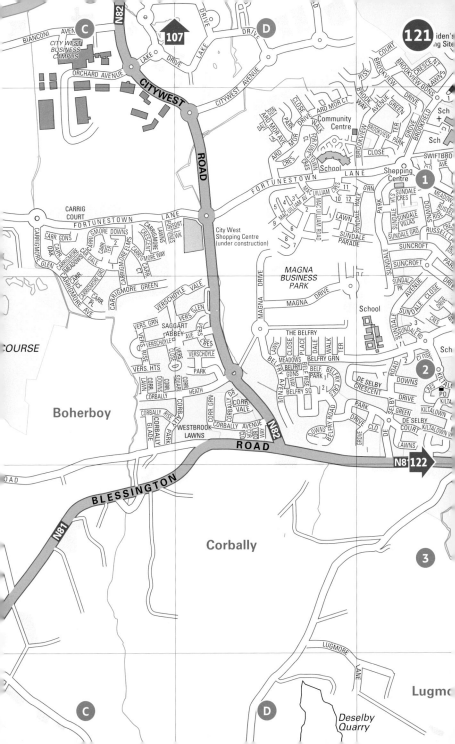

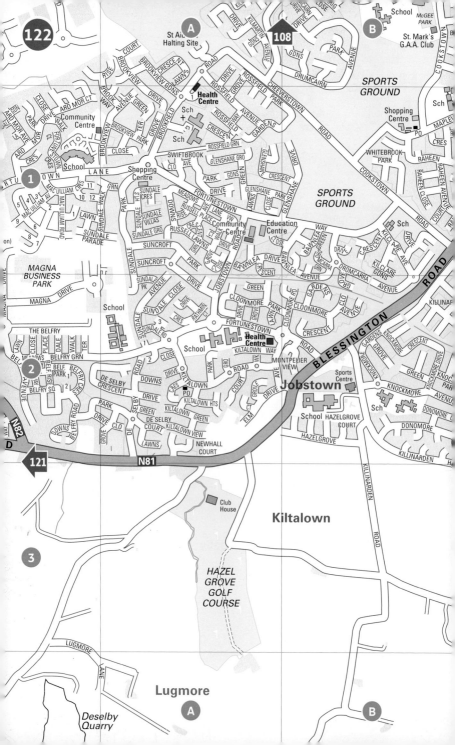

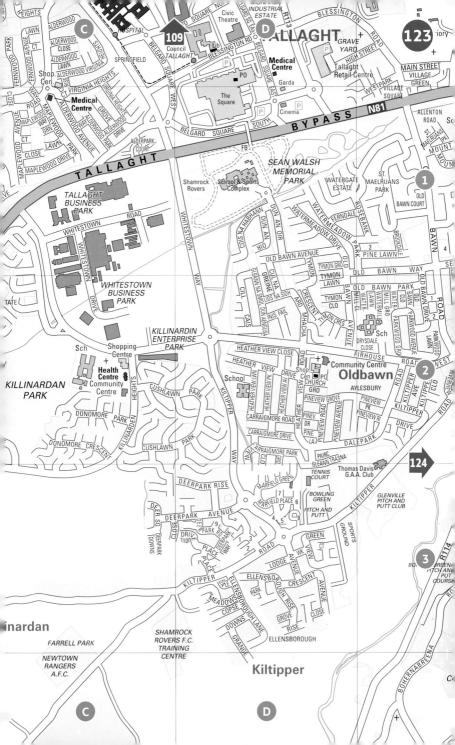

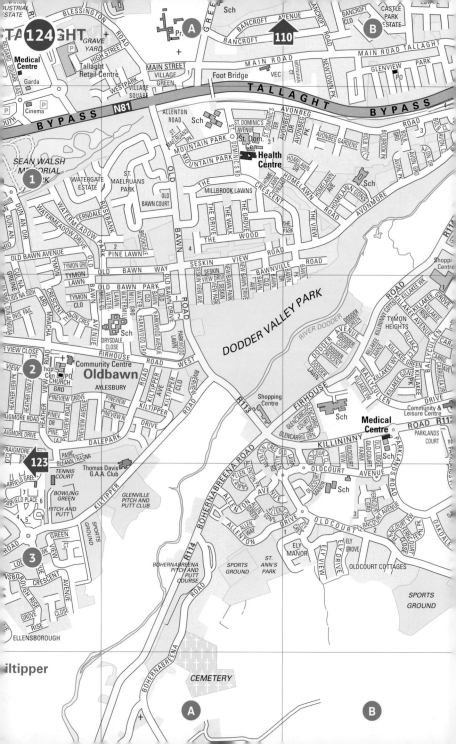

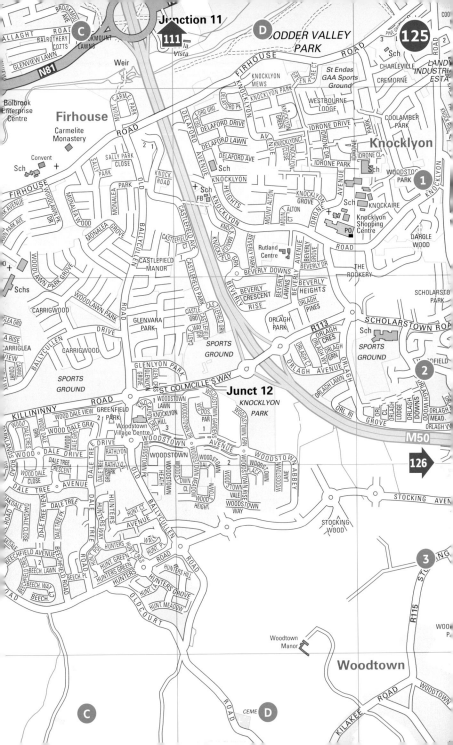

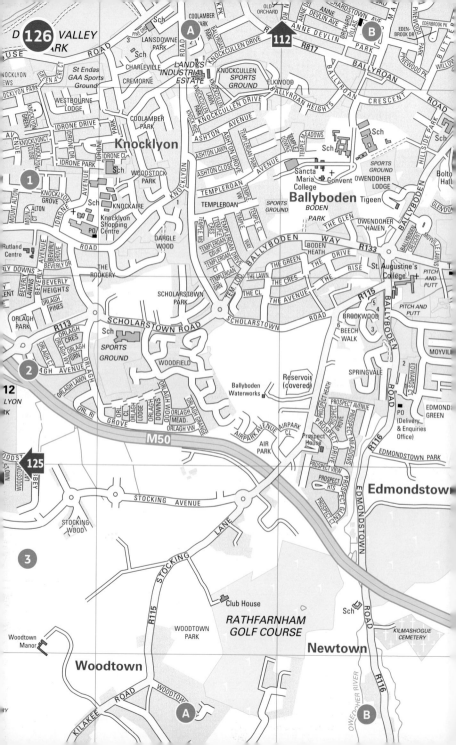

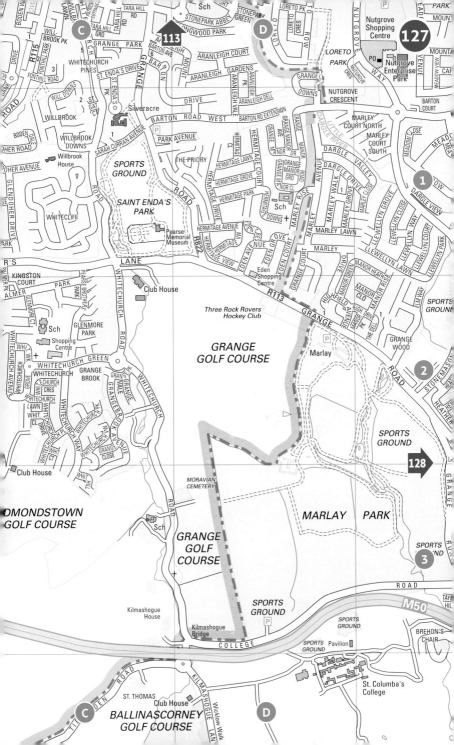

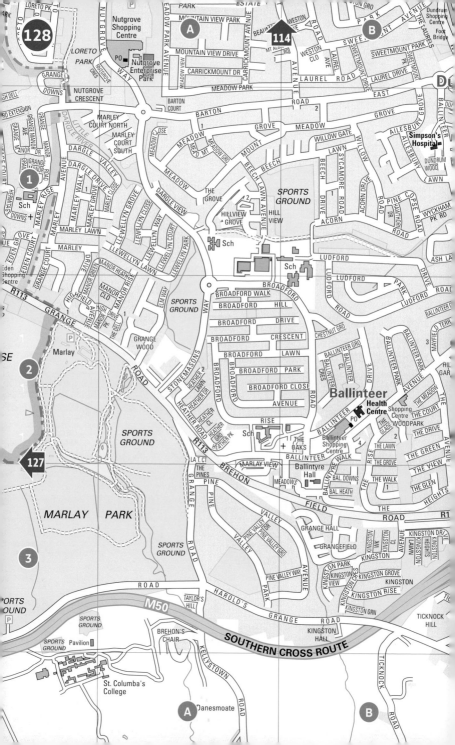

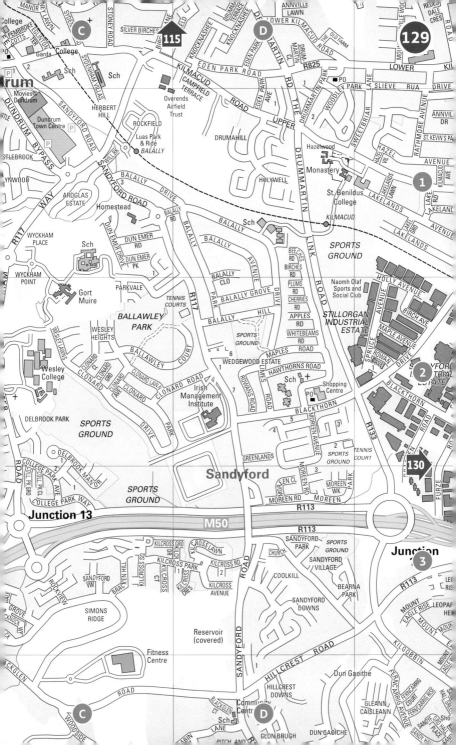

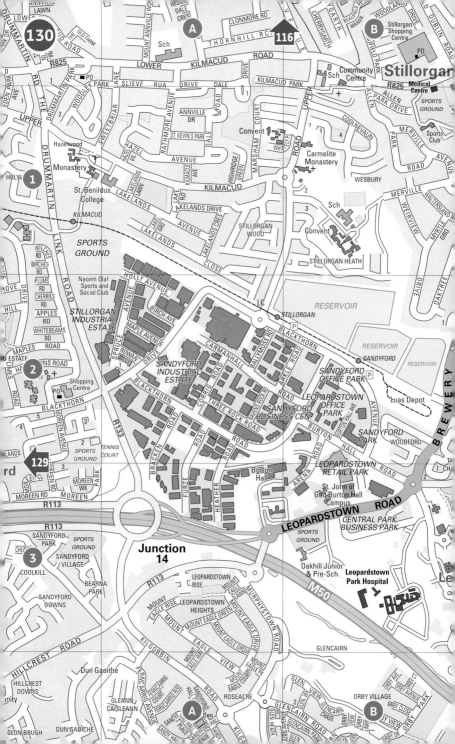

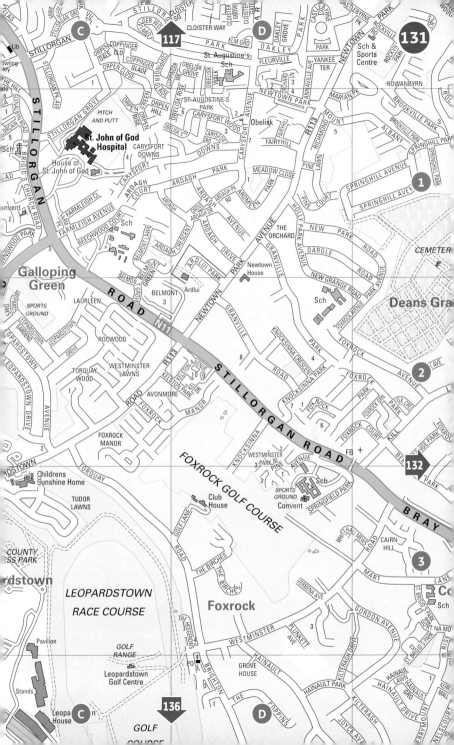

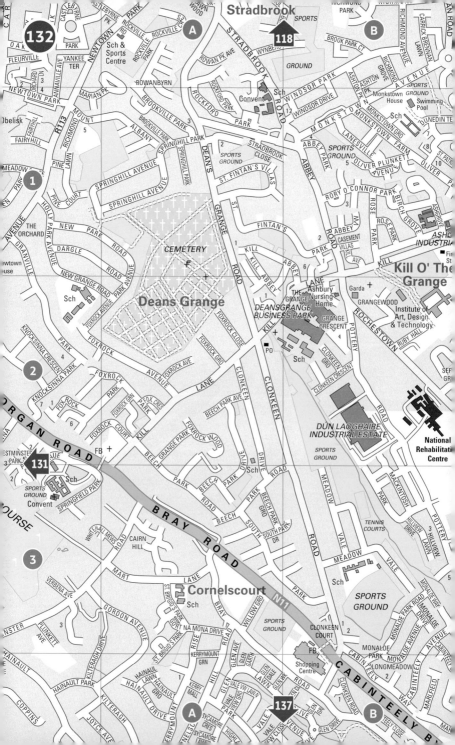

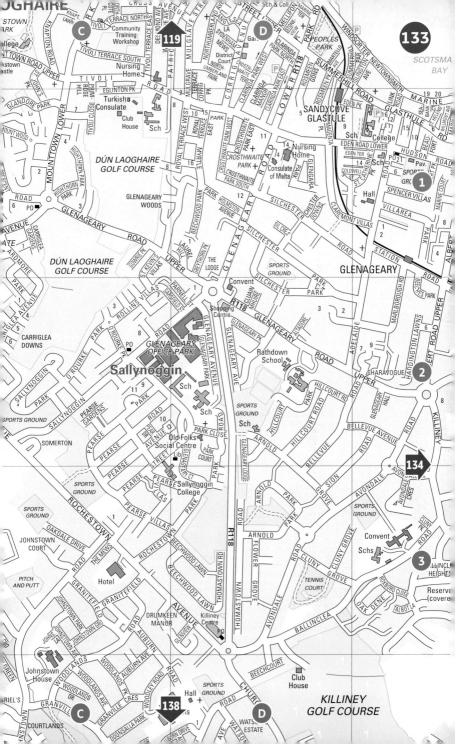

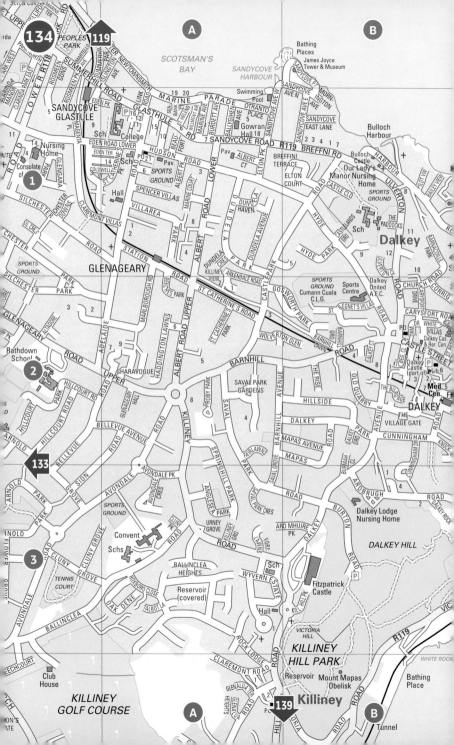

Place

Schs

Loreto
Abbey School

LORETO AVENUE

LESLIE AVENUE

SPORTS
GROUNDS

3

COLIEMORE

10

6

ROAD

ROCKCLIFF AVENUE

HEANY AVE

MAIDEN ROCK

Pier

MORE RD

11

8

RENTO

TO DRIVE

N

4

VICTORIA ROAD

DALKEY AVENUE

2

5

7

DALKEY SOUND

GREEN RD

COLIEMORE

Martello
Tower

Coliemore
Harbour

LAMB ISLAND

MUGLINS

DALKEY SOUND

R119

ROAD

KNOCK-NA-CREE
GROVE

ROAD

2

1

NERANO RD

NERANO RD

Tunnel

SORRENTO
PARK

ROAD

SORRENTO ROAD

Promontory
Fort
+

Martello
Tower

K-NA-CREE

MOUNT SALUS RD

ROAD

ROAD

DALKEY ISLAND

3

SORRENTO
POINT

HAWK CLIFF

CASTLE

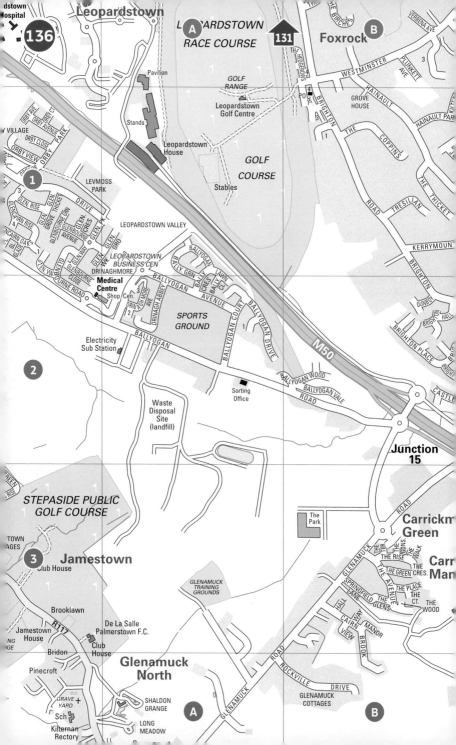

ABBERLEY
COURT
NORWOOD
CARR
ACHILL ROAD
ARAN AVENUE
ARAN CV
AMBACH
ARAN CL
9
BAYVIEW CT
BAYVIEW GRN
BAYVIEW LAWNS
CASTLECOURT
DRUID
BAY GRO
BAY CRES
BAYVIEW
BAYVIEW
CROMLECH
FIELDS
GLEN DRUID
HACKETSLAND
BROOKDENE
wn
SPORTS
GROUND
ROAD
R119 ROAD
MILL LANE
CLIFTON
PARK
SHANGANAGH
CLIFFS
SPORTS
GROUND
LAWN
SEAVIEW PARK
BROOKFIELD
COURT
FIELD
RATHSALLAGH
GROVE
RATHSALLAGH
BRIDGE
AZELWOOD
WD
PARK
SHANGANAGH
RATHSALLAGH PARK
RATHS AVE
RATHSALLAGH DRIVE
SHANGANAGH WOOD
SEAFIELD
CORBAWN AVE
EATON BRAE
FB
CORBAWN
LANE
CORB
DALE
CORBAWN
GRO
Sch
SHANKILL
SPORTS
GROUND
ATHGOE
CORBAWN
CLANMAWR
CORBAWN
CT
CORBAWN
DRIVE
HANKILL
USINESS
ENTRE
BEECH MANOR
WINDRUSH
R119
PO
Shankill
Shop. Cen.
Garda
HOLLY PARK
CORBAWN
CORBAWN
CLOSE
CORBAWN
GLADE
hankil
DORNEY
COURT
EATON WOOD AVENUE
EATON WOOD
CT
CORBAWN
WOOD
CORBAWN
LAWN
DORNEY
THE
BRIDGE
EATON WOOD GREEN
Shankill Tennis &
Bowling Club
LFORD
TER
ROAD
FOXES
EATON WOOD GRO
CL NA GR CT
SPORTS
GROUND
R ROAD
LOWER
ROAD
AUBREY PK
AUBREY GRO
ROAD
DUBLIN
QUINN'S
ST ANNE'S PARK
SHANGANAGH GROVE
OAD
SHREWSBURY RD
CHERRING DR
RING.
SHREWSBURY HALL
CAS FM
WOOD
R119
CASTLE FARM
Shanganagh
Castle
SHANGANAGH
PARK
GOLF
LINKS
AR
SPORTS
GROUND
DUBLIN ROAD
St.
Josephs
Centre
CEMETERY
P
Sewage
Disposal
Works
SHANGANAGH
CEMETERY

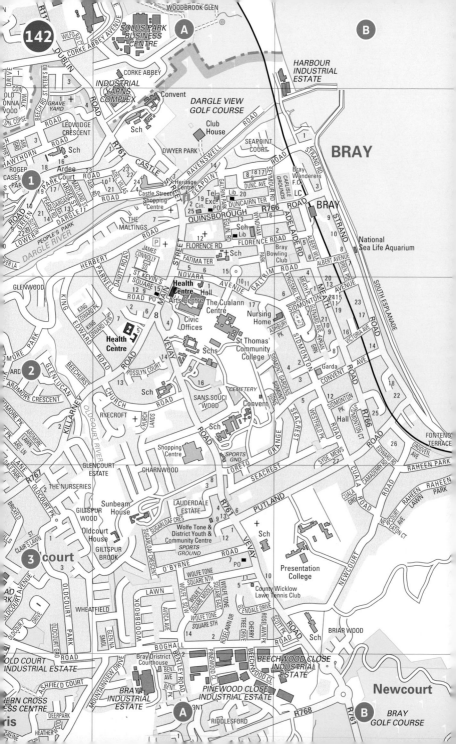

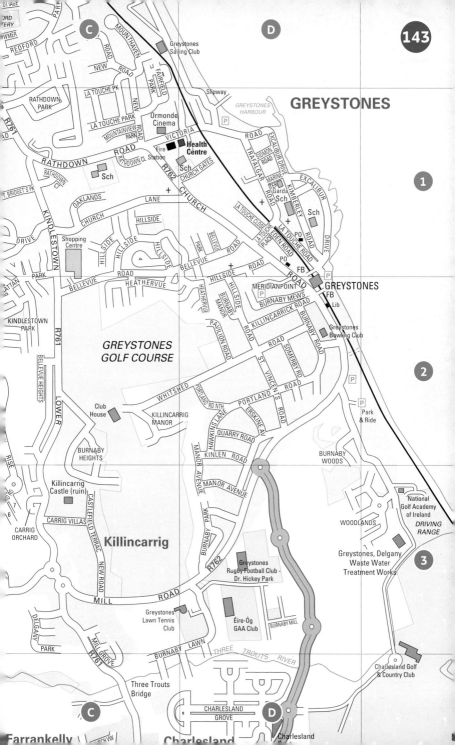

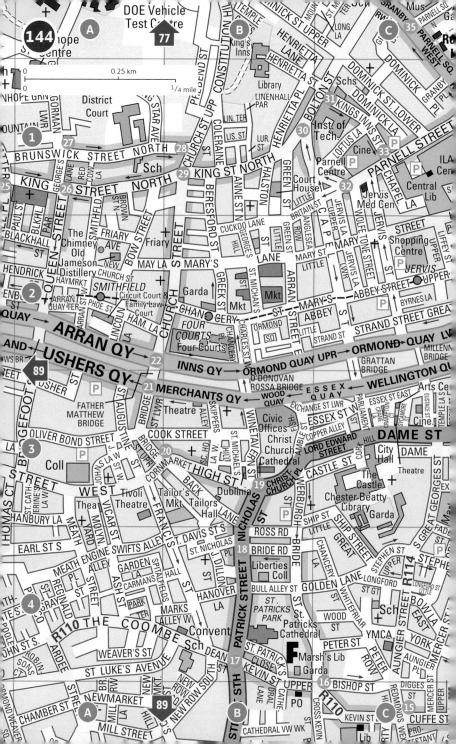

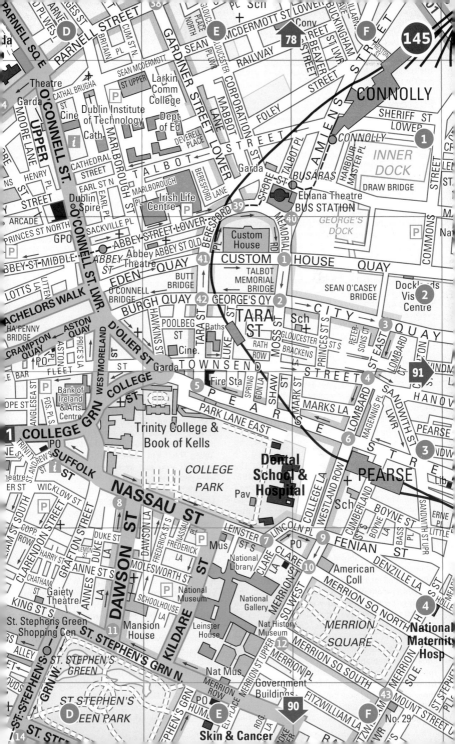

Guide to central Dublin

The telephone numbers beginning with '01' are Dublin numbers. To telephone these numbers from the UK replace the initial '0' with '00 353'

History

The ford over the River Liffey has been important since Celtic times and there was a thriving Christian community here from the 5thC, following their conversion by St Patrick in AD448. Marauding Vikings landed here in AD840, established a garrison port by the Dark Pool or Dubbh Linn, and within a few years had built a fortified town on the high ground above the estuary. Originally a base for raiding sorties, Dublin soon became a flourishing trading port as well, until Viking dominance was curtailed following a defeat by Brian Boru at the Battle of Clontarf in 1014.

Many of the Vikings had inter-married with the Irish and converted to Christianity but they were finally driven out by the Anglo-Normans under Strongbow, who took Dublin by storm and executed the Viking leader Hasculf. In 1170 Henry II arrived in Dublin, defeated Strongbow and received the submission of the Irish chieftains on the site of College Green. Henry granted the city by charter to the citizens of Bristol, thereby establishing English authority in Ireland.

The city and surrounding area, established as the seat of English government and protected by an enclosing wall and strategic castles, was known as The Pale. Frequently attacked during the 12thC and 13thC by the Irish clans based in the Wicklow Mountains, it was assaulted unsuccessfully by Edward Bruce in 1316. The city witnessed the crowning of Lambert Simnel, pretender to the English throne, in Christ Church in 1486. Unmoved by the rebellion of 'Silken' Thomas Fitzgerald in 1534, the inhabitants remained loyal to the English crown, supporting King Charles during the Civil Wars. Parliamentarians captured Dublin in 1647 and at this time the city was in decline. Following the Restoration of Charles I, however, Dublin underwent a great economic and architectural expansion.

By the end of the 17thC Dublin had become a flourishing commercial centre and during the following century the city was transformed into one of the most beautiful Georgian cities in Europe. The 'Wide Streets Commission' was established in 1757 and in 1773 the Paving Board was formed. New, elegantly spacious streets and squares were planned and palatial town houses built. In 1783 the Irish Parliament led by Henry Grattan was granted a short-lived autonomy but there was growing political unrest, which erupted in the unsuccessful uprising of 1798. Lord Edward Fitzgerald died of wounds sustained resisting arrest and in 1800 the detested Act of Union was established and the fortunes of the city began to wane.

With government now in London, few of the noblemen required their fine mansions and many returned to their country estates or left for London. Bitterness increased; in 1803 the Lord Chief Justice was assassinated and Robert Emmet, the leader of an abortive insurrection, was hanged. The newspaper The Nation was established by Charles Gavan Duffy in 1842, the heyday of the Repeal Movement. Daniel O'Connell was elected Lord Mayor in 1841 but only three years later he was interned in Richmond Gaol for campaigning for the repeal of the Union and the restoration of Grattan's 'Irish Parliament'. In 1873 the first great Home Rule Conference was held and in 1879 the Land League was formed, whose leaders, including Parnell and Davitt, were imprisoned as a consequence. In 1882 the new Chief Secretary, Lord Frederick Cavendish, and his Under-Secretary were assassinated in Phoenix Park by the Invincibles, a new terrorist organisation.

As the campaign for Home Rule gathered momentum, the Gaelic League, which started the Irish literary renaissance, was established by Douglas Hyde and Eóin MacNeill in 1893. Conceived as a means of reviving interest in the Irish language and traditional Irish life, the Gaelic League was also responsible for a remarkable literary revival resulting in the formation of the Abbey Theatre in 1904, where plays by J M Synge, Sean O'Casey and W B Yeats, amongst others, were performed.

In 1905 the Sinn Fein movement was formed, in 1909 the Irish Transport and General Workers Union was set up under the leadership of James Connolly, and in 1913 there was a massive strike, paralysing the city. The Irish Volunteers came into being in 1914, largely to combat the Ulster Volunteers who had been raised by Edward Carson in January 1913 to defend the right of Ulster to remain united with Great Britain. In 1916 the Irish Volunteers seized the General Post Office in Lower O'Connell Street as their headquarters and the Easter Rising had begun. It was quickly crushed, but so brutally that public conscience, clearly appalled, overwhelmingly elected Sinn Fein at the general election of December 1918 with Eamon de Valera as the new president.

Whilst the Dublin faction was openly in support of the guerrilla bands operating across the country, the Ulster Unionists set up their own provisional government, and the ambushes and assassinations which characterised the Anglo-Irish

War, featuring the notorious Black and Tans, began in bloody earnest. The war ended in the truce of July 1921. Despite the ratification of the Irish Free State in January 1922, a large and dissatisfied faction of leaders in the Irish movement took up arms against their former comrades and seized the Four Courts, which they held for two months. The subsequent shelling ordered by the new Dublin Government destroyed much of O'Connell Street but by the 1930s Dublin was emerging as a modern capital city and most of the public buildings had been restored.

Visiting Dublin www.visitdublin.com

Passports
Citizens of the European Union need either a valid national identity card or passport to enter the Republic of Ireland. It is recommended that visitors from the UK bring a passport as a means of identification. Nationals of other countries require a passport and may require a visa. Enquiries should be made with a travel agent or Irish Embassy before travelling. The address of the Irish Embassy in London is 17 Grosvenor Place, SW1X 7HR ☎ 020 7235 2171
The Irish Passport & Visa Office is at Montpelier House, 106 Brompton Road, London SW3 1JJ ☎ 020 7225 7700
www.dfa.ie

Banks
In February 2002 the Irish Punt (IEP) was withdrawn from circulation and the Euro (€) became the Irish unit of currency.
Banks open Monday–Friday from 10.00–16.00 and in Dublin most branches remain open until 17.00 on Thursdays. Major banks have 24 hour ATM machines which accept Plus and Cirrus symbols. All major credit cards are widely accepted in shops, petrol stations, restaurants and hotels. Personal cheques from banks outside the Republic of Ireland are not accepted in the country without prior arrangement.

Bureaux de Change
Banks and Bureaux de Change generally offer the best exchange rates, although post offices, hotels, travel agents and some department stores offer exchange facilities.
There is a Bureau de Change at Dublin Airport and Dún Laoghaire ferry terminal. Dublin Airport also has a 24 hour Bank of Ireland foreign currency note exchanger and multi-currency Pass machines. Foreign exchange facilities are also to be found at the central bus station (Busárus), Connolly railway station and at the Dublin Tourism Centre in Suffolk Street.

Language
English is spoken by everyone in Ireland. The country is officially bilingual with Irish (Gaelic) also spoken.

Customs and excise
The Republic of Ireland is a member of the European Union and, in accordance with EU regulations, travellers within the Community can import 90 litres of wine, 110 litres of duty paid beer and 800 cigarettes without question. Duty free sales of goods amongst European community members are now abolished. There are restrictions on taking certain food items into Ireland and checks should be made beforehand with the Irish Embassy or travel agent. Pets may not be brought into the country unless travelling from the UK, all other animals entering the country have to undergo quarantine.

Emergency
If you are involved in an emergency and require the services of the Police, Fire Brigade, Ambulance Service, or Coastguard, dial 999 or 112.

Medical treatment
Visitors to Ireland from European Community countries are entitled to free treatment by a general practitioner, medicines on prescription and treatment on a public ward in a hospital. British citizens need only show some form of identification such as a passport or driving licence to the doctor or hospital and request treatment under the EU health agreement. Visitors from other EU countries need to present form EIII (available from social security offices prior to departure). Health Insurance is recommended for visitors from outside the EU. No inoculations are required for travellers to Ireland.

Disabled visitors
The Irish Wheelchair association can offer advice and can arrange wheelchair hire.
☎ 01 818 6400 (Mon–Fri 09.00–17.00).
www.iwa.ie
Irish Rail publishes a 'Guide for Mobility Impaired Passengers' which details the accessibility of all railway and DART stations. Obtainable at all manned stations or from the Access and Liaison officer, ☎ 01 703 2634. Most of the Dublin Bus fleet is low floor easy access, and the buses run by Bus Éireann – Ireland's national bus company – are largely wheelchair accessible. Discounts on many ferry sailings from Britain are available to disabled drivers who wish to take their own car to Ireland. Drivers should contact the Disabled Drivers' Association or Motor Club in Britain to obtain the relevant form. This form should then be sent to the ferry company.

Phones

Most calls are dialled direct with cheaper call charge rates between 18.00 and 08.00 Mon–Fri and all day Saturday, Sunday and bank holidays. The dialling code for Dublin is *01* and so for calls within Dublin omit *01* at the beginning of a number. To dial Dublin from abroad dial the access code for Ireland *(00353)* plus the area code for Dublin *(01)* but omit the zero. For directory enquiries, including Northern Ireland, dial *11811*; for Great Britain or International numbers dial *11818*. For operator assistance dial *10* (Ireland and UK) or *114* for the international operator. Card phones are cheaper than payphones and are widely available. Callcards are obtainable at post offices, newsagents and supermarkets. Mobile phones can be brought into Ireland but visitors need to ensure their phone company has a roaming agreement with the Irish network operators.

Transport

Driving

Driving is on the left-hand side of the road in Ireland as in the UK; at roundabouts give way to traffic from the right. All drivers and front seat passengers must wear seat belts, and rear belts if they are fitted. Children under twelve must have a suitable restraint. Helmets are compulsory for motorcyclists. The maximum speed limit is 97kph (60mph) outside urban areas and the motorway speed limit is 110kph (70mph). In urban areas the limit is usually 50kph (30mph). There are on-the-spot fines for speeding and drink driving laws are strict. Parking infringements are taken seriously and illegally parked cars in Dublin City are liable to be clamped or towed away to the Corporation pound with a recovery charge payable.

Distances and speed limits are now both measured in kilometres (speed limit signs changed on 20th January 2005). Place names are generally in English and Irish. Unleaded petrol and diesel are widely available. Recorded weather information is available for Dublin by calling the Meteorological Service ☎ *1550 123 854*. There is a charge for this call.

Car hire

Car hire is readily available in Dublin, although in July and August there is a high demand and it is best to book in advance. You must have held a full licence for 2 years and be under 70 and over 23. Some companies make exceptions to this but charges may be higher. A full valid driving licence of your country of residence (which you must have held for at least two years without endorsements) must be presented at the time of hiring. Most international car rental companies have offices in Dublin and cars can also be hired at the airport and Dún Laoghaire ferry terminal. The cost of hire will depend on the type of car and time of year and it is worthwhile shopping around. It is important, however, to check the insurance details and ensure Collision Damage Waiver is included. A deposit is usually payable at the time of booking or before you drive away. Fly-drive or rail-sail-drive packages arranged by travel agents or the air and ferry companies can be an economical and easy way of hiring a car.

Public transport

Dublin is linked with the cities and towns of Ireland by a network of rail and bus services overseen by Córas Iompair Éireann (CIE), which is Ireland's National Transport Authority. The CIE organises Iarnód Éireann (Irish Rail), Bus Éireann (Irish Bus) and Dublin Bus. Bus and rail timetables can be bought at most newsagents. Unlimited use period tickets are available for use on rail and/or bus services.

Bus and coach travel

Dublin Bus (Bus Átha Cliath) operates the public bus services in Dublin and the surrounding area. Pre-paid tickets can be bought for periods of time ranging from one day to one month and are good value for money. They can be bought at any of the many bus ticket agencies in the city, from the CIE information desk at Dublin Airport or at Dublin Bus head office at 59 O'Connell Street Upper. Many routes operate an exact fare only policy. Dublin Bus also operates late night services (Nitelink) to most suburban areas on Thursdays, Fridays and Saturdays; some services also operate Monday to Wednesday. They also operate links to the airport (Airlink), ferry ports, railway stations and sightseeing tours.

59 O'Connell Street ☎ *01 872 0000*
Open Mon 08.30-17.30; Tues-Fri 09.00-17.30; Sat 09.00-13.00.
Information ☎ *01 873 4222*
Mon-Sat 09.00-19.00
www.dublinbus.ie

Irish Bus (Bus Éireann) and many private companies operate national bus services between Dublin, Dublin Airport and many major cities and towns. Bus Éireann also operate combined bus and ferry services between Britain and Ireland. This service operates under the 'Eurolines' brand www.eurolines.com
Dublin Bus Station (Busáras), Store Street.
☎ *01 836 6111*
www.buseireann.ie

Scheduled daily hop-on hop-off city sightseeing tours are operated by Gray Line www.grayline.com and City Sightseeing www.guidefriday.com. Buses depart every 6-15 minutes 09.30-17.30; also available are seasonal half and full day excursions further afield including to Newgrange and the Boyne Valley, Powerscourt Gardens, Glendalough and Wicklow. 3 & 4 day trips to Kerry and Dingle are also available. Information and tickets from the Desk 1 at the Dublin Tourism Centre, Suffolk Street.

☎ 01 605 7705
www.irishcitytours.com
Email: info@irishcitytours.com

Taxis

Taxis are available at taxi ranks or by phoning one of the many radio-linked taxi companies. There are numerous taxi ranks including ones on O'Connell Street, Dame Street, and St. Stephen's Green West.

Taxi companies are listed in the Golden Pages classified telephone directory.

Rail travel

Dublin Connolly and Dublin Heuston are the two mainline railway stations and Irish Rail (Iarnród Éireann) operates an excellent service to most towns and cities in Ireland. Irish rail also operates the suburban rail network in Dublin and DART (Dublin Area Rapid Transit) with 26 stations between Howth on the north of Dublin Bay to Bray in the south.

☎ 01 850 366222
www.irishrail.ie

LUAS is the Light Rail Transit System in Dublin operated by Veolia Transport Ireland. There are two lines; the red line runs from Tallaght to Connolly Station and the green line runs from Sandyford to St. Stephen's Green. Tickets are available at each stop at vending machines.

☎ 1800 300 604 (Freephone, Dublin only) Mon-Fri from 07.00-19.00; Sat 10.00-14.00.

Bike hire

Belfield Bike Shop, University College Dublin.
☎ 01 260 0749
www.cyclingsafaris.com
Cycleways, 185/186 Parnell Street
☎ 01 873 4748
www.cycleways.com
Hollingworth Cycles, Templeogue Road, Templeogue
☎ 01 490 5094
Drumartin Road, Kilmacaud Road Lower, Stillorgan
☎ 01 296 0225
www.hollingsworth.ie
Tracks Bikes, Botanic Road, Glasnevin.
☎ 01 850 0252

Lost property

Enquire at the nearest police station or: Dublin Airport. Open 07.30-22.30.
☎ 01 814 5555

Dublin Bus. Open Mon-Fri 08.45-17.00.
☎ 01 703 1321
Irish Bus. Open Mon-Fri 09.00-17.00.
☎ 01 836 6111
Irish Rail (Connolly Station). Open Mon-Fri 09.00-17.00.
☎ 01 703 2362
Irish Rail (Heuston Station). Open Mon-Fri 09.00-17.00. ☎ 01 703 2102 / 2126

Places of interest

Arbour Hill Cemetery, Arbour Hill.
The leaders of the Easter Rising are buried here.

Bank of Ireland, College Green.
Designed by Sir Edward Lovett Pearce in 1729, it was later enlarged by James Gandon and Robert Parke between 1785-1794. Originally the Parliament House, the first of a series of great public buildings erected in 18thC Dublin, it was taken over by the Bank of Ireland in 1804. A statue of Henry Grattan, leader of the Irish parliament of 1782, stands outside on the lawn of College Green. Two huge 18thC tapestries commemorating the Siege of Londonderry and the Battle of the Boyne hang in the oak-panelled chamber of the former House of Lords.
There are guided tours of the House of Lords on Tuesdays at 10.30, 11.30, and 13.45. The House of Commons is now the banking hall.
Admission free. Disabled access.
☎ 01 671 1488

Bank of Ireland Arts Centre, Foster Place.
An arts centre which presents classical concerts and recitals and houses an interactive museum. The museum illustrates the history of the adjoining College Green buildings where many of the dramatic events of Irish history were played out in the Irish parliament. The museum also reflects the role played by the Bank of Ireland in the economic and social development of Ireland.
Open Tues-Fri 10.00-16.00.
Disabled access.
☎ 01 671 1488

Belvedere House, North Great George's Street.
One of the best 18thC mansions in Dublin. Taken over by Jesuit Belvedere College in 1841; James Joyce went to school here between 1893-1898. Not open to the public.

Casino, off Malahide Road, Marino.
A miniature 18thC neo-classical masterpiece designed by Sir William Chambers and recently restored. Casino means 'small house'. It was built as a pleasure house beside Marino House (now demolished), Lord Charlemont's country residence, for the enormous sum of £60,000. It is a compact building, remarkably containing 16 rooms, with

many interesting architectural features. The interior circular hall, ringed by columns, is crowned by a coffered dome. The graceful roof urns disguise chimneys while the columns conceal drainpipes.

Open May-Oct daily 10.00-17.00 (Jun-Sept 18.00); Jan-Apr, Nov-Dec Sat & Sun only 12.00-16.00 (Apr 17.00). Access by guided tour only. Last tour leaves 45 mins before closing. Access to interior by stairway.

☎ 01 833 1618

City Hall, Dame Street.
Completed in 1779, this fine building was designed as The Royal Exchange. Subsequent use included a prison and corn exchange before being taken over by the city in 1852. Presently used by Dublin City Council. It features a beautiful Corinthian coffered dome and portico. The archives include the original charter of 1171 in which Henry II granted Dublin to the citizens of Bristol.

Open Mon-Sat 10.00-17.15, Sun 14.00-17.00.

☎ 01 222 2204

Custom House Visitor Centre,
Custom House Quay.
The Custom House, with a magnificent long river frontage, is an architectural masterpiece designed by James Gandon and completed in 1791. Exhibits relate to James Gandon and the history of the Custom House itself, with illustrations of how the building was restored after it was gutted by fire in 1921. The building is best viewed from the south bank of the River Liffey.

Open: Wed-Fri (Nov-16 Mar) & Mon-Fri (17 Mar-Nov) 10.00-12.30, Sat & Sun 14.00-17.00. Disabled access by prior arrangement.

☎ 01 888 2538

Drimnagh Castle, Long Mile Road.
Ireland's only castle with a flooded moat. This Norman castle has a fully restored Great Hall, medieval undercroft and 17thC style formal garden.

Open Wed 12.00-17.00; Sun 14.00-17.00. Open at other times by appointment.

☎ 01 450 2530

Email: drimnaghcastle@eircom.net

Dublin Castle, off Dame Street.
The Castle was originally built between 1204-1228 as part of Dublin's defensive system. The Record Tower is the principal remnant of the 13thC Anglo-Norman fortress and has walls 5 metres (16ft) thick but what remains today is largely the result of 18thC and 19thC re-building. It now contains the Garda (Police) Museum. The 15thC Bermingham Tower was once the state prison where Red Hugh O'Donnell was interned in the 16thC; it was rebuilt in the 18thC. The State Apartments, Undercroft and ornate Chapel Royal are open to the public. The State Apartments, dating from the British Administration, were once the residence of the English Viceroys and are now used for Presidential Inaugurations and state receptions. Within these apartments are the magnificent throne room and St Patrick's Hall, 25 metres (82ft) long with a high panelled and decorated ceiling. In the undercroft can be seen the remains of a Viking fortress, part of the original moat, and part of the old city wall. The Chester Beatty Library exhibits art treasures from around the world.

Open: Mon-Fri 10.00-16.45, Sat & Sun 14.00-16.45. Access by guided tour only. Disabled access/toilets.

☎ 01 645 8813

www.dublincastle.ie

Email: info@dublincastle.ie

Dublin Writers Museum, Parnell Square.
Tracing the history of Irish literature from its earliest times to the 20thC, this museum is a celebration of this literary heritage. Writers and playwrights including Jonathan Swift, George Bernard Shaw, Oscar Wilde, W B Yeats, James Joyce and Samuel Beckett are brought to life through personal items, portraits, their books and letters. There is also a room dedicated to children's authors. The museum is housed in a restored 18thC Georgian mansion with decorative stained-glass windows and ornate plaster-work.

Open Mon-Sat 10.00-17.00 (18.00 Jun-Aug), Sun 11.00-17.00. Disabled access to ground floor. Last entry 45 mins before closing.

☎ 01 872 2077

www.writersmuseum.com

Email: writers@dublintourism.ie

Dublinia & Viking World,
Christ Church, St. Michael's Hill.
A multi-media recreation of Dublin life in medieval times from the Anglo-Norman arrival in 1170 to the dissolution of the monasteries in 1540. There is a scale model of the medieval city, a life size reconstruction of a merchant's house, and numerous Viking and Norman artefacts from excavations at nearby Wood Quay. The building is the old Synod Hall and is linked to Christ Church Cathedral by an ornate Victorian pedestrian bridge.

Open Mon-Fri 10.00-17.00 (Oct-Mar 11.00-16.00); Sat & Sun 10.00-16.00. Disabled access.

☎ 01 679 4611

www.dublinia.ie

Email: marketing@dublinia.ie

Dublin Zoo, Phoenix Park.
The Zoo is well known for its captive-breeding programme and is committed to the conservation and protection of endangered species. The 'big

cats', living in enclosures which simulate their natural habitats, include lions, tigers, jaguars and snow leopards. Attractive gardens surround two natural lakes where pelicans, flamingos, ducks and geese abound, while the islands in the lakes are home to chimps, gibbons, spider monkeys and orang-utans. A recent development 'Fringes of the Arctic' has provided a state of the art enclosure for the polar bears and is home to wolves, arctic foxes and snowy owls. The zoo doubled in size in 2000 and an African Plains area has been developed providing greater space and freedom for giraffe, hippo, rhino and other African animals and birds. The city farm and pets' corner provide encounters with Irish domestic animals. Other attractions include a zoo train, discovery centre, and 'meet the keeper' programme.

Open: Mon-Sat 09.30–17.30, Sun 10.30–17.30. Last admission 1hr before closing. Closes at dusk in winter.

☎ 01 474 8900

www.dublinzoo.ie

Email: info@dublinzoo.ie

Dunsink Observatory, Castleknock, Dublin 15.
Founded in 1783, it is one of the oldest observatories in the world and houses the astronomy section of the School of Cosmic Physics. Public open nights are held on the first and third Wednesdays of each month from October to March inclusive at 20.00. Requests for tickets for the open nights must be made by post to the Observatory.

☎ 01 838 7911

www.dunsink.dias.ie

Email: cwoods@dunsinkdias.ie

Four Courts, Inns Quay.
Originally designed by James Gandon in 1785, it was partially destroyed by a fire in 1922 in the struggle for Irish independence but restored again by 1932. The Four Courts has a 137 metre (450ft) river frontage and the building is fronted by a Corinthian portico with six columns. The square central block with circular hall is crowned by a copper-covered lantern-dome. Housed here are the Irish Law Courts and Law Library.

☎ 01 888 6000

www.courts.ie

Fry Model Railway, Malahide Castle, Malahide.
Covering 233 square metres (2,500sq.ft) this is one of the world's largest working miniature railways and is a delight for children and adults alike. Besides the track, the railway has stations, bridges, trams, buses and barges and includes the Dublin landmarks of Heuston station and O'Connell Bridge. On display are the hand constructed models of Irish trains by Cyril Fry, draughtsman and railway engineer, who made

them from the 1930s until his death in 1974. Perfectly engineered, the models represent the earliest trains to those of more modern times. Situated in the grounds of Malahide Castle, 13km (8 miles) north of Dublin city centre.

Open (Apr-Sept) Mon-Sat 10.00-17.00 closed Fridays; Sun & public holidays 14.00–18.00; Closed 13.00-14.00 and Oct-Mar.

☎ 01 846 3779

www.malahidecastle.com

GAA Museum, Croke Park.
The Gaelic Athletic Association (GAA) is Ireland's largest sporting and cultural organisation and is dedicated to promoting the games of hurling, Gaelic football, handball, rounders and camogie. The museum is at Croke Park, home of Irish hurling and football, and traces the history of Gaelic sports and their place in Irish culture right up to the present day. Interactive exhibits allow visitors the chance to try out the skills of the games for themselves. National trophies and sports equipment are also on display.

Open Mon-Sat 09.30-17.00, Sun 12.00-17.00. Last admission ½ hour before closing. Open for Cusack Stand ticket holders only on match days. All groups must be pre-booked.

☎ 01 819 2323

www.gaa.ie/museum

Email: gaamuseum@crokepark.ie

Heraldic Museum, Kildare Street.
Part of the National Library of Ireland, the museum illustrates the uses of heraldry with displays of coat of arms and banners and a collection of heraldic glass, seals, stamps, and coins. Open Mon-Wed 10.00-20.30; Thurs-Fri 10.00-16.30; Sat 10.00-12.30. Admission is free.

☎ 01 603 0311

www.nli.ie

Email: herald@nli.ie

General Post Office, O'Connell Street.
Designed by Francis Johnston and completed in 1818. A century later the GPO became the headquarters of the 1916 Easter Rising and the Proclamation of the Irish Republic was read from the steps by Patrick Pearse. Bullet marks can still be seen on the pillars. Badly damaged in 1922 in the fight for independence, it was restored in 1929. A bronze sculpture, The Death of Cúchulainn by Oliver Sheppard, stands within the building.

☎ 01 705 7600

Email: customer.service@anpost.ie

Guinness Storehouse, St. James's Gate.
The story of Guinness is told from its beginnings in 1759, how it is made and the advertising campaigns used to make it internationally famous. Housed in St James's Gate Brewery and

spread over six floors, on the highest of which can be found the bar 'Gravity', from which a 360° view of Dublin can be enjoyed. Open all year 09.30-17.00 (last admission); Jul-Aug 09.30-19.00. Closed Christmas Eve, Christmas Day, Boxing Day, Good Friday. Disabled access.

☎ 01 408 4800

www.guinness-storehouse.com

Email: guinness-storehouse@guinness.com

Ha'penny Bridge, Crampton Quay.

An elegant cast-iron pedestrian bridge spanning the Liffey; it was first opened in 1816 and the name derives from the toll once charged.

Irish Jewish Museum, Walworth Road

Opened by President Herzog of Israel in 1985, exhibits relate to the Jewish community in Ireland including synagogue fittings and the reconstruction of a typical Dublin Jewish kitchen of 100 years ago. Open (May–Sept) Sun, Tues, Thurs 11.00–15.30; (Oct–Apr) Sun 10.30–14.30. Admission is free.

☎ 01 490 1857

Irish Museum of Modern Art,

Military Road, Kilmainham.

Opened in the 17thC Royal Hospital building and grounds in 1991, the museum is an important institution for the collection of modern and contemporary art. A wide variety of work by major established 20thC figures and that of younger contemporary artists is presented in an ever changing programme of exhibitions, drawn from the museum's own collection and from public and private collections world-wide.

Open Tues–Sat 10.00–17.15, Sun & some bank holidays 12.00–17.15. Admission is free.

☎ 01 612 9900

www.modernart.ie

Email: info@imma.ie

James Joyce Centre, North Great George's Street.

A museum in a restored Georgian town house, built in 1784, devoted to the great novelist and run by members of his family. Dennis J Maginni, dancing master in Joyce's novel Ulysses, ran his dancing school from this house. The library contains editions of Joyce's work and that of other Irish writers as well as biographical and critical writing. There is a set of biographies of real Dublin people fictionalised in Ulysses, and also the door from the house occupied by the central character of the novel, Leopold Bloom and his wife Molly. The centre hosts readings, lectures and debates on all aspects of Joyce and his literature and conducts guided city tours.

Open Tues–Sat 10.00–17.00.

☎ 01 878 8547

www.jamesjoyce.ie

Email: info@jamesjoyce.ie

James Joyce Museum, Sandycove.

The museum is housed in the Martello Tower which Joyce used as the setting for the opening chapter of Ulysses, his great work of fiction which immortalised Dublin. Joyce stayed here briefly in 1904 and the living room and view from the gun platform remains much as he described it in the novel. The museum collection includes personal possessions, letters, photographs, first editions and items that reflect the Dublin of Joyce. Situated 13km (8 miles) south of Dublin city centre, the tower was one of 15 defensive towers built along Dublin Bay in 1804 to withstand a threatened invasion from Napoleon.

Open (Mar–Oct) Mon–Sat 10.00–17.00, Sun 14.00–18.00. Closed 13.00–14.00.

Open Nov-Mar by arrangement.

☎ 01 280 9265

Kilmainham Gaol, Inchicore Road, Kilmainham.

Built as a gaol in 1796, Kilmainham is now dedicated to the Irish patriots imprisoned there from 1792–1924, including Emmet and his United Irishmen colleagues, the Fenians, the Invincibles and the Irish Volunteers of the Easter Rising. Patrick Pearse and James Connolly were executed in the prison yard and Eamon de Valera, later Prime Minister and then President of Ireland, was one of the last inmates. After its closure in 1924 Kilmainham re-opened as a museum in 1966. It is one of the largest unoccupied gaols in Europe with tiers of cells and overhead catwalks. Access is by guided tour only and features an exhibition and audio-visual show on the political and penal history of the gaol.

Open daily (May–Sept) 09.30–17.00; (Oct–Mar) Mon–Fri 09.30–16.00, Sun 10.00–17.00. Disabled toilets. Tours for visitors with special needs by prior arrangement.

☎ 01 453 5984

King's Inns, Henrietta Street.

The Dublin Inns of Court is a glorious classical building, partly built to the plans of James Gandon at the end of the 19thC. The library was founded in 1787 and contains a large legal collection with about 100,000 books. The courtyard opens into Henrietta Street, where Dublin's earliest Georgian mansions remain.

☎ 01 872 6048

www.kingsinns.ie

Leinster House, Kildare Street.

Originally a handsome town mansion designed by Richard Castle for the Duke of Leinster in 1745; it has been a Parliament House since 1922. The Dáil Éireann (House of Representatives) and Seanad Éireann (Senate) sit here. The house has two contrasting facades: an imposing formal side facing Kildare Street while from Merrion Square the building has more of the appearance of a country residence. Anybody wanting a tour of Irish Parliament must contact their respective embassy in Dublin where arrangements can be made. Advance notice is required.

☎ 01 618 3000

Malahide Castle, Malahide.

Originally built in 1185, it was the seat of the Talbot family until 1973 when the last Lord Talbot died; the history of the family is detailed in the Great Hall alongside many family portraits. Malahide also has a large collection of Irish portrait paintings, mainly from the National Gallery, and is furnished with fine period furniture. Within the 100 hectares (250 acres) of parkland surrounding the castle is the Talbot Botanic Gardens, largely created by Lord Milo Talbot between 1948 and 1973. The grounds include walled gardens and a shrubbery with a collection of southern hemisphere plants. Malahide is situated 13km (8 miles) north of Dublin city centre.

Open Mon-Sat 10.00-17.00; Sundays & Bank Holidays 11.00-17.00 (18.00 Apr-Sept); Closed for tours 13.00-14.00.

Combined tickets with Fry Model Railway are available.

☎ 01 846 2184

www.malahidecastle.com

Email: malahidecastle@dublintourism.ie

Mansion House, Dawson Street.

Built in 1705, this Queen Anne style house has been the official residence of the Lord Mayor of Dublin since 1715. The first Irish parliament assembled here in 1919 to adopt Ireland's declaration of Independence and ratify the 1916 proclamation of the Irish Republic. Not open to the public.

National Museum of Ireland

☎ 01 677 7444 / 1890 687 386

www.museum.ie

Open Tues-Sat 10.00-17.00, Sun 14.00-17.00. Admission is free. A Museumlink bus linking the three sites of the National Museum operates regularly throughout the day.

The three national museum sites are:

Archæology and History, Kildare Street.

Houses a fabulous collection of national antiquities including prehistoric gold ornaments, and outstanding examples of Celtic and medieval art. The 8thC Ardagh Chalice and Tara Brooch are amongst the treasures. The entire history of Ireland is reflected in the museum with 'The Road to Independence Exhibition' illustrating Irish history from 1916-1921. Additionally, there is an Ancient Egypt exhibition.

Decorative Arts and History (Collins Barracks), Benburb Street.

Ireland's museum of decorative arts and economic, social, political and military history, based in the oldest military barracks in Europe. Major collections include Irish silver, Irish country furniture, and costume jewellery and accessories. The work of museum restoration and conservation is explained and the Out of Storage gallery provides visitors with a view of artefacts in storage.

Natural History, Merrion Street.

First opened in 1857 and hardly changed since then, the museum houses a large collection of stuffed animals and the skeletons of mammals and birds from both Ireland and the rest of the world. The exhibits include three examples of the Irish Great Elk which became extinct over 10,000 years ago and the skeleton of a Basking Shark. Fascinating glass reproductions of marine specimens, known as the Blaschka Collection, are found on the upper gallery.

National Print Museum, Haddington Road.

Situated in the former Garrison Chapel in Beggars Bush Barracks, the museum illustrates the development of printing from the advent of printing to the use of computer technology with a unique collection of implements and machines from Ireland's printing industry.

Open Mon-Fri 09.00-17.00, Sat-Sun 14.00-17.00. Closed Bank Holiday weekends.

☎ 01 660 3770

National Sea Life Centre, Bray.

Features marine life from the seas around Ireland including stingrays, conger eels, and sharks; also freshwater fish from Irish rivers and streams. A touch pool gives children the opportunity to pick up small creatures such as starfish, crabs and sea anemones. By way of contrast is the fascinating 'Danger in the Depths' tank with many sea creatures from around the world which have proved harmful or fatal to humans.

Open (May-Sept) Mon-Fri 10.00-18.00, Sat & Sun 10.00-18.30; (Oct-Apr) Mon-Fri 11.00-17.00, Sat & Sun 11.00-18.00.

☎ 01 286 6939

www.sealifeeurope.com

National Transport Museum, Howth.

A collection of buses, trams, trucks, tractors and fire engines, some dating back to 1880, along with other memorabilia from the transport industry.

Open (Jun-Aug) Mon-Fri 10.00-17.00, Sat & Sun 14.00-17.00; (Sept-May) Sat & Sun only 14.00-17.00. Bank holidays 14.00-17.00.

☎ 01 848 0831

www.nationaltransportmuseum.org

Email: info@nationaltransportmuseum.org

National Wax Museum, Grafton Street.
Over 300 life-size wax figures of well-known people and personalities from the past and present ranging from Eamon De Valera to Elvis Presley. Also a dimly lit Chamber of Horrors.
Open Mon-Sat 10.00-17.30; Sun 12.00-17.30
☎ 01 872 6340

Newbridge House, Donabate.
Built in 1737 for Archbishop Charles Cobbe, and still the residence of his descendants, Newbridge has one of the most beautiful period manor house interiors in Ireland and is set within 142 hectares (350 acres) of parkland. A fully restored 18thC farm lies on the estate together with dairy, forge, tack room, and estate worker's house. Situated 19km (12 miles) north of Dublin.
Open (Apr-Sept) Tues-Sat 10.00-17.00, Sun & bank holidays 14.00-18.00; (Oct-Mar) Sat, Sun & bank holidays 12.00-17.00.
☎ 01 843 6534

Newman House, St Stephen's Green.
Newman House is made up of two splendid Georgian mansions, No 85 and No 86, which were once part of the buildings of the Catholic University of Ireland and named after Cardinal Newman, the first rector of the university. They are now owned by University College Dublin. No 86 was built in 1765 for Richard Whaley MP with marvellous stucco by Robert West, the house has also been owned by the celebrated gambler Buck Whaley. The smaller house, No 85, was designed by Richard Castle in 1739 with beautiful plasterwork by the Swiss La Franchini brothers and includes the Apollo Room with a figure of the god above the mantle. Gerald Manley Hopkins was Professor of Classics here at the end of the 19thC and his study is on view. Also open to the public is a classroom furnished as it would have been when James Joyce was a pupil here from 1899-1902. A guided tour explains the history and heritage of the house and how it was restored.
Open (Jun, Jul, Aug) Tues-Fri 14.00-17.00.
☎ 01 716 7422

Number 29, Lower Fitzwilliam Street.
This elegant four-storey house has been restored and furnished exactly as it would have been between 1790-1820 by any well-to-do middle class family. Everything in the house is authentic with period items from the National Museum. The wallpaper was hand-made for Number 29 using 18thC methods. Among the rooms in the house are a kitchen, pantry, governess' room, nursery and boudoir.
Open Tues-Sat 10.00-17.00, Sun 13.00-17.00. Closed for about 2 weeks preceding Christmas.
☎ 01 702 6165

Old Jameson Distillery,
Bow Street, Smithfield Village.
The art of Irish Whiskey making shown through an audio-visual presentation, working models of the distilling process, and guided tour of the old distillery which was in use between 1780-1971.
Open daily 09.30-17.30 (tours only). Disabled access.
☎ 01 807 2355

Pearse Museum,
St. Enda's Park, Grange Road, Rathfarnham.
Housed in the former school run by nationalist Patrick Pearse from 1910-1916, it includes an audio-visual presentation and a nature study room with displays on Irish flora and fauna. Pearse was executed in 1916 for his part in the Easter Rising. Due to reopen mid 2008 after renovation. Open (Feb-Apr) 10.00-17.00; (May-Aug) 10.00-17.30; (Sept-Oct) 10.00-17.00; (Nov-Jan) 10.00-16.00; closed 13.00-14.00. Admission is free. Disabled access to ground floor/toilet.
☎ 01 493 4208

Phoenix Park Visitor Centre, Phoenix Park.
The visitor centre illustrates the history and wildlife of the park with an audio-visual display, a variety of fascinating exhibits and temporary exhibitions. Adjoining the centre is a restored medieval tower house, Ashtown Castle. On Saturdays there are free guided tours to the Irish President's House which is situated in the Park.
Open (Mar-Oct) daily 10.00-17.30 (18.00 Apr-Sept); (Nov-Sept) Wed-Sun 10.00-17.00. Last admission 45 minutes before closing. Toilet for people with disabilities.
☎ 01 677 0095

Powerscourt Centre, South William Street.
A lively three storey centre of craft shops, galleries, boutiques and cafés, converted from Powerscourt Townhouse, a classical style mansion designed by Robert Mack and built between 1771-74. It features the original grand wooden staircase and finely detailed plasterwork.
Open Mon-Fri 10.00-18.00 (Thurs 20.00), Sat 09.00-21.00, Sun 12.00-18.00.
☎ 01 671 7000
www.powerscourtcentre.com

Powerscourt House & Gardens,
County Wicklow.
First laid out in the 1740s, the 18 hectare (45 acre) gardens, perhaps the finest in Ireland, include sweeping terraces cut into a steep hillside, statues and ornamental lakes. A spectacular Italian style stairway leading down to the main lake was added in 1874. Secluded Japanese gardens with bamboo and walled gardens are also notable and there is a huge variety of trees and shrubs. The house

suffered a serious fire in 1974 and is no longer lived in. Visitors may walk through the old ballroom, and an exhibition area illustrates the history of the construction of the house and there are models of some of the rooms as they would have been before the fire. The house dates back to the 18thC when in 1731 architect Richard Castle was commissioned by Richard Wingfield to transform the medieval Powerscourt Castle into a grand Palladian style mansion; the castle walls were used to form the main structure and the central courtyard was converted into an entrance hall. Powerscourt is in the foothills of the Wicklow mountains, 19km (12 miles) south of Dublin.
Open daily 09.30–17.30.

Powerscourt Waterfall is a separate attraction and is the highest in Ireland at 121m (398ft). Open daily 09.30-17.30. Gardens & waterfall close at dusk in the winter.
☎ 01 204 6000
www.powerscourt.ie

Rathfarnham Castle, Rathfarnham.
Dating from around 1583, this castle has 18thC interiors by Sir William Chambers and James Stuart and is presented to visitors as a castle undergoing conservation. Restricted access to the castle for people with disabilities.
Open daily from May–Oct 09.30–17.30 (last tour 16.30).
☎ 01 493 9462

Royal Hospital, Military Road, Kilmainham.
The Royal Hospital was built as a home for army pensioners and invalids by Charles I, and continued in use for almost 250 years. Designed by Sir William Robinson in 1684, it has a formal facade and large courtyard and bears similarities to Les Invalides in Paris and The Royal Hospital in Chelsea. The restored building has one of Dublin's finest interiors and houses the Irish Museum of Modern Art in which there is an audio-visual presentation "The Story of the Royal Hospital Kilmainham". The grounds, including a formal garden, are open to the public.
Open (Jun-Sept) Tues-Sat 12.00-17.30, Sun & bank holidays 12.00-17.30
☎ 01 612 9900

Shaw Birthplace, Synge Street.
This delightful Victorian terrace home was the birthplace of one of Ireland's four Nobel prize-winners for literature, George Bernard Shaw. Restored to give the feeling that the Shaw family is still in residence, the home provides an insight into the domestic life of Victorian Dubliners.
Open (May–Sept) Mon–Fri 10.00–17.00, Sat & Sun 14.00–17.00. Closed Weds & 13.00–14.00.
☎ 01 475 0854

Tara's Palace, Malahide Castle.
The centrepiece of this museum is the one-twelfth size scale model house reflecting the splendour of 18thC Irish mansions. Conceived by Ronald and Doreen McDonnell in 1980, it was ten years in the making. Irish craftsmen paid meticulous attention to detail, with unique miniature furniture and paintings adorning the walls. The museum also has rare pieces of porcelain, miniature glass and silver. Dolls houses of the 18thC and 19thC are displayed, together with dolls and antique toys.
Open (all year) Sat, Sun, bank holidays 11.30-17.30, (Apr-Sept) Mon-Fri 10.45-16.45.
☎ 01 846 3779

Temple Bar
Named after a 17thC landowner, Sir William Temple, this charming neighbourhood is Dublin's cultural quarter. With its narrow cobbled streets running close to the Liffey, Temple Bar is full of character and home to many artists and musicians. The area has been regenerated in recent years and boasts a wide variety of cultural venues and events and an eclectic mix of studios, galleries, shops, markets and eating-places. Modern architecture now blends with the historic. Many free open-air events take place in summer at Meeting House Square and Temple Bar Square, including circus acts, concerts and the outdoor screening of films. Temple Bar is bounded by the south quays of the Liffey, Dame Street, Westmoreland Street and Fishamble Street.
Temple Bar Information Centre, 12 Essex Street East.
Open Mon-Fri 09.00-17.30 (19.00 Jun-Sept), Sat 10.00-18.00, Sun 12.00-16.00 (18.00 Jun-Sept).
☎ 01 677 2255
www.temple-bar.ie

The Chimney, Smithfield Village.
Originally built in 1895, this 53 metre (175ft) chimney which belonged to the Jameson Whiskey Distillery now provides a 360 degree panoramic viewpoint over the city. A glass walled lift takes visitors up the side of the chimney to two viewing galleries at the top.
Open daily 10.00–17.30 (opens 11.00 on Sundays).
☎ 01 817 3838

Trinity College, College Green.
The original Elizabethan college was founded in 1592 but the present building was largely built between 1755–1759. The cruciform complex surrounding cobbled quadrangles and peaceful gardens has an impressive 91 metre (300ft) Palladian facade designed by Henry Keene and John Sanderford. One of the most notable features within the main college square is the 30 metre (98ft) Campanile or bell tower built in 1853 by Sir

Charles Lanyon. The oldest surviving part of the college is the red brick apartment building from 1700 known as The Rubrics. Originally a Protestant College, Catholics did not start entering Trinity until the 1970s. The Library has over a million books and a magnificent collection of early illuminated manuscripts, including the famous Book of Kells; areas open to the public include the Colonnades, the Treasury, and the Long Room Library. Edmund Burke, Oliver Goldsmith and Samuel Beckett are among famous former Trinity College students.

www.tcd.ie

Waterways Visitor Centre, Grand Canal Quay.
A modern centre built on piers over the Grand Canal, housing an exhibition about Ireland's inland waterways. Working models of various engineering features are displayed and there is an interactive multimedia presentation.
Open (Jun–Sept) daily 09.30-17.30; (Oct–May) Wed–Sun 12.30-17.00. Last admission 45 minutes before closing. Access to ground floor for people with disabilities.
☎ 01 677 7510

Cathedrals and churches

Augustinian Church, Thomas Street.
Designed by E W Pugin and G C Ashlin in 1862, it has a mountainous exterior with lofty side aisles to the nave and a 49 metre (160ft) high tower crowned by a spire.

Christ Church Cathedral, Christchurch Place.
The Cathedral was established by Strongbow and Archbishop Laurence O'Toole in 1173 on the site of the cathedral founded around 1030 by the Norse King Sitric Silkenbeard. Lambert Simnel, pretender to the English throne, was crowned here as Edward VI in 1487. It was extensively restored between 1871–78 by George Edmund Street and is one of the best examples in Ireland of early Gothic architecture. The medieval crypt is one of the oldest and largest in Ireland.
Open 09.45-17.00 (Jun-Aug 09.00-18.00).
☎ 01 677 8099
www.cccdub.ie
Email: welcome@cccdub.ie

Franciscan Church,
(Adam and Eve's) Merchants Quay.
Designed by Patrick Byrne in 1830.

St. Ann's Church, Dawson Street.
Designed by Isaac Wells in 1720 with a Romanesque-style facade added by Sir Thomas Deane in 1868. Much of the colourful stained glass dates back to the mid 19thC. Wooden shelves behind the altar were once used to take bread for distribution to the poor. Music recitals are held in the church.
☎ 01 676 7727
www.stannschurch.ie

St. Audoen's Church, High Street.
Dublin's only surviving medieval parish church, with a 12thC font and portal. The bell tower, restored in the 19thC, has three 15thC bells. The guild chapel has an exhibition on the importance of the church in the life of the medieval city. Dublin's only surviving city gate, known as St. Audoen's Arch, stands nearby.
Open Jun–Sept 09.30 (10.15 on Sun)–16.45. Toilet for people with disabilities and church partly accessible.
☎ 01 677 0088

St. Audoen's RC Church, High Street.
Designed by Patrick Byrne in 1841–47, it has a monumental, cliff-like exterior with a huge Corinthian portico added by Stephen Ashlin in 1898.

St. George's, Temple Street.
This neo-classical church was designed by Francis Johnston in 1802 and has a 61 metre (200ft) high steeple modelled on St. Martin-in-the-Fields, London.

St. Mary's Church, Mary Street.
A handsome galleried church designed by Thomas Burgh in 1627. Wolfe Tone, leader of the United Irishmen, was baptised here in 1763 and Sean O'Casey in 1880.

St. Mary's Abbey, Meetinghouse Lane.
Established originally as a Benedictine foundation in 1139, it became Cistercian seven years later. Until the 16thC it was one of the largest and most important monasteries in Ireland. The remains include a fine vaulted Chapter House of 1190 and there is an interesting exhibition about the history of the abbey.
Open mid June–mid Sept, Wed and Sat 10.00-17.00. Last admission 45 minutes before closing.
☎ 01 872 1490

St. Mary's Pro-Cathedral, Marlborough Street.
A Greek Doric style building with the interior modelled on the Church of St. Philippe de Roule in Paris, designed by John Sweetman and built between 1815–1825. St. Mary's is Dublin's most important Catholic Church and is used on State occasions. Tenor John McCormack was once a member of the Palestrina choir that sings a Latin mass every Sunday at 11.00.
Open Mon-Fri 07.30-18.45, Sat 07.30-19.15, Sun 09.00-13.45 and 17.30-19.45.
☎ 01 874 5441
www.procathedral.ie

St. Michan's Church, Church Street.
Founded in 1095 as a Viking parish church, largely rebuilt in 1685 and restored in 1828. Famous for the 17thC mummified bodies in the crypt which are preserved with skin and hair because of the dry atmosphere created by the limestone walls. Handel is thought to have played on the organ which dates from 1724.
Open (March/April–Oct) Mon–Fri 10.00–12.45 and 14.00–16.45; (Nov–March) Mon–Fri 12.30–15.30; all Saturdays 10.00–12.45. Vaults closed on Sundays.
☎ 01 872 4154

St. Patrick's Cathedral, St. Patrick's Close.
The National Cathedral of the Church of Ireland, it was built in the late 12thC on the site of the pre-Norman parish church of St. Patrick. It gained and lost cathedral status more than once in its chequered history and Cromwellian soldiers stabled horses here in the Civil War. Architect John Semple added a spire in 1749 and St. Patrick's was fully restored in the 19thC with finance from the Guinness family. The massive west tower houses the largest ringing peel of bells in Ireland. The cathedral is full of memorial brasses, busts and monuments to famous Irishmen. Jonathan Swift was Dean here from 1713–1745; there are memorials to Swift and his beloved Stella (Esther Johnson) and Swift's pulpit contains his writing table and chair, and portrait.
Usually open daily 09.00–17.00. Wheelchair access by arrangement.
☎ 01 453 9472
www.stpatrickscathedral.ie
Email: admin@stpatrickscathedral.ie

St. Saviour's, Dominick Street.
Designed by J J McCarthy in 1858, this extravagant French style Gothic edifice has a bold west door under a triangular hood, crowned by a large rose window.

St. Stephen's (Pepper Canister),
Mount Street Crescent.
This handsome neo-classical church, designed by John Bowden in 1824, has a Greek style portico.
www.peppercanister.ie

St. Werburgh's Church, Werburgh Street.
Originally the site of an Anglo-Norman foundation, the present church was built in 1715–19 and rebuilt in 1759 following a fire. St. Werburgh's was the Chapel Royal until 1790. Lord Edward Fitzgerald, one of the leaders of the 1798 rebellion, is buried in the vaults.

Whitefriar Street Carmelite Church,
Aungier Street.
19thC church standing on the site of a 16thC Carmelite Priory. The remains of Saint Valentine are buried here and there is a 15thC oak statue of the Virgin and Child, thought to be the only surviving Pre-reformation statue of its kind.
☎ 01 475 8821

Libraries

Central Catholic Library, Merrion Square.
Of religious and general interest, with a large Irish section.
Open Mon–Fri 11.00–18.00, Sat 11.00–17.30.
☎ 01 676 1264
www.catholiclibrary.ie

Central Library, Ilac Centre.
☎ 01 873 4333.
Enquiries about other Dublin City Public Libraries (lending, reference and special collections).
Open Mon–Thurs 10.00–20.00, Fri-Sat 10.00-17.00, Sun closed.
☎ 01 674 4800
Email: dublinpubliclibraries@dublincity.ie

Chester Beatty Library,
Dublin Castle, Dame Street.
Reopened in 2000 in a purpose designed home in the Clock Tower building of Dublin Castle, the library is a treasure of manuscripts, books, prints and textiles collected by American scholar Sir Alfred Chester Beatty. It has some of the rarest original manuscripts still in existence. The collection reflects the art of manuscript production and printing from many parts of the world and from early to modern times with picture scrolls, jade books and woodblock prints from the Far East, around 4,000 Islamic manuscripts, and fine books, bindings and manuscripts from Western Europe. With many Early Christian papyri, the library is a major resource for the study of the Old and New Testaments.
Open Mon–Fri 10.00–17.00, Sat 11.00–17.00, Sun 13.00–17.00. Oct-Apr closed Mondays. Admission is free.
☎ 01 407 0750
www.cbl.ie
Email: info@cbl.ie

Genealogical Office, Kildare Street.
Part of the National Library, the genealogical office offers a service to assist in the task of tracing family history, familiarising people with the relevant records and procedures.
Open Mon–Fri 10.00–17.00, Sat 10.00–12.30.
☎ 01 603 0200

Gilbert Library, Pearse Street.
Books and manuscripts relating to Dublin which were accumulated by 19thC Dublin historian Sir John T Gilbert and now in the care of Dublin Corporation. The collection includes rare early Dublin newspapers, 18thC bindings, Irish Almanacs,

manuscripts of the municipal records of the City of Dublin and the records of the Dublin guilds.
☎ 01 674 4800

Goethe Institute Library, Merrion Square.
German cultural information centre and reference library.
Open Tues-Thurs 12.00–20.00, Fri 10.00-14.30, Sat 10.00-13.30.
☎ 01 661 1155
www.goethe.de

Irish Architectural Archive, Merrion Square.
Records of Irish architecture are preserved and can be examined free of charge with no appointment at the discretion of the staff.
Open Tues–Fri 10.00-17.00.
☎ 01 663 3040
www.iarc.ie

Marsh's Library, St Patrick's Close.
Given to the city by Archbishop Narcissus Marsh and opened in 1701, this is Ireland's oldest public library containing many rare books still in their original carved bookcases. The building was designed by Sir William Robinson who was also the architect of the Royal Hospital, Kilmainham. To prevent the theft of rare books readers were locked in wire cages and three of these cages survive.
Open Mon-Fri 10.00-17.00 (closed 13.00-14.00); Sat 10.30-13.00; closed Tuesdays.
☎ 01 454 3511
www.marshlibrary.ie
Email: keeper@marshlibrary.ie

National Library of Ireland, Kildare Street.
Offers over half a million books, a vast collection of maps, prints and manuscripts and an invaluable collection of Irish newspapers and periodicals. The impressive Victorian building has been home to the Library since 1890, and there is a large domed reading room. Holds temporary exhibitions on Irish writers and books.
Open: Mon-Wed 10.00–21.00,
Thurs–Fri 10.00–17.00, Sat 10.00-13.00.
☎ 01 603 0200
www.nli.ie Email: info@nli.ie

National Photographic Archive,
Meeting House Square.
Only established in 1998, it has over 600,000 photographs recording people, political events, and scenes of Irish cities, towns and countryside. Images from the collection are always on view. There is also a reading room and darkrooms.
Open: Mon–Fri 10.00–17.00. Sat 10.00-14.00 (exhibition only) Admission is free. Disabled access/toilet.
☎ 01 603 0374
www.nli.ie/fr_arch.htm
Email: photoarchive@nli.ie

Royal Irish Academy Library, Dawson Street.
One of the largest collections of ancient Irish manuscripts in the country with one usually on display together with a small exhibition. Access may be restricted depending on Royal Academy meetings and large groups need to make a prior arrangement to visit.
Open Mon–Fri 10.00–17.30 (Fri 17.00).
Admission is free.
☎ 01 676 2570
www.ria.ie

Trinity College Library, College Green.
The oldest and most famous of Dublin's libraries dating from the late 16thC. Entitled to receive a copy of every book published in Ireland, the library also contains an extensive collection of Irish manuscripts including the Book of Kells, a beautifully illuminated copy of the gospels written on vellum in Latin around the year AD800. The Book of Kells is now bound in four volumes and two are always on display in the Treasury, one open at a major ornamental page and the other to show two pages of script. An exhibition explains how the Book of Kells and other manuscripts such as the Book of Durrow (AD675) and Book of Armagh (AD807) were created and illustrates monastic life in the 8thC.
The impressive Old Library or Long Room Library is lined with marble busts of scholars and is nearly 64 metres (210ft) long. It rises two storeys with a high barrel vaulted ceiling and contains over 200,000 of the college's books.
Open Mon–Sat 09.30–17.00; Sun 09.30–16.30 (Jun–Sept), Sun 12.00–16.30 (May–Oct). Last admission 30 minutes before closing.
☎ 01 896 1661
www.tcd.ie/Library

Arts centres, galleries, and concert halls

Douglas Hyde Gallery, Trinity College.
Showing mainly temporary exhibitions of contemporary art.
Open Mon-Sat 11.00-18.00 (Thurs 19.00, Sat 16.45)
☎ 01 896 1116
www.douglashydegallery.com
Email: dhgallery@tcd.ie

Gallery of Photography,
Meeting House Square.
Exhibitions of contemporary photography. Roof terrace has views over the square.
Open Tues-Sat 11.00-18.00, Sun 13.00-18.00.
☎ 01 671 4654
www.irish-photography.com
Email: gallery@irish-photography.com

Hugh Lane Municipal Gallery of Modern Art,
Parnell Square North.

19thC and 20thC paintings, mainly Impressionist works, bequeathed by Sir Hugh Lane who was drowned in the Lusitania in 1915, form the nucleus of this collection. The Lane Collection is split with the Tate Gallery in London; each half is alternated between the galleries every 5 years. There is an extensive range of Irish and international paintings, sculpture and stained glass and the acquisition of contemporary work is ongoing. Included is the London studio of Dublin-born artist Francis Bacon, which was carefully dismantled and reconstructed here. Regular 'Sundays at Noon' Concerts are held at the gallery (apart from July and August) with everything from early music to commissioned new works; the music is often arranged to complement one of the temporary exhibitions. The classical building which houses the gallery, Charlemont House, was designed by William Chambers in 1763 for James Caulfield, later 1st Earl Charlemont. It was reconstructed in 1929 to house the Lane Collection and opened in 1933.

Open Tues–Thurs 10.00–18.00, Fri & Sat 10.00–17.00, Sun 11.00–17.00. Admission free except for special exhibitions. Disabled access.

☎ 01 222 5550

www.hughlane.ie

Email: info.hughlane@dublincity.ie

National Concert Hall, Earlsfort Terrace.
Home of the National Symphony Orchestra of Ireland, but also a venue for international artists and orchestras, jazz, contemporary and traditional Irish music. The classical building was designed for the Great Exhibition of 1865, then became the centrepiece of University College Dublin before opening as Ireland's National Concert Hall in 1981. Booking office open Mon–Sat 10.00–19.00. Disabled access/toilet.

☎ 01 417 0000

www.nch.ie

Email:info@nch.ie

National Gallery of Ireland, Merrion Square.
Paintings by illustrious 20thC European artists such as Morrisot, Bonnard, Picasso and Monet hang in the National Gallery as well as the work of Old Masters including Titian, Caravaggio, Rembrandt and Vermeer. There is the National Collection of Irish art, a room dedicated to the work of Jack B Yeats, English paintings, and over 250 sculptures. William Dargan organised the 1853 Dublin Exhibition on this site and used the proceeds to found the collection; his statue stands on the lawn.

Open Mon–Sat 09.30–17.30, Thurs 09.30–20.30, Sun 12.00–17.30. Admission free. Disabled access/toilet.

☎ 01 661 5133

www.nationalgallery.ie

Email: info@ngi.ie

Royal Dublin Society, Ballsbridge.
Venue for large events including craft and antiques fairs and Ideal Homes exhibitions.

☎ 01 668 0866

www.rds.ie

Royal Hibernian Academy Gallagher Gallery,
Ely Place.

Showing both traditional and innovative work from both Irish and international artists.

☎ 01 661 2558

www.royalhibernianacademy.com

Email: www.rhagallery@eircom.net

Solomon Gallery, Powerscourt Centre.
One of Ireland's leading contemporary art galleries, situated in an 18thC Georgian townhouse.

Open Mon–Fri 10.00–17.30, Sat 11.00–14.00. Admission free.

☎ 01 679 4237

www.solomongallery.com

Email: info@solomongallery.com

Temple Bar Gallery and Studios, Temple Bar.
A large complex with studios and exhibition spaces.

Open Tues-Sat 10.00-18.00 (Thurs 19.00).

☎ 01 671 0073

www.templebargallery.com

Email: info@templebargallery.com

Temple Bar Music Centre, Curved Street.
Live music venue with recording and rehearsal studios.

☎ 01 670 9202

www.tbmc.ie

Email: info@tbmc.ie

Taylor Galleries, Kildare Street.
Contemporary art gallery, mainly Irish, with the emphasis on painting and sculpture.

☎ 01 676 6055

The Ark, Eustace Street.
A cultural centre for children aged between 3 and 14 with a programme of events and workshops from the worlds of literature, visual arts and music & dance. Plays, exhibitions, festivals, concerts, opera and dance are regularly featured with participation and interaction encouraged. Open to school groups during school times and individuals and family groups at all other times.

Open Mon-Fri 10.00-17.00 and for weekend performances and workshops.

☎ 01 670 7788

www.ark.ie Email: boxoffice@ark.ie

Parks and gardens

Garden of Remembrance, Parnell Square East.
The Garden of Remembrance, opened in 1966, is dedicated to all those who died in the cause of Irish Freedom.
Open (Oct-Mar) 09.30-1600, (Apr-Sept) 08.30-18.00.
☎ *01 874 3074 / 01 647 2498*

Iveagh Gardens, Clonmel Street.
Designed by Ninian Niven in 1863, this is one of the least known and most tranquil of Dublin's parks. Features include a rustic grotto, cascade, fountains, maze, archery grounds, wilderness and woodlands. Opening according to daylight hours.
☎ *01 475 7816*

Marlay Park, Rathfarnham.
This large park situated at the foot of the Dublin Mountains contains areas of woodland, a large pond, nature trail and model railway. It is also a popular open-air music venue.

National Botanic Gardens, Glasnevin.
Established in 1795, these magnificent gardens occupy an area of 20 hectares (49 acres) and contain a fabulous collection of plants, shrubs and trees. Many of the plants come from tropical Africa and South America and are housed in large Victorian glasshouses. Features include a rose garden, rockery and wall plants, herbaceous borders, vegetable garden and arboretum.
Open Mon-Sun 09.00-18.00 (Feb-Oct), 09.00-16.30 (Nov-Jan). Admission is free but there is a small charge for the car park. Toilet for people with disabilities, and gardens largely accessible.
☎ *01 857 0909*
www.botanicgardens.ie

Phoenix Park
Phoenix Park, covering over 712 hectares (1,760 acres), is Europe's largest enclosed city park. Its name is thought to derive from the Irish meaning "clear water" and a spring does rise in the park. Enclosed by an 11km (7 mile) long stone wall, the park was laid out in the mid 18thC and was the scene of the Phoenix Park murders in 1882, when the Chief Secretary and the Under-Secretary for Ireland were assassinated. A more recent event was when the Pope celebrated mass in the park in front of 1 million people; a 27 metre (90ft) steel cross marks the spot. The park includes a number of buildings, the most important of which is Áras an Uachtaráin; the Viceroy's Lodge built in 1751 but later becoming the official house of the President of Ireland when Dr Douglas Hyde moved there in 1938. Other important buildings are the American ambassador's residence and the Ordnance Survey Office. A 60 metre (205 ft) high obelisk, erected in 1817, is a memorial to the Dublin-born Duke of Wellington. The People's Garden by the main entrance on Parkgate Street is laid out with ornamental planting in ribbon borders, much as it would have been in Victorian times. Dublin Zoo is in the south-east corner. The open space known as Fifteen Acres (but actually covering more than 200) was used in the 18thC as a duelling ground. Phoenix Park is open to the public at all times but the People's Gardens usually close at sunset.

St. Anne's Park, Dollymount.
Once part of the Guinness family estate, the park covers over 110 hectares (270 acres) and is wooded with oak, pine, beech, chestnut and lime. There is a lovely rose garden, opened in 1975.

St. Enda's Park, Grange Road, Rathfarnham.
The park surrounds the Pearse Museum and includes a walled garden, riverside walks and waterfall. Open daily from 10.00, closing time varies according to daylight hours. Limited access for people with disabilities.

St. Stephen's Green
In the heart of the city, St Stephen's Green was originally an open common but was enclosed in 1663. Opened to the general public in 1877, it is laid out as a public park with flowerbeds, an ornamental pond and several sculptures. There is a garden for the visually impaired and there are summer lunchtime concerts at the bandstand.
Open daily 08.00 (Sun & bank Holidays 10.00); closes according to daylight hours.
☎ *01 475 7816*

War Memorial Gardens,
South Circular Road, Islandbridge.
Dedicated to the memory of the Irish soldiers who died in the First World War, these gardens include a sunken rose garden and herbaceous borders. They were designed by Sir Edward Lutyens. The names of the 49,400 soldiers who died between 1914-1918 are contained in the granite bookrooms in the gardens, access to which is only by arrangement with the management.
Open Mon-Fri 08.00, Sat & Sun 10.00; closes according to daylight hours.
☎ *01 677 0236 (gardens)*
☎ *01 647 2498 (head office)*

Theatres

The **Dublin Theatre Festival**, held at many venues throughout the city, runs for two weeks every October.
☎ *01 677 8439, Box office 01 677 8899*
www.dublintheatrefestival.com

The **Fringe Festival** runs for two to three weeks each September presenting theatre, dance, music

and the visual arts. Although concentrating on new and emerging local artists, contemporary international artists are usually also featured.
☎ *01 872 9433*
www.fringefest.com

Abbey Theatre, Lower Abbey Street.
Ireland's National Theatre, founded by Lady Gregory and W B Yeats in 1904. The Abbey quickly became world renowned, staging plays by J M Synge and Sean O'Casey, and played a significant role in the renaissance of Irish culture. It also provoked controversy in Dublin and even riots. The present theatre was built in 1966 to replace the previous building which had been destroyed by fire. The Abbey stages classic Irish plays, while the Peacock theatre downstairs presents new and experimental drama.
☎ *01 878 7222*
www.abbeytheatre.ie

Andrews Lane Theatre and Studio,
Andrews Lane.
A wide variety of works shown both in the theatre and studio.
☎ *01 679 5720*
www.andrewslane.com

Civic Theatre, Tallaght.
Stages everything from drama to variety shows
☎ *01 462 7477*
www.civictheatre.ie

Focus Theatre,
Pembroke Place, Pembroke Street.
Small theatre presenting classics and new writing.
☎ *01 676 3071*

Gaiety Theatre, South King Street.
Restored Victorian building and Dublin's oldest theatre, founded in 1837.
☎ *01 677 1717*
www.gaietytheatre.net

Gate Theatre, Cavendish Row.
Modern Irish and classical drama, also international plays. Founded in 1928.
☎ *01 874 4045*
www.gate-theatre.ie

Lambert Puppet Theatre,
Clifton Lane, Monkstown.
☎ *01 280 0974*
www.lambertpuppettheatre.com

Olympia Theatre, Dame Street.
Comedy, drama, pantomime, musicals, concerts.
☎ *0818 719330*

Peacock Theatre, Lower Abbey Street.
New and experimental work.
☎ *01 878 7222*
www.abbeytheatre.ie

Point, The North Wall Quay.
Theatre and concert venue including ballet.
☎ *01 836 3633*
www.livenation.ie

Project Arts Centre, 39 East Essex Street.
Moved in 2000 into new custom designed building with performance and gallery space; generally innovative new work and everything from drama and visual arts to talks and events.
☎ *01 881 9613*
www.project.ie

Samuel Beckett Theatre, Trinity College.
Trinity College School of Drama theatre with a variety of student productions during term and touring companies at other times. Venue for Festival Fringe events.
☎ *01 608 2461*

Sugar Club, Lower Leeson Street.
Multimedia theatre with wide range of entertainment; drama, film, cabaret, comedy, music, events.
☎ *01 678 7188*
www.thesugarclub.com

Cinemas

Cineworld, Parnell Street
☎ *01 872 8444*. 17 screens.
www.cineworld.ie

IMC, Dún Laoghaire
☎ *01 230 1399*. 12 screens.
www.imc-cinemas.com

Irish Film Institute, Eustace Street
Art house with 2 screens and restaurant converted from old Quaker meeting house.
☎ *01 679 3477*   www.irishfilm.ie

Movies@Dundrum, Dundrum town centre
☎ *01 291 6802*. 12 screens.
www.movies-at.ie

Movies@Swords, Pavilions Shopping Centre
☎ *01 870 3600*. 11 screens.
www.movies-at.ie

Omniplex, Santry
☎ *01 842 8844*. 11 screens.
www.omniplex.ie

Ormonde Cinema, Stillorgan
☎ *01 707 4100*. 7 screens.
www.ormondecinemas.com

Savoy Cinema, O'Connell Street Upper
☎ *01 874 6000*. 6 screens.
www.savoy.ie

Screen Cinema, D'Olier Street
☎ *01 672 5500*. 3 screens.
www.screencinema.ie

UCI Cinema, Blanchardstown
☎ 01 8222 624. 9 screens.

UCI Cinema, Coolock
☎ 01 848 5122. 10 screens.

UCI Cinema, Tallaght
☎ 01 459 8400. 12 screens.

Vue Dublin, Liffey Valley Shopping Centre, Fonthill Road
☎ 1520 501 000. 14 screens.

Shopping

Opening hours are generally 09.00–18.00 Mon–Sat. Many city centre shops and shopping centres remain open until 20.00 or 21.00 on Thursdays and Fridays and open 12.00–18.00 on Sundays.

The main city centre shopping areas are around Grafton Street and Nassau Street to the south of the Liffey and around Henry Street (off O'Connell Street) to the north of the river. Both Grafton Street and Henry Street are pedestrianised. Many up-market and international designer stores can be found in Grafton Street, while shops around Henry Street are generally less expensive. The Temple Bar area has a number of craft and specialist shops.

Department stores

Arnotts, Henry Street, ☎ 01 805 0400.

Brown Thomas, Grafton Street,
☎ 01 605 6666.

Clery and Co, O'Connell Street Lower,
☎ 01 878 6000.

Debenhams, Jervis Centre, ☎ 01 878 1222.

Dunnes Stores, Henry Street, ☎ 01 872 3911.

Guiney & Co, Talbot Street, ☎ 01 878 8835.

Marks & Spencers, Grafton Street,
☎ 01 679 7855.

Penneys Stores, Mary Street, ☎ 01 872 7788.

Roches Stores, Henry Street, ☎ 01 873 0044.

Shopping centres

Dún Laoghaire Shopping Centre, Marine Road,
☎ 01 280 2981.

Ilac Centre, Henry Street, ☎ 01 704 1460.

Irish Life Shopping Mall, Abbey Street,
☎ 01 704 1452.

Jervis Shopping Centre, Jervis Street,
☎ 01 878 1323.

Powerscourt Centre, South William Street,
☎ 01 679 4144.

St. Stephen's Green Centre, ☎ 01 478 0888.

There are also shopping centres at Clondalkin (Liffey Valley), Blanchardstown, and Tallaght on the outskirts of Dublin.

Markets

Blackrock
Sat, Sun & bank holidays 11.00–17.30 (bric-a-brac, china and antiques).
☎ 01 283 3522

George's Street Market Arcade
Second hand clothes, jewellery, records.
☎ 01 280 8683

Liberty Market
Clothes, fabrics, household goods, Meath Street.
☎ 01 280 8683

Moore Street Market
Mon–Sat (flower, fruit and vegetables), off Henry Street.

St. Michan's Street Vegetable Market
Fruit, vegetables, fish and flowers).

Temple Bar Square
Food market is open every Saturday from 09.30–18.00 selling organic fruit and vegetables, bread, cheeses, oysters, and smoked fish. Book Market is open on Saturdays from 09.30. There is also a craft and furniture market on Sundays 12.00-18.00.
☎ 01 677 2255

Sport and leisure

International sports venues:

Athletics
Irishtown Stadium, Irishtown
☎ 01 669 7211

Gaelic Football and Hurling
Croke Park
(Also rugby and soccer while redevelopment of Lansdowne Road takes place)
☎ 01 836 3222

Golf (18-hole golf clubs):

Balcarrick Golf Club, Donabate, 16km (10m) north of city centre.
☎ 01 843 6957
www.balcarrickgolfclub.com

Ballinascorney, 13km (8m) south west of city centre.
☎ 01 493 7755
www.ballinascorneygc.com

Beaverstown Golf Club, Donabate, 16km (10m) north of city centre.
☎ 01 843 6439
www.beaverstown.com

Castle Golf Club, Rathfarnham, 6km (4m) south of city centre.
☎ 01 490 4207
www.castlegc.ie

Citywest Golf Resort, Saggart, 16km (10m) south west of city centre.
☎ 01 401 0500
www.citywesthotel.ie

Corballis Golf Links, Donabate,16km (10m) north of city centre.
☎ 01 843 6583
www.golfdublin.com/corballis

Deerpark Hotel and Golf Courses, Howth, 14km (9m) north east of city centre.
☎ 01 832 6039
www.deerpark–hotel.ie

Druids Glen, Newmountkennedy, 32km (2m) south east of city centre.
☎ 01 287 3600
www.druidsglen.ie

Edmondstown Golf Club, Rathfarnham, 11km (7m) south of city centre.
☎ 01 493 1082
www.edmondstowngolfclub.ie

Elmgreen Golf Centre, Castleknock, 8km (5m) north west of city centre.
☎ 01 820 0797
www.golfdublin.com/elmgreen

Elm Park Golf Club, Donnybrook, 5km (3m) south of city centre.
☎ 01 269 3438
www.elmparkgolfclub.ie

Forrest Little Golf Club, Cloghean, 9km (6m) north of city centre, near to airport.
☎ 01 840 1763
www.forrestlittle.ie

Grange Castle, Clondalkin, 8km (5m) south west of city centre.
☎ 01 464 1043
www.grange-castle.com

Grange Golf Club, Rathfarnham, 6km (4m) south of city centre.
☎ 01 493 2889
www.grangegolfclub.ie

Hermitage Golf Club, Lucan, 11km (7m) west of city centre.
☎ 01 626 8491
www.hermitagegolf.ie

Howth Golf Club, Sutton, 14km (9m) north east of city centre.
☎ 01 832 3055
www.howthgolfclub.ie

Island Golf Club, Corballis, Donabate, 14km (9m) north of city centre.
☎ 01 843 6205
www.theislandgolfclub.com

Luttrellstown Castle, Castleknock, 10 km (6m) west of city centre.
☎ 01 808 9988
www.luttrellstowngc.com

Malahide Golf Club, 13km (8m) north of city centre.
☎ 01 846 1611
www.malahidegolfclub.ie

Portmarnock Golf Club, 11km (7m) north east of city centre.
☎ 01 846 2968
www.portmarnockgolfclub.ie

Portmarnock Hotel and Golf Links, 11km (7m) north east of city centre.
☎ 01 846 1800
www.portmarnock.com

Royal Dublin Golf Club, Dollymount, 5km (3m) north east of city centre.
☎ 01 833 6346
www.theroyaldublingolfclub.com

St. Anne's Golf Club, Dollymount, 5km (3m) north east of city centre.
☎ 01 833 6471
www.stanneslinksgolf.com

St. Margaret's Golf Club, 11km (7m) north of city centre.
☎ 01 864 0400
www.stmargaretsgolf.com

Swords Open Golf Course, 13km (8m) north of city centre.
☎ 01 840 9819
www.swordsgolfclub.com

Greyhound racing

Shelbourne Park Stadium, Ringsend, (Wed, Thurs, Sat at 20.00).
☎ 01 668 3502
www.shelbournepark.com

Harold's Cross Stadium, (Mon, Tues & Fri at 20.00).
☎ 01 497 1081

Horse racing

Leopardstown
10km (6 miles) south of Dublin. National Hunt and Flat racing with 22 meetings including 4 day Christmas National Hunt Festival.
☎ 01 289 0500
www.leopardstown.com

Fairyhouse
19km (12 miles) north west of Dublin. Home of the
Irish Grand National.
☎ 01 825 6167
www.fairyhouseracecourse.ie

Sailing

The Irish Sailing Association, Dún Laoghaire
☎ 01 280 0239
www.sailing.ie

Sports centres

Aughrim Street, ☎ 01 838 8085

Glin Road, Coolock, ☎ 01 847 8177

Coolmine Sports Complex, Coolmine
☎ 01 821 4549

Swimming pools

Ballymun, Town Centre, ☎ 01 862 3510

Coolock, Northside Shopping Centre,
☎ 01 847 7743

Crumlin, Windmill Road, ☎ 01 455 5792

Finglas, Mellowes Road, ☎ 01 864 2584

Markievicz Pool, Townsend Street,
☎ 01 672 9121

Rathmines, Lower Rathmines Road,
☎ 01 496 1275

Sean McDermott Street
☎ 01 872 0752

Help and advice

Embassies

Apostolic Nunciature, Navan Road.
☎ 01 838 0577

Argentina, Ailesbury Drive. ☎ 01 269 1546

Australia, Fitzwilton House, Wilton Terrace.
☎ 01 664 5300

Austria, Ailesbury Road. ☎ 01 269 4577

Belgium, Shrewsbury Road. ☎ 01 205 7100

Brazil, Harcourt Street. ☎ 01 475 6000

Bulgaria, Burlington Road. ☎ 01 660 3293

Canada, St. Stephen's Green. ☎ 01 417 4100

Chile, Wellington Road. ☎ 01 667 5094

China, Ailesbury Road. ☎ 01 269 1707

Croatia, Chambers Street. ☎ 01 476 7181

Cuba, Adelaide Road. ☎ 01 475 0899 / 2999

Cyprus, Lower Leeson Street. ☎ 01 676 3060

Czech Republic, Northumberland Road.
☎ 01 668 1135

Denmark, St. Stephen's Green.
☎ 01 475 6404 / 6405

Egypt, Clyde Road. ☎ 01 660 6566

Estonia, Ailesbury Road. ☎ 01 219 6730

Ethiopia, Fitzwilliam Street Lower.
☎ 01 678 7062 / 3

Finland, St. Stephen's Green. ☎ 01 478 1344

France, Ailesbury Road. ☎ 01 277 5000

Germany, Trimleston Avenue.
☎ 01 269 3011

Greece, Pembroke Street Upper.
☎ 01 676 7254

Hungary, Fitzwilliam Place. ☎ 01 661 2902

India, Leeson Park. ☎ 01 497 0959

Iran, Mount Merrion Avenue. ☎ 01 288 0252

Israel, Pembroke Road. ☎ 01 230 9400

Italy, Northumberland Road. ☎ 01 660 1744

Japan, Merrion Centre. ☎ 01 202 8300

Korea, Clyde Road. ☎ 01 660 8800

Latvia, Lower Leeson Street. ☎ 01 662 1610

Lesotho, Clanwilliam Square. ☎ 01 676 2233

Lithuania, Merrion Road. ☎ 01 668 8292

Malaysia, Shelbourne Road. ☎ 01 667 7280

Malta, Earlsfort Terrace. ☎ 01 676 2340

Mexico, Ailesbury Road. ☎ 01 260 0699

Morocco, Raglan Road. ☎ 01 660 9449

Netherlands, Merrion Road. ☎ 01 269 3444

Nigeria, Leeson Park. ☎ 01 660 4366

Norway, Molesworth Street. ☎ 01 662 1800

Pakistan, Ailesbury Road. ☎ 01 261 3032 / 3

Poland, Ailesbury Road. ☎ 01 283 0855

Portugal, Knocksinna Mews. ☎ 01 289 4416

Romania, Waterloo Road. ☎ 01 668 1085

Russian Federation, Orwell Road.
☎ 01 492 3492

Slovak Republic, Clyde Road. ☎ 01 660 0008

Slovenia, Nassau Street. ☎ 01 670 5240

South Africa, Earlsfort Terrace.
☎ 01 661 5553

Spain, Merlyn Park. ☎ 01 269 1640

Sweden, Dawson Street. ☎ 01 474 4400

Switzerland, Ailesbury Road. ☎ 01 218 6382

Turkey, Clyde Road. ☎ 01 668 5240

Ukraine, Elgin Road. ☎ *01 668 8601 / 5189*

United Kingdom, Merrion Road. ☎ *01 205 3700*

USA, Elgin Road. ☎ *01 668 8777*

Health centres and pharmacies

Grafton Street Centre, Open Mon-Thurs 08.30-18.30, Fri 08.30-18.00.
☎ *01 671 2122*

Mercer's Medical Centre, Stephen Street Lower, Open: Mon–Thurs 09.00–17.30, Fri 09.00–16.30 (closed 12.30-14.00).
☎ *01 402 2300*

O'Connell's Late Night Pharmacy,
O'Connell Street Lower.
Open daily Mon-Fri 07.30-22.00, Sat 08.00-22.00, Sun 10.00–22.00.
☎ *01 873 0427*

Garda Síochána (Police)

City centre Garda stations:

Pearse Street station, ☎ *01 666 9000*

Store Street station, ☎ *01 666 8000*

Dublin Metropolitan Area Headquarters,
Harcourt Square, ☎ *01 666 9500*

Greater Dublin Area Headquarters,
Phoenix Park, ☎ *01 666 0000*

Dún Laoghaire station, ☎ *01 666 5000*
www.garda.ie

Post Offices

General Post Office, O'Connell Street.
Open Mon–Sat 08.00-20.00.
☎ *01 705 7000*
www.anpost.ie

Post offices are usually open Mon–Fri 09.00–17.30 (closed 13.00–14.15) and from 09.00–13.00 on Saturdays.

Welfare organisations

Citizens Information Centre (Comhairle),
13a O'Connell Street Upper.
☎ *01 809 0633*
www.citizensinformation.ie

Irish Tourist Assistance Service,
Garda Headquarters, Harcourt Square.
All referrals must go through the Garda.
☎ *01 478 5295*
www.itas.ie

Samaritans, 112 Marlborough Street.
☎ *01 872 7700 or callsave 1850 609 090*
www.samaritans.org

Social Welfare Services, Store Street.
☎ *01 874 8444*

Hospitals

The Adelaide & Meath Hospital Incorporating the National Children's Hospital, Tallaght.
☎ *01 414 2000* www.amnch.ie

Beaumont, Beaumont Road.
☎ *01 809 3000* www.beaumont.ie

Blackrock Clinic (private), Rock Road.
☎ *01 283 2222* www.blackrock-clinic.ie

Bon Secours Private Hospital, Glasnevin.
☎ *01 837 5111* www.bonsecoursireland.org

Cappagh National Orthopaedic, Cappagh Road.
☎ *01 814 0400* www.cappagh.ie

Dental Hospital, Lincoln Place.
☎ *01 612 7200* www.dentalscience.tcd.ie

James Connolly Memorial Hospital,
Blanchardstown.
☎ *01 646 5000* www.connollyhospital.ie

Mater Misericordiae, Eccles Street.
☎ *01 803 2000* www.mater.ie

Mater Private, Eccles Street.
☎ *01 885 8888* www.materprivate.ie

National Maternity, Holles Street.
☎ *01 637 3100* www.nmh.ie

Our Lady's Hospital for Sick Children, Crumlin.
☎ *01 409 6100* www.olhsc.ie

Rotunda Hospital, Parnell Square.
☎ *01 873 0700* www.rotunda.ie

Royal Victoria Eye and Ear, Adelaide Road.
☎ *01 664 4600*

St. James's, James's Street.
☎ *01 410 3000* www.stjames.ie

St. Mary's Hospital, Phoenix Park.
☎ *01 677 8132*

St. Michael's,
George's Street Lower, Dún Laoghaire.
☎ *01 280 6901*

St. Patrick's, James's Street.
☎ *01 249 3200* www.stpatrickshosp.ie

St.Vincent's University Hospital, Elm Park.
☎ *01 221 4000* www.st-vincents.ie

Index to place names

Archerstown	11	D3
Artane	54	B3
Ashbourne	10	B2
Ashtown	49	C3
Balgriffin	41	D1
Balgriffin Park	42	A2
Ballealease North	13	D1
Ballealease South	13	D2
Ballinteer	128	B2
Ballisk	13	D2
Ballisk Common	13	D1
Ballsbridge	103	D1
Ballyboden	126	B1
Ballybrack	139	C2
Ballyfermot	86	B2
Ballymacartle	24	B2
Ballymastone	13	D2
Ballymount	98	A2
Ballymun	38	A3
Barrogstown West	65	D3
Beaumont	53	C1
Beechwood	26	A2
Blackrock	117	D1
Blanchardstown	47	D2
Bluebell	98	B1
Bohammer	25	C3
Boherboy	121	C2
Booterstown	116	B1
Bray	142	B1
Burgage	41	C1
Cabinteely	137	D1
Cabra	77	C2
Carpenterstown	46	A3
Carrickmines	137	C2
Castleknock	73	D1
Celbridge	66	B2
Chapelizod	86	B1
Churchtown	114	A2
Clare Hall	41	D3
Cloghran	23	C1
Clondalkin	96	A2
Clonee	30	A1
Clongriffin	42	B2
Clonshaugh	40	B1
Clonsilla	45	D2
Clonskeagh	103	C3
Clontarf	80	A2
Confey	68	B1
Cookstown	10	A1
Coolock	54	B1
Corballis	13	D3
Corbally	121	D3
Corduff	33	D3
Cornelscourt	132	A3
Crumlin	99	D2
Dalkey	134	B1
Darndale	41	C2
Deans Grange	132	A2
Dollymount	81	D2
Donabate	13	C1
Donnybrook	103	C2
Drimnagh	99	D1
Drumcondra	78	A1
Drumnigh	42	B1
Dublin Airport	22	B2
Dunboyne	28	B2
Dundrum	114	B3
Dún Laoghaire (Dunleary)	119	C3
Dunleary (Dún Laoghaire)	119	C3
Dunreagh	11	C1
Edmondstown	126	B3
Feltrim	25	C1
Finglas	51	C2
Finglas East	50	B1
Firhouse	125	C1
Foxrock	131	D3
Galloping Green	131	C1
Glasnevin	52	A3
Glasnevin North	51	D1
Glebe	24	A2
Goatstown	115	C3
Goldenbridge	87	D3
Grange	26	A1
Greenhills	110	B1
Greenwood	24	B2
Harold's Cross	101	C1
Hartstown	45	C1
Hazelbrook	25	D2
Hilltown	16	A2
Howth	60	B2
Inchicore	87	D2
Irishtown	91	D3
Islandbridge	88	A1
Jobstown	122	B2
Kilbarrack	57	C2
Kildonan	50	A1
Killegland	10	B3
Killester	54	B3
Killinardan	122	B3
Killincarrig	143	C3
Killiney	139	D1
Kill O' The Grange	132	B1
Kilmainham	88	A2
Kilmore	39	D3
Kilnamanagh	109	D2
Kiltalown	122	A3
Kimmage	100	B3
Kingswood	107	D2
Kinsaley	25	C2
Knocklyon	126	A1
Laraghbryan East	64	A1
Leixlip	69	C2
Leopardstown	130	B3
Loughlinstown	140	B1
Lucan	82	A1
Malahide	20	A1
Malahide Demesne	19	D3
Marino	79	C2
Mayeston Hall	37	C2
Maynetown	43	C1
Maynooth	65	C1
Merrion	104	A3
Milltown (Dublin 6)	102	B3
Milltown (Ashbourne)	11	C2
Monkstown	118	B3
Mooretown	14	A3
Mount Merrion	116	A2
Mulhuddart	32	B2
Newtown (Dublin 16)	126	B3
Newtown (Swords)	15	C1
Northwood	38	A2
Oldbawn	123	D2
Oldtown	14	B1
Outlands	14	B2
Palmerston	73	D3
Pelletstown	49	C3
Phibsborough	77	D2
Poppintree	37	C2
Portmarnock	27	C2
Raheny	56	A3
Railpark	65	D2
Ranelagh	102	B1
Rathfarnham	113	C2
Rathgar	101	D3
Rathmichael	140	A2
Rathmines	102	A2
Ringsend	91	D2
Ronanstown	84	A3
Rossmore	111	D2
Saggart	120	B2
Saintdoolaghs (east)	42	A1
St. Doolagh's (west)	41	D1
Sallynoggin	133	C2
Sandyford	129	D3
Sandymount	92	A3
Santry	38	B3
Shankill	141	C2
Shielmartin	62	B2
Slade	120	B3
Snugborough	42	B2
Stapolin	43	C2
Stillorgan	116	B3
Stockhole	23	D3
Stradbrook	118	A3
Sutton	58	A1
Swords	18	A1
Tallaght	109	D3
Templeogue	112	A2
Terenure	113	C1
Wainsfort	112	A1
Walkinstown	98	B2
Whitehall	52	B3
Willbrook	112	B3
Williamstown	117	D1
Windmill Lands	16	A1
Windy Arbour	115	C2
Yellow Walls	19	C2

Index to street names

General abbreviations

All	Alley	Dws	Dwellings	Junct	Junction	Rd	Road
Apts	Apartments	E	East	La	Lane	Ri	Rise
Av/Ave	Avenue	Ex	Exchange	Lo	Lodge	S	South
Bk	Bank	Ext	Extension	Lwr	Lower	Sch	School
Bldgs	Buildings	Fld	Field	Mans	Mansions	Sq	Square
Boul	Boulevard	Flds	Fields	Mkt	Market	St.	Saint
Br/Bri	Bridge	Fm	Farm	Ms	Mews	St	Street
Cem	Cemetery	Gdn	Garden	Mt	Mount	Sta	Station
Cen	Central, Centre	Gdns	Gardens	N	North	Ter	Terrace
		Gra	Grange	No	Numbers	Vil	Villa, Villas
Cl/Clo	Close	Grd	Ground	Par	Parade	Vw	View
Coll	College	Grn	Green	Pas	Passage	W	West
Cotts	Cottages	Gro	Grove	Pk	Park	Wd	Wood
Cres	Crescent	Ho	House	Pl	Place	Wds	Woods
Ct	Court	Hosp	Hospital	Prom	Promenade	Wk	Walk
Dr	Drive	Hts	Heights	Rbt	Roundabout	Yd	Yard

District abbreviations

Abb.	Abberley	Clons.	Clonsilla	Kill.	Killiney	Mulh.	Mulhuddart
Ashb.	Ashbourne	Collins.	Collinstown	Kilsh.	Kilshane	Palm.	Palmerston
B'brack	Ballybrack	Cool.	Coolmine	Kilt.	Kiltipper	Port.	Portmarnock
Balg.	Balgriffin	Corn.	Cornelscourt	Kings.	Kingswood	R'coole	Rathcoole
Black.	Blackrock	D'bate	Donabate	Kins.	Kinsaley	Ronan.	Ronanstown
Boot.	Booterstown	D.L.	Dún Laoghaire	Leix.	Leixlip	Sagg.	Saggart
Cabin.	Cabinteely	Dunb.	Dunboyne	Leo.	Leopardstown	Sally.	Sallynoggin
Carp.	Carpenterstown	Fox.	Foxrock	Lou.V.	Louisa Valley	Sandy.	Sandyford
Carrick.	Carrickmines	G'geary	Glenageary	Lough.	Loughlinstown	Shank.	Shankill
Castle.	Castleknock	Gra M.	Grange Manor	Mala.	Malahide	Still.	Stillorgan
Celbr.	Celbridge	Grey.	Greystones	Manor.	Manorfields		
Clond.	Clondalkin	Jobs.	Jobstown	Mayn.	Maynooth		

Some streets are not named on the map due to insufficient space. In some of these cases the nearest street that does appear on the map is listed in italics. In other cases they are indicated on the map by a number which is listed here in **bold**.

Name	Page	Grid
1 Branch Rd N	92	A1
1 Branch Rd S	92	A1
2 Branch Rd N	92	B1
2 Branch Rd N Ext	92	B1
2 Branch Rd S	92	B1
3 Branch Rd N	92	A1
4 Branch Rd S	92	B1

A

Name	Page	Grid
Abberley	139	C3
Abbey Cotts		
off Abbey St Upr	144	C2
Abbey Ct Dublin 5	54	B3
Abbey Ct 1 D.L.	132	B1
Abbeydale	83	D2
Abbeydale Cl	83	D2
Abbeydale Cres	83	D2
Abbeydale Gdns	83	D2
Abbeydale Pk	83	D2
Abbeydale Ri	83	D2
Abbeydale Wk	83	D2
Abbey Dr	76	A1
Abbeyfarm	66	A3
Abbeyfield Dublin 5	54	B3
Abbeyfield Dublin 6	102	B3
Abbeyfield Ct	83	C2
Abbeylea Av	14	B3
Abbeylea Cl	14	B3
Abbeylea Dr	15	C3
Abbeylea Grn	14	B3
Abbey Pk Dublin 5	54	A3
Abbey Pk Dublin 13	57	C1
Abbey Pk D.L.	132	B1
Abbey Rd	132	B1
Abbey St	61	C2
Abbey St Lwr	145	D2
Abbey St Mid	145	D2
Abbey St Old	145	E2
Abbey St Sta	145	D2
Abbey St Upr	144	C2
Abbey Thea	145	D2
Abbeyvale Av	14	A3
Abbeyvale Cl	14	A3
Abbeyvale Ct	14	A3
Abbeyvale Cres	14	A3
Abbeyvale Dr	14	A3
Abbeyvale Grn	14	A3
Abbeyvale Gro	14	A3
Abbeyvale Lawn	14	A3
Abbeyvale Pl	14	A3
Abbeyvale Ri	14	A3
Abbeyvale Vw	14	A3
Abbeyvale Way	14	A3
Abbey Vw	132	B1
Abbeywood	83	D2
Abbeywood Av	83	D2
Abbeywood Cl	83	D2
Abbeywood Cres	83	D2
Abbeywood Pk	83	D2
Abbeywood Way	83	D2
Abbots Hill	20	B2
Abbotstown Av (Ascal Bhaile An Abba)	49	D1
Abbotstown Dr	49	D1
Abbotstown Rd	50	A1
Abercorn Rd	91	C1
Abercorn Sq	87	D2
Abercorn Ter Dublin 7	77	C3
Abercorn Ter Dublin 8	87	D2
Aberdeen St	88	B1
Abington	19	C3
Achill Rd Dublin 9	78	B1
Achill Rd Lough.	139	C3
Acorn Dr	128	B1
Acorn Rd	128	B1
Acres Rd	75	D3
Adair	103	D1
Adam Ct off Grafton St	145	D4
Adamstown Rd	70	A3
Adare Av	54	A1
Adare Dr	54	B1
Adare Grn	54	B1
Adare Pk	54	B1
Adare Rd	40	B3
Addison Av	51	D3
Addison Dr	51	D3
Addison Pl	78	A1
Addison Rd	79	C2
Addison Ter	78	A1
Adelaide Ms	104	B2
Adelaide Rd Dublin 2	90	A3
Adelaide Rd Bray	142	B1
Adelaide Rd D.L.	134	A2
Adelaide St	119	D3
Adelaide Ter Dublin 8		
off Brookfield St	88	B2
Adelaide Ter 1 D.L.	134	A1
Adelaide Vil Bray	142	A1
Adelaide Vil 2 D.L.	134	A1
Admiral Ct 7	43	D3
Admiral Pk	43	D3
Adrian Av	101	C2
Advance Business Pk	39	C1
Aideen Av	100	B3
Aideen Dr	100	B3
Aideen Pl	100	B3
Aikenhead Ter	91	D2
Ailesbury	52	A1
Ailesbury Cl	103	D2
Ailesbury Ct	103	D2
Ailesbury Gdns	104	A2
Ailesbury Gro Dublin 4	103	D2
Ailesbury Gro Dublin 16	128	B1
Ailesbury Lawn	128	B1
Ailesbury Ms	104	B2
Ailesbury Pk	104	A2
Ailesbury Rd	103	D2
Ailsbury Gro	128	B1
Ailsbury Lawn	128	B1
Airfield Cl	103	D3
Airfield Ct	103	D3
Airfield Manor	103	D3
Airfield Pk	103	D3
Airfield Rd	101	D3
Airfield Ter	103	D3
Air Pk	126	A2
Airpark Av	126	A2
Airpark Cl	126	B2
Airport Business Pk	23	C2
Airport Ind Est	39	C2
Airside Business Pk	17	C2
Airside Retail Pk	17	C2
Airton Cl	110	A3
Airton Rd	109	D3
Airton Ter	110	A3
Airways Ind Est	39	C2
Albany Av	118	B3
Albany Ct	139	C3
Albany Rd	102	B2
Albert Av	142	B1
Albert Coll Av	52	A2
Albert Coll Cres	52	A2
Albert Coll Dr	52	A2
Albert Coll Lawn	52	A2
Albert Coll Pk	52	A2
Albert Coll Ter	52	A2
Albert Ct	134	A1
Albert Ct E	91	C2
Albert Pk	134	A1
Albert Pl		
off Inchicore Rd	88	A2
Albert Pl E	91	C2
Albert Pl W	90	A3
Albert Rd Lwr	134	A1
Albert Rd Upr	134	A2
Albert Ter		
off Albert Pl W	90	A3
Albert Vil		
off Morehampton Rd	103	C1
Albert Wk	142	B1
Albion Ter		
off Inchicore Rd	88	A2
Aldborough Par	79	C3
Aldborough Pl	78	B3
Aldborough Sq	78	B3
Aldemere	45	C2
Alden Dr	56	B1
Alden Pk	57	C1
Alden Rd	56	B1
Alderbrook Downs	11	C3
Alderbrook Glen	11	C3
Alderbrook Pk	11	C3
Alderbrook Ri	11	C3
Alderbrook Rd	11	C3
Alderbrook Vale	11	C3
Alder Ct 1	27	C1
Alderpark Ct	123	C1
Alders, The	118	A3
Alderwood Av	123	C1
Alderwood Cl	109	C3
Alderwood Ct	123	C1
Alderwood Dr	123	C1
Alderwood Grn	109	C3
Alderwood Gro	123	C1
Alderwood Lawn	109	C3
Alderwood Pk	123	C1
Alderwood Ri	109	C3
Aldrin Wk	54	A1
Alexander Ter Dublin 1	91	C1
Alexander Ter Dublin 8	89	D3
Alexander Ter 1 Bray	142	A2
Alexandra Quay	92	A1
Alexandra Rd	91	D1
Alexandra Rd Ext	93	C1
Alexandra Ter Dublin 3		
off Clontarf Rd	81	C3
Alexandra Ter Dublin 6	101	D3
Alexandra Ter (Dundrum) Dublin 14	114	B3
Alfie Byrne Rd	79	D3
Allendale Cl	45	C1
Allendale Copse	45	C1
Allendale Ct	45	C1
Allendale Dr	45	C1
Allendale Elms	45	C1
Allendale Glen	45	C1
Allendale Grn	45	C1
Allendale Gro	45	C1
Allendale Heath	45	C1
Allendale Lawn	45	C1
Allendale Pl	45	C1
Allendale Ri	45	C1
Allendale Sq	45	C1
Allendale Ter	45	C1
Allendale Vw	45	C1
Allendale Wk	45	C1
Allen Pk Dr	130	B1
Allen Pk Rd	130	B1
Allenton Av	124	A3
Allenton Cres	124	A3
Allenton Dr	124	A3
Allenton Gdns	124	A3
Allenton Grn	124	A3
Allenton Lawns	124	A3
Allenton Pk	124	A2
Allenton Rd (Oldcourt) Dublin 24	124	A2
Allenton Rd (Tallaght) Dublin 24	124	A1
Allenton Way	124	A3
All Hallows Coll	78	B1
All Hallows La off Drumcondra Rd Upr	78	B1
Allied Ind Est	86	B3
Allingham St	89	C2
All Saints Dr	55	D3
All Saints Pk	55	D3
All Saints Rd	55	C3
Alma Pl	118	B3
Alma Rd	118	A2
Almeida Av		
off Brookfield St	88	B2
Almeida Ter		
off Brookfield St	88	B2
Alone Wk	54	B3
Alpine Hts	96	A2
Alpine Ri	108	B2
Altadore	133	D2
Altona Ter	77	C3
Alverno	80	A2
Amber Vale	108	B3
Amiens St	145	F1
Anastasia La	135	C2
Anfield Cl	46	A3
Anfield Ct	72	A1
Anfield Cres	72	A1
Anfield Dr	72	A1
Anfield Lawn 1	72	A1
Anfield Vw 2	72	A1
Anglesea Av	117	D2
Anglesea Br	103	D2
Anglesea Fruit Mkt		
off Green St Little	144	B2
Anglesea La	119	D3
Anglesea Pk	134	A3
Anglesea Rd	103	D2
Anglesea Row	144	B2
Anglesea St	145	D3
Anley Ct	71	C3
Annabeg 1	138	B2
Annadale Av	79	C2
Annadale Cres	79	C1
Annadale Dr	79	C1
Annagh Ct	47	D1
Annaly Cl	45	C1
Annaly Gro	45	C1
Annaly Rd	77	C2
Annaly Ter	45	C1
Annamoe Dr	77	C2
Annamoe Par	77	C3
Annamoe Pk	77	C3
Annamoe Rd	77	C3
Annamoe Ter	77	C3
Anna Vil	102	B2
Annaville Av	131	D1
Annaville Gro	114	B2
Annaville Pk	114	B2
Annaville Ter		
off Annaville Gro	115	C2
Anne Devlin Av	112	B3
Anne Devlin Dr	112	B3
Anne Devlin Pk	112	B3
Anne Devlin Rd	112	B3
Anner Rd	88	A2
Annes La	145	D4
Annesley Av	79	C3
Annesley Br	79	C2
Annesley Br Rd	79	C2
Annesley Pk	102	B2
Annesley Pl	79	C2
Anne St N	144	B1
Anne St S	145	D4
Annsbrook	115	C1
Annville Dr	130	A1
Apollo Way	54	A1
Appian Way, The	102	B1
Apples Rd	129	D2
Applewood Av	15	C2
Applewood Cl	15	C2
Applewood Cres	14	B2
Applewood Dr	14	B2
Applewood Gro	14	B2
Applewood Main St	14	B2
Applewood Sq	15	C2
Aran Av	139	C3
Aran Cl	139	C3
Aran Dr	139	C3
Aranleigh Ct	113	D3
Aranleigh Dell	127	D1
Aranleigh Gdns	113	D3
Aranleigh Mt	113	C3
Aranleigh Pk	113	D3
Aranleigh Vale	113	D3
Áras An Uachtaráin	75	D2
Aras Naclunne	97	C1
Aravon Ct 8	142	B2
Arbour Hill	89	C1
Arbour Pl	89	C1
Arbour Ter	89	C1
Arbutus Av	101	C1
Arbutus Pl	89	D3
Arcade	145	D2
Archerstown Rd	11	D2
Archers Wd	32	A2
Arches, The 11 Lough.	139	C3
Arches, The Mayn.	65	C2
Ardagh Av	131	D1
Ardagh Cl 1	131	D1
Ardagh Ct	131	C1
Ardagh Cres	131	D1
Ardagh Dr	131	D1
Ardagh Gro	131	C1
Ardagh Pk	131	D1
Ardagh Pk Rd	131	D1
Ardagh Rd	100	B1
Ardara Av	42	A3
Ardbeg Cres	54	B2
Ardbeg Dr	54	B2
Ardbeg Pk	54	B2
Ardbeg Rd	54	B2
Ardbrugh Cl 1	134	B3
Ardbrugh Rd	134	B3
Ardbrugh Vil 2	134	B3
Ardcian Pk	14	B3
Ardcollum Av	54	A2
Ardee Gro	102	A1
Ardeen	70	A3
Ardee Rd	102	A1
Ardee St	144	A4
Ardeevin Av	70	A3
Ardeevin Ct	70	A3
Ardeevin Dr	70	A3
Ardeevin Rd	134	B2

Ardenza Pk	
off Seapoint Av	118 A2
Ardenza Ter	118 A2
Ardglas Est	129 C1
Ardilaun	27 C2
Ardilaun Rd	78 B3
Ardilea Downs	115 D2
Ardlea Rd	54 A2
Ard Lorcain	131 C1
Ard Lorcain Vil 1	131 C1
Ardlui Pk	131 D1
Ardmeen Pk	131 D1
Ard Mhacha	123 D2
Ard Mhuire Pk	134 A3
Ard Mor Av	121 D1
Ard Mor Cl	121 D1
Ard Mor Ct	121 D1
Ard Mor Cres	121 D1
Ard Mor Dale	121 D1
Ard Mor Dr	121 D1
Ardmore Av	77 C3
Ardmore Cl	53 D2
Ardmore Cres	54 A2
Ardmore Dr	53 D2
Ardmore Gro	53 D2
Ardmore Pk Dublin 5	54 A2
Ardmore Pk D.L.	133 C1
Ard Mor Gdn	121 D1
Ard Mor La	121 D1
Ard Mor Pk	121 D1
Ard Mor Wk	121 D1
Ard Na Mara	19 C2
Ard Na Meala	38 A3
Ardpatrick Rd	76 A2
Ard Ri Pl	
off Ard Ri Rd	89 C1
Ard Ri Rd	89 C1
Ardtona Av	114 B2
Arena Rd	130 B3
Argyle Rd	103 C1
Arkendale Ct 1	134 A2
Arkendale Rd	134 A1
Arkendale Wds 2	134 A2
Arkle Hill	11 C3
Arkle Rd	130 B3
Arkle Sq 1	130 B3
Arklow Rd	77 C3
Armagh Rd	100 A2
Armstrong St	
off Harolds Cross Rd	101 D1
Armstrong Wk	54 A1
Arnold Gro	133 D2
Arnold Pk	133 D3
Arnott St	89 D3
Arran Ct	47 D1
Arran Grn	142 B2
Arranmore Av	78 A2
Arranmore Rd	103 C1
Arran Quay	144 A2
Arran Quay Ter	144 A2
Arran Rd	78 B1
Arran St E	144 B2
Arran St W	144 A2
Arthur Griffith Pk	82 B1
Arundel	118 B3
Ascal An Charrain Chno	
(Nutgrove Av)	113 D3
Ascal Bhaile An Abba	
(Abbotstown Av)	49 D1
Ascal Bhaile Thuaidh	
(Ballyhoy Av)	55 D3
Ascal Dun Eanna	
(Ennafort Av)	55 C3
Ascal Measc (Mask Av)	54 B2
Ascal Phairc An Bhailtini	
(Villa Park Av)	76 A2
Ascal Ratabhachta	
(Ratoath Av)	49 D2
Asgard Pk	61 C2
Asgard Rd	61 C2
Ashberry	82 A2
Ashbourne Ind Pk	10 A1
Ashbrook Dublin 3	80 A1
Ashbrook Dublin 7	75 C1
Ashbury Pk	142 A3
Ashcroft	55 D2

Ashcroft Gro 1	32 A3
Ashdale Av	101 C3
Ashdale Cl	18 A2
Ashdale Cres	11 C2
Ashdale Gdns	101 C3
Ashdale Pk	101 C3
Ashdale Rd Dublin 6W	101 C3
Ashdale Rd Swords	18 B3
Ashes, The	10 B1
Ashfield (Templeogue)	112 A2
Ashfield Av Dublin 6	102 B2
Ashfield Av Dublin 24	109 D1
Ashfield Cl Dublin 6W	
off Ashfield	112 A2
Ashfield Cl Dublin 24	109 D1
Ashfield Ct	32 A3
Ashfield Dr	109 D1
Ashfield Gdns	32 A3
Ashfield Grn	32 A2
Ashfield Gro	32 A2
Ashfield Lawn	32 A2
Ashfield Pk (Templeogue)	
Dublin 6W off Ashfield	112 A2
Ashfield Pk (Terenure)	
Dublin 6W	101 C3
Ashfield Pk Dublin 24	109 D1
Ashfield Pk Boot.	116 A1
Ashfield Pk 7 Mulh.	32 A3
Ashfield Pk (Ranelagh)	102 B2
Ashfield Way	32 A3
Ashford Cotts	
off Ashford St	77 C3
Ashford Pl	
off Ashford St	77 C3
Ashford St	76 B3
Ashgrove Dublin 24	109 C3
Ashgrove Celbr.	66 A1
Ashgrove D.L.	132 B1
Ashgrove Ind Est	132 B1
Ashgrove Lo	75 D1
Ashgrove Ter 1	115 C3
Ashington Av	76 A1
Ashington Cl	49 D3
Ashington Ct	76 A1
Ashington Dale	76 A1
Ashington Gdns	76 A1
Ashington Grn	76 A1
Ashington Ms	50 A3
Ashington Pk	75 D1
Ashington Ri	49 D3
Ash Lawn Dublin 16	128 B1
Ashlawn B'brack	138 B2
Ashleaf Shop Cen	99 D3
Ashleigh Grn	47 D3
Ashleigh Gro Dublin 15	47 D2
Ashleigh Gro Mayn.	64 A2
Ashleigh Lawn	20 A3
Ashley Av	17 D1
Ashley Dr 5	17 D1
Ashley Gro 4	17 D1
Ashley Ri	27 C1
Ashling Cl	100 B1
Ashling Hts	47 C1
Ash Pk Av	82 B2
Ash Pk Ct	83 C2
Ash Pk Gro	83 C1
Ash Pk Heath	83 C1
Ash St	144 A4
Ashton Av	126 A1
Ashton Cl	126 A1
Ashton Gro	126 A1
Ashton Lawn	126 A1
Ashton Pk	118 B3
Ashtown Br	48 B2
Ashtown Gate Rd	75 C1
Ashtown Gro	75 D1
Ashtown Rd	49 C3
Ashtown Sta	49 C3
Ashurst	139 C3
Ashville Cl	71 C3
Ashwood Av	95 D1
Ashwood Cl	95 D1
Ashwood Dr	96 A1
Ashwood Lawns	96 A1
Ashwood Pk	96 A1
Ashwood Rd	96 A1
Ashwood Way	96 A1
Aspen Dr	18 B2
Aspen Pk 1 D.L.	133 C2
Aspen Pk Swords	18 B2
Aspen Rd	18 A2
Aspen Wds	46 A2

Aspen Wds Av	46 A2
Aspen Wds Lawn	46 A2
Assumpta Pk	140 B3
Asthown Av	14 B1
Asthown Cl	14 B1
Asthown Ct	14 B1
Asthown Dr	14 B1
Asthown Grn	14 B1
Asthown Gro	14 B1
Asthown Lawns	14 B1
Asthown Ri	14 B1
Aston Pl	145 D2
Aston Quay	145 D2
Athgoe Dr	141 C2
Athgoe Rd	141 C2
Athlumney Vil	102 A1
Atmospheric Rd 3	134 A2
Aubrey Gro	141 C2
Aubrey Pk	141 C2
Auburn Av Dublin 4	103 C2
Auburn Av Dublin 15	74 A1
Auburn Av Cabin.	138 B1
Auburn Cl Dublin 15	48 A3
Auburn Cl Cabin.	138 B1
Auburn Dr Dublin 15	48 A3
Auburn Dr Cabin.	138 A1
Auburn Grn	48 A3
Auburn Gro	19 C3
Auburn Pk	48 A2
Auburn Rd Dublin 4	
off Auburn Av	103 C2
Auburn Rd Cabin.	133 C3
Auburn St	77 D3
Auburn Vil	101 D3
Auburn Wk	77 C3
Aughavanagh Rd	101 C1
Aughrim La	77 C3
Aughrim Pl	77 C3
Aughrim St	77 C3
Aughrim Vil	
off Aughrim St	77 C3
Augustine Vil 1	142 B2
Aulden Gra	39 D3
Aungier Pl	144 C4
Aungier St	144 C4
Austins Cotts	
off Annesley Pl	79 C2
Avalon 1	133 C2
Ave Maria Rd	89 C3
Avenue, The Dublin 6W	112 A2
Avenue, The (Ballinteer)	
Dublin 16	128 B2
Avenue, The (Ballyboden)	
Dublin 16	126 A2
Avenue, The (Carrick.)	136 B3
Avenue, The (Primrose Hill)	
Celbr.	66 B3
Avenue, The (The Drive)	
Celbr.	66 B2
Avenue, The Clons.	30 B3
Avenue, The	
(Dunboyne Castle)	
Dunb.	28 B3
Avenue, The (Lutterell Hall)	
Dunb.	28 B1
Avenue, The (Plunkett Hall)	
Dunb.	28 A1
Avenue, The Gra M.	82 B2
Avenue, The Kins.	18 A2
Avenue, The Lou.V.	68 A1
Avenue, The 4 Mala.	21 C3
Avenue, The Manor.	31 C3
Avenue, The Mulh.	32 A2
Avenue, The Swords	15 D3
Avenue Rd	89 D3
Avila Apts 2	131 D1
Avila Pk	49 D1
Avoca Av Black.	117 C2
Avoca Av Bray	142 A3
Avoca Pk	117 C3
Avoca Pl	117 D2
Avoca Rd	117 C3
Avonbeg Ct 1	124 A1
Avonbeg Dr	124 B1
Avonbeg Gdns	124 B1
Avonbeg Ind Est	98 B1
Avonbeg Pk	124 B1
Avonbeg Rd	124 B1
Avondale	68 B1
Avondale Av	77 D3
Avondale Business Pk	117 D3
Avondale Ct 4	134 A1

Avondale Cres	134 A3
Avondale Lawn	117 D3
Avondale Lawn Ext	117 D3
Avondale Pk Dublin 5	56 A3
Avondale Pk Dalkey	134 A3
Avondale Rd Dublin 7	77 D2
Avondale Rd Dalkey	134 A3
Avondale Sq	28 B2
Avondale Ter	99 D3
Avonmore	131 C2
Avonmore Av 1	124 B1
Avonmore Cl	124 B1
Avonmore Dr	124 B1
Avonmore Gro	124 B1
Avonmore Pk	124 B1
Avonmore Rd	124 B1
Aylesbury	124 A2
Ayrefield Av	55 C1
Ayrefield Cl	55 C1
Ayrefield Dr	55 C1
Ayrefield Gro	55 C1
Ayrefield Pl	55 C1

B

Bachelors Wk Dublin 1	145 D2
Bachelors Wk Ashb.	11 C3
Back La Dublin 8	144 B3
Back La 3 Dublin 13	43 D3
Back La Mayn.	65 C1
Back Rd	19 D3
Baggot Cl	
off Baggot St Lwr	90 B3
Baggot Ct	90 B3
Baggot La	91 C3
Baggot Rd	75 D2
Baggot St Lwr	90 B3
Baggot St Upr	91 C3
Baggot Ter	
off Blackhorse Av	75 D2
Bailey, The	10 B3
Bailey Grn Rd	63 D2
Bailey's Row	78 B3
Bailey Vw	134 B1
Balally Av	129 D2
Balally Cl	129 D2
Balally Dr	129 C1
Balally Gro	129 D2
Balally Hill	129 D2
Balally Pk	129 D1
Balally Rd	129 C1
Balally Sta	129 C1
Balally Ter 1	129 D2
Balbutcher Dr	37 D2
Balbutcher La	37 D3
Balbutcher Way	37 D2
Balcurris Cl	38 A3
Balcurris Gdns	38 A3
Balcurris Pk E	38 A3
Balcurris Pk W	37 D3
Balcurris Rd	37 D3
Baldonnell Business Pk	106 B3
Baldoyle Ind Est	57 C1
Baldoyle Rd	58 A1
Balfe Av	99 D2
Balfe Rd	99 D2
Balfe Rd E	99 D2
Balfe St	
off Chatham St	145 D4
Balgaddy Rd	83 D2
Balglass Est	60 B2
Balglass Rd	61 C2
Balgriffin Cotts	41 D2
Balgriffin Rd	41 D2
Balheary Br	15 D2
Balheary Ind Pk	15 D2
Balheary Rd	15 D2
Balkill Pk	60 B2
Balkill Rd	61 C3
Ballawley Ct	129 C2
Ballinclea Hts	134 A3
Ballinclea Rd	133 D3
Ballinteer Av	128 B2
Ballinteer Cl	128 B2
Ballinteer Ct 2	128 B2
Ballinteer Cres	128 B2
Ballinteer Dr	128 B2
Ballinteer Gdns	128 B2
Ballinteer Gro	128 B2
Ballinteer Pk	128 B2
Ballinteer Rd	128 B2
Ballinteer Shop Cen	128 B2
Ballintrane Wd	17 C1

Ballintyre Downs 128 B3
Ballintyre Heath 128 B3
Ballintyre Meadows 128 A3
Ballintyre Wk 128 B3
Balliskcourt 13 C2
Ball's Br 103 D1
Ballsbridge Av 103 D1
Ballsbridge Pk 103 D1
Ballsbridge Ter
    off Merrion Rd 103 D1
Ballsbridge Wd 91 D3
Ballybin Rd 10 A2
Ballyboden Cres 126 B1
Ballyboden Rd
    Dublin 14 126 B1
Ballyboden Rd
    Dublin 16 126 B1
Ballyboden Way 126 A1
Ballyboggan Ind Est 50 A3
Ballyboggan Rd 50 B3
Ballybough Av
    off Kings Av 79 C3
Ballybough Br 79 C2
Ballybough Ct
    off Kings Av 79 C3
Ballybough Rd 78 B3
Ballybrack Shop Cen 138 B2
Ballybride 140 B3
Ballybride Rd 140 B3
Ballycoolin Business &
    Tech Pk 34 A2
Ballycoolin Rd 34 A3
Ballycullen Av 124 B2
Ballycullen Dr 125 C2
Ballydowd Dr 83 C1
Ballydowd Gro 71 C3
Ballydowd Manor 83 C1
Ballyfermot Av 86 A3
Ballyfermot Br 98 A1
Ballyfermot Cres 86 B2
Ballyfermot Dr 86 A2
Ballyfermot Par 86 A2
Ballyfermot Rd (Bothar
    Baile Thormod) 86 A2
Ballygall Av 51 C1
Ballygall Cres 50 B2
Ballygall Par 50 B2
Ballygall Pl 51 C2
Ballygall Rd E 51 D2
Ballygall Rd W 50 B2
Ballygihen Av 134 A1
Ballygihen Vil 5 134 A1
Ballygoran Vw 66 A1
Ballyhoy Av (Ascal Bhaile
    Thuaidh) 55 D3
Ballymace Grn 112 A3
Ballymanagin La 1 96 B1
Ballymoss Par 2 130 B3
Ballymoss Rd 130 A2
Ballymount Av
    Dublin 12 110 B1
Ballymount Av
    Dublin 24 110 B1
Ballymount Cross 98 A3
Ballymount Cross
    Ind Est 97 D3
Ballymount Dr 98 B3
Ballymount Ind Est 98 B3
Ballymount Lwr Rd 98 A3
Ballymount Rd 109 D1
Ballymount Rd Ind Est 98 B2
Ballymount Rd Upr 98 A3
Ballymount Trd Est 99 C3
Ballymun Business &
    Tech Pk 37 D2
Ballymun Ind Est 37 D2
Ballymun Rd 52 A3
Ballymun Rd N 38 A2
Ballymun Shop Cen 38 A3
Ballyneety Rd 87 C2
Ballyogan Av 136 A2
Ballyogan Cl 136 A2
Ballyogan Ct 136 A2
Ballyogan Cres 136 A2
Ballyogan Dr 136 A2
Ballyogan Est 136 A1
Ballyogan Grn 136 A1
Ballyogan Lawn 136 A1
Ballyogan Rd 1 136 A2
Ballyogan Vale 136 B2
Ballyogan Wd 136 A2

Ballyolaf Manor 1 129 C1
Ballyowen Av 71 D3
Ballyowen Castle Shop &
    Med Cen 83 C1
Ballyowen Ct 71 D3
Ballyowen Cres 71 D3
Ballyowen Dr 71 D3
Ballyowen Grn 71 D3
Ballyowen Gro 71 D3
Ballyowen La 71 D3
Ballyowen Lawn 71 D3
Ballyowen Rd 71 D3
Ballyowen Vw 71 D3
Ballyowen Way 71 D3
Ballyroan Ct 1 112 A3
Ballyroan Cres 112 B3
Ballyroan Hts 126 A1
Ballyroan Pk 112 A3
Ballyroan Rd 112 A3
Ballyshannon Av 53 D1
Ballyshannon Rd 53 D1
Ballytore Rd 113 D1
Balnagowan 102 B3
Balrothery Cotts 111 C3
Balrothery Est 110 B3
Balscadden Rd 61 C2
Bancroft Av 110 A3
Bancroft Cl 110 B3
Bancroft Gro 110 B3
Bancroft Pk 110 A3
Bancroft Rd 110 B3
Bangor Dr 100 B1
Bangor Rd 100 B1
Bank of Ireland 145 D3
Bankside Cotts 114 B1
Bannow Rd 76 B3
Bann Rd 50 B3
Bantry Rd 52 A3
Banville Av 86 A3
Barclay Ct 117 D2
Bargy Rd 79 D3
Barnacoille Pk 134 B1
Barnamore Cres 50 B3
Barnamore Gro 50 B3
Barnamore Pk 50 B3
Barnewall Av 13 D1
Barnewall Cres 13 C1
Barnewall Dr 37 D3
Barnhill Av 70 A3
Barnhill Cross Rds 70 A3
Barnhill Gro 134 B2
Barnhill Lawn 134 B2
Barnhill Pk 4 134 A2
Barnhill Rd 134 A2
Barnville Pk 85 C3
Barren Hill Cross Rds 62 B2
Barrett St 119 C3
Barrow Rd 77 C1
Barrow St 91 C2
Barry Av 36 A3
Barry Dr 36 A3
Barry Grn 50 A1
Barry La 44 B1
Barry Pk 50 A1
Barry Rd 50 A1
Barryscourt Rd 54 A1
Barton Av 113 C3
Barton Ct 128 A1
Barton Dr 113 C3
Barton Rd E 128 A1
Barton Rd Ext 127 D1
Barton Rd W (Willbrook) 127 C1
Bartra Rock 6 134 B1
Basin St Lwr 89 C2
Basin St Upr 89 C2
Baskin Vw Ter 77 D3
Baskin Cotts 24 B2
Baskin La 24 A2
Bass Pl 145 F4
Bath Av Dublin 4 91 D3
Bath Av Mala. 20 A3
Bath Av Gdns 91 D3
Bath Av Pl 91 D3
Bath La 78 A3
Bath Pl 117 D2
Bath St 91 D2
Bawn, The 20 A3
Bawn Gro, The 20 A3
Bawnlea Av 122 B1
Bawnlea Cl 122 A1
Bawnlea Cres 122 A1

Bawnlea Dr 122 A1
Bawnlea Grn 122 B1
Bawnogue Cotts 1 95 D2
Bawnville Av 124 A2
Bawnville Cl 124 A2
Bawnville Dr 124 B1
Bawnville Pk 124 B3
Bawnville Rd 124 A1
Baymount Pk 81 D1
Bayshore La 139 C3
Bayside Boul N 57 C1
Bayside Boul S 57 C1
Bayside Pk 57 C1
Bayside Sq E 57 C1
Bayside Sq N 57 C1
Bayside Sq S 57 C1
Bayside Sq W 57 C1
Bayside Sta 57 D1
Bayside Wk 57 C1
Bayswater Ter 7 134 B1
Bayview Dublin 4
    off Pembroke St 91 D2
Bayview 2 Bray 142 A1
Bayview Lough. 139 C3
Bayview Av 79 C3
Bayview Cl 139 C3
Bayview Ct 139 C3
Bayview Cres 141 C1
Bayview Dr 141 C1
Bayview Glade 141 C1
Bayview Glen 4 141 C1
Bayview Grn 139 C3
Bayview Gro 141 C1
Bayview Lawn 139 C3
Bayview Pk 139 C3
Bayview Ri 3 141 C1
Beach Av 92 A3
Beach Dr 92 A3
Beach Pk 27 C2
Beach Rd 92 A3
Beach Vw 57 C2
Beaconsfield Ct
    off The Belfry 88 A2
Bearna Pk 129 D3
Beatty Gro 66 B1
Beatty Pk 66 A2
Beattys Av 103 D1
Beaufield 64 B3
Beaufield Ave 64 B3
Beaufield Cl 64 B3
Beaufield Cres 64 B3
Beaufield Dr 64 B3
Beaufield Gdns 64 B3
Beaufield Grn 64 B3
Beaufield Gro 64 B3
Beaufield Lawn 64 B3
Beaufield Manor 116 B3
Beaufield Pk 116 B3
Beaufort 134 A1
Beaufort Downs 113 C3
Beaumont Av 114 A3
Beaumont Cl 114 A3
Beaumont Cres 53 D2
Beaumont Dr 114 B3
Beaumont Gdns 117 C2
Beaumont Gro 53 C2
Beaumont Rd 53 C2
Beau Pk Av 42 B3
Beau Pk Cres 42 B3
Beau Pk Rd 42 B3
Beau Pk Row 42 B3
Beau Pk Sq 42 B3
Beau Pk St 42 B3
Beau Pk Ter 42 B3
Beauvale Pk 54 A2
Beaver Row 103 C3
Beaverstown Orchard 13 C1
Beaver St 78 B3
Beckett Way 97 C1
Bedford Row
    off Temple Bar 145 D3
Beechbrook Gro 7 42 A3
Beechcourt 138 B1
Beechdale 29 C3
Beechdale Ms 102 A2
Beech Dr 128 B1
Beeches, The
    Dublin 13 56 A1
Beeches, The 6
    Dublin 14 113 C3
Beeches, The 12 Abb. 139 C3
Beeches, The Black. 118 B3

Beeches Pk 134 A2
Beeches Rd 129 D1
Beechfield 30 B2
Beechfield Av
    Dublin 12 99 D3
Beechfield Av
    Dublin 24 125 C3
Beechfield Cl
    Dublin 12 99 D3
Beechfield Cl 1
    Dublin 24 125 C3
Beechfield Cl Dunb. 30 B3
Beechfield Ct Dublin 24 125 C3
Beechfield Ct Clons. 30 B3
Beechfield Cres 125 C3
Beechfield Dr 30 B2
Beechfield Grn 30 B2
Beechfield Haven 1 141 C2
Beechfield Hts 30 B3
Beechfield Lawn
    Dublin 24 125 C3
Beechfield Manor Clons. 31 C2
Beechfield Manor 141 C2
Beechfield Meadows 30 B2
Beechfield Pk 2 125 C3
Beechfield Pl Dublin 24 125 C3
Beechfield Pl Clons. 31 C2
Beechfield Ri 31 C2
Beechfield Rd
    Dublin 12 99 D3
Beechfield Rd
    Dublin 24 125 C3
Beechfield Rd (Hartstown)
    Clons. 30 B3
Beechfield Vw 30 B2
Beechfield Way
    Dublin 24 125 C3
Beechfield Way Clons. 30 B2
Beech Gro Boot. 116 B1
Beech Gro Lucan 70 B3
Beech Hill
    off Beech Hill Rd 103 C3
Beech Hill Av 103 D2
Beech Hill Cres 103 D3
Beech Hill Dr 103 D2
Beech Hill Rd 103 C3
Beech Hill Ter 103 D3
Beech Hill Vil
    off Beech Hill Ter 103 D3
Beech Lawn Dublin 16 128 A1
Beechlawn Boot. 116 B2
Beechlawn Av Dublin 5 54 B1
Beech Lawn Av
    Dublin 16 128 A1
Beechlawn Cl 54 B1
Beechlawn Grn 54 B1
Beechlawn Gro 54 B1
Beechlawn Ind Complex 99 C3
Beechmount Dr 115 C1
Beech Pk Dublin 15 48 A3
Beech Pk Cabin. 138 A2
Beech Pk Lucan 70 B3
Beech Pk Av Dublin 5 54 B1
Beech Pk Av Dublin 15 48 A3
Beech Pk Av Deans Gra 132 A2
Beechpark Ct 54 B1
Beech Pk Cres 48 A3
Beech Pk Dr 132 A3
Beech Pk Gro 132 A3
Beech Pk Lawn 48 A3
Beech Pk Rd 132 A2
Beech Rd Dublin 12 98 A2
Beech Rd 3 Shank. 141 C3
Beech Row 3 Clond. 96 B2
Beech Row Ronan. 84 A3
Beechview 1 126 B2
Beech Wk 126 B2
Beechwood Av Lwr 102 B2
Beechwood Av Upr 102 B2
Beechwood Cl Bray 142 A3
Beechwood Cl Manor. 31 D3
Beechwood Ct 131 C1
Beechwood Downs 31 D3
Beechwood Gro 133 D1
Beechwood Lawn 133 D3
Beechwood Pk Dublin 6 102 A2

Beechwood Pk *D.L.*	133 D1
Beechwood Rd	102 B2
Beechwood Sta	102 B2
Belcamp Av	40 B3
Belcamp Cres	40 B2
Belcamp Gdns	40 B2
Belcamp Grn	41 C3
Belcamp La	41 C3
Belclare Av	37 D3
Belclare Cres	37 D3
Belclare Dr	37 D3
Belclare Grn	37 D3
Belclare Gro	37 D3
Belclare Lawns	37 D3
Belclare Pk	37 C3
Belclare Ter	37 C3
Belclare Way	37 D3
Belfield Cl	115 C1
Belfield Ct	103 D3
Belfield Downs	115 C2
Belfield Office Pk	103 C3
Belfry, The *Dublin 8*	88 A2
Belfry, The *Jobs.*	121 D2
Belfry Av	121 D2
Belfry Cl	121 D2
Belfry Dale	121 D2
Belfry Downs	121 D2
Belfry Dr	121 D2
Belfry Gdns	121 D2
Belfry Grn	121 D2
Belfry Gro	122 A2
Belfry Lawn	121 D2
Belfry Meadows	121 D2
Belfry Pk	121 D2
Belfry Pl	121 D2
Belfry Ri	121 D2
Belfry Rd	121 D2
Belfry Sq	121 D2
Belfry Ter	121 D2
Belfry Wk	121 D2
Belfry Way	121 D2
Belgard Cl **1**	109 D2
Belgard Grn	108 B3
Belgard Hts	109 C2
Belgard Ind Est	109 D2
Belgard Rd	109 D2
Belgard Sq E	109 D3
Belgard Sq N	109 C3
Belgard Sq S	123 D1
Belgard Sq W	109 C3
Belgard Sta	109 C2
Belgrave Av	102 A2
Belgrave Pl	102 A2
Belgrave Rd *Dublin 6*	102 A2
Belgrave Rd *Black.*	118 A2
Belgrave Sq E *Dublin 6*	102 A2
Belgrave Sq E *Black.*	118 B3
Belgrave Sq N *Dublin 6*	102 A2
Belgrave Sq N *Black.*	118 A2
Belgrave Sq S *Dublin 6*	102 A2
Belgrave Sq S *Black.*	118 A2
Belgrave Sq W *Dublin 6*	102 A2
Belgrave Sq W *Black.*	118 A2
Belgrave Ter *Black.*	
off Belgrave Rd	118 A2
Belgrave Ter **9** *Bray*	142 B2
Belgrave Vil **10**	142 B2
Belgrove Lawn	74 B3
Belgrove Pk	86 B1
Belgrove Rd	80 B2
Bella Av	
off Bella St	78 B3
Bella St	78 B3
Belle Bk	89 C2
Belleville	75 C1
Belleville Av	101 D3
Bellevue	89 C2
Bellevue Av *Boot.*	104 B3
Bellevue Av *Dalkey*	133 D2
Bellevue Copse	104 B3
Bellevue Ct	104 B3
Bellevue Hts	143 C2
Bellevue Pk *Boot.*	104 A3
Bellevue Pk *Grey.*	143 D1
Bellevue Pk Av	104 B3
Bellevue Rd *Dalkey*	133 D3
Bellevue Rd *Grey.*	143 D1
Bellmans Wk	
off Ferrymans	
Crossing	91 C1
Belmont	131 C2
Belmont Av	103 C2
Belmont Ct	
off Belmont Av	103 C2
Belmont Gdns	103 C2
Belmont Grn	131 C1
Belmont Gro	131 C1
Belmont Lawn	131 C1
Belmont Pk *Dublin 4*	103 C2
Belmont Pk *Dublin 5*	56 A2
Belmont Vil	103 C2
Belton Pk Av	53 D3
Belton Pk Gdns	53 D3
Belton Pk Rd	53 D3
Belton Pk Vil	53 D3
Belton Ter **3**	142 A1
Belvidere Av	78 A3
Belvidere Ct	78 A3
Belvidere Pl	78 A3
Belvidere Rd	78 A2
Belview Bldgs	
off School St	89 C2
Belvue	108 B3
Benbulbin Av	100 A1
Benbulbin Rd	88 A3
Benburb St	89 C1
Beneavin Ct	51 C2
Beneavin Dr	51 C1
Beneavin Pk	51 C1
Beneavin Rd	51 C1
Ben Edar Rd	77 C3
Bengal Ter	77 D1
Ben Inagh Pk	117 D1
Benmadigan Rd	88 A3
Benson St	91 D1
Benson St Enterprise	
Cen	91 C2
Bentley Rd	142 A3
Beresford	78 B1
Beresford Av	78 B1
Beresford La	145 E1
Beresford Lawn	78 B1
Beresford Pl	145 E2
Beresford St	144 B1
Berkeley Rd	77 D2
Berkeley St	78 A3
Berkeley Ter	91 C3
Berryfield	82 A3
Berryfield Cres	50 A2
Berryfield Dr	50 A2
Berryfield Rd	50 A2
Berwick	113 D3
Berwick Av	14 A3
Berwick Ct	14 A3
Berwick Cres	14 A3
Berwick Dr	14 A3
Berwick Gro	14 A3
Berwick Hall	113 D3
Berwick Lawn	14 A3
Berwick Pl	14 A3
Berwick Ri	14 A3
Berwick Vw	14 A3
Berwick Wk	14 A3
Berwick Way	14 A3
Berystede	
off Leeson Pk	102 B1
Bessborough Av	79 C3
Bessborough Par	102 A1
Besser Dr	84 B3
Bethesda Pl	
off Dorset St Upr	78 A3
Bettyglen	56 B3
Bettysford **7**	96 B2
Bettystown Av	55 D3
Beverly Av	125 D2
Beverly Cres	125 D2
Beverly Downs	125 D1
Beverly Dr	125 D1
Beverly Gro	125 D1
Beverly Hts	125 D2
Beverly Lawns	125 D2
Beverly Pk	125 D1
Beverly Ri	125 D2
Beverton Av	13 C1
Beverton Cl	13 C1
Beverton Cres	13 C1
Beverton Dr	13 C1
Beverton Grn	13 C1
Beverton Gro	13 C1
Beverton Lawn	13 C1
Beverton Pk	13 C1
Beverton Way	13 C1
Bewley	71 C3
Bewley Av	83 C1
Bewley Dr	71 C3
Bewley Gro	83 C1
Bewley Lawn	71 C3
Bianconi Av	107 C3
Big Br	113 C1
Bigger Rd	99 D2
Big La	66 B2
Binn Eadair Vw	58 A1
Binns Br	78 A3
Birch Av	130 A2
Birch Dale **2** *D.L.*	133 C2
Birch Dale **1** *Fox.*	131 D3
Birchdale Cl	18 B2
Birchdale Dr	18 B2
Birchdale Pk	18 B2
Birchdale Rd	18 B2
Birches, The	131 D3
Birches Rd	129 D1
Birchfield	115 D3
Birchgrove	132 B1
Birchs La	115 C3
Birchview Av	110 A2
Birchview Cl	110 A2
Birchview Ct	
off Birchview Dr	110 A2
Birchview Dr	110 A2
Birchview Hts	
off Birchview Dr	110 A2
Birchview Lawn	
off Birchview Av	110 A2
Birchview Ri	
off Birchview Dr	110 A2
Birchwood Cl	109 C3
Birchwood Dr	109 C3
Birchwood Hts	109 C3
Bird Av	115 C1
Biscayne	21 C2
Bishop St	90 A3
Bisset's Strand	145 E1
Black Av, The	69 C2
Blackberry La *Dublin 6*	102 A1
Blackberry La *Port.*	27 C2
Blackberry Ri	27 C2
Blackcourt Rd	33 C3
Blackditch Dr	85 D2
Blackditch Rd	86 A2
Blackhall Par	144 A2
Blackhall Pl	89 C1
Blackhall St	89 C1
Blackheath Av	80 B2
Blackheath Ct	81 C2
Blackheath Dr	80 B2
Blackheath Gdns	80 B2
Blackheath Gro	80 B2
Blackheath Pk	80 B2
Blackhorse Av	76 A2
Blackhorse Br	87 D3
Blackhorse Gro	76 B3
Blackhorse Ind Est	76 B3
Blackhorse Sta	87 D3
Blackpitts	89 D3
Blackrock Business Pk	117 D2
Blackrock Coll	117 C1
Blackrock Shop Cen	117 D1
Blackrock Sta	117 D1
Black St	88 B1
Blackthorn Av	130 A2
Blackthorn Cl *Port.*	27 C2
Blackthorn Cl **1** *Still.*	130 A2
Blackthorn Ct **3**	129 D2
Blackthorn Dr	129 D2
Blackthorn Grn **4**	129 D2
Blackthorn Gro **2**	129 D2
Blackthorn Rd	130 A2
Blackwater Rd	77 C1
Blackwood	30 B3
Blackwood Cl	44 B1
Blackwood Cres	30 B3
Blackwood Dr	30 B3
Blackwood La	26 B1
Blackwood Lawn	44 B1
Blackwood Ms	30 B3
Blackwood Pk	44 B1
Blackwood Pl	30 B3
Blakesfield	31 D3
Blakestown Cotts	46 A1
Blakestown Dr	32 A3
Blakestown Rd	46 A1
Blakestown Way	32 B3
Blanchardstown Business	
& Tech Park	33 D3
Blanchardstown Bypass	47 C1
Blanchardstown Cen	46 B1
Blanchardstown	
Corporate Pk	33 D2
Blanchardstown Ind Pk	33 D2
Blanchardstown Rd N	33 C3
Blanchardstown Rd S	46 A2
Blarney Pk	100 B2
Blasket Sq	47 D1
Blessington Ct	
off Blessington St	78 A3
Blessington Rd	
Dublin 24	109 D3
Blessington St *Jobs.*	122 B2
Blessington St	77 D3
Bloom Cotts	89 D3
Bloomfield Av (Donnybrook)	
Dublin 4	102 B1
Bloomfield Av *Dublin 8*	89 D3
Bloomfield Pk	101 D1
Bluebell Av	86 B3
Bluebell Ind Est	98 A1
Bluebell Rd	99 C1
Bluebell Sta	99 C1
Blunden Dr	41 D3
Blythe Av	
off Church Rd	91 C1
Boden Dale	127 C1
Boden Heath	126 B1
Boden Mill **2**	126 B2
Boden Pk	126 B1
Boden Wd	113 C3
Boeing Rd	39 C2
Boghall Rd	142 A3
Boherboy Rd	120 B3
Bohernabreena Rd	124 A3
Bolbrook Av **2**	124 B1
Bolbrook Cl	124 B1
Bolbrook Dr **3**	124 B1
Bolbrook	
Enterprise Cen	125 C1
Bolbrook Gro	124 B1
Bolbrook Pk	124 B1
Bolbrook Vil	124 B1
Bolton St	144 B1
Bond Dr	92 A1
Bond Rd	79 D3
Bond St	89 C2
Bonham St	89 C2
Boolavogue Rd	91 D1
Booterstown Av	116 B1
Booterstown Pk	116 B2
Booterstown Sta	105 C3
Boot Rd	96 B3
Boroimhe Alder	16 B3
Boroimhe Ash	16 B3
Boroimhe Aspen	16 B2
Boroimhe Beech	16 B3
Boroimhe Birches	16 B2
Boroimhe Blackthorn	16 B2
Boroimhe Cedars	16 B2
Boroimhe Cherry	16 B2
Boroimhe Elms	17 C3
Boroimhe Hawthorns	16 B2
Boroimhe Hazel	17 C3
Boroimhe Laurels	16 B2
Boroimhe Maples	17 C3
Boroimhe Oaks	17 C3
Boroimhe Pines	17 C2
Boroimhe Poplars	17 C2
Boroimhe Willows	17 C2
Botanic Av	78 A1
Botanic Gdns	77 D1
Botanic Ms	77 D1
Botanic Pk	78 A1
Botanic Rd	77 D2
Botanic Vil	
off Botanic Rd	78 A1
Bothar An Easa	
(Watermill Rd)	55 D3
Bothar Baile Thormod	
(Ballyfermot Rd)	86 A2
Bothar Chille Na Manac	
(Walkinstown Rd)	99 C2
Bothar Cloiginn	
(Cleggan Rd)	85 D2

Name	Page	Grid
Bothar Coilbeard (Con Colbert Rd) *Dublin 8*	88	A2
Bothar Coilbeard (Con Colbert Rd) *Dublin 10*	87	D2
Bothar Dhroichead Chiarduibh (Cardiffsbridge Rd)	50	A1
Bothar Drom Finn (Drumfinn Rd)	86	A2
Bothar Loch Con (Lough Conn Rd)	86	A1
Bothar Phairc An Bhailtini (Villa Park Rd)	76	A2
Bothar Raitleann (Rathland Rd)	100	B3
Boundary Rd	80	A3
Bourne Av	10	B3
Bourne Ct	10	B3
Bourne Vw	10	B3
Bow Br	88	B2
Bow La E	144	C4
Bow La W	88	B2
Bow St	144	A2
Boyne La	145	F4
Boyne Rd	50	B3
Boyne St	145	F3
Brabazon Cotts 4	142	A1
Brabazon Row	89	D3
Brabazon Sq off Gray St	144	A4
Brabazon St off The Coombe	144	A4
Bracetown Business Pk	29	D1
Brackenbush Pk	138	B1
Brackenbush Rd	138	B2
Bracken Dr	27	C1
Bracken Hill	129	C3
Bracken Rd	130	A3
Brackens La	145	E2
Brackenstown Av	17	C1
Braeburn Ter	15	C2
Braemor Av	114	A2
Braemor Dr	114	A2
Braemor Gro	114	A2
Braemor Pk	114	A1
Braemor Rd	114	A2
Brainborough Ter off South Circular Rd	89	C3
Braithwaite St	89	C2
Bramblefield	31	D2
Bramblefield Ct	31	D2
Bramblefield Cres	31	D2
Bramblefield Dr	31	D2
Bramblefield Pk	32	A2
Bramblefield Vw	32	A2
Bramblefield Wk	31	D2
Bramley Av	73	C1
Bramley Ct	73	C1
Bramley Cres	73	C1
Bramley Garth	73	C1
Bramley Grn	47	C3
Bramley Gro	47	C3
Bramley Heath	73	C1
Bramley Pk	73	C1
Bramley Rd	47	C3
Bramley Ter	15	C2
Bramley Vw	47	C3
Bramley Wk	46	B3
Bramley Way	73	C1
Brandon Rd	99	D1
Bray Head Ter 1	142	A3
Bray Rd *Cabin.*	138	A2
Bray Rd *Corn.*	132	A3
Bray Sta	142	B1
Breakwater Rd S	92	B1
Breffni Ter	134	A1
Breffni Rd	134	B1
Bregia Rd	77	C2
Brehon Fld Rd	128	A3
Brehon's Chair	128	A3
Bremen Av	92	A3
Bremen Gro	92	A2
Bremen Rd	92	A2
Brendan Behan Ct off Russell St	78	B3
Brendan Rd	103	C2
Brennans Par	142	B1
Brennans Ter 7	142	B1
Brennanstown Av	137	D2
Brennanstown Rd	137	D2
Brennanstown Sq	137	D2
Brennanstown Vale	137	C2
Brewery Rd	130	B2
Brian Av	79	C1
Brian Boru Av	81	C3
Brian Boru St	81	C2
Brian Rd	79	C2
Brian Ter	79	C2
Briarfield Gro	56	B2
Briarfield Rd	56	A2
Briarfield Vil	56	B2
Briars, The	73	C3
Briar Wk	27	C1
Briar Wd	142	B3
Briarwood Av	32	A3
Briarwood Cl	32	A3
Briarwood Gdns	32	A3
Briarwood Grn	32	A3
Briarwood Lawn	32	A3
Briarwood Pk 2	32	A3
Briarwood Rd 3	32	A3
Brickfield Dr	88	B3
Brickfield La	89	C3
Bride Rd	144	B4
Bride's Glen Av	14	B2
Bride's Glen Pk	14	B2
Brides Glen Rd	140	A1
Bride St	144	B4
Bridge, The	141	C2
Bridgecourt Office Pk	98	B2
Bridgefoot St	144	A4
Bridge St *Dublin 4*	91	D2
Bridge St *Ashb.*	11	C3
Bridge St *Swords*	17	C1
Bridge St Lwr	144	A3
Bridge St Upr	144	A3
Bridgeview 1	85	C2
Bridgewater Quay	88	A1
Brighton Av *Dublin 3*	79	D2
Brighton Av *Dublin 6*	101	D3
Brighton Av *Black.*	118	B3
Brighton Av *Carrick.*	136	B1
Brighton Cotts 2	136	B1
Brighton Ct	136	B2
Brighton Gdns	101	D3
Brighton Grn	101	C3
Brighton Hall	136	B2
Brighton Lo 3	136	B1
Brighton Pl	136	B2
Brighton Rd *Dublin 6*	101	D3
Brighton Rd *Fox.*	136	B1
Brighton Sq	101	D3
Brighton Ter 7	134	A1
Brighton Vale	118	A2
Brindley Pk Cres	10	B2
Brindley Pk Gdn	10	B2
Brindley Pk Sq	10	B2
Britain Pl	78	A3
Britain Quay	91	D2
Broadford Av	128	A2
Broadford Cl	128	A2
Broadford Cres	128	A2
Broadford Dr	128	A2
Broadford Hill	128	A2
Broadford Lawn	128	A2
Broadford Pk	128	A2
Broadford Ri	128	A2
Broadford Rd	128	A2
Broadford Wk	128	A2
Broadmeadow	15	C3
Broad Meadow Castle	11	C3
Broadmeadow Grn	10	B3
Broadmeadow Rd *Ashb.*	11	C3
Broadmeadow Rd *Swords*	15	C3
Broadstone	77	D3
Broadstone Av off Royal Canal Bk	77	D3
Broadway Dr	46	B2
Broadway Gro	46	B2
Broadway Pk	46	B2
Broadway Rd	46	B2
Brompton Ct	47	C2
Brompton Grn	47	C2
Brompton Gro	47	C2
Brompton Lawn	47	C2
Brookdale	124	A1
Brookdale Av	16	A1
Brookdale Cl	16	A1
Brookdale Ct	16	A1
Brookdale Dr	16	A1
Brookdale Grn	16	A1
Brookdale Gro	16	A1
Brookdale Lawns	16	A1
Brookdale Pk	16	A1
Brookdale Rd	16	A2
Brookdale Wk	16	A1
Brookdale Way	16	A1
Brookdene	141	C1
Brookfield *Dublin 5*	55	C2
Brookfield *Dublin 6*	102	B3
Brookfield *Black.*	117	C2
Brookfield *Lucan*	82	A2
Brookfield Av *Black.*	117	D2
Brookfield Av 25 *Bray*	142	B2
Brookfield Av *Mayn.*	64	B3
Brookfield Ct 1	122	A1
Brookfield Est	100	B3
Brookfield Pk	64	B3
Brookfield Rd *Dublin 8*	88	B2
Brookfield Rd *Dublin 24*	122	A1
Brookfield St	88	B2
Brookfield Ter	117	D2
Brookhaven Dr	33	C3
Brookhaven Gro	33	C3
Brookhaven Lawn	33	C3
Brookhaven Pk	33	C3
Brookhaven Ri	33	C3
Brooklands	104	A2
Brooklawn *Dublin 3*	80	A2
Brooklawn *Black.*	117	C2
Brooklawn *Lucan*	82	A2
Brooklawn Av	118	A3
Brooklawn Wd	118	A3
Brookmount Av	111	C3
Brookmount Lawns	111	C3
Brookpark	82	A2
Brook Pk Ct	118	B3
Brookstone La 4	43	D3
Brookstone Rd	43	D3
Brookvale	70	B3
Brookvale Downs	113	C1
Brookvale Rd *Dublin 4*	103	C2
Brookvale Rd *Dublin 14*	113	C2
Brookview Av	122	A1
Brookview Cl	122	A1
Brookview Cres	108	A3
Brookview Dr	108	A3
Brookview Gdns	108	A3
Brookview Grn	122	A1
Brookview Gro	122	A1
Brookview Lawns	108	A3
Brookview Ri	108	A3
Brookview Ter	122	A1
Brookview Way	122	A1
Brookville *Dublin 11*	50	B1
Brookville *Ashb.*	11	C2
Brookville Cres	54	B1
Brookville Pk (Artane) *Dublin 5*	54	B2
Brookville Pk (Coolock) *Dublin 5*	55	C1
Brookville Pk *D.L.*	132	A1
Brookwood	126	B2
Brookwood Av	54	B3
Brookwood Cres	55	C3
Brookwood Dr	54	B3
Brookwood Glen	55	C3
Brookwood Gro	54	B3
Brookwood Hts	55	C3
Brookwood Lawn	55	C3
Brookwood Meadow	54	B3
Brookwood Pk	54	B3
Brookwood Ri	55	C3
Brookwood Rd	54	B3
Broombridge Rd	76	B1
Broombridge Sta	76	B1
Broomfield	20	A3
Broomfield Ct	141	C1
Broomhill Business Complex	109	D2
Broomhill Business Pk	110	A2
Broom Hill Cl	109	D3
Broomhill Rd	110	A2
Broom Hill Ter	110	A3
Brownsbarn Ct	107	D2
Brownsbarn Gdns	107	D2
Brownsbarn Orchard	107	D2
Brown St N	144	A1
Brown St S	89	C3
Brunswick Pl off Pearse St	91	C2
Brunswick St N	144	A1
Brusna Cotts	117	D2
Buckingham St Lwr	78	B3
Buckingham St Upr	78	B3
Buckleys La	68	B2
Buirg An Ri Glen	83	D2
Buirg An Ri Ter	83	D2
Bulfin Gdns	88	A2
Bulfin Rd	88	A2
Bulfin St	88	A3
Bull All St	144	B4
Bullock Steps 8	134	B1
Bunbury Gate Av	14	B2
Bunbury Gate Cres	14	B2
Bunratty Av	54	B1
Bunratty Dr	54	B1
Bunratty Rd	54	A1
Bunting Rd	99	C2
Burdett Av	134	A1
Burgage, The	134	B2
Burgess La off Haymarket	144	A2
Burgh Quay	145	D2
Burke Pl	88	B2
Burleigh Ct	90	B3
Burlington Gdns	90	B3
Burlington Rd	102	B1
Burmah Cl	134	B3
Burnaby Hts	143	C2
Burnaby Manor	143	D2
Burnaby Ms	143	D2
Burnaby Mill	143	D3
Burnaby Pk	143	D3
Burnaby Rd	143	D2
Burnaby Wds	143	D2
Burnell Pk Av	73	C1
Burnell Pk Grn	73	C1
Burren Ct	37	D3
Burris Ct off School Ho La W	144	B3
Burrow Ct	27	C2
Burrowfield Rd	58	A1
Burrow Rd	58	B1
Burton Hall Av	130	B2
Burton Hall Rd	130	B2
Burton Rd	134	B3
Busáras Sta	145	F1
Bushes La	101	D2
Bushfield	96	A3
Bushfield Av	103	C2
Bushfield Dr	108	A1
Bushfield Grn	96	A3
Bushfield Gro	108	A1
Bushfield Lawns	108	A1
Bushfield Pl	102	B1
Bushfield Ter	102	B2
Bushy Pk Gdns	113	C1
Bushy Pk Rd	113	C1
Buterly Business Pk	54	A2
Butt Br	145	E2
Buttercup Cl 1	41	C3
Buttercup Dr	41	C3
Buttercup Pk 2	41	C3
Buttercup Sq 3	41	C3
Butterfield Av	112	B2
Butterfield Cl	112	B3
Butterfield Ct	113	C2
Butterfield Cres	113	C3
Butterfield Dr	113	C3
Butterfield Gro	112	B2
Butterfield Meadow	113	C3
Butterfield Orchard	113	C3
Butterfield Pk	112	B3
Byrnes La	144	C2

C

Name	Page	Grid
Cabinteely Av	137	D1
Cabinteely Bypass	137	D1
Cabinteely Cl	137	D1
Cabinteely Ct 4	132	B3
Cabinteely Cres	132	B3
Cabinteely Dr	132	B3
Cabinteely Grn	132	B3
Cabinteely Pk 2	137	D1

Name	Page	Grid
Cabinteely Way	132	B3
Cabra Dr	77	C2
Cabra Gro	77	C2
Cabra Pk	77	D2
Cabra Rd	76	B2
Caddell	26	B3
Cadogan Rd	79	C2
Cairn Brook	136	B3
Cairn Brook Hall	136	B3
Cairn Brook Manor	136	B3
Cairn Brook Vw	136	B3
Cairn Brook Way	136	B3
Cairn Ct	37	D3
Cairn Hill	132	A3
Cairnwood	108	B3
Cairnwood Av	108	B3
Cairnwood Ct	108	B3
Cairnwood Grn	108	B3
Calderwood Av	53	C3
Calderwood Gro	53	C3
Calderwood Rd	79	C1
Caledon Rd	79	C3
Callaghan Br	45	D2
Callary Rd	116	A2
Calmount Business Pk	98	B3
Calmount Rd	98	B3
Camac Ct	88	A2
Camac Pk	98	B1
Camac Ter		
off Bow Br	88	B2
Camaderry Rd	142	B3
Camberley Elms	114	A2
Camberley Oaks	114	A3
Cambridge Av	92	A2
Cambridge La	101	D2
Cambridge Rd *Dublin 4*	91	D2
Cambridge Rd		
(Rathmines) *Dublin 6*	102	A2
Cambridge Sq	91	D2
Cambridge Ter	102	B1
Cambridge Vil		
off Belgrave Rd	102	A2
Camden Av	49	D3
Camden Lock		
off South Docks Rd	91	D2
Camden Mkt		
off Camden St Lwr	90	A3
Camden Pl	90	A3
Camden Rd	49	D3
Camden Row	90	A3
Camden St Lwr	90	A3
Camden St Upr	90	A3
Cameron Sq	88	B2
Cameron St	89	C3
Campbell's Ct		
off Little Britain St	144	B1
Campbells Row		
off Portland St N	78	B3
Campfield Ter	115	D3
Canal Bk	97	D1
Canal Rd	102	A1
Canal Ter	87	C3
Canal Turn	96	B1
Canal Wk	86	A3
Cannonbrook	82	B1
Cannonbrook Av	82	B1
Cannonbrook Ct	82	B1
Cannonbrook Lawn	82	B1
Cannonbrook Pk	82	B1
Cannon Rock Vw	61	C2
Canon Lillis Av	79	C3
Canon Mooney Gdns		
off Cambridge Rd	91	D2
Canon Troy Ct	86	B1
Capel St	144	C1
Cappagh Av	50	A1
Cappagh Dr	50	A1
Cappaghmore	96	A1
Cappagh Rd	50	A1
Cappoge Cotts	35	C3
Captains Av	100	A2
Captains Dr	100	A2
Captain's Hill	68	B2
Captains Rd	100	A2
Caragh Rd	76	B3
Cara Pk	40	B2
Carberry Rd	53	C3
Cardiff Br		
off Phibsborough Rd	77	D3
Cardiff Castle Rd	50	A1
Cardiffsbridge Av	49	D2
Cardiffsbridge Gro		
off Cappagh Rd	50	A1
Cardiffsbridge Rd		
(Bothar Dhroichead		
Chiarduibh)	50	A1
Cardiffs La	91	C2
Cards La		
off Townsend St	145	E3
Caritas Convalescent Cen &		
St. Mary's La	104	B3
Carleton Rd	79	D2
Carlingford Par	91	C2
Carlingford Pl		
off Carlingford Par	91	C2
Carlingford Rd	78	A2
Carlisle Av	103	C1
Carlisle St	89	D3
Carlisle Ter **2** *D.L.*	133	D1
Carlisle Ter *Mala.*	20	A2
Carlton Ct *Dublin 3*	80	A2
Carlton Ct *Swords*	17	C2
Carlton Ms		
off Shelbourne Av	91	D3
Carlton Ter **5**	142	A1
Carlton Vil **6**	142	A1
Carmanhall Rd	130	A2
Carmans Hall	144	A4
Carmelite Cen	103	C1
Carmelite Monastery		
Dublin 14	115	D1
Carmelite Monastery		
Still.	130	B1
Carna Rd	85	D2
Carndonagh Dr	56	B1
Carndonagh Lawn	56	B1
Carndonagh Pk	56	B1
Carndonagh Rd	56	B1
Carne Ct	31	D3
Carnew St	77	C3
Carnlough Rd	76	B2
Caroline Row		
off Bridge St	91	D2
Carpenterstown Av	47	C3
Carpenterstown Pk E	46	B3
Carpenterstown Rd	73	C1
Carraig Glen	137	D1
Carraig Grennane	139	C2
Carraigmore Cl	123	D2
Carraigmore Dr	123	D2
Carraigmore Gro	123	D2
Carraigmore Pk	123	D2
Carraigmore Vw	123	D2
Carraroe Av	54	B1
Carrickbrack Heath	59	C2
Carrickbrack Hill	59	C3
Carrickbrack Lawn	59	C3
Carrickbrack Pk	59	C3
Carrickbrack Rd	59	C3
Carrick Brennan Lawn	118	B3
Carrickbrennan Rd	118	B3
Carrick Ct	27	C2
Carrickhill Cl	27	C1
Carrickhill Dr	27	C2
Carrickhill Hts	27	C2
Carrickhill Ri	27	C1
Carrickhill Rd	27	C3
Carrickhill Rd Mid	27	C2
Carrickhill Rd Upr	27	C1
Carrickhill Wk	27	C1
Carrick Lawn **1**	129	D1
Carrickmines	137	C2
Carrickmines Av	137	C2
Carrickmines Chase	137	C2
Carrickmines Dale	137	C2
Carrickmines Garth	137	C2
Carrickmines Grn	136	B3
Carrickmines Little	137	C2
Carrickmines Oaks	137	C2
Carrickmount Av	114	A3
Carrickmount Dr	114	A3
Carrick Ter	88	B3
Carrigallen Dr		
off Carrigallen Rd	50	B3
Carrigallen Pk		
off Carrigallen Rd	50	B3
Carrigallen Rd	50	B3
Carriglea	125	C2
Carriglea Av *Dublin 24*	124	B2
Carriglea Av *D.L.*	133	C2
Carriglea Ct *Dublin 24*	125	C2
Carriglea Ct **1** *D.L.*	133	C2
Carriglea Downs		
Dublin 24	124	B2
Carriglea Downs *D.L.*	133	C2
Carriglea Dr	124	B2
Carriglea Gdns	133	C1
Carriglea Gro	124	B2
Carriglea Ind Est	99	C1
Carriglea Ri	124	B2
Carriglea Vw	124	B2
Carriglea Wk	125	C2
Carrigmore Av	121	C2
Carrigmore Cl	121	C1
Carrigmore Ct	121	C1
Carrigmore Cres, The	121	C1
Carrigmore Dale	121	C1
Carrigmore Downs	121	C2
Carrigmore Elms	121	C2
Carrigmore Gdns	121	C1
Carrigmore Glen	121	C1
Carrigmore Grn	121	C2
Carrigmore Gro	121	C2
Carrigmore Lawns **2**	121	C1
Carrigmore Manor **1**	121	C1
Carrigmore Meadows	121	C1
Carrigmore Oak	121	C2
Carrigmore Pl	121	C2
Carrigmore Ter	121	C1
Carrigmore Way	121	C1
Carrig Orchard	143	C3
Carrig Rd	37	D3
Carrig Vil	143	C3
Carrigwood	125	C2
Carrow Rd	87	D3
Carrs Mill	13	D1
Carton Av	65	C1
Carton Ct *Dublin 11*	37	D2
Carton Ct *Mayn.*	65	C2
Carton Dr	37	D2
Carton Rd	37	D2
Carton Ter	37	D2
Carysfort Av	117	C2
Carysfort Downs	131	C1
Carysfort Dr	134	B2
Carysfort Gro	131	D1
Carysfort Hall	117	D3
Carysfort Pk	117	D3
Carysfort Rd	134	B2
Carysfort Wd	131	C1
Casana Vw	61	C3
Casement Cl	50	A1
Casement Dr	50	A1
Casement Grn	50	A1
Casement Gro	50	A1
Casement Pk	50	A1
Casement Rd (Finglas S)		
Dublin 11	50	B2
Casement Rd (Finglas W)		
Dublin 11	50	A1
Casement Vil	132	B1
Cashel Av	100	B2
Cashel Business Cen	100	B3
Cashel Rd	100	A2
Casimir Av	101	C2
Casimir Ct	101	D2
Casimir Rd	101	C2
Casino Pk	79	D1
Casino Rd	79	C1
Castaheany	31	C2
Castilla Pk	81	C2
Castle Av *Dublin 3*	80	B2
Castle Av *Clond.*	96	B2
Castle Av *Swords*	17	D1
Castlebridge	65	C2
Castlebrook	129	C1
Castlebyrne Pk	117	D3
Castle Cl *Ashb.*	11	C3
Castle Cl *Clond.*	96	B1
Castle Cl *D.L.*	134	B1
Castle Ct *Dublin 3*	80	A1
Castle Ct **2** *Dublin 16*	129	C1
Castle Ct *Boot.*	116	B1
Castle Ct *Lough.*	139	C3
Castle Cove **2** *Dalkey*	134	B2
Castle Cove *Mala.*	19	C3
Castle Cres *Ashb.*	11	C3
Castle Cres **6** *Clond.*	96	B1
Castlecurragh Heath	32	B2
Castlecurragh Pk	32	B2
Castlecurragh Vale	32	B2
Castle Dawson	64	A2
Castledawson Av	117	C1
Castle Down Cft **4**	19	C1
Castle Down Gro	19	C1
Castle Down Rd	19	C1
Castle Dr *Clond.*	96	B2
Castle Dr *Swords*	17	D1
Castle Elms	54	B1
Castle Fm *Shank.*	141	C3
Castlefarm *Swords*	15	C3
Castlefarm Wd	141	C3
Castlefield	125	D1
Castlefield Ct *Dublin 16*	125	C1
Castlefield Ct *Clons.*	45	D2
Castlefield Dr	125	D2
Castlefield Grn	125	D2
Castlefield Gro	125	D2
Castlefield Lawn **1**	125	D1
Castlefield Manor		
Dublin 24	125	C1
Castlefield Manor *Mala.*	20	A3
Castlefield Pk *Dublin 16*	125	D1
Castlefield Pk *Clons.*	45	D2
Castlefield Ter	143	C3
Castlefield Way	125	D2
Castlefield Wds	125	D1
Castleforbes Ind Est	91	C1
Castleforbes Rd	91	D1
Castle Gate *Dublin 15*	74	B1
Castlegate *Shank.*	140	A3
Castlegate Chase	82	A3
Castlegate Cres	82	A3
Castlegate Dene	82	A3
Castlegate Elms	82	A3
Castlegate Grn	82	A3
Castlegate Gro	82	A3
Castlegate Pk	82	A3
Castlegate Pl	82	A3
Castlegate Sq	82	A3
Castlegate Wk	82	A3
Castlegate Way	82	A3
Castle Golf Course	113	C2
Castlegrange *Clons.*	95	C2
Castlegrange Av *Clons.*	31	C3
Castlegrange Av *Swords*	15	C3
Castlegrange Cl *Clond.*	95	C2
Castlegrange Cl *Swords*	15	D3
Castlegrange Ct	95	C2
Castlegrange Dale	31	C3
Castlegrange Dr *Clond.*	95	C2
Castlegrange Dr *Clons.*	31	C3
Castlegrange Gdns	31	C3
Castlegrange Grn *Clond.*	95	C2
Castlegrange Grn *Clons.*	31	C3
Castlegrange Gro	31	C3
Castlegrange Hts	15	C3
Castlegrange Hill	15	D3
Castlegrange Lawn		
Clond.	95	C2
Castlegrange Lawn		
Clons.	31	C3
Castlegrange Rd *Clond.*	95	C2
Castlegrange Rd *Swords*	15	D3
Castlegrange Row	31	C3
Castlegrange Sq *Clond.*	95	C2
Castlegrange Sq *Clons.*	31	C3
Castlegrange Way	15	C3
Castle Gro *Dublin 3*	80	B1
Castle Gro *Clond.*	96	B2
Castle Gro *Swords*	17	D1
Castle Heath	19	C2
Castlekevin Rd	54	A1
Castleknock Av	47	D3
Castleknock Brook	47	D3
Castleknock Cl	47	C3
Castleknock Coll	73	D1
Castleknock Cres	47	D3
Castleknock Dale	47	D3
Castleknock Downs	47	C3
Castleknock Dr	47	D3
Castleknock Elms	47	D3
Castleknock Glade	47	D3
Castleknock Gra	47	C3
Castleknock Grn	74	A1
Castleknock Laurels	47	D3
Castleknock Lo	74	A1
Castleknock Meadows	47	D3
Castleknock Oaks	47	D3
Castleknock Pk	74	A1

Name	Page	Grid
Castleknock Parklands	47	D3
Castleknock Ri	47	C3
Castleknock Rd	74	B1
Castleknock Sta	47	D2
Castleknock Vale	47	C3
Castleknock Vw	47	C3
Castleknock Village Cen	74	A1
Castleknock Wk	47	C3
Castleknock Way	47	C3
Castleknock Wd	47	D3
Castlelands 9 *Dalkey*	134	B1
Castlelands, The		
Dublin 14	113	D2
Castlelands Gro	134	B1
Castle Lawns	19	C1
Castle Lawns Est	110	B3
Castle Mkt		
off Drury St	144	C4
Castlemoyne	42	A2
Castle Pk *Dublin 24*	110	B3
Castle Pk *Ashb.*	11	C3
Castle Pk *Black.*	118	B3
Castle Pk *Clond.*	96	B2
Castle Pk *Leix.*	68	B2
Castle Pk *Swords*	17	D1
Castle Pk Est	110	B3
Castlepark Rd	134	A2
Castle Riada	83	C1
Castle Riada Av	83	C1
Castle Riada Cres	83	C1
Castle Riada Dr	83	C2
Castle Riada Gro	83	C1
Castle Rd *Dublin 3*	80	B2
Castle Rd *Lucan*	83	C1
Castle Rosse	43	C3
Castlerosse Cres	43	C3
Castlerosse Dr	43	C3
Castlerosse Vw	43	D3
Castle Shop Cen	17	D1
Castleside Dr	113	D2
Castle St *Dublin 2*	144	B3
Castle St *Ashb.*	10	B3
Castle St *Bray*	142	A1
Castle St *Dalkey*	134	B2
Castle St Shop Cen	142	A1
Castle Ter	20	A2
Castletimon Av	53	D1
Castletimon Dr	53	D1
Castletimon Gdns	53	D1
Castletimon Grn	53	D1
Castletimon Pk	53	D1
Castletimon Rd	53	D1
Castletown Ct	66	B2
Castletown Gro	66	B1
Castletown Lawn	66	B1
Castletymon Gro	110	B3
Castleview *Dublin 5*	54	A2
Castleview 3 *Dublin 16*	128	B1
Castle Vw *Carrick.*	136	B2
Castleview *Swords*	14	B2
Castleview Av	14	B2
Castleview Cl	14	B2
Castleview Ct	14	B2
Castleview Cres	14	B2
Castleview Dr	14	B2
Castleview Est	28	B2
Castleview Grn	14	B2
Castleview Gro	14	B2
Castleview Heath	14	B2
Castleview Hts	14	B1
Castleview Lawns	14	B2
Castleview Meadows	14	B2
Castleview Pk *Mala.*	19	D2
Castleview Pk *Swords*	14	B2
Castleview Pl	14	B2
Castleview Ri	14	B2
Castle Vw Rd	96	B2
Castleview Row	14	B2
Castleview Wk	14	B2
Castleview Way	14	B2
Castle Village Av	66	A1
Castle Village Cl	66	A1
Castle Village Ct	66	A1
Castle Village Cres	66	A1
Castle Village Dr	66	A1
Castle Village Lawns	66	A1
Castle Village Pk	66	A1
Castle Village Ri	66	A1
Castle Village Wk	66	A1
Castle Village Way	66	A1
Castle Village Wds	66	A1
Castle Vil 3	134	B2
Castle Way	11	C3
Castlewood	31	D3
Castlewood Av	102	A2
Castlewood Cl		
off Castlewood Av	102	A2
Castlewood La	102	A2
Castlewood Pk	102	A2
Castlewood Pl	102	A2
Castlewood Ter	102	A2
Cathal Brugha St	145	D1
Cathedral La	89	D3
Cathedral St	145	D1
Cathedral Vw Ct		
off Cathedral Vw Wk	89	D3
Cathedral Vw Wk	89	D3
Catherines La		
off Church St Upr	144	B1
Catherine St		
off Ash St	144	A4
Cats Ladder 3	135	C3
Causeway Rd	105	D1
Cavalry Row	89	C1
Cavendish Row		
off Parnell St	78	A3
Ceannchor Rd	62	C3
Ceannt Fort	88	B2
Cecil Av	79	D2
Cecilia St		
off Temple La S	144	C3
Cedar Av	109	D1
Cedar Brook Av	85	C3
Cedar Brook Pl	85	C3
Cedar Brook Wk	85	C3
Cedar Brook Way	85	C3
Cedar Ct *Dublin 6W*	101	C3
Cedar Ct *Dunb.*	29	C2
Cedar Ct *Lough.*	138	B3
Cedar Dr *Dunb.*	29	C2
Cedar Dr *Palm.*	73	C3
Cedar Gro 1	46	A1
Cedar Hall		
off Prospect La	103	C3
Cedarhurst Rd	75	C1
Cedar Lo 6	126	B2
Cedarmount Rd	116	A3
Cedar Pk *Dublin 13*	56	A1
Cedar Pk *Leix.*	68	A2
Cedars, The 13 *Abb.*	139	C3
Cedars, The *D.L.*	118	A3
Cedar Sq	117	C3
Cedar Wk	56	A2
Cedarwood	66	B2
Cedarwood Av	51	C1
Cedarwood Cl	51	C1
Cedarwood Grn	37	C3
Cedarwood Gro	51	C1
Cedarwood Pk	51	C1
Cedarwood Ri	51	C1
Cedarwood Rd	37	C3
Ceder Pk	16	A2
Ceder Vw	16	A2
Ceide Dun Eanna		
(Ennafort Dr)	55	C3
Ceide Gleannaluinn		
(Glenaulin Dr)	86	A1
Ceide Phairc An Bhailtini		
(Villa Park Dr)	76	A2
Celbridge Abbey	66	A3
Celbridge Rd *Leix.*	68	A2
Celbridge Rd *Lucan*	69	D3
Celbridge Rd *Mayn.*	65	D3
Celestine Av	91	D2
Celtic Pk Av	53	D3
Celtic Pk Rd	53	D3
Cenacle Gro	139	C3
Central Pk Business Pk	130	B3
Centre Pt Business Pk	97	D2
Century Business Pk	36	B3
Chalet Gdns	71	C3
Chalfont Av	19	D1
Chalfont Dr	19	D2
Chalfont Pl	19	D2
Chalfont Rd	19	D2
Chamber St	89	D3
Chancery La	144	C4
Chancery Pl	144	B2
Chancery St	144	B2
Chanel Av	54	B2
Chanel Gro	54	B1
Chanel Rd	54	A2
Chapel Av	91	D2
Chapelizod Bypass	86	A1
Chapelizod Ct	86	A1
Chapelizod Hill Rd	86	A1
Chapelizod Ind Est	86	B1
Chapelizod Rd		
Dublin 8	87	C1
Chapelizod Rd		
Dublin 20	87	C1
Chapel La *Dublin 1*	144	C1
Chapel La *Swords*	17	C1
Chapel Rd	25	D2
Charlemont	53	D3
Charlemont Av	119	D3
Charlemont Ct	102	A1
Charlemont Gdns		
off Charlemont St	90	A3
Charlemont Mall	102	A2
Charlemont Par	79	C3
Charlemont Pl	102	A1
Charlemont Rd	79	D2
Charlemont Sq		
off Charlemont St	90	A3
Charlemont Sta	102	A1
Charlemont St	90	A3
Charles La	78	B3
Charles St Gt	78	B3
Charles St W	144	B2
Charleston Av	102	A2
Charleston Rd	102	A2
Charlestown	36	B2
Charlestown Av	36	B2
Charlestown Ct	36	B2
Charlestown Dr	36	B2
Charlestown Grn	36	B2
Charlestown Pk	36	B2
Charlestown Way	36	B2
Charleville *Dublin 14*	114	B2
Charleville *Dublin 16*	112	A3
Charleville Av	78	B3
Charleville Mall	78	B3
Charleville Rd *Dublin 6*	101	C2
Charleville Rd *Dublin 7*	77	C2
Charleville Sq	112	B2
Charlotte Quay	91	C2
Charlotte Ter 2	135	C2
Charlotte Way	90	A3
Charlton Lawn	115	D2
Charnwood *Bray*	142	A3
Charnwood *Clons.*	45	D2
Charnwood Av	45	D2
Charnwood Cts	45	D2
Charnwood Dale	45	D2
Charnwood Gdns	45	D2
Charnwood Grn	46	A2
Charnwood Gro	45	D2
Charnwood Heath	45	D2
Charnwood Meadows	45	D2
Charnwood Pk	45	D2
Chase, The	130	B2
Chatham Row		
off William St S	145	D1
Chatham St	145	D4
Chaworth Ter		
off Hanbury La	144	A3
Cheaters La		
off Redmonds Hill	90	A3
Cheeverstown	112	A3
Cheeverstown Rd	108	A3
Chelmsford La	102	B1
Chelmsford Rd	102	B1
Chelsea Gdns	81	C2
Cheltenham Pl		
off Canal Rd	102	A1
Cherbury Ct	116	B2
Cherbury Gdns	116	B2
Cherbury Ms	116	B2
Cherbury Pk Av	82	B1
Cherbury Pk Rd	82	B1
Cherries, The 1	128	A2
Cherries Rd	129	D2
Cherrington Cl	141	C3
Cherrington Dr	141	C3
Cherrington Rd	140	B3
Cherry Av *Carp.*	46	B3
Cherry Av *Swords*	16	B2
Cherry Ct *Dublin 6W*	101	C3
Cherry Ct 6 *Grey.*	143	C3
Cherry Ct 2 *Lough.*	138	B3
Cherry Dr	46	B3
Cherryfield Av		
Dublin 6	102	B2
Cherryfield Av		
Dublin 12	99	D3
Cherryfield Cl	45	D1
Cherryfield Ct	45	C1
Cherryfield Dr	99	D3
Cherryfield Lawn	45	D1
Cherryfield Pk	45	D1
Cherryfield Rd	99	C3
Cherryfield Vw	45	C1
Cherryfield Wk	31	D3
Cherry Gdns 7	143	C3
Cherrygarth *Still.*	116	B3
Cherry Garth *Swords*	16	B2
Cherry Gro *Dublin 12*	99	D3
Cherry Gro *Swords*	16	B2
Cherry Lawn	46	B3
Cherry Lawns	82	A1
Cherrymount Cres	79	D1
Cherrymount Gro	79	D1
Cherrymount Pk	77	D2
Cherry Orchard Av	85	D3
Cherry Orchard Ct	85	D3
Cherry Orchard Cres	85	D3
Cherry Orchard Dr	85	D3
Cherry Orchard Grn	85	C2
Cherry Orchard Gro	85	D3
Cherry Orchard Ind Est	85	D1
Cherry Orchard Par 1	85	D3
Cherry Orchard Pk	85	D3
Cherry Orchard Sta	85	D3
Cherry Orchard Way		
off Cherry Orchard Av	85	D3
Cherry Pk *Carp.*	46	B3
Cherry Pk *Swords*	16	B2
Cherry Ri	143	C2
Cherry Tree Dr	142	A3
Cherrywood *Celbr.*	66	B1
Cherry Wd *Lough.*	138	B3
Cherrywood Av	96	A2
Cherrywood Business Pk	140	A1
Cherrywood Cres	95	D3
Cherrywood Dr	95	D2
Cherrywood Gro	96	A2
Cherrywood Lawn	95	D3
Cherrywood Pk *Clond.*	95	D2
Cherrywood Pk *Lough.*	138	B3
Cherrywood Rd	140	B1
Cherrywood Vil	95	D2
Chester Downs	133	D1
Chesterfield Av		
Dublin 8	75	D3
Chesterfield Av		
Dublin 15	74	B1
Chesterfield Cl	74	B1
Chesterfield Copse	74	B1
Chesterfield Gro	74	B1
Chesterfield Pk	74	B1
Chesterfield Vw	74	B1
Chester Rd	102	A1
Chester Sq 8	134	A1
Chestnut Ct	53	D2
Chestnut Gro *Dublin 16*	128	B2
Chestnut Gro *Dublin 24*	109	D1
Chestnut Gro *Celbr.*	66	B2
Chestnut Gro *Dunb.*	29	C3
Chestnut Pk 2	131	D2
Chestnut Rd *Dublin 12*	98	A2
Chestnut Rd *Still.*	116	A2
Chipping Row	30	B3
Chipping Ter 3	30	B3
Christ Ch Cath	144	B3
Christchurch Pl	144	B3
Church Av (Irishtown)		
Dublin 4	91	D3
Church Av (Rathmines)		
Dublin 6	102	A2
Church Av *Dublin 8*	88	B3
Church Av (Glasnevin)		
Dublin 9	52	A3
Church Av (Blanchardstown)		
Dublin 15	47	C2
Church Av *Kill.*	139	C2
Church Av 2 *Port.*	26	B3
Church Av N		
(Drumcondra)	78	B1
Church Ct	74	A1
Churchfields	114	B1
Church Gdns	102	A2

Churchgate Av	80	B3
Church Gates	143	D1
Church Gro	123	D2
Churchill Ms **10**	134	B1
Churchill Ter	103	D1
Church Lands *Bray*	142	A2
Churchlands *Sandy.*	129	D3
Church La *Dublin 2*		
off College Grn	145	D3
Church La (Rathfarnham)		
Dublin 14	113	C2
Church La *Grey.*	143	C1
Church La S		
off Kevin St Lwr	90	A3
Church Pk Av	101	C2
Church Pk Ct	101	C2
Church Pk Dr	101	C2
Church Pk Lawn	101	C2
Church Pk Vw	101	C2
Church Pk Way	101	C2
Church Rd *Dublin 3*	91	C1
Church Rd (Finglas)		
Dublin 11	50	B2
Church Rd *Dublin 13*	58	B2
Church Rd *Bray*	142	A2
Church Rd *Celbr.*	66	A3
Church Rd *Dalkey*	134	B2
Church Rd *Grey.*	143	D1
Church Rd *Kill.*	138	B1
Church Rd *Mala.*	20	A2
Church Rd *Mulh.*	32	B2
Church Rd *Swords*	17	C1
Church St *Dublin 7*	144	B2
Church St (Finglas)		
Dublin 11	50	B2
Church St (Howth)		
Dublin 13	60	B2
Church St E	91	C1
Church St Upr	144	B1
Church Ter *Dublin 7*		
off Church St	144	B2
Church Ter **7** *Bray*	142	A1
Churchtown		
Business Pk	114	A3
Churchtown Cl	114	B1
Churchtown Dr	114	B1
Churchtown Rd Lwr	114	B1
Churchtown Rd Upr	114	B3
Church Vw **1**	96	A3
Churchview Av	138	B1
Churchview Dr	138	B1
Churchview Pk	138	B1
Churchview Rd	138	B2
Cianlea	14	B3
Cian Pk	78	B1
Cill Cais	123	D2
Cilldara Cl	66	B2
Cill Eanna	55	D3
Cill Manntan Pk **2**	142	A2
City Junct Business Pk	41	D2
Citylink Business Pk	98	B1
City Quay	145	F2
Citywest Br	121	D1
City W Br	107	C3
City W Business		
Campus	107	C3
City W Shop Cen	121	D1
Claddagh Grn	85	D2
Claddagh Rd	85	D2
Claddagh Ter **8**	142	B1
Clanboy Rd	54	A3
Clanbrassil Cl	101	C1
Clanbrassil St Lwr	89	D3
Clanbrassil St Upr	101	C1
Clancarthy Rd	80	A1
Clancy Av	50	B1
Clancy Rd	51	C1
Clandonagh Rd	54	A3
Clanhugh Rd	80	A1
Clanmahon Rd	54	A3
Clanmaurice Rd	54	A3
Clanmawr	141	C2
Clanmoyle Rd	80	A1
Clanranald Rd	54	A3
Clanree Rd	54	A3
Clanwilliam Pl	91	C3
Clare Hall Av	41	D3
Clarehall Shop Cen	41	D3
Clare La	145	E4
Claremont Av	51	D3
Claremont Ct	77	C1
Claremont Dr	51	D2
Claremont Gro **1**	139	C1
Claremont Pk		
(Pairc Clearmont)	92	A3
Claremont Rd *Dublin 4*	92	A3
Claremont Rd *Dublin 13*	59	C1
Claremont Rd *Cabin.*	137	C1
Claremont Rd *Kill.*	139	C1
Claremont Vil	133	D1
Claremount Pines	137	C1
Claremount Ter **11**	142	B2
Clarence Mangan Rd	89	D3
Clarence St	119	C3
Clarendon Mkt		
off Chatham St	145	D4
Clarendon Row		
off Clarendon St	145	D4
Clarendon St	145	D4
Clare Rd	52	B3
Clare St	145	E4
Clare Village	41	D3
Clareville Ct	77	D1
Clareville Gro	77	D1
Clareville Pk	77	D1
Clareville Rd	101	C2
Clarinda Manor	133	D1
Clarinda Pk E	133	D1
Clarinda Pk N	119	D3
Clarinda Pk W	133	D1
Clarke Ter	89	C3
Clarkeville Ter **1**	73	D3
Classons Br	114	B1
Claude Rd	78	A2
Cleggan Av	85	D2
Cleggan Pk	85	D2
Cleggan Rd		
(Bothar Cloiginn)	85	D2
Clifden Dr	85	D2
Clifden Rd	86	A2
Cliffords La	18	A1
Cliff Ter **1**	134	B1
Cliff Wlk (Fingal Way)	61	D2
Clifton Av	118	B3
Clifton La	118	B3
Clifton Ms	102	A1
Clifton Pk	141	C1
Clifton Ter	118	B3
Cliftonville Rd	78	A1
Clinches Ct	79	C3
Clogher Rd	100	B1
Cloister Av	117	D3
Cloister Ct	76	A1
Cloister Gate	117	D3
Cloister Grn	117	D3
Cloister Gro	117	D3
Cloister Pk	117	C3
Cloisters, The		
Dublin 6W	101	C3
Cloisters, The *Dublin 9*	53	C3
Cloister Sq	117	D3
Cloister Way	117	D3
Clonard Av	129	C2
Clonard Cl	129	C2
Clonard Dr	129	C2
Clonard Gro	129	C2
Clonard Lawn	129	C2
Clonard Pk	129	C2
Clonard Rd *Dublin 12*	100	A1
Clonard Rd *Dublin 16*	129	C2
Clonasleigh **2**	141	C2
Clondalkin		
Business Cen	85	C3
Clondalkin		
Commercial Pk	84	B3
Clondalkin		
Enterprise Cen	84	A3
Clondalkin Sta	84	B3
Clonee Br	30	B1
Clonee Bypass	30	B1
Clonfadda Wd	116	B2
Clonfert Rd	100	B2
Clonkeen Ct	132	B3
Clonkeen Cres	132	B2
Clonkeen Dr	132	A2
Clonkeen Gro	132	B3
Clonkeen Lawn **1**	132	B3
Clonkeen Rd	132	A2
Clonlara Av	106	B3
Clonlara Rd (Ringsend)		
Dublin 4	92	A2
Clonlara Rd *Kings.*	106	B3
Clonlea	128	B2
Clonlea Wd **1**	128	B2
Clonliffe Av	78	B2
Clonliffe Gdns	78	B2
Clonliffe Rd	78	B2
Clonmacnoise Gro	100	B2
Clonmacnoise Rd	100	B2
Clonmellon Gro **6**	42	A3
Clonmel Rd	51	D1
Clonmel St	90	A3
Clonmore Rd *Dublin 3*	78	B3
Clonmore Rd *Still.*	116	A3
Clonmore Ter	78	B3
Clonrosse Ct		
off Clonrosse Dr	55	D1
Clonrosse Dr	55	D1
Clonrosse Pk		
off Clonrosse Dr	55	D1
Clonshaugh Av	40	A3
Clonshaugh Business &		
Tech Pk	39	D3
Clonshaugh Cl	40	A2
Clonshaugh Ct **1**	40	A2
Clonshaugh Cres	40	A2
Clonshaugh Dr	40	B2
Clonshaugh Grn	40	B2
Clonshaugh Gro	40	B2
Clonshaugh Hts	40	A2
Clonshaugh Ind Est	40	A3
Clonshaugh Lawns	40	B2
Clonshaugh Meadow	40	A2
Clonshaugh Pk	40	A2
Clonshaugh Ri **2**	40	B2
Clonshaugh Rd	40	A3
Clonshaugh Wk	40	B2
Clonsilla Cl	47	C2
Clonsilla Pk	47	C2
Clonsilla Rd	47	C2
Clonsilla Sta	45	C2
Clonskeagh Dr	103	C3
Clonskeagh Dr	103	C3
Clonskeagh Rd		
Dublin 6	103	C2
Clonskeagh Rd		
Dublin 14	103	C3
Clonskeagh Sq	103	C3
Clontarf Castle		
off Castle Av	80	B2
Clontarf Golf Course	80	A1
Clontarf Pk	81	C3
Clontarf Prom	80	A2
Clontarf Rd	79	D2
Clontarf Rd Sta	79	D2
Clonturk Av	78	B2
Clonturk Gdns	78	B1
Clonturk Pk	78	B2
Cloonlara Cres	50	B3
Cloonlara Dr		
off Cloonlara Rd	50	B3
Cloonlara Rd	50	B3
Cloonmore Av	122	B2
Cloonmore Cl	122	B2
Cloonmore Cres	122	B2
Cloonmore Dr	122	A2
Cloonmore Gdns	122	B2
Cloonmore Grn	122	A2
Cloonmore Gro	122	A2
Cloonmore Lawn	122	A2
Cloonmore Pk	122	A2
Cloonmore Rd	122	B2
Close, The *Dublin 6W*	112	A2
Close, The *Dublin 9*	53	D1
Close, The (Ballinteer)		
Dublin 16	128	B2
Close, The (Ballyboden)		
Dublin 16	126	A2
Close, The (Kilnamanagh)		
Dublin 24	109	D2
Close, The (Tallaght) **4**		
Dublin 24	124	A1
Close, The (Oldtown Mill Rd)		
Celbr.	66	A2
Close, The (Wolstan Haven Av)		
Celbr.	66	A2
Close, The (Dunboyne Castle)		
Dunb.	28	B3
Close, The (Lutterell Hall)		
Dunb.	28	B2
Close, The (Plunkett Hall)		
Dunb.	28	A1
Close, The *Gra M.*	82	B2
Close, The *Kins.*	18	A2
Close, The **8** *Mala.*	21	C3
Close, The *Manor.*	31	C3
Close, The *Still.*	116	A2
Clover Hill Dr	86	A3
Cloverhill Ind Est	84	B3
Clover Hill Rd *Dublin 10*	86	A3
Cloverhill Rd *Clond.*	84	B3
Cloyne Rd	100	B2
Cluain Aoibhinn	64	B3
Cluain Mhuire	133	D2
Cluain Na Greine Ct	141	C2
Cluain Rí	83	D1
Cluain Ri	10	B2
Club Rd	98	A2
Clune Rd	50	B1
Cluny Gro	133	D3
Cluny Pk	134	A3
Clyde La	103	C1
Clyde Rd	103	C1
Cnoc Aoibhean	69	C3
Coast Rd *Dublin 13*	43	D2
Coast Rd *Mala.*	20	B2
Coates La **2**	65	C2
Coburg Pl	79	C3
Cois Coillte **3**	138	B3
Cois Inbhir	13	D1
Cois Na hAbhann	123	D1
Colbert's Fort	109	D3
Colberts Fort Cotts	109	D2
Coldcut Rd	84	B1
Coldwater Lakes	120	B2
Coldwell St	133	D1
Colepark Av	86	A2
Colepark Dr	86	B2
Colepark Grn	86	B2
Colepark Rd	86	A2
Coleraine St	144	B1
Coliemore Rd	135	C2
Coliemore Vil **3**	135	C2
College Business &		
Tech Pk	33	C2
College Cres	112	A1
College Dr	112	A1
Collegefort	73	D1
College Gate	73	D1
College Grn *Dublin 2*	145	D3
College Grn *Mayn.*	64	B3
College Gro	73	D1
College La	145	F3
College Pk *Dublin 6W*	112	A1
College Pk *Dublin 15*	74	A1
College Pk Av	129	C2
College Pk Cl	129	C3
College Pk Ct **1**	129	C3
College Pk Dr **2**	129	C3
College Pk Gro	129	C3
College Pk Way	129	C3
College Rd *Dublin 15*	74	A1
College Rd (Ballinteer)		
Dublin 16	127	D3
College Sq	112	A1
College St *Dublin 2*	145	D3
College St *Dublin 13*	43	D3
College Vw **1**	110	A3
Collegewood	73	D1
Colliers Av	102	B2
Collins Av	53	D3
Collins Av E	54	A3
Collins Av Ext	52	A1
Collins Av W	52	B2
Collins Br	70	A1
Collins Ct *Dublin 9*	53	D3
Collins Ct *Black.*		
off Sweetmans Av	117	D2
Collins Dr	51	C1
Collins Grn	51	C1
Collins Pk	53	D3
Collins Pl	51	C1
Collins Row	51	C2
Collinstown Business Pk **3**	91	C1
Collinstown Cres **1**	84	A3
Collinstown Cross		
Ind Est	39	C1
Collinstown Gro	84	B3
Collinstown Rd	84	B2
Collins Wd	53	C2

Colthurst	83	D1
Colthurst Cl	83	D1
Colthurst Cres	83	D1
Colthurst Gdns	83	D1
Colthurst Grn	83	D1
Colthurst Ms	83	D1
Colthurst Pk	83	D1
Colthurst Ri	83	D1
Colthurst Rd	83	D1
Colthurst Way	83	D1
Comeragh Rd	99	D1
Commons Rd *Clond.*	96	A3
Commons Rd *Lough.*	140	B1
Commons St	145	F2
Con Colbert Rd (Bothar Coilbeard) *Dublin 8*	88	A2
Con Colbert Rd (Bothar Coilbeard) *Dublin 10*	87	D2
Congress Gdns **10**	134	A1
Congress Hall	28	B3
Congress Pk	28	B3
Connaught St	77	D2
Connaught Ter off *Rathgar Rd*	101	D3
Connolly Av *Dublin 8*	88	A2
Connolly Av *Mala.*	25	D1
Connolly Cres	25	D1
Connolly Gdns	88	A2
Connolly Luas Sta	145	F1
Connolly Sta	145	F1
Conor Clune Rd	75	D1
Conquer Hill Rd	81	C3
Conquer Hill Ter	81	C3
Constellation Rd	39	C2
Constitution Hill	144	B1
Convent Av *Dublin 3*	79	C3
Convent Av *Bray*	142	B2
Convent Ct **1**	130	B1
Convent La *Dublin 14*	113	C3
Convent La *Port.*	27	D1
Convent Lawns	86	A2
Convent Rd *Black.*	117	D2
Convent Rd *Dalkey*	135	C2
Convent Rd *D.L.*	119	C3
Convent Vw **12** *Bray*	142	B2
Convent Vw *Clond.*	96	B3
Convent Vw Cotts *Dublin 7*	76	A1
Convent Vw Cotts *Clond.*	96	A3
Convent Way	76	A1
Conway Ct off *Macken St*	91	C2
Conyngham Rd	88	A1
Cookstown Br	10	A2
Cookstown Est Rd	109	C2
Cookstown Ind Est	109	C3
Cookstown Rd	108	B2
Cookstown Sta	109	C3
Cookstown Way	109	C3
Cook St	144	A3
Coolamber Ct **2**	112	A3
Coolamber Pk	112	A3
Coolatree Cl	53	D2
Coolatree Pk	53	C2
Coolatree Rd	53	D2
Cooldrinagh La	69	C3
Cooldrinagh Ter	69	C2
Cooleen Av	53	C1
Coolevin	138	B2
Coolevin La off *Long La*	89	D3
Cooley Rd	99	D1
Coolgariff Rd	53	C2
Coolgreena Cl	53	C2
Coolgreena Rd	53	D2
Coolkill	129	D3
Coolmine Boul	46	B2
Coolmine Cl	46	B2
Coolmine Cotts	32	B3
Coolmine Ct	46	B3
Coolmine Grn	46	B2
Coolmine Ind Est	46	B2
Coolmine Lawn	46	B2
Coolmine Ms **1**	46	B2
Coolmine Pk	46	B3
Coolmine Rd	46	B3
Coolmine Sta	46	B3
Coolmine Wds	46	B2
Coolnevaun	130	B1
Coolock Dr	54	B1
Coolock Ind Est	55	C1
Coolock La	39	C3
Coolock Village	54	B2
Coolrua Dr	53	C1
Coombe, The	144	A4
Copeland Av	79	D1
Copeland Gro	79	D1
Cope St	145	D3
Copper All	144	B3
Coppice, The	73	C3
Coppinger Cl	117	C3
Coppinger Glade	117	C3
Coppinger Row	145	D4
Coppinger Wk	117	C3
Coppinger Wd	117	C3
Coppins, The *Celbr.*	66	B2
Coppins, The *Fox.*	136	B1
Corballis Row off *Kevin St Upr*	144	B4
Corbally Av	121	D2
Corbally Cl	121	D2
Corbally Downs	121	C2
Corbally Dr	121	D2
Corbally Glade	121	C2
Corbally Grn	121	C2
Corbally Heath	121	C2
Corbally Lawn	121	C2
Corbally Pk	121	D2
Corbally Ri	121	C2
Corbally Sq	121	D2
Corbally Vale	121	D2
Corbally Way	121	D2
Corbawn Av	141	D1
Corbawn Cl	141	D2
Corbawn Ct	141	D2
Corbawn Dale	141	D2
Corbawn Dr	141	D2
Corbawn Glade	141	D2
Corbawn Gro	141	D2
Corbawn La	141	C2
Corbawn Lawn	141	C2
Corbawn Wd	141	C2
Corcaill	26	B1
Corduff Av	33	D3
Corduff Cl	33	D3
Corduff Cotts	47	C1
Corduff Cres	33	D3
Corduff Gdns	33	D3
Corduff Grn	33	C3
Corduff Gro	33	C3
Corduff Pk	33	C3
Corduff Pl	33	D3
Corduff Way	33	D3
Corkagh Vw	96	A3
Cork Hill	144	C3
Cork St	89	C3
Cormac Ter	113	C1
Cornelscourt Hill Rd	137	C1
Corn Ex Pl off *Burgh Quay*	145	E2
Cornmarket	144	A3
Corporation St	145	E1
Cornb Rd	100	B3
Corrig Av	133	D1
Corrig Cl off *Lugaquilla Av*	110	B1
Corrig Pk	133	D1
Corrig Rd *Dalkey*	134	B2
Corrig Rd *D.L.*	133	D1
Corrig Rd *Still.*	130	A2
Corrybeg	112	A2
Cottage Pl off *Portland Pl*	78	A2
Coulson Av	101	D3
Coultry Av	38	B3
Coultry Cres	38	A3
Coultry Dr	38	A3
Coultry Gdns	38	B3
Coultry Gro	38	B3
Coultry Lawn	38	B3
Coultry Pk	38	B3
Coultry Rd	38	A3
Coultry Way	38	A3
Coundon Ct	138	B2
Court, The *Dublin 3* off *Clontarf Rd*	80	A2
Court, The *Dublin 5*	56	A3
Court, The *Dublin 6W*	112	A2
Court, The *Dublin 9*	53	C3
Court, The *Dublin 13*	58	A1
Court, The *Dublin 16*	128	B2
Court, The *Dublin 17*	39	D3
Court, The (Cookstown) *Dublin 24*	109	C2
Court, The (Kilnamanagh) *Dublin 24*	109	D1
Court, The *Carrick.*	136	B3
Court, The *Celbr.*	66	A2
Court, The (Dunboyne Castle) *Dunb.*	28	B3
Court, The (Lutterell Hall) *Dunb.*	28	B2
Court, The (Plunkett Hall) *Dunb.*	28	A1
Court, The (Sadleir Hall) *Dunb.*	28	B2
Court, The (Ballyowen) *Lucan*	83	D1
Court, The **7** *Mala.*	21	C3
Court, The *Mulh.*	32	A2
Court, The *Swords*	15	D3
Courthill Dr	28	B2
Court Ho Sq **3**	65	C2
Courtlands	138	A1
Courtyard, The *Dublin 14*	113	D2
Courtyard, The *Celbr.*	66	A3
Courtyard, The *Cool.*	46	A3
Courtyard, The **6** *Fox.*	131	D2
Courtyard, The **1** *Mala.*	21	C3
Courtyard Business Pk, The	94	B2
Cove, The **1**	19	D1
Cowbooter La	61	C2
Cowley Pl	78	A2
Cow Parlour	89	C3
Cowper Downs	102	A3
Cowper Dr	102	B3
Cowper Gdns	102	B3
Cowper Rd	102	A3
Cowper St	77	C3
Cowper Village	102	A3
Crag Av	96	B1
Crag Av Business Pk	96	B1
Crag Av Ind Cen	96	B1
Crag Cres	85	C3
Crag Ter	96	B1
Craigford Av	54	A3
Craigford Dr	54	A3
Craiglands **4**	135	C2
Craigmore Gdns	118	A2
Crampton Bldgs off *Temple Bar*	144	C3
Crampton Ct	144	C3
Crampton Quay	145	D2
Crampton Rd	91	D3
Crane La	144	C3
Crane St	89	C2
Cranfield Pl	91	D3
Cranford Ct	104	A3
Cranmer La	91	C3
Crannagh	103	C3
Crannagh Castle	113	C2
Crannagh Ct	113	C2
Crannagh Gro	113	D2
Crannagh Pk	113	C2
Crannagh Rd	113	C2
Crannagh Way	113	D2
Crannoque Cl	37	D3
Crannoque Rd	37	D3
Crawford Av	78	A2
Creighton St	145	F3
Cremona Rd	86	A2
Cremore Av	51	D3
Cremore Cres	51	D3
Cremore Dr	51	D3
Cremore Hts off *Ballygall Rd E*	51	D2
Cremore Lawn	51	D3
Cremore Pk	51	D3
Cremore Rd	51	D3
Cremore *Dublin 5*	101	D3
Cremore *Dublin 16*	112	A3
Crescent, The *Dublin 3*	79	D3
Crescent, The (Donnybrook) *Dublin 4*	103	C3
Crescent, The (Beaumont) *Dublin 9*	53	C2
Crescent, The (Whitehall) *Dublin 9*	53	C3
Crescent, The *Dublin 13*	58	A1
Crescent, The (Ballinteer) **1** *Dublin 16*	128	B3
Crescent, The (Ballyboden) *Dublin 16*	126	A2
Crescent, The *Dublin 17*	39	D3
Crescent, The *Dublin 24*	124	A1
Crescent, The (Cookstown) *Dublin 24*	109	C2
Crescent, The (Kilnamanagh) *Dublin 24*	109	D1
Crescent, The *Carrick.*	136	B3
Crescent, The (Abbeyfarm) *Celbr.*	66	A3
Crescent, The (Oldtown Mill) *Celbr.*	66	A2
Crescent, The (St. Wolstan's Abbey) *Celbr.*	66	B3
Crescent, The *Clons.*	30	B3
Crescent, The (Dunboyne Castle) *Dunb.*	28	B3
Crescent, The (Lutterell Hall) *Dunb.*	28	B2
Crescent, The (Plunkett Hall) *Dunb.*	28	A1
Crescent, The *Gra M.*	82	B2
Crescent, The *Kins.*	18	A3
Crescent, The *Lucan*	69	D3
Crescent, The **5** *Mala.*	21	C3
Crescent, The **3** *Swords*	17	D1
Crescent, The (Seatown Pk) *Swords*	15	D3
Crescent Gdns	79	C3
Crescent Pl	79	D2
Crescent Vil	78	A1
Crestfield Av	52	B2
Crestfield Cl	52	B2
Crestfield Dr	52	B2
Crestfield Pk off *Crestfield Cl*	52	B2
Crestwood Av	10	B3
Crestwood Grn	10	B3
Crestwood Pk	10	B3
Crestwood Rd	10	B3
Crinan Strand	91	C1
Crinken Glen	140	B3
Crinken La	140	B3
Croaghpatrick Rd	76	A2
Crodaun Ct	66	A1
Croft, The	66	B1
Crofton Av	119	C3
Crofton Rd	119	C3
Crofton Ter	119	C2
Croftwood Cres	85	D3
Croftwood Dr	85	D3
Croftwood Gdns	85	D3
Croftwood Grn	86	A3
Croftwood Gro	85	D3
Croftwood Pk	86	A3
Croke Pk Ind Est	78	B3
Cromcastle Av	54	A1
Cromcastle Dr	54	A1
Cromcastle Grn	54	A1
Cromcastle Pk	54	A1
Cromcastle Rd	54	A1
Cromlech Ct	37	D3
Cromlech Flds	141	C1
Cromwells Fort Rd	99	C2
Cromwells Quarters	88	B2
Cross & Passion Coll	53	C3
Cross Av *Boot.*	117	C1
Cross Av *D.L.*	119	C3
Crossbeg Ind Est	98	A3
Cross Guns Br	77	D2
Cross Kevin St	90	A3
Crosslands Ind Est	98	A3
Cross La	65	C1
Crosstrees	61	C2
Crosthwaite Pk E	133	D1
Crosthwaite Pk S	133	D1
Crosthwaite Pk W	133	D1
Crosthwaite Ter	119	C3
Crotty Av	99	D2
Crown All off *Temple Bar*	144	C3
Crow St	144	C3

Croydon Gdns	79	C1
Croydon Grn	79	C2
Croydon Pk Av	79	C1
Croydon Ter	79	C1
Cruiserath Business Pk	33	D1
Crumlin Pk	100	A1
Crumlin Rd	100	A1
Crumlin Shop Cen	88	B3
Cuala Gro	142	B3
Cuala Rd *Dublin 7*	77	C2
Cuala Rd *Bray*	142	B3
Cuckoo La	144	B2
Cuffe La	90	A3
Cuffe St	90	A3
Cullenswood Gdns	102	B2
Cullenswood Pk	102	B2
Culmore Pk	85	D1
Culmore Rd	85	D1
Cul Na Greine	123	D1
Cumberland Rd	90	B3
Cumberland St	119	C3
Cumberland St N	78	A3
Cumberland St S	145	F4
Cunningham Dr	134	B3
Cunningham Rd	134	B2
Curlew Rd	99	D1
Curragh Av **3**	32	B1
Curragh Cres **1**	33	C1
Curragh Dr **2**	33	C1
Curragh Grn **1**	32	B1
Curragh Hall	32	B1
Curragh La **4**	32	B1
Curragh Ms **2**	32	B1
Curragh Rd **4**	33	C1
Curved *off Eustace St*	144	C1
Curzon St	89	D3
Cushlawn Pk	123	C2
Custom Ho	145	E2
Custom Ho Quay	145	E2
Cymric Rd	92	A2
Cypress Av **3**	126	B2
Cypress St	138	B3
Cypress Downs	112	A2
Cypress Dr	112	A2
Cypress Garth	112	A2
Cypress Gro N	112	A2
Cypress Gro Rd	112	A2
Cypress Gro S	112	A2
Cypress Lawn	112	A2
Cypress Pk	112	A2
Cypress Rd	116	A2

D

Dakota Av	39	C2
Dalcassian Downs	77	D2
Dale, The (Cookstown) *Dublin 24*	109	C2
Dale, The (Kilnamanagh) *Dublin 24*	109	C1
Dale, The *Celbr.*	66	A2
Dale, The *Dunb.*	28	B1
Dale, The *Manor.*	31	C3
Dale Cl **1**	130	A1
Dale Dr	116	A3
Dalepark Rd	123	D2
Dale Rd	116	A3
Dales, The	136	B3
Dale Tree	125	C3
Dale Tree Av	125	C3
Dale Tree Cres	125	C3
Dale Tree Dr	125	C3
Dale Tree Gro	125	C3
Dale Tree Pk	125	C3
Dale Tree Rd	125	C3
Dale Tree Vw	125	C3
Dale Vw	138	B2
Dale Vw Pk **3**	138	B2
Dale Vw Rd	14	B3
Dalkey Av	134	B3
Dalkey Ct	134	B2
Dalkey Gro	134	B2
Dalkey Pk	134	B2
Dalkey Rock	134	B3
Dalkey Sound	135	C2
Dalkey Sta	134	B2
Dal Riada	21	C3

Damastown Av	31	D1
Damastown Cl	32	A2
Damastown Ct	32	A1
Damastown Grn	31	D2
Damastown Ind Pk	31	D1
Damastown Rd	31	D1
Damastown Wk	31	C1
Damastown Way	32	A2
Dame Ct	144	C3
Dame La	144	C3
Dame St	144	C3
Dane Rd	37	D3
Danes Ct	81	D2
Danesfort	80	B2
Daneswell Rd	78	A1
Dangan Av	100	A3
Dangan Dr	100	A3
Dangan Pk	100	A3
Danieli Dr	54	B3
Danieli Rd	54	B3
Daniel St	89	D3
Dara Ct	66	B2
Dara Cres	66	B2
Dargan Ct **13**	142	B2
Dargle Dr	127	D1
Dargle Lo **1**	126	A1
Dargle Rd *Dublin 9*	78	A2
Dargle Rd *Black.*	131	D1
Dargle Valley	127	D1
Dargle Vw	128	A1
Dargle Wd	126	A1
Darley Cotts **3**	142	A2
Darley St	101	D1
Darleys Ter	89	C3
Darling Est	75	D1
Dartmouth Ho Ind Est	86	B3
Dartmouth La	102	A1
Dartmouth Pl	102	A1
Dartmouth Rd	102	A1
Dartmouth Sq	102	B1
Dartmouth Ter	102	A1
Dartmouth Wk *off Dartmouth Ter*	102	A1
Dartry Cotts	114	A1
Dartry Pk	102	A3
Dartry Rd	102	A3
David Pk	77	D2
David Rd	78	A2
Davis Pl *off Thomas Davis St S*	144	B4
Davitt Pk	138	B2
Davitt Rd *Dublin 12*	88	A3
Davitt Rd *Bray*	142	A2
Dawson Ct *Dublin 2*		
off Stephen St	144	C4
Dawson Ct *Black.*	117	C2
Dawson La	145	E4
Dawson St	145	D4
Deans Ct **1**	132	A2
Deansgrange Business Pk	132	A2
Dean's Gra Rd	132	A1
Deansrath Av	95	C1
Deansrath Cres	95	C1
Deansrath Gro	95	C1
Deansrath Lawn	95	D1
Deansrath Pk	95	C1
Deansrath Rd	95	C1
Deanstown Av	49	D2
Deanstown Dr	50	A2
Deanstown Grn	50	A2
Deanstown Pk	50	A2
Deanstown Rd	50	A4
Dean St	144	B4
Dean Swift Grn	51	D2
Dean Swift Rd	51	D2
Dean Swift Sq *off Francis St*	144	A4
De Burgh Rd	88	B1
Decies Rd	86	A4
De Courcy Sq	77	D1
Deerhaven	31	D3
Deerhaven Av	31	D2
Deerhaven Cl	31	D2
Deerhaven Cres	31	D3
Deerhaven Grn	31	D3
Deerhaven Pk	31	D2
Deerhaven Vw	31	D2
Deerhaven Wk	31	D3
Deerpark	11	C3
Deerpark Av *Dublin 15*	74	B1
Deerpark Av *Kilt.*	123	C3

Deerpark Cl *Dublin 15*	74	B1
Deerpark Cl *Kilt.*	123	C3
Deerpark Downs	123	C3
Deerpark Dr *Dublin 15*	74	B1
Deerpark Dr *Kilt.*	123	D3
Deerpark Grn **9**	123	D3
Deerpark Lawn	74	B1
Deerpark Pl	123	D3
Deerpark Ri	123	D3
Deerpark Rd *Dublin 15*	74	B1
Deerpark Rd *Kilt.*	123	C3
Deerpark Rd *Still.*	116	A2
Deerpark Sq	123	C3
Deerpark Ter **10**	123	D3
Deerpark Way	123	D3
Deey Br	67	D1
Delafield Av	125	D1
Delaford Dr	125	D1
Delaford Gro	125	D1
Delaford Lawn	125	D1
Delaford Pk	125	D1
Delbrook Manor	129	C2
Delbrook Pk	129	C2
Delgany Pk	143	C3
Delhurst Av	44	B1
Delhurst Cl	44	B1
Delhurst Ms	44	B1
Delhurst Ter	44	B1
Dell, The	128	A2
Del Val Av	57	C2
Del Val Ct	57	C2
Delville Rd	51	D2
Delvin Rd	77	C2
Delwood Cl	47	C3
Delwood Dr	47	C3
Delwood Gro	46	B3
Delwood Lawn	46	B3
Delwood Pk	47	C3
Delwood Rd	47	C3
Delwood Wk	47	C3
Demesne	80	B1
Denmark St Gt	78	A3
Denville Ct	138	B2
Denzille La	145	F4
Denzille Pl *off Denzille La*	145	F4
Department of Defence (Infirmary Rd) *Dublin 7*	88	B1
Department of Defence (St. Mobhi Rd) *Dublin 9*	78	A1
Dermot O'Hurley Av	91	D2
Derravaragh Rd	100	B3
Derry Av	100	A2
Derry Dr	100	A2
Derrynane Gdns	91	D2
Derrynane Par	78	A2
Derry Pk	100	A2
Derry Rd	100	A2
De Selby	122	A2
De Selby Cl	122	A2
De Selby Ct	122	A2
De Selby Cres	122	A2
De Selby Downs	122	A2
De Selby Dr	122	A2
De Selby Grn	122	A2
De Selby La **2**	122	A2
De Selby Lawns	122	A2
De Selby Pk	121	D2
De Selby Ri **1**	122	A2
De Selby Rd	122	A2
Desmond Av	119	C3
Desmond Cotts **4**	134	B3
Desmond St	89	D3
Devenish Rd	100	B2
Deverell Pl	145	E1
Deverys La	77	D2
De Vesci Ter	119	C3
Devitt Vil **11**	134	A1
Devon Cl **6**	132	B1
Devoy Rd	88	A3
Dewberry Pk	27	C1
Digges La		
off Stephen St	144	C4
Digges St	90	A3
Digges St Lwr *off Cuffe La*	90	A3
Dillon's Row	65	C1
Dingle, The	73	C3
Dingle Rd	76	B2
Dispensary La *Dublin 14*	113	C3

Dispensary La **1** *Lucan*	70	A3
Distillery La	68	B1
Distillery Rd	78	B2
Distributor Rd	36	B3
Diswellstown Rd	46	A3
Dixon Vil **12**	134	A1
Docklands Innovation Pk	79	D3
Dock Pl S *off Dock St S*	91	C2
Dock St S	91	C2
Doctor's La	65	C2
Dodder Av	124	B2
Dodderbank	102	B3
Dodder Ct	124	B2
Dodder Cres	124	B2
Dodder Dale	113	C2
Dodder Grn	124	B2
Dodder Lawn	124	B2
Dodder Pk Dr	113	D1
Dodder Pk Gro	113	D1
Dodder Pk Rd	113	C1
Dodder Ter	91	D2
Dodder Vw Rd	113	C2
D'Olier St	145	D2
Dollymount Av	81	D2
Dollymount Gro	81	C2
Dollymount Pk	81	D2
Dollymount Ri	81	D2
Dolmen Ct	37	D3
Dolphin Av	89	C3
Dolphin Mkt *off Dolphin's Barn St*	89	C3
Dolphin Rd	88	B3
Dolphin's Barn	89	C3
Dolphin's Barn St	89	C3
Dominican Conv	76	A1
Dominick La	144	C1
Dominick Pl	144	C1
Dominick St	119	C3
Dominick St Lwr	144	C1
Dominick St Upr	77	D3
Domville Dr	112	A2
Domville Gro **2**	139	C3
Domville Rd	112	A2
Donabate Sta	13	C2
Donaghmede Av	56	B1
Donaghmede Dr	56	B1
Donaghmede Pk	56	B1
Donaghmede Rd	56	A1
Donaghmede Shop Cen	56	A1
Donard Rd	99	D1
Donelan Av	88	B2
Donnybrook Castle Ct	103	D2
Donnybrook Cl	103	D3
Donnybrook Grn	103	D3
Donnybrook Manor	103	C2
Donnybrook Rd	103	C2
Donnycarney Rd	53	D2
Donnycastle	103	D2
Donomore Av	122	B2
Donomore Cres	123	C2
Donomore Grn	122	B2
Donomore Pk	123	C2
Donore Av	89	C3
Donore Rd	89	C3
Donore Ter *off Brown St S*	89	C3
Donovan La *off Clanbrassil St Lwr*	89	D3
Doonamana Rd	138	A1
Doonanore Pk	138	A1
Doon Av	77	C3
Doon Ct	37	D3
Doonsalla Dr	138	A1
Doonsalla Pk	138	A1
Doris St	91	C2
Dornden Pk	104	B3
Dorney Ct	141	C2
Dorset La	78	A3
Dorset Pl *off Dorset St Lwr*	78	A3
Dorset St Lwr	78	A3
Dorset St Upr	78	A3
Double La	65	C1
Dowkers La	89	C3
Dowland Rd	99	D2
Dowling's Ct *off Lombard St E*	145	F2
Dowling's Ct S *off Lombard St E*	145	F2
Downpatrick Rd	100	B1

Name	Page	Grid
Downs, The *Celbr.*	66	B3
Downs, The *Dunb.*	28	A3
Dowth Av	77	C2
Doyle's La	81	D2
Drapier Grn	51	D2
Drapier Rd	51	D2
Drayton Cl	118	B3
Drimnagh Castle	99	C1
Drimnagh Rd	99	D1
Drimnagh Sta	87	D3
Drinagh Abbey	136	A2
Drinagh More Av	136	A2
Drinagh More Cl **2**	136	A2
Drinagh More Ct **3**	136	A2
Drive, The (Ballinteer) *Dublin 16*	128	B2
Drive, The (Ballyboden) *Dublin 16*	126	B1
Drive, The *Dublin 24*	124	A1
Drive, The (Castletown) *Celbr.*	66	B2
Drive, The (Oldtown Mill) *Celbr.*	66	A2
Drive, The (Lutterell Hall) *Dunb.*	28	B1
Drive, The (Sadleir Hall) *Dunb.*	28	A2
Drive, The *Gra M.*	82	B2
Drive, The *Kins.*	18	A2
Drive, The *Manor.*	31	C3
Drive, The *Mulh.*	32	A2
Drive, The *Swords*	15	D3
Droim Na Coille Ct **4**	83	D1
Dromard Rd	99	D1
Dromawling Rd	53	D2
Dromcarra Av	122	B1
Dromcarra Dr	122	B1
Dromcarra Grn	122	B1
Dromcarra Gro	122	B2
Dromdawn Av	53	C2
Dromeen Av	53	D2
Dromheath Av	32	B2
Dromheath Dr	32	B2
Dromheath Gdns	32	B2
Dromheath Gro	32	B2
Dromheath Pk	32	B2
Dromlee Cres	53	D2
Dromnanane Pk	53	D2
Dromnanane Rd	53	D2
Dromore Rd	100	A1
Druid Ct	37	D3
Druid Valley	138	A3
Drumahill	129	D1
Drumalee Av *off Drumalee Rd*	77	C3
Drumalee Ct *off Drumalee Rd*	77	C3
Drumalee Dr *off Drumalee Rd*	77	C3
Drumalee Gro *off Drumalee Rd*	77	C3
Drumalee Pk	77	C3
Drumalee Rd	77	C3
Drumcairn Av	108	B3
Drumcairn Dr	108	B3
Drumcairn Gdns	108	B3
Drumcairn Pk	108	B3
Drumcliffe Dr	76	B2
Drumcliffe Rd	76	B2
Drumcondra Pk	78	B2
Drumcondra Rd Lwr	78	A2
Drumcondra Rd Upr	78	B1
Drumcondra Sta	78	B2
Drumfinn Av	85	D1
Drumfinn Pk	86	A2
Drumfinn Rd (Bothar Drom Finn)	86	A2
Drumkeen Manor	133	C3
Drummartin Cl	115	D3
Drummartin Cres **1**	115	D3
Drummartin Link Rd, The *Dublin 14*	129	D1
Drummartin Link Rd, The *Dublin 16*	129	D1
Drummartin Pk	129	D1
Drummartin Rd	115	D3
Drummartin Ter	115	D3
Drummond Pl *off Mount Drummond Av*	101	D1
Drumnigh Rd	42	B1
Drumnigh Wd	42	B1
Druncondra Br	78	B1
Drury St	144	C4
Drynam Cl **1**	18	A3
Drynam Ct	17	D2
Drynam Cres	18	A3
Drynam Dr	18	A3
Drynam Glen **3**	18	B3
Drynam Grn **4**	18	B3
Drynam Gro	18	A3
Drynam Pl	18	A3
Drynam Ri	18	A3
Drynam Rd	17	D1
Drynam Sq	18	A3
Drynam Vw **2**	18	B3
Drynam Wk **2**	18	B3
Drynam Way **3**	18	A3
Drysdale Cl	124	A2
Dubber Cross	36	B2
Dublin City Uni	52	A2
Dublin Corporation Food Mkt *off St. Michan's St*	144	B2
Dublin Ind Est	51	C3
Dublin Port Tunnel	79	D3
Dublin Rd *Dublin 13*	57	C2
Dublin Rd *Ashb.*	11	C3
Dublin Rd *Celbr.*	66	B3
Dublin Rd *Dunb.*	29	C3
Dublin Rd *Mala.*	19	C3
Dublin Rd *Mayn.*	65	D2
Dublin Rd *Shank.*	140	B1
Dublin Rd *Swords*	23	C1
Dublin St *Dublin 13*	43	D3
Dublin St *Swords*	17	C1
Dublin Zoo	76	A3
Dufferin Av	89	D3
Duggan Pl *off Rathmines Rd Upr*	102	A2
Duke La	145	D4
Duke La Lwr *off Duke St*	145	D3
Duke Row *off Summerhill*	78	B3
Duke St	145	D4
Dun Aengusa	123	D2
Dunamase	117	C1
Dún An Óir	123	D1
Dunard Av	76	B3
Dunard Ct	76	B2
Dunard Dr	76	B2
Dunard Pk	76	B2
Dunard Rd	76	B3
Dunard Wk	76	B3
Dunawley Av	96	A1
Dunawley Dr	96	A1
Dunawley Gro	96	A1
Dunawley Way	96	A1
Dunbo Ter *off Church St*	60	B2
Dunboy	136	B2
Dunboyne Business Pk	28	B1
Dunboyne Castle	28	B3
Dunbur Ter **8**	142	A1
Duncairn Av	142	A1
Duncairn Ter	142	A1
Duncarrig	59	C2
Dundaniel Rd	53	D1
Dundela Av	134	A1
Dundela Cres	134	A1
Dundela Haven	134	A1
Dundela Pk	134	A1
Dundrum Business Pk	115	C1
Dundrum Bypass	129	C1
Dundrum Castle	128	B1
Dundrum Gate Apts **4**	128	B1
Dundrum Rd	114	B1
Dundrum Shop Cen	114	B3
Dundrum Sta	115	C3
Dundrum Town Cen	129	C1
Dundrum Wd	128	B1
Dunedin Ct **7**	132	B1
Dunedin Dr **8**	132	B1
Dunedin Pk	132	B1
Dunedin Ter	132	B1
Dun Emer Dr	129	C1
Dun Emer Pk	129	C1
Dun Emer Rd	129	C1
Dunes, The	27	C3
Dungar Ter *off Northumberland Av*	119	D3
Dungriffan Rd	61	C3
Dun Laoghaire Ind Est	132	B2
Dun Laoghaire Sta	119	D2
Dunleary Hill	119	C3
Dunleary Rd	119	C2
Dunluce Rd	80	B1
Dunmanus Rd	76	B2
Dunmore Gro	109	D1
Dunmore Lawn	109	D1
Dunmore Pk	109	D1
Dunne St	78	B3
Dunree Pk	55	C1
Dunsandle Ct	74	A1
Dunsandle Gro	74	A1
Dunseverick Rd	80	B1
Dunsink Av	50	A2
Dunsink Dr	50	A2
Dunsink Gdns	50	B2
Dunsink Grn	50	A2
Dunsink La	49	C2
Dunsink Observatory	49	C2
Dunsink Pk	50	A2
Dunsink Rd	50	B2
Dunsoghly Av	49	D1
Dunsoghly Cl	49	D1
Dunsoghly Ct	49	D1
Dunsoghly Dr	49	D1
Dunsoghly Grn	49	D1
Dunsoghly Gro	49	D1
Dunsoghly Pk	49	D1
Dunstaffnage Hall Apts **2**	131	C1
Dunville Av	102	A2
Dunville Ter *off Mountpleasant Av Upr*	102	A1
Durham Pl **8**	133	D1
Durham Rd	104	A1
Durrow Rd	100	B2
Dursey Row	47	D1
Dwyer Pk	142	A1
E		
Eagle Hill	117	D2
Eagle Hill Av	101	C3
Eagle Pk	54	A1
Eagle Ter **2**	115	C3
Eaglewood **1**	133	C3
Earl Pl	145	D4
Earls Ct	76	B2
Earlscourt Ind Est	114	A3
Earlsfort	83	D2
Earlsfort Av	83	D2
Earlsfort Cl	83	D1
Earlsfort Ct	83	D1
Earlsfort Dr	83	D2
Earlsfort Gdns	83	D1
Earlsfort Grn	83	D2
Earlsfort Gro	83	D2
Earlsfort La	83	D2
Earlsfort Lawn	83	D1
Earlsfort Mans *off Adelaide Rd*	90	A3
Earlsfort Meadows	83	D1
Earlsfort Pk	83	D1
Earlsfort Ri	83	D2
Earlsfort Rd	83	D2
Earlsfort Ter	90	A3
Earlsfort Vale	83	D2
Earlsfort Vw	83	D2
Earlsfort Way	83	D2
Earl St N	145	D1
Earl St S	144	A4
Eastern Breakwater	92	B2
East Link	91	D2
Eastmoreland La	91	C3
Eastmoreland Pl	91	C3
East Oil Jetty	92	B2
East Pt Business Pk	79	D3
East Rd	91	D1
East Rd Ind Est	91	D1
East Wall Rd	79	C2
Eastwood Cl	49	D2
Eastwood Cres	49	D2
Eastwood Pk	49	D2
Eaton Brae *Dublin 14*	114	A1
Eaton Brae *Shank.*	141	C2
Eaton Ct	142	B3
Eaton Pl	118	A2
Eaton Rd	101	C3
Eaton Sq *Dublin 6W*	101	C3
Eaton Sq *Black.*	118	A2
Eaton Wd Av	141	C2
Eaton Wd Ct	141	C2
Eaton Wd Grn	141	C2
Eaton Wd Gro	141	C2
Ebenezer Ter	89	C3
Eblana Av	119	D3
Eblana Vil *off Grand Canal St Lwr*	91	C2
Eccles Ct *off Eccles Pl*	78	A3
Eccles Pl	78	A3
Eccles St	78	A3
Echlin St	89	C2
Eden Av	127	D1
Edenbrook Ct **1**	113	C3
Edenbrook Dr	112	B3
Edenbrook Pk	112	B3
Eden Ct	127	D1
Eden Cres	127	D1
Eden Gro *Dublin 16*	127	D1
Eden Gro *D'bate*	13	C1
Edenmore Av	55	C2
Edenmore Cres	55	D2
Edenmore Dr	55	D2
Edenmore Gdns	55	D2
Edenmore Grn	55	D2
Edenmore Gro	55	D2
Edenmore Pk	55	C2
Eden Pk	133	D1
Eden Pk Av	129	D1
Eden Pk Dr	115	D3
Eden Pk Rd	115	D3
Eden Quay	145	D2
Eden Rd	143	D1
Eden Rd Lwr	133	D1
Eden Rd Upr	133	D1
Eden Shop Cen	127	D1
Eden Ter	133	D1
Edenvale Rd	102	B2
Eden Vil **3**	133	D1
Edgewood Lawns	33	C3
Edmondsbury Ct **1**	71	C3
Edmondstown Grn	126	B2
Edmondstown Pk	126	B2
Edmondstown Rd	126	B3
Edward Rd	142	B2
Edwards Ct	126	B2
Edwin Ct **5**	134	A2
Effra Rd	101	D2
Eglington Rd	142	A1
Eglinton Ct	103	C2
Eglinton Pk *Dublin 4*	103	C2
Eglinton Pk *D.L.*	133	C1
Eglinton Rd	103	C2
Eglinton Sq	103	C2
Eglinton Ter *Dublin 4*	103	C2
Eglinton Ter *Dublin 14*	115	C3
Eglinton Wd	103	C2
Elderberry	82	A2
Elderwood Rd	73	C3
Eldon Ter *off South Circular Rd*	89	C3
Elgin Rd	103	C1
Elizabeth St	78	B2
Elkwood	112	A3
Ellenfield Rd	53	C2
Ellensborough	123	D3
Ellensborough Av	123	D3
Ellensborough Cl	123	D3
Ellensborough Copse	123	D3
Ellensborough Ct	123	D3
Ellensborough Cres	123	D3
Ellensborough Dale	123	D3
Ellensborough Downs	123	D3
Ellensborough Gra	123	D3
Ellensborough Grn	123	D3
Ellensborough Gro	123	D3
Ellensborough La	123	D3
Ellensborough Lo	123	D3
Ellensborough Meadows	123	D3
Ellensborough Pk	123	D3
Ellensborough Ri	123	D3
Ellensborough Vw	123	D3
Ellensborough Wk	123	D3
Ellesmere **1**	130	B2
Ellesmere Av	77	C3
Ellis Quay	89	C1
Ellis St *off Benburb St*	89	C1
Elmbrook	83	C1

178

Name	Page	Grid
Elmbrook Cres	83	C1
Elmbrook Lawn	83	C1
Elmbrook Wk	83	C1
Elmcastle Cl	110	A2
Elmcastle Ct	110	A2
Elmcastle Dr	110	A2
Elmcastle Grn	110	A2
Elmcastle Pk	110	A2
Elmcastle Wk	110	A2
Elm Cl	83	C2
Elm Ct *Jobs.*	122	A2
Elm Ct *Lucan*	83	C2
Elmdale Cl	85	D2
Elmdale Cres	85	D2
Elmdale Dr	85	D2
Elmdale Pk	85	C2
Elm Dene	83	C2
Elm Dr *Jobs.*	122	A2
Elm Dr *Lucan*	83	C2
Elmfield Av	42	A3
Elmfield Cl **5**	42	A3
Elmfield Cl **4**	42	A3
Elmfield Cres **1**	42	A3
Elmfield Dr **2**	42	A3
Elmfield Grn	42	A3
Elmfield Gro	42	A3
Elmfield Ind Est	96	B1
Elmfield Lawn	42	A3
Elmfield Pk		
off Elmfield Av	42	A3
Elmfield Ri	42	A3
Elmfield Vale **3**	42	A3
Elmfield Wk	42	A3
Elmfield Way	42	A3
Elm Grn	82	B2
Elmgrove *B'brack*	138	B2
Elm Gro *Black.*	117	D3
Elm Gro *Jobs.*	122	A2
Elm Gro *Lucan*	83	C2
Elm Gro Cotts		
off Blackhorse Av	76	A2
Elmgrove Ter **9**	142	A1
Elm Mt Av	53	D3
Elm Mt Cl	53	D3
Elm Mt Ct	54	A3
Elm Mt Cres	53	D2
Elm Mt Dr	53	D2
Elm Mt Gro	53	D2
Elm Mt Hts	53	D2
Elm Mt Lawn	53	D2
Elm Mt Pk	53	D2
Elm Mt Ri	53	D2
Elm Mt Rd	53	D3
Elm Mt Vw	53	D2
Elm Pk *Dublin 4*	104	A2
Elm Pk *Celbr.*	66	B2
Elmpark Av	102	B1
Elmpark Ter	101	C3
Elm Rd *Dublin 9*	53	D2
Elm Rd *Dublin 12*	98	A2
Elms, The *Dublin 4*	104	A3
Elms, The **14** *Abb.*	139	C3
Elms, The *Black.*	117	C2
Elms, The *Celbr.*	66	B1
Elms, The *Dunb.*	29	C2
Elms, The *Shank.*	141	C3
Elm Vale	83	C2
Elm Way *Dublin 16*	128	A2
Elm Way *Lucan*	83	C2
Elm Wd	83	C2
Elmwood Av Lwr		
off Elmwood Av Upr	102	B1
Elmwood Av Upr	102	B2
Elmwood Cl	45	C1
Elmwood Ct	14	B3
Elmwood Dr	14	B3
Elmwood Pk	14	B3
Elmwood Rd	14	B3
Elner Ct	27	C1
Elton Ct *Dublin 13*		
off Clonrosse Dr	55	D1
Elton Ct *Dunb.*	29	C2
Elton Ct *D.L.*	134	B1
Elton Ct *Leix.*	68	A2
Elton Dr *Dublin 13*	55	D1
Elton Dr *Dunb.*	29	C2

Name	Page	Grid
Elton Gro	29	C2
Elton Pk *Dublin 13*	55	D1
Elton Pk *D.L.*	134	A1
Elton Wk		
off Clonrosse Dr	55	D1
Ely Cres	124	B3
Ely Dr	124	B3
Ely Grn **1**	124	B3
Ely Gro	124	B3
Ely Manor	124	B3
Ely Pl	90	B3
Ely Pl Upr *off Ely Pl*	90	B3
Ely Vw	124	B3
Embassy Lawn	115	C1
Emerald Cotts	91	C3
Emerald Pl		
off Sheriff St Lwr	91	C1
Emerald Sq	89	C3
Emerald St	91	C1
Emily Pl		
off Sheriff St Lwr	145	F1
Emmet Ct	87	D3
Emmet Rd	87	D2
Emmet Sq	117	C1
Emmet St *Dublin 1*	78	B3
Emmet St (Haroldscross)		
Dublin 6	101	D1
Emmet St **1** *Sally.*	133	D2
Emor St	89	D3
Emorville Av	89	D3
Emorville Sq		
off South Circular Rd	89	C3
Empress Pl	78	A3
Enaville Rd	79	C2
Engine All	144	A4
English Row	66	B3
Ennafort Av		
(Ascal Dun Eanna)	55	C3
Ennafort Ct	55	C3
Ennafort Dr		
(Ceide Dun Eanna)	55	C3
Ennafort Gro	55	C3
Ennafort Pk	55	C3
Ennafort Rd	55	C3
Ennel Av	55	C2
Ennel Ct **3**	139	C3
Ennel Dr	55	C2
Ennel Pk	55	C2
Ennis Gro	91	D3
Enniskerry Rd	77	D2
Erne Pl	91	C2
Erne Pl Little	145	F3
Erne St Lwr	91	C2
Erne St Upr	91	C2
Erne Ter Front		
off Erne St Upr	91	C2
Erne Ter Rere		
off Erne St Upr	91	C2
Errigal Gdns	99	D1
Errigal Rd	99	D1
Erris Rd	77	C2
Erskine Av	143	D2
Esker Dr	82	A1
Esker La (north) *Lucan*	71	C1
Esker La (south) *Lucan*	83	C1
Esker Lawns	70	B3
Esker Lo	83	C1
Esker Lo Av	83	C1
Esker Lo Cl	83	C1
Esker Lo Vw	83	C1
Esker Manor	82	B1
Esker Meadow	83	C1
Esker Meadow Cl	83	C1
Esker Meadow Ct	83	C1
Esker Meadow Grn	83	C1
Esker Meadow Gro	83	C1
Esker Meadow Lawn	83	C1
Esker Meadow Ri	83	C1
Esker Meadow Vw	83	C1
Esker Pk	83	C1
Esker Pines	71	C3
Esker Rd	82	B1
Esker S	82	B2
Esker Wds Ct	83	C1
Esker Wds Dr	83	C1
Esker Wds Gro	83	C1
Esker Wds Ri	83	C1
Esker Wds Vw	83	C1
Esker Wds Wk	83	C1
Esmond Av	79	C2
Esplanade Ter **14**	142	B2
Esposito Rd	99	D2

Name	Page	Grid
Essex Quay	144	B3
Essex St E	144	C3
Essex St W	144	B3
Estate Av	104	B3
Estate Cotts	91	C3
Estuary Business Pk	15	D3
Estuary Ct	15	D3
Estuary Rd	19	C2
Estuary Rbt	15	D3
Estuary Row	20	A1
Estuary Wk	19	C2
Eugene St	89	C3
Eustace St	144	C3
Everton Av	77	C3
Evora Cres	60	B2
Evora Pk	60	B2
Evora Ter		
off St. Lawrence Rd	60	B2
Ewington La	89	C2
Excalibur Dr	143	D1
Exchange Ct		
off Dame St	144	C3
Exchange St Lwr	144	B3
Exchange St Upr		
off Lord Edward St	144	C3
Exchequer St	144	C3

F

Name	Page	Grid
Faber Gro **3**	132	B1
Fade St	144	C4
Fagan's La **1**	65	C2
Fairbrook Lawn	113	C3
Fairfield Av	79	C3
Fairfield Pk	101	D3
Fairfield Rd (Glasnevin)	78	A1
Fairgreen	120	B2
Fairgreen Ct **10**	142	A1
Fairgreen Ter **11**	142	A1
Fair Haven **1**	20	A2
Fairlawn Pk		
off Fairlawn Rd	50	B2
Fairlawn Rd	50	B2
Fairlawns	134	A2
Fairview	79	C2
Fairview Av (Irishtown)	91	D2
Fairview Av Lwr	79	C2
Fairview Av Upr	79	C2
Fairview Grn	79	C2
Fairview Lawn	138	A3
Fairview Pas		
off Fairview Strand	79	C2
Fairview Strand	79	C2
Fairview Ter	79	C2
Fairways *Dublin 14*	112	B2
Fairways, *D'bate*	13	D2
Fairways, *The. Port.*	26	A3
Fairways Av	51	C2
Fairways Grn	51	C2
Fairways Gro	51	C2
Fairy Hill	131	D1
Faith Av	79	C3
Falcarragh Rd	52	B2
Falls Rd	140	B1
Farmhill Dr	115	C2
Farmhill Pk	115	D3
Farmhill Rd	115	C2
Farmleigh Av *Dublin 15*	74	A1
Farmleigh Av *Black.*	131	C1
Farmleigh Cl *Dublin 15*	74	A1
Farmleigh Cl *Black.*	131	C1
Farmleigh Ct	74	A1
Farmleigh Pk *Dublin 15*	74	A1
Farmleigh Pk *Black.*	131	C1
Farmleigh Vw	74	A1
Farmleigh Wds	74	A1
Farney Pk	92	A3
Farnham Cres	50	B2
Farnham Dr	50	B2
Farrenboley Cotts	114	B1
Farrenboley Pk	114	B1
Father Colohan Ter **4**	142	A1
Father Kitt Ct	100	A2
Father Matthew Br	144	A3
Fatima Mans	88	B3
Fatima Sta	89	C3
Fatima Ter	142	A1
Faughart Rd	100	B2
Faussagh Av	76	B1
Faussagh Rd	77	C2
Feltrim Ind Pk	18	A2
Feltrim Rd	18	B3

Name	Page	Grid
Fenian St	145	F4
Ferguson Rd	78	A1
Fergus Rd	113	C1
Ferncourt Av	124	B3
Ferncourt Cl	124	B3
Ferncourt Cres **2**	124	B3
Ferncourt Dr **3**	124	B3
Ferncourt Grn	124	B3
Ferncourt Pk	124	B3
Ferncourt Vw	124	B3
Ferndale *Dublin 24*	123	D1
Ferndale *Manor.*	31	D3
Ferndale Av	51	C2
Ferndale Glen	140	B3
Ferndale Hill	140	B3
Ferndale Rd *Dublin 11*	51	C2
Ferndale Rd *Shank.*	140	B3
Fernhill Av	111	D1
Fernhill Pk	111	D1
Fernhill Rd	111	D1
Fernleigh	72	A1
Fernvale Dr	99	D1
Fernleigh Cl	46	A3
Fernleigh Ct	72	A1
Fernleigh Dale	72	A1
Fernleigh Dr	46	A3
Fernleigh Grn	72	A1
Fernleigh Gro	72	A1
Fernleigh Pk	72	A1
Fernleigh Pl **3**	72	A1
Fernleigh Vw	72	A1
Ferns Rd	100	B2
Fernwood Av	109	C3
Fernwood Cl	123	C1
Fernwood Ct	109	C3
Fernwood Lawn	109	C3
Fernwood Pk	109	C3
Fernwood Way	123	C1
Ferrard Rd	101	D3
Ferrycarrig Av	40	B3
Ferrycarrig Dr	40	B3
Ferrycarrig Grn **2**	40	B3
Ferrycarrig Pk	40	B3
Ferrycarrig Rd	40	B3
Ferrymans Crossing	91	C1
Fertullagh Rd	77	C2
Fettercairn Rd	108	B3
Fey Yerra **1**	131	C2
Fforester	83	C1
Fforester Cl	83	C1
Fforester Ct	83	C1
Fforester Lawn	83	C1
Fforester Pk	83	C1
Fforester Wk	83	C1
Fforester Way	83	C1
Field Av	99	D2
Fields Ter		
off Ranelagh Rd	102	B1
Finches Ind Pk	99	C1
Findlater Pl		
off Marlborough St	145	D1
Findlaters St	88	B1
Findlater St **14**	134	A1
Fingal Pl	77	C3
Fingal St	89	C3
Finglas Business Cen	36	B3
Finglas Business Pk	51	C3
Finglas Pk	51	C1
Finglas Pl	50	B2
Finglas Rd	51	C3
Finglas Rd Old	51	D3
Finglas Shop Cen	50	B1
Finglaswood Rd	50	A1
Finlay Sq	116	A2
Finneber Fort	50	B2
Finneber Fort Sq **1**	50	B2
Finnscourt	82	A3
Finnsgreen	82	A3
Finnsgrove	82	A2
Finnslawn	82	A3
Finnspark	82	A3
Finnstown Fairways	82	A2
Finn St	77	C3
Finnsvale	82	A2
Finnsview	82	A2
Finnswood	82	A3
Finsbury Grn	114	B3
Finsbury Pk	114	B3
Firgrove **1**	139	C3
Firhouse Rd *Dublin 16*	111	D3
Firhouse Rd *Dublin 24*	111	D3
Firhouse Rd W	123	D2

First Av *Dublin 1*	91 C1
First Av (Inchicore) *Dublin 10*	87 C2
First Av *Dublin 24*	109 C2
Fishamble St	144 B3
Fitzgerald Pk **2**	133 C1
Fitzgerald St	101 D1
Fitzgibbon La	78 B3
Fitzgibbon St	78 B3
Fitzmaurice Rd *Dublin 11*	51 D2
Fitzmaurice Rd *R'coole*	120 A1
Fitzroy Av	78 A2
Fitzwilliam Ct *off Pembroke St Upr*	90 B3
Fitzwilliam La	90 B3
Fitzwilliam Pl	90 B3
Fitzwilliam Quay	91 D2
Fitzwilliam Sq E	90 B3
Fitzwilliam Sq N	90 B3
Fitzwilliam Sq S	90 B3
Fitzwilliam Sq W	90 B3
Fitzwilliam St (Ringsend)	91 D2
Fitzwilliam St Lwr	90 B3
Fitzwilliam St Upr	90 B3
Fleet St	145 D3
Fleming Pl	90 B3
Fleming Rd	78 A1
Flemings La *off Haddington Rd*	91 C3
Flemingstown Pk	114 B2
Fleurville	117 D3
Floraville Av	96 B3
Floraville Dr	97 C3
Floraville Est	96 B3
Floraville Lawn	97 C2
Florence Rd	142 A1
Florence St *off Lennox St*	102 A1
Florence Ter **2**	142 B1
Florence Vil **12**	142 A1
Flower Gro	133 D3
Foley St	145 E1
Fontenoy St	77 D2
Fontenoy Ter	142 B2
Fonthill Abbey **2**	113 C3
Fonthill Ct **3**	113 C3
Fonthill Pk	113 C3
Fonthill Retail Pk	84 A1
Fonthill Rd *Dublin 14*	113 C3
Fonthill Rd *Clond.*	84 A1
Fonthill Rd S	96 B3
Forbes La	89 C2
Forbes St	91 C2
Forest Av *Dublin 24*	110 A1
Forest Av *Swords*	16 B2
Forest Boul	110 A1
Forest Cl	16 A2
Forest Ct	16 A2
Forest Cres	16 B2
Forest Dale	16 B2
Forest Dr *Dublin 24*	110 A1
Forest Dr *Swords*	16 B2
Forest Flds Rd	16 B2
Forest Grn *Dublin 24*	110 A1
Forest Grn *Swords*	16 B2
Forest Gro	16 A2
Forest Lawn	110 A1
Forest Pk *Dublin 24*	110 A1
Forest Pk *Leix.*	68 A2
Forest Pk *Swords*	16 B2
Forest Rd	16 A3
Forest Vw **1**	16 B2
Forest Wk	16 B2
Forest Way **2**	16 B2
Forestwood Av	38 A3
Forestwood Cl	38 B3
Fortfield Av	112 B1
Fortfield Ct	112 B1
Fortfield Dr	112 B1
Fortfield Gdns	102 A3
Fortfield Gro	112 B1
Fortfield Pk	112 B1
Fortfield Rd	112 B1
Fortfield Sq	112 B1
Fortfield Ter	102 A3
Forth Rd	79 D2
Fortlawn	46 A1
Fortlawn Av	46 A1
Fortlawn Dr	46 A1
Fortlawn Pk	46 A1
Fortlawns	134 A3
Fortrose Pk	112 A2
Fortunestown Cl	121 D1
Fortunestown Cres	121 D1
Fortunestown Grn	121 C1
Fortunestown Lawns	121 C1
Fortunestown Rd	122 A2
Fortunestown Wk	121 C1
Fortview Av	81 C3
Fosterbrook	116 B1
Foster Cotts *off Phibsborough Rd*	77 D3
Foster Pl S	145 D3
Fosters, The	116 A2
Fosters Av	116 A2
Foster Ter	78 B3
Fountain Pl	89 C1
Fountain Rd	88 B1
Four Cts (Courts of Justice)	144 B2
Four Cts Sta	144 B2
Fownes St	145 D3
Foxborough Av	83 C2
Foxborough Cl	83 D2
Foxborough Ct	83 C3
Foxborough Cres **1**	83 C2
Foxborough Downes	83 C2
Foxborough Dr	83 C2
Foxborough Gdns	83 D2
Foxborough Glen	83 D2
Foxborough Grn	83 D2
Foxborough Gro	83 D2
Foxborough Hts	83 D2
Foxborough Hill	83 C2
Foxborough La	83 D2
Foxborough Lawn	83 D3
Foxborough Meadows	83 C2
Foxborough Pk	83 C2
Foxborough Pl	83 C2
Foxborough Ri	83 C2
Foxborough Rd	83 C3
Foxborough Row	83 D2
Foxborough Wk	83 D2
Foxborough Way	83 C3
Foxdene Av	83 D3
Foxdene Dr	84 A3
Foxdene Gdns	83 D2
Foxdene Grn	84 A2
Foxdene Gro	84 A2
Foxdene Pk	84 A2
Foxes Gro	141 C2
Foxfield	82 A2
Foxfield Av	56 A2
Foxfield Cres	56 B2
Foxfield Dr	56 B2
Foxfield Grn	56 B2
Foxfield Gro	56 A2
Foxfield Hts	56 B2
Foxfield Lawn	56 B2
Foxfield Pk	56 B2
Foxfield Rd	56 A2
Foxfield St. John	56 B2
Foxford	83 D1
Foxhill Av	55 D1
Foxhill Cl	55 D1
Foxhill Ct	55 D1
Foxhill Cres	55 D1
Foxhill Dr	55 D1
Foxhill Grn	41 D3
Foxhill Gro	41 D3
Foxhill Lawn	55 D1
Foxhill Pk	55 D1
Foxhill Way	55 D1
Foxpark	82 A2
Foxrock Av	131 D2
Foxrock Cl	132 A2
Foxrock Ct	131 D2
Foxrock Cres	132 A2
Foxrock Grn	132 A2
Foxrock Gro	132 A2
Foxrock Manor	131 C2
Foxrock Mt **1**	131 D2
Foxrock Pk	131 D2
Foxrock Wd	132 A2
Foxs La	56 B3
Foxwood *Lucan*	82 A2
Foxwood *Swords*	17 D1
Foyle Rd	79 C2
Francis St	144 A3
Frankfort	114 B2
Frankfort Av	101 D2
Frankfort Ct	101 D3
Frankfort Pk	114 B2
Frascati Pk	117 D2
Frascati Rd	117 D2
Frascati Shop Cen	117 D2
Frederick Ct *off Hardwicke St*	78 A3
Frederick La	145 E4
Frederick La N	78 A3
Frederick St	10 B2
Frederick St N	78 A3
Frederick St S	145 E4
Frenchmans La *off Gardiner St Lwr*	145 E1
Fnarsland Av	115 C2
Fnarsland Rd	115 C2
Friar's Wk **8**	96 B2
Fnary Av	144 A2
Fnel Av	86 A3
Fumbally La	89 D3
Furry Pk Rd	80 B1
Furry Pk Ind Est	38 B2
Furry Pk Rd	80 B1
Furze Rd *Dublin 8*	74 B2
Furze Rd *Sandy.*	130 A3

G

Gables, The *Clond.*	95 C2
Gables, The **4** *Fox.*	131 D3
Gaelic St	79 C3
Gailtrim Gra	26 A1
Gainsborough	18 B2
Gainsborough Av	19 C2
Gainsborough Cl **3**	19 C2
Gainsborough Ct	18 B2
Gainsborough Cres	18 B2
Gainsborough Downs	18 B2
Gainsborough Grn	18 B2
Gainsborough Lawn	19 C2
Gainsborough Pk	19 C2
Gairdini Sheinleasa	52 A1
Gallaun Rd	37 D3
Gallery, The	13 C2
Galloping Grn **3**	131 C2
Galmoy Rd	77 C2
Galtrim Pk	142 A1
Galtrim Rd	142 A2
Galtymore Cl	87 D3
Galtymore Dr	88 A3
Galtymore Pk	99 D1
Galtymore Rd	88 A3
Gandon Cl	101 D1
Gandon Ms	70 B3
Garden Croath	117 D3
Garden La	144 A4
Gardens, The	136 B3
Gardiner La	78 B3
Gardiner Row	78 A3
Gardiner's Pl	78 A3
Gardiner St Lwr	78 B3
Gardiner St Mid	78 A3
Gardiner St Upr	78 A3
Gardini Lein (Lein Gdns)	55 D3
Gardini Phairc An Bhailtin (Villa Park Gdns)	76 A2
Garnett Hall	28 A2
Garnish Sq	47 D1
Garrynisk Cl	109 D2
Garrynisk Est	109 D2
Garrynure	102 B3
Garryowen Rd	86 B2
Gartan Av	78 A2
Garter La	120 B1
Garth, The *Dublin 24*	109 D1
Garth, The (Cookstown) *Dublin 24*	109 C2
Garville Av	101 D3
Garville Av Upr	101 D3
Garville Rd	101 D3
Gas Yd La	20 A1
Gateway Ct **4**	52 A1
Gateway Cres	52 A1
Gateway Gdns **3**	52 A1
Gateway Ms **2**	52 A1
Gateway Pl **1**	52 A1
Gateway Vw **5**	52 A1
Gaybrook Lawns	19 C2
Gaywood Ind Est	32 B1
Geoffrey Keating Rd *off O'Curry Rd*	89 D3
George's Av	117 D2
George's Hill	144 B2
George's La	144 A1
George's Pl *Dublin 1*	78 A3
George's Pl *Black.*	117 D2
George's Pl *D.L.*	119 C3
George's Quay	145 E2
Georges Rd	50 B1
George's St Lwr	119 C3
George's St Upr	119 D3
Georgian Hamlet	43 D3
Georgian Village	74 A1
Geraldine Ct **4**	65 C2
Geraldine St	77 D3
Geraldine Ter	102 B3
Geraldstown Wds	38 A3
Geraldstown Wds Apts **1**	38 A3
Gerald St	91 C2
Gilbert Rd	89 D3
Gilford Av	104 A1
Gilford Ct	104 A1
Gilford Dr	104 A1
Gilford Pk	104 A1
Gilford Rd	104 A1
Giltspur Brook	142 A3
Glade, The *Dublin 16*	128 B2
Glade, The (Cookstown) *Dublin 24*	109 C2
Glade, The (Oldtown Mill) *Celbr.*	66 A1
Glade, The (St. Wolstan's Abbey) *Celbr.*	66 B3
Glade, The *Palm.*	73 C3
Glandore Pk	133 C1
Glandore Rd	53 C3
Glasanoon Ct *off Glasanoon Pk*	51 C2
Glasanoon Pk	51 C2
Glasanoon Rd	51 C1
Glasaree Rd	51 D2
Glasilawn Av	51 D2
Glasilawn Rd	51 C3
Glasmeen Rd	51 C3
Glasmore Pk	14 B3
Glasnamana Pl	51 C2
Glasnamana Rd	51 C1
Glasnevin Av	51 C1
Glasnevin Br	77 D1
Glasnevin Business Pk	50 A3
Glasnevin Ct	51 C3
Glasnevin Downs	51 C3
Glasnevin Dr	51 D2
Glasnevin Hill	52 A3
Glasnevin Pk	51 D1
Glasnevin Wds	51 C3
Glasson Ct	114 B1
Glasthule Bldgs **15**	134 A1
Glasthule Rd	134 A1
Glaunsharoon	103 C2
Gleann Na Ri	138 A3
Gleann Na Smol *Dublin 24*	123 D1
Gleann Na Smol *D.L.*	118 A3
Glebe, The	82 B1
Glebe Vw	50 B1
Gledswood Av	115 C1
Gledswood Cl	115 C1
Gledswood Dr	115 C1
Gledswood Pk	115 C1
Glen, The (Ballinteer) *Dublin 16*	128 B3
Glen, The (Ballyboden) *Dublin 16*	126 B1
Glen, The *D.L.*	133 D1
Glen, The *Lou.V.*	68 A2
Glenaan Rd	52 B2
Glen Abbey Complex	109 D2
Glenabbey Rd	116 A3
Glenageary Av	133 D2
Glenageary Ct	133 D2
Glenageary Hall	134 A2
Glenageary Lo	133 D2
Glenageary Office Pk	133 C2
Glenageary Pk	133 D2
Glenageary Rd Lwr	133 D1

Glenageary Rd Upr	133	C1
Glenageary Sta	133	D1
Glenageary Wds	133	C1
Glenalbyn Rd	131	C1
Glenalua Hts	139	C1
Glenalua Rd	139	C1
Glenalua Ter	139	C1
Glenamuck Rd	137	C2
Glenanne	100	B3
Glenard Av *Dublin 7*	77	C3
Glenard Av *Bray*	142	B2
Glenarm Av	78	B2
Glenarm Sq	78	A2
Glenarriff Rd	75	C1
Glenart Av	117	C3
Glenaulin	74	A3
Glenaulin Dr		
(Ceide Glennaluinn)	86	A1
Glenaulin Grn	85	D1
Glenaulin Pk		
(Pairc Gleannaluinn)	74	A3
Glenaulin Rd	85	D1
Glen Av	137	C1
Glenavon Pk	138	B3
Glenavy Pk	100	B3
Glenayle Rd	55	D1
Glenayr Rd	113	D1
Glenbeigh Pk	76	B3
Glenbeigh Rd	76	B3
Glenbourne Gro	136	A1
Glenbower Pk	114	B3
Glenbrook Pk	113	C3
Glenbrook Rd	49	D3
Glencairn	130	B3
Glencarr Ct **4**	139	C3
Glencarrig	59	C1
Glencarrig Ct	124	B2
Glencarrig Dr	124	B2
Glencarrig Grn	124	A2
Glencarr Lawn	139	C3
Glencar Rd	76	B3
Glen Cl	137	D1
Glencloy Rd	52	B2
Glencorp Rd	53	C2
Glen Dale *Cabin.*	137	C1
Glendale *Leix.*	68	B1
Glendale Dr	142	B3
Glendale Meadows	69	C1
Glendale Pk	112	A1
Glendalough Rd	78	A1
Glendhu Pk	49	D3
Glendhu Rd	49	D3
Glendoher Av	127	C1
Glendoher Cl	126	B1
Glendoher Dr	127	C1
Glendoher Pk	127	C1
Glendoher Rd	126	B1
Glendoo Cl		
off Lugaquilla Av	110	B1
Glendown Av	111	D1
Glendown Cl		
off Glendown Gro	111	D1
Glendown Ct	111	D1
Glendown Cres	111	D1
Glendown Grn		
off Glendown Gro	112	A1
Glendown Gro	111	D1
Glendown Lawn	112	A1
Glendown Pk	111	D1
Glendown Rd	111	D2
Glen Dr	137	D1
Glen Druid	141	C1
Glendun Rd	52	B2
Glenealy Downs	31	D3
Glenealy Rd	101	C1
Gleneaston Av	67	D1
Gleneaston Gdns	67	D2
Gleneaston Gro	67	D2
Gleneaston Pk	67	D2
Gleneaston Ri	67	D2
Gleneaston Wds	67	D1
Glen Ellan Av	15	C2
Glen Ellan Cl	15	C3
Glen Ellan Ct	15	C3
Glen Ellan Cres	15	C3
Glen Ellan Dr	15	C2
Glen Ellan Gdns	14	B2
Glen Ellan Grn	15	C2
Glen Ellan Gro	14	B2
Glen Ellan Pk	15	C2
Glen Ellan Pines	15	C2
Glen Ellan Wk	14	B2
Glenfarne Rd	55	C1
Glenfield Av	84	A1
Glenfield Cl	84	A1
Glenfield Dr	84	A1
Glenfield Gro	84	A1
Glenfield Pk	84	A1
Glengara Cl **4**	133	D1
Glengara Pk	133	D1
Glengariff Par	78	A2
Glen Garth	137	C1
Glen Gro	137	D1
Glenhill Av	51	C2
Glenhill Ct	51	C2
Glenhill Dr	50	B2
Glenhill Gro	51	C2
Glenhill Rd	50	B2
Glenhill Vil		
off Glenhill Rd	50	B2
Glen Lawn Dr	137	C1
Glenlyon Cres	125	C2
Glenlyon Gro	125	C2
Glenlyon Pk	125	C2
Glenmalure Pk	88	B3
Glenmalure Sq	102	B3
Glenmaroon Pk	85	D1
Glenmaroon Rd	85	D1
Glenmore Ct	127	C2
Glenmore Pk	127	C2
Glenmore Rd	76	B3
Glen Na Smol	142	A3
Glenomena Gro	116	A1
Glenomena Pk	104	A3
Glenpark Cl	73	C3
Glenpark Dr	73	C3
Glenpark Rd	73	C3
Glens, The	136	B3
Glenshane Cl	122	A1
Glenshane Cres	122	A1
Glenshane Gdns	122	A1
Glenshane Grn	122	A1
Glenshane Gro	122	B1
Glenshane Lawns	122	A1
Glenshane Pk	122	A1
Glenshesk Rd	53	C2
Glenside Vil **2**	73	D3
Glen Ter **16**	134	A1
Glenties Dr	50	A2
Glenties Pk	50	A3
Glentow Rd	52	B2
Glentworth Pk	41	D3
Glenvale	83	C2
Glenvara Pk	125	C2
Glenvar Pk	117	C2
Glenview	133	D3
Glenview Dr **4**	124	B1
Glenview Ind Est	88	B3
Glenview Lawn	111	C3
Glenville Av	47	C2
Glenville Ct	46	B3
Glenville Dr	46	B2
Glenville Garth	46	B3
Glenville Grn	47	C2
Glenville Gro	47	C2
Glenville Ind Est	116	A2
Glenville Lawn	46	B2
Glenville Rd	46	B3
Glenville Way	47	C2
Glen Wk	137	C1
Glenwood Rd	55	C1
Glin Av	40	B3
Glin Cres	40	B3
Glin Dr	40	B3
Glin Glen	40	B3
Glin Gro	40	B3
Glin Pk	40	B3
Glin Rd	40	B3
Gloucester La *off Sean McDermott St Lwr*	78	B3
Gloucester Pl	78	B3
Gloucester Pl Lwr	78	B3
Gloucester Pl N	78	B3
Gloucester Pl Upr		
off Gloucester Pl	78	B3
Gloucester St S	145	E2
Glovers All	144	C4
Goatstown Av	115	C2
Goatstown Rd	115	D2
Gofton Hall	50	B1
Golden Br	87	D2
Goldenbridge Av	88	A3
Goldenbridge Gdns	88	A3
Goldenbridge Sta	88	A3
Goldenbridge Ter		
off Connolly Av	88	A3
Golden La	144	B4
Goldsmith St	77	D3
Goldsmith Ter **13**	142	A1
Golf La	131	D3
Golf Links Rd	27	C3
Gordon Av	132	A3
Gordon Pl		
off Richmond St S	90	A3
Gordon St	91	C2
Gorsefield Ct	55	C2
Gortbeg Av	50	B3
Gortbeg Dr	50	B3
Gortbeg Pk	50	B3
Gortbeg Rd	50	B3
Gortmore Av	50	B3
Gortmore Dr	50	B3
Gortmore Pk		
off Gortmore Rd	50	B3
Gortmore Rd	50	B3
Gort Na Mona Dr	132	A3
Gosworth Pk	134	A2
Government Bldgs	90	B3
Gowrie Pk	133	C1
Gracefield Av	55	C3
Gracefield Ct	54	B3
Gracefield Rd	54	B2
Grace O'Malley Dr	60	B2
Grace O'Malley Rd	60	B2
Grace Pk Av	78	B1
Grace Pk Ct	53	C2
Grace Pk Gdns	78	B1
Grace Pk Hts	53	C3
Grace Pk Meadows	53	D3
Grace Pk Rd	78	B1
Grace Pk Ter	79	C1
Grafton St	145	D4
Graham Ct	78	A3
Graigue Ct	37	D2
Granard Br	47	D2
Granby La	78	A3
Granby Pl	144	C1
Granby Row	78	A3
Grand Canal Bk *Dublin 8*	89	C2
Grand Canal Bk (Ranelagh) *Dublin 8*	102	A1
Grand Canal Business Cen	87	C3
Grand Canal Dock Sta	91	C2
Grand Canal Harbour *off James's St*	88	B2
Grand Canal Pl N	89	C2
Grand Canal Quay	91	C2
Grand Canal St Lwr	91	C2
Grand Canal St Upr	91	C3
Grand Canal Vw	88	A3
Grand Par	102	B1
Grange, The *Deans Gra*	132	B2
Grange, The *Still.*	131	C1
Grange Abbey Cres	42	B3
Grange Abbey Dr	42	B3
Grange Abbey Gro	42	B3
Grange Abbey Rd	42	B3
Grange Av	43	C3
Grange Brook	127	C2
Grangebrook Av	127	C2
Grangebrook Cl	127	C2
Grangebrook Pk	127	C2
Grangebrook Vale	127	C2
Grange Castle Int Business Park	94	B1
Grange Cl *Dublin 13*	57	C2
Grange Cl *Sally.*	133	C3
Grange Cotts **1**	132	A1
Grange Ct	127	D2
Grange Cres	132	B2
Grange Downs	113	D3
Grange Dr	57	C1
Grangefield	128	B3
Grangegorman Lwr	144	A1
Grangegorman Upr	77	C3
Grange Gro **2**	132	A1
Grange Hall	128	B3
Grange Lo Av	42	B3
Grange Manor	82	B2
Grange Manor Av	127	D1
Grange Manor Cl	127	D1
Grange Manor Dr	127	D1
Grange Manor Gro	127	D1
Grange Manor Rd	127	D1
Grangemore	42	A3
Grangemore Av	42	A3
Grangemore Ct	42	A3
Grangemore Cres	42	A3
Grangemore Dr	42	A3
Grangemore Gro	42	A3
Grangemore Lawn	42	A3
Grangemore Pk	42	A3
Grangemore Ri	42	A3
Grangemore Rd	42	A3
Grange Par	57	C1
Grange Pk *Dublin 13*	43	C3
Grange Pk *Dublin 14*	113	C3
Grange Pk *Corn.*	132	A2
Grange Pk Av	56	A2
Grange Pk Cl	56	A2
Grange Pk Cres	56	A2
Grange Pk Dr	56	A2
Grange Pk Grn	56	A2
Grange Pk Gro	56	A2
Grange Pk Par	56	A2
Grange Pk Ri	56	A2
Grange Pk Rd	56	A2
Grange Pk Wk	56	A2
Grange Ri	43	C3
Grange Rd *Dublin 13*	56	A1
Grange Rd (Baldoyle) *Dublin 13*	42	B3
Grange Rd *Dublin 14*	113	C2
Grange Rd *Dublin 16*	113	C3
Grange Vw Cl	95	C1
Grange Vw Ct	95	C1
Grange Vw Grn	95	C1
Grange Vw Gro	95	C1
Grange Vw Lawn	95	C2
Grange Vw Pk	95	C2
Grange Vw Rd	95	C1
Grange Vw Wk	95	C1
Grange Vw Way	95	C1
Grange Vw Wd	95	C1
Grange Way	57	C1
Grange Wd *Dublin 16*	128	A2
Grangewood *D.L.*	132	B2
Granitefield	133	C3
Granite Hall **5**	133	D1
Granite Pl	103	D1
Granite Ter *off Inchicore Ter S*	87	D2
Grantham Pl	90	A3
Grantham St	90	A3
Grants Row	91	C2
Granville Cl	138	A1
Granville Cres	138	A1
Granville Pk	131	D1
Granville Rd *Cabin.*	138	A1
Granville Rd *Deans Gra*	131	D2
Grattan Br	144	C2
Grattan Ct E *off Grattan St*	91	C2
Grattan Cres	87	D2
Grattan Hall	42	A3
Grattan Lo	42	A3
Grattan Par	78	A2
Grattan Pk	143	C2
Grattan Pl *off Grattan St*	91	C2
Grattan St	91	C2
Gray Sq *off Gray St*	144	A4
Gray St	144	A4
Great Clarence Pl	91	C2
Great Western Av *off North Circular Rd*	77	D3
Great Western Sq	77	D3
Great Western Vil	77	D3
Greek St	144	B2
Green, The *Dublin 9*	53	D1
Green, The (Ballinteer) *Dublin 16*	128	B2
Green, The (Ballyboden) *Dublin 16*	126	A1
Green, The *Dublin 17*	39	D3
Green, The *Dublin 24*	109	D1
Green, The *Ashb.*	11	C3
Green, The *Carrick.*	136	B3

Green, The *Celbr.*	66	A2
Green, The (Dunboyne Castle)		
Dunb.	28	B3
Green, The (Lutterell Hall)		
Dunb.	28	B1
Green, The *Kins.*	18	A3
Green, The *Mala.*	20	A2
Green, The (Robswall) **2**		
Mala.	21	C3
Green, The *Manor.*	31	C3
Green, The *Mayn.*	64	A1
Green, The *Mulh.*	32	A2
Green, The *Swords*	15	D3
Greenacre Ct	111	D3
Greencastle Av	54	B1
Greencastle Cres	40	B3
Greencastle Dr	40	B3
Greencastle Par	55	C1
Greencastle Pk	40	B3
Greencastle Rd	40	B3
Greendale Av	56	B2
Greendale Rd	56	B2
Greendale Shop Cen	56	B2
Greenfield Cl	64	B3
Greenfield Cres	103	D3
Greenfield Dr	65	C3
Greenfield Gro	11	C3
Greenfield Manor	103	D3
Greenfield Pk *Dublin 4*	103	D3
Greenfield Pk *Dublin 24*	125	C2
Greenfield Rd *Dublin 13*	58	B1
Greenfield Rd *Still.*	116	B2
Greenfort Av	84	A1
Greenfort Cl	84	B1
Greenfort Cres	84	B1
Greenfort Dr	84	A1
Greenfort Gdns	84	B1
Greenfort Lawns	84	B1
Greenfort Pk	84	A1
Greenhills Business Cen	110	B2
Greenhills Business Pk	110	B3
Greenhills Ind Est	99	C3
Greenhills Rd *Dublin 12*	98	B3
Greenhills Rd *Dublin 24*	110	B2
Green Isle Business Pk	108	A1
Green Isle Ct **1**	108	A1
Greenlands *Dublin 16*	129	D2
Greenlands, The		
Dublin 14	113	D2
Green La	68	A2
Greenlawns **1**	40	B3
Greenlea Av	112	B1
Greenlea Dr	112	B1
Greenlea Gro	112	B1
Greenlea Pk	112	B1
Greenlea Rd	112	B1
Greenmount Av	101	D1
Greenmount Ct		
off Greenmount Av	101	D1
Greenmount La	101	D1
Greenmount Lawns	113	C1
Greenmount Rd	101	D3
Greenmount Sq		
off Greenmount La	101	D1
Greenore Ter		
off Hogan Av	91	C2
Green Pk	114	A1
Greenridge Ct	47	C1
Green Rd *Black.*	117	C2
Green Rd, The *Dalkey*	135	C2
Green St	144	B1
Green St E	91	D2
Green St Little	144	B2
Greentrees Dr	111	D1
Greentrees Pk	99	D3
Greentrees Rd	99	D3
Greenview	26	A3
Greenville Av	89	D3
Greenville Rd	118	A3
Greenville Ter	89	D3
Greenwich Ct	102	A2
Greenwood Av	41	D3
Greenwood Cl	41	D3
Greenwood Ct	41	D3
Greenwood Dr	41	D3
Greenwood Lawn		
off Greenwood Dr	41	D3
Greenwood Pk **2**	41	D3
Greenwood Wk	41	D3
Greenwood Way	41	D3
Grenville La	78	A3
Grenville St	78	A3

Greygates	116	B2
Greyhound Racing		
Stadium	101	D1
Greys La	61	C3
Greystones Sta	143	D2
Greythorn Pk	133	D1
Griffeen	83	C2
Griffeen Av	82	B2
Griffeen Glen Av	82	B2
Griffeen Glen Boul	83	C2
Griffeen Glen Chase	82	B2
Griffeen Glen Ct	83	C2
Griffeen Glen Ct Yd	83	C2
Griffeen Glen Cres	82	B2
Griffeen Glen Dale	82	B2
Griffeen Glen Dene	82	B2
Griffeen Glen Dr	83	C2
Griffeen Glen Grn	82	B2
Griffeen Glen Gro	83	C2
Griffeen Glen Lawn	82	B2
Griffeen Glen Pk	82	B2
Griffeen Glen Rd (east)		
Lucan	83	C2
Griffeen Glen Rd (west)		
Lucan	82	B2
Griffeen Glen Vale	83	C2
Griffeen Glen Vw	82	B2
Griffeen Glen Way	83	C2
Griffeen Rd	83	C2
Griffeen Way	83	C1
Griffith Av *Dublin 9*	52	B3
Griffith Av *Dublin 11*	51	D3
Griffith Br	88	A3
Griffith Cl	51	C3
Griffith Ct	79	C1
Griffith Downs	52	B3
Griffith Dr	51	C2
Griffith Hts	51	C3
Griffith Lawns	52	A3
Griffith Par	51	C2
Griffith Rd	51	C2
Griffith Sq		
off Wesley Pl	89	D3
Griffith Sq S		
off South Circular Rd	89	C3
Griffith Wk	79	C1
Grosvenor Av	142	B2
Grosvenor Ct *Dublin 3*	80	B1
Grosvenor Ct *Dublin 6W*	112	A1
Grosvenor Lo	101	D2
Grosvenor Pk	101	D2
Grosvenor Pl	101	D2
Grosvenor Rd	101	D2
Grosvenor Sq	101	D1
Grosvenor Ter **5** *Dalkey*	135	C2
Grosvenor Ter *D.L.*	119	C3
Grosvenor Vil	101	D2
Grotto Av	117	C1
Grotto Pl	116	B1
Grove, The *Dublin 5*	56	A3
Grove, The *Dublin 9*	53	C3
Grove, The (Ballinteer)		
Dublin 16	128	B2
Grove, The (Meadow Mt)		
Dublin 16	128	A1
Grove, The *Dublin 24*	124	A1
Grove, The (Cookstown)		
Dublin 24	109	C2
Grove, The (Kilnamanagh)		
Dublin 24	109	C1
Grove, The *Celbr.*	66	B3
Grove, The (Abbeyfarm)		
Celbr.	66	A3
Grove, The (Dunboyne Castle)		
Dunb.	28	B3
Grove, The (Lutterell Hall)		
Dunb.	28	B1
Grove, The (Plunkett Hall)		
Dunb.	28	A1
Grove, The (Sadleir Hall)		
Dunb.	28	A2
Grove, The *Gra M.*	82	B2
Grove, The *Kins.*	18	A3
Grove, The *Lou.V.*	68	A1
Grove Av *Dublin 6*		
off Grove Rd	101	D1
Grove Av (Finglas)		
Dublin 11	51	C1
Grove Av *Black.*	117	C2
Grove Av *Mala.*	20	B2

Grove Ct **1**	16	A1
Grove Ho	136	B1
Grove Ho Gdns	117	C3
Grove Ind Est	36	B1
Grove La	41	D3
Grove Lawn *Black.*	117	C3
Grove Lawn *Mala.*	20	B2
Grove Pk *Dublin 6*	101	D1
Grove Pk *Dublin 13*	41	D3
Grove Pk Av	51	C1
Grove Pk Cres	51	D1
Grove Pk Dr	51	C1
Grove Pk Rd	51	C1
Grove Rd (Rathmines)		
Dublin 6	101	D1
Grove Rd (Finglas)		
Dublin 11	51	C1
Grove Rd (Blanchardstown)		
Dublin 15	46	B2
Grove Rd *Mala.*	20	A2
Grove Wd	51	C1
Guild St	91	C1
Guilford Ter	141	C2
Guinness Brewery	89	C2
Guinness Enterprise Cen	89	C2
Gulistan Cotts	102	A1
Gulistan Pl	102	A1
Gulistan Ter	102	A1
Gullivers Retail Pk	38	A2
Gurteen Av	86	A2
Gurteen Pk	86	A2
Gurteen Rd	86	A1

H

Hacketsland	141	C1
Haddington Lawns	134	A2
Haddington Pk **6**	134	A2
Haddington Pl	91	C3
Haddington Rd	91	C3
Haddinton Ter	119	D3
Haddon Pk		
off Seaview Av N	80	A2
Haddon Rd	80	A2
Hadleigh Ct	48	A3
Hadleigh Grn	48	A3
Hadleigh Pk	48	A3
Hagans Ct	90	B3
Haigh Ter	119	D3
Hainault Dr	137	C1
Hainault Gro	137	C1
Hainault Lawn	137	C1
Hainault Pk	136	B1
Halliday Rd	89	C1
Halliday Sq	89	C1
Halston St	144	B1
Hamilton Ct **1**	29	C2
Hamilton Hall	29	C3
Hamilton St	89	C3
Hammond La	144	A2
Hammond St	89	D3
Hampstead Av	52	A2
Hampstead Ct	52	A2
Hampstead Pk	52	A3
Hampton Ct	81	C1
Hampton Cres	116	B1
Hampton Grn	76	B2
Hampton Hermitage &		
Theresian Trust	79	C1
Hampton Pk	116	B2
Hampton Wd Av	37	C2
Hampton Wd Ct	37	C2
Hampton Wd Cres	37	C2
Hampton Wd Dr	37	C2
Hampton Wd Grn	37	C2
Hampton Wd Lawn	37	C2
Hampton Wd Pk	37	C2
Hampton Wd Rd	37	C2
Hampton Wd Sq	37	C2
Hampton Wd Way	37	C2
Hanbury La *Dublin 8*	144	A3
Hanbury La **2** *Lucan*	70	A3
Hannaville Pk	101	C3
Hanover La	144	B4
Hanover Quay	91	C2
Hanover Sq W		
off Hanover La	144	B4
Hanover St E	145	F3
Hanover St W		
off Carmans Hall	144	A4
Hansfield	31	C3
Hansfield Rd	30	B3

Hansted Cl **1**	82	A3
Hansted Cres	82	A3
Hansted Dale	82	A3
Hansted Pk	82	A3
Hansted Pl **2**	82	A3
Hansted Rd	82	A3
Hansted Way	82	A3
Ha'penny Br	145	D2
Harbour Ct		
off Marlborough St	145	D2
Harbour Cres	134	B2
Harbourmaster Pl	145	F1
Harbour Rd *Dublin 13*	60	B1
Harbour Rd *Dalkey*	134	B1
Harbour Rd *D.L.*	119	C2
Harbour Ter	119	C2
Harbour Vw		
off St. Lawrence Rd	61	C2
Harcourt Grn	90	A3
Harcourt La		
off Adelaide Rd	90	A3
Harcourt Rd	90	A3
Harcourt Sta	90	A3
Harcourt St	90	A3
Harcourt Ter	90	A3
Harcourt Ter La	90	B3
Hardbeck Av	99	C2
Hardiman Rd	78	A1
Hardwicke Pl	78	A3
Hardwicke St	78	A3
Harelawn Av	84	B2
Harelawn Cres	84	B2
Harelawn Dr	84	B1
Harelawn Grn	84	B2
Harelawn Gro	84	B1
Harelawn Pk	84	B2
Harlech Cres	115	D2
Harlech Downs	115	D2
Harlech Gro	115	D2
Harlech Vil	115	D2
Harman St	89	C3
Harmonstown Rd	55	C3
Harmonstown Sta	55	C3
Harmony Av	103	C2
Harmony Row	91	C2
Harold Rd	89	C1
Harolds Cross Rd	101	D1
Harold's Gra Rd	128	A3
Haroldville Av	89	C3
Harrington St	90	A3
Harrison Row	101	D3
Harry St	145	D4
Hartstown Rd	45	D1
Harty Av	99	D2
Harty Ct	99	D2
Harty Pl	89	D3
Harvard	115	D2
Hastings St	91	D2
Hastings Ter **17**	134	A1
Hatch La	90	A3
Hatch Pl		
off Hatch La	90	B3
Hatch St Lwr	90	A3
Hatch St Upr	90	A3
Havelock Pl		
off Bath Av	91	D3
Havelock Sq E	91	D3
Havelock Sq N	91	D3
Havelock Sq S	91	D3
Havelock Sq W	91	D3
Havelock Ter		
off Bath Av	91	D3
Haven, The *Dublin 9*	52	A3
Haven, The *Mala.*	19	D1
Haven Vw **2**	19	D1
Haverty Rd	79	D2
Hawkins La	143	D2
Hawkins St	145	E2
Hawthorn Av	79	C3
Hawthorn Dr	128	B1
Hawthorn Lawn	48	A3
Hawthorn Lo	48	A3
Hawthorn Manor **1**	117	D3
Hawthorn Pk	17	C2
Hawthorn Rd	97	D2
Hawthorns, The **15** *Abb.*	139	C3

181

182

Hawthorns, The *Ashb.* 11 C2
Hawthorns Rd 129 D2
Hawthorn Ter 79 C3
Hawthorn Vw 66 A1
Hayden's La 82 A2
Haydens Pk 82 B3
Haydens Pk Av 82 B3
Haydens Pk Cl 82 B2
Haydens Pk Dale 82 B3
Haydens Pk Dr 82 B3
Haydens Pk Glade 82 B3
Haydens Pk Grn 82 B3
Haydens Pk Gro 82 B3
Haydens Pk Lawn 82 B3
Haydens Pk Vw 82 B3
Haydens Pk Wk 82 B3
Haydens Pk Way 82 B3
Hayden Sq 116 A2
Haymarket 144 A2
Hayworth Dr 44 B1
Hayworth Ms 44 B1
Hayworth Ter 44 B1
Hazel Av 130 A1
Hazelbrook Ct 101 C3
Hazelbrook Dr 100 B3
Hazelbrook Pk 110 B2
Hazelbrook Rd 100 B3
Hazelbury Grn 31 C2
Hazelbury Pk 31 C3
Hazel Ct 6 26 B3
Hazelcroft Gdns 50 B2
Hazelcroft Pk 50 B2
Hazelcroft Rd 50 B2
Hazeldene 103 D2
Hazelgrove *Jobs.* 122 B2
Hazel Gro *Port.* 26 B3
Hazelgrove Ct 122 B2
Hazel Lawn (Blanchardstown)
   Dublin 15 47 C2
Hazel Lawn 5 *D.L.* 133 C2
Hazel Pk 100 B3
Hazel Rd 53 D3
Hazel Vil 130 A1
Hazelwood *D'bate* 13 C1
Hazelwood *Shank.* 141 C2
Hazelwood Av 45 D1
Hazelwood Cl 96 A3
Hazelwood Ct *Dublin 5* 54 A1
Hazelwood Ct *Clons.* 45 D1
Hazelwood Cres *Clond.* 96 A3
Hazelwood Cres *Clons.* 45 D1
Hazelwood Dr 54 A2
Hazelwood Grn 45 D1
Hazelwood Gro 54 A2
Hazelwood La 96 A3
Hazelwood Pk 54 A2
Hazelwood Vw 96 A3
Headford Gro 114 A3
Healthfield Rd 101 D3
Healy St
   off Rutland Pl N 78 B3
Heaney Av 85 D3
Heany Av 135 C2
Heath, The *Dublin 6W* 112 A2
Heath, The *Dublin 24* 109 C2
Heath Cres 75 D1
Heather Cl 128 A2
Heather Dr 128 A2
Heather Gdns 27 D1
Heather Gro *Dublin 16* 128 A2
Heather Gro *Palm.* 85 C1
Heather Lawn 128 A2
Heather Pk 128 A2
Heather Rd *Dublin 16* 128 A2
Heather Rd *Sandy.* 130 A3
Heather Vw Av 123 D2
Heather Vw Cl 123 D2
Heather Vw Dr 123 D2
Heather Vw Lawn 123 D2
Heather Vw Pk 123 D2
Heather Vw Rd 123 D2
Heathervue 143 C2
Heather Wk 27 D1
Heathfield 118 B3
Heath Gro 76 A3
Hedgerows, The 131 D3

Heidelberg 115 D2
Heights, The *Dublin 16* 128 B3
Heights, The *Dunb.* 28 B3
Heights, The *Kins.* 18 A3
Heights, The *Mala.* 20 B3
Hellers Copse 117 C3
Hendrick La
   off Benburb St 89 C1
Hendrick Pl 89 C1
Hendrick St 89 C1
Henley Ct 114 B2
Henley Pk 114 B2
Henley Vil 114 B2
Henrietta La 77 D3
Henrietta Pl 144 B1
Henrietta St 144 B1
Henry Pl 145 D1
Henry Rd 86 A3
Henry St 144 C1
Herbert Av 104 B3
Herbert Cotts 103 D1
Herbert Hill 129 C1
Herbert La 91 C3
Herberton Dr 88 B3
Herberton Pk 88 B3
Herberton Rd *Dublin 8* 88 B3
Herberton Rd *Dublin 12* 88 B3
Herbert Pk 91 C3
Herbert Pl 91 C3
Herbert Rd *Dublin 4* 91 C3
Herbert Rd (Blanchardstown)
   Dublin 15 47 D2
Herbert St 90 B3
Hermitage Av 127 D1
Hermitage Cl 127 D1
Hermitage Cres 127 D1
Hermitage Downs 127 D1
Hermitage Dr 127 D1
Hermitage Gdn 71 D3
Hermitage Grn 71 D3
Hermitage Gro 127 D1
Hermitage Lawn 127 D1
Hermitage Manor 71 D3
Hermitage Pk
   Dublin 16 127 D1
Hermitage Pk *Lucan* 71 D3
Hermitage Pl 71 D3
Hermitage Rd 71 D3
Hermitage Valley 71 D3
Hermitage Vw 127 D1
Hermitage Way 71 D3
Heuston Luas Sta 89 C1
Heuston Sta 88 B1
Hewardine Ter
   off Killarney St 78 B3
Heytesbury La 103 C1
Heytesbury Pl
   off Long La 89 D3
Heytesbury St 90 A3
Hibernian Av 79 C3
Hibernian Ind Est 110 A3
Highfield Av 127 D2
Highfield Cl 17 C1
Highfield Ct 101 D3
Highfield Cres 17 C1
Highfield Downs 17 C1
Highfield Dr 127 D2
Highfield Grn 17 C1
Highfield Gro 102 A3
Highfield Lawn 17 C1
Highfield Pk *Dublin 14* 114 B2
Highfield Pk *Leix.* 68 A3
Highfield Rd 101 D3
Highland Av 137 C1
Highland Gro 137 C1
Highland Lawn 137 C1
Highland Vw 137 C1
High Pk 53 C3
Highridge Grn 130 A1
High St *Dublin 8* 144 B3
High St *Dublin 24* 109 D3
Highthorn Pk 133 C1
Highthorn Wds 3 133 C1
Hill, The *Dublin 16* 128 B3
Hill, The *Black.* 119 C3
Hill, The *Mala.* 20 A3
Hill, The 6 *Mulh.* 32 A3
Hill, The *Still.* 117 C3
Hillbrook Wds 46 A1
Hill Cotts 1 139 D1
Hill Ct 27 C1

Hillcourt Pk 133 D2
Hillcourt Rd 133 D2
Hillcrest *Dublin 6W* 112 A3
Hillcrest *Lucan* 82 A1
Hillcrest (Mooretown) 1
   Swords 19 C1
Hillcrest Av 82 A1
Hillcrest Ct 82 A1
Hillcrest Dr 82 A1
Hillcrest Grn 82 A1
Hillcrest Gro 82 A1
Hillcrest Hts 82 A1
Hillcrest Lawns 82 A1
Hillcrest Pk *Dublin 11* 51 D1
Hillcrest Pk *Lucan* 82 A1
Hillcrest Rd 82 A1
Hillcrest Vw 82 A1
Hillcrest Wk 82 A1
Hillcrest Way 82 A1
Hill Dr 20 A3
Hillsbrook Av 99 D3
Hillsbrook Cres 99 D3
Hillsbrook Dr 100 A3
Hillsbrook Gro 99 D3
Hillside *Dalkey* 134 B2
Hillside *Grey.* 143 C1
Hillside Dr 113 D2
Hillside Pk 126 B1
Hillside Rd 143 D2
Hillside Vw 57 C2
Hills Ind Est 70 B2
Hill St 78 A3
Hilltop Lawn 140 B3
Hilltop Shop Cen 55 D2
Hilltown Cl 16 B1
Hilltown Ct 4 16 B1
Hilltown Grn 5 16 B1
Hilltown Gro 16 B1
Hilltown Lawn 16 B1
Hilltown Pk 16 B1
Hilltown Rd 16 B1
Hilltown Way 16 B1
Hill Vw 128 A1
Hillview Cotts 3 132 B3
Hillview Dr 132 B3
Hillview Glade 2 128 A1
Hillview Gro 128 A1
Hillview Lawn 132 B3
Hilton Gdns 128 B2
Hoeys Ct
   off Castle St 144 B3
Hogan Av 91 C2
Hogan Pl 91 C2
Hole In The Wall Rd,
   The 42 A2
Holles Row 145 F4
Holles St 145 F4
Hollows, The 7 70 A3
Holly Av 130 A2
Hollybank Av 102 B2
Hollybank Rd 78 A1
Hollybrook Ct
   off Hollybrook Rd 80 A2
Hollybrook Ct Dr 80 A2
Hollybrook Gro 79 D2
Hollybrook Pk 80 A2
Hollybrook Rd 80 A2
Holly Ct 138 B3
Holly Pk 141 C2
Holly Pk Av 131 D1
Holly Rd *Dublin 9* 79 D1
Holly Rd *Dublin 12* 97 D2
Hollyville Lawn 73 C3
Hollywell 37 C3
Hollywood Dr 115 D2
Hollywood Pk 115 D3
Holmston Av 133 D1
Holmwood 137 D2
Holycross Av 78 B2
Holy Cross Coll 78 B2
Holyrood Pk
   off Sandymount Av 104 A1
Holywell *Dublin 14* 129 D1
Holywell *Swords* 17 D3
Holywell Av *Dublin 13* 56 A1
Holywell Av *Swords* 17 D2
Holywell Cl 18 A3
Holywell Ct 1 17 D2
Holywell Cres *Dublin 13* 56 A1
Holywell Cres *Swords* 17 D2
Holywell Dr 17 D2
Holywell Gdns 17 D2

Holywell Glen 18 A3
Holywell Gro 18 A3
Holywell Heath 17 D3
Holywell Pk 17 D3
Holywell Pl 2 17 D3
Holywell Ri 17 D3
Holywell Rd *Dublin 13* 56 A1
Holywell Rd *Swords* 17 D3
Holywell Row 17 D3
Holywell Sq 18 A2
Holywell Vw 18 A3
Holywell Wk 17 D3
Holywell Way 18 A3
Holywell Wd 17 D3
Home Fm Pk 78 B1
Home Fm Rd 52 A3
Homelawn Av 124 B1
Homelawn Dr 124 B1
Homelawn Gdns 124 B1
Homelawn Rd 124 B1
Homelawn Vil 124 A1
Homeleigh 72 B1
Homeville *Dublin 6* 102 A2
Homeville, The 1
   Dublin 24 125 C1
Homeville Ct 4 125 C1
Honey Pk 8 133 C2
Hope Av 79 C3
Hope St 91 C2
Hopkins Sq 116 A2
Horseman's Row
   off Parnell St 78 A3
Horton Ct 113 C1
Hospital Sta 109 C3
Hotel Yd 144 C2
House of Retreat 87 D3
House of St. John
   of God 131 C1
Howard St 91 C2
Howth Castle 59 D2
Howth Golf Course 59 D3
Howth Junct 56 B1
Howth Rd *Dublin 3* 79 D2
Howth Rd *Dublin 5* 55 C3
Howth Rd (Howth)
   Dublin 13 59 D1
Howth Sta 60 B1
Howth Vw Pk 56 A1
H.S. Reilly Br 50 A3
Huband Br 91 C3
Huband Rd 99 C1
Hudson Rd 134 A1
Hughes Rd E 99 D2
Hughes Rd N 99 D2
Hughes Rd S 99 D2
Hume Av 97 D1
Hume Cen 86 A3
Hume St 90 B3
Hunters Av 125 C3
Hunters Ct 125 C3
Hunters Cres 125 C3
Hunters Grn 125 C3
Hunters Gro 125 C3
Hunters Hill 125 C3
Hunters La *Dublin 24* 125 C3
Hunters La *Ashb.* 11 C2
Hunters Meadow 125 C3
Hunters Par 125 C3
Hunters Pl 125 C3
Hunters Rd 125 C3
Hunter's Run 31 D2
Hunter's Run The Cl 31 D2
Hunter's Run The Dr 31 D2
Hunter's Run The Glade 31 D2
Hunter's Run The Gro 31 C2
Hunter's Run The Pk 31 D2
Hunter's Run The Ri 31 D3
Hunter's Run The Vw 31 D2
Hunter's Run The Way 31 D3
Hunters Wk 125 C3
Hunters Way 125 C3
Huntsgrove 11 C2
Huntstown Av 31 D3
Huntstown Cl 32 A3
Huntstown Ct 31 D3
Huntstown Dr 31 D3
Huntstown Glen 31 D3
Huntstown Grn 32 A3
Huntstown Gro 32 A3
Huntstown Lawn 32 A3
Huntstown Pk 32 A3

Huntstown Ri 32 A3
Huntstown Rd 32 A3
Huntstown Way 32 A3
Huntstown Wk 31 D3
Huxley Cres 89 C3
Hyacinth St 79 C3
Hyde Pk *Dublin 6W* 112 B2
Hyde Pk *D.L.* 134 B1
Hyde Pk Av 117 C2
Hyde Pk Gdns 117 C2
Hyde Rd 134 B1
Hyde Sq 116 A2

I

I.D.A. Ind Cen 77 C2
I.D.A. Small Ind Cen 39 D3
Idrone Av 125 D1
Idrone Cl 126 A1
Idrone Dr 125 D1
Idrone Pk 125 D1
Idrone Ter 117 D2
ILAC Cen 144 C1
Imaal Rd 77 C2
Inagh Ct 139 C3
Inagh Rd 86 A2
Inbhir Ide 19 D2
Inbhir Ide Cl 19 D1
Inbhir Ide Dr 19 D1
Inchicore Par 87 D2
Inchicore Rd 88 A2
Inchicore Sq 87 D2
Inchicore Ter N 87 D2
Inchicore Ter S 87 D2
Infirmary Rd 88 B1
Inglewood 45 D1
Inglewood Cl 45 D1
Inglewood Cres 45 D1
Inglewood Dr 46 A1
Inglewood Rd 46 A1
Ingram Rd 89 D3
Inis Fail 123 D2
Innisfallen Par 78 A2
Innishmaan Rd 52 B2
Innismore 99 D2
Inns Quay 144 B2
Invermore Gro
　off Carraroe Av 56 A1
Inverness Rd 79 C2
Inver Rd 76 B2
Iona Cres 78 A1
Iona Dr 78 A2
Iona Pk 78 A2
Iona Rd 77 D2
Iona Vil 78 A1
Iris Gro 116 A2
Inishtown Rd 91 D2
Irvine Cres
　off Church Rd 91 C1
Irvine Ter 91 C1
Irwin Ct 88 B2
Irwin St 88 B2
Island St 89 C1
Island Vw *Dublin 5* 57 C2
Island Vw *Mala.* 20 B2
Island Vil
　off Hogan Av 91 C1
Isolda Rd 92 A2
Ivar St 89 C1
Iveagh Bldgs
　off Kevin St Upr 89 D3
Iveagh Gdns 100 A1
Iveleary Rd 52 B2
Iveragh Ct 91 C1
Iveragh Rd 52 B2

J

James Connolly Pk 96 B1
James Connolly Sq 142 A1
James Joyce Ct 57 C2
James Larkin Rd
　Dublin 3 105 C1
James Larkin Rd
　Dublin 5 56 A3
James McCormack Gdns 58 A1
James Pl E 90 B3
James's Gate
　off James's St 88 B2
James's Sta 88 B2
James's St 88 B2
James's St E 90 B3
James's Ter **6** 20 A2
James St N 79 C3

Jamestown Av 87 C3
Jamestown Business Pk 50 B1
Jamestown Ind Est 87 C3
Jamestown Rd (Inchicore)
　Dublin 8 87 C3
Jamestown Rd (Finglas)
　Dublin 11 50 B1
Jamestown Sq 87 C3
Janelle Shop Cen 50 B2
Jane Ville
　off Tivoli Rd 119 C3
Jerome Connor Pl
　off Sullivan St 88 B1
Jervis La Lwr 144 C2
Jervis La Upr 144 C1
Jervis Sta 144 C2
Jervis St 144 C1
Jetty Rd 92 B1
Jobstown Rd 122 A2
John Dillon St 144 B4
John F. Kennedy Av 98 A1
John F. Kennedy Dr 98 B1
John F. Kennedy Ind Est 98 A1
John F. Kennedy Pk 98 A1
John F. Kennedy Rd 98 A1
John McCormack Av 99 D2
Johnsbridge 82 B2
Johnsbridge Av 82 B2
Johnsbridge Cl 82 B2
Johnsbridge Grn 82 B2
Johnsbridge Gro 82 B2
Johnsbridge Meadows 82 B2
Johnsbridge Pk 82 B2
Johnsbridge Wk 82 B2
Johns La W 144 A3
Johnsons Ct
　off Grafton St 145 D4
Johnsons Pl
　off William St S 145 D4
Johnstown Av 133 C3
Johnstown Ct 133 C3
Johnstown Gro 133 C3
Johnstown La 133 C3
Johnstown Pk
　Dublin 11 51 D2
Johnstown Pk *Corn.* 133 C3
Johnstown Rd 138 A1
John St S 89 C2
John St W 144 A3
Jones's Rd 78 B2
Jones Ter **15** 142 B2
Josephine Av
　off Leo St 78 A3
Joshua La
　off Dawson St 145 D4
Joyce Av 136 B1
Joyce Rd 78 A1
Joyce Way 97 D1
Joy St *off Barrow St* 91 C2
Jugback Cl 15 C2
Jugback Cres 15 C3
Jugback Grn 15 C2
Jugback La 15 C2

K

KCR Ind Est 100 B3
Keadeen Av 110 B1
Kearns Pl 88 B2
Keeper Rd 88 B3
Kells Rd 100 B2
Kelly's Av 119 C3
Kelly's La 64 B2
Kellys Row 78 A3
Kellystown Rd 128 A3
Kelston Av 131 D2
Kelston Dr 131 D2
Kelston Hall **9** 131 D2
Kelston Pk 131 C2
Kelston Vw **10** 131 D2
Kelvin Cl 27 C1
Kempton Av 75 D1
Kempton Ct 75 D1
Kempton Grn 75 C1
Kempton Gro 75 D1
Kempton Heath 75 D1
Kempton Lawn 75 D1
Kempton Pk 75 D1
Kempton Ri 75 D1
Kempton Vw 75 D1
Kempton Way 75 D1
Kenah Hill 139 C1
Kenilworth La 101 D2

Kenilworth Pk 101 C2
Kenilworth Rd 101 D2
Kenilworth Sq E 101 D2
Kenilworth Sq N 101 D2
Kenilworth Sq S 101 D2
Kenilworth Sq W 101 D2
Kenmare Par
　off Killarney Par 78 A2
Kennedy Pk **2** 142 A3
Kennelsfort Grn 85 C1
Kennelsfort Rd 85 C1
Kennelsfort Rd Lwr 73 D3
Kennelsfort Rd Upr 85 C1
Kennington Cl 111 C2
Kennington Cres 111 C2
Kennington Lawn 111 D2
Kennington Rd 111 C2
Kentfield 140 B1
Keogh Sq 87 D2
Kerlogue Rd 92 A2
Kerrymount Av 136 B1
Kerrymount Cl **1** 137 C1
Kerrymount Grn 137 C1
Kerrymount Mall 137 C1
Kerrymount Ri 137 C1
Kettles La 17 D3
Kevanagh Av 86 A3
Kevin St Lwr 90 A3
Kevin St Upr 144 B4
Kew Pk 69 D3
Kew Pk Av 69 D3
Kew Pk Cres 69 D3
Kickam Rd 88 A2
Kilakea Cl
　off Tibradden Dr 110 B1
Kilakea Dr
　off Tibradden Dr 110 B1
Kilbarrack Av 56 B2
Kilbarrack Gdns 57 C2
Kilbarrack Gro 56 B2
Kilbarrack Ind Est 56 B1
Kilbarrack Par 56 B1
Kilbarrack Rd 56 A1
Kilbarrack Shop Cen 56 A1
Kilbarrack Sta 56 A2
Kilbarrack Way 56 B1
Kilbarron Av 53 D1
Kilbarron Dr 53 D1
Kilbarron Pk 53 D1
Kilbarron Rd 53 D1
Kilbegnet Cl 134 B2
Kilbogget Gro 138 A2
Kilbogget Vil **1** 138 A1
Kilbride Rd 80 B1
Kilbrina 28 B2
Kilcarberry Av 95 D2
Kilcarberry Cl 95 D2
Kilcarberry Ct 95 D2
Kilcarberry Ind Est 94 B2
Kilcarberry Ind Pk 95 C2
Kilcarberry Lawn 95 D2
Kilcarrig Av 108 B3
Kilcarrig Cl 108 B3
Kilcarrig Cres 108 B3
Kilcarrig Grn 108 B3
Kilclare Av 122 B1
Kilclare Cres 122 B1
Kilclare Dr 122 B1
Kilclare Gdns 122 B1
Kilcock Maynooth
　Leixlip Bypass 68 A3
Kilcock Rd 64 A2
Kilcolman Ct **7** 134 A2
Kilcronan Av 95 C1
Kilcronan Cl 95 C1
Kilcronan Ct 95 C1
Kilcronan Cres 95 C1
Kilcronan Gro 95 C1
Kilcronan Lawns **1** 95 C1
Kilcronan Vw 95 C1
Kilcross Av 129 D3
Kilcross Cl **2** 129 D3
Kilcross Ct 129 D3
Kilcross Cres 129 D3
Kilcross Dr 129 D3
Kilcross Gro 129 D3
Kilcross Lawn 129 D3
Kilcross Pk 129 D3
Kilcross Rd 129 D3
Kilcross Sq 129 D3
Kilcross Way **1** 129 D3
Kildare Br 65 D1

Kildare Pk 100 A1
Kildare Rd 100 B1
Kildare St 145 E4
Kilderry Hall 10 B2
Kildonan Av 50 A1
Kildonan Dr 50 A1
Kildonan Rd 50 A1
Kilfenora Dr 42 A3
Kilfenora Rd 100 B2
Kilgobbin Rd 130 A3
Kilkieran Ct 76 B1
Kilkieran Rd 76 B1
Kill Abbey 132 A1
Killakee Av 124 B2
Killakee Ct 124 B2
Killakee Gdns 124 B2
Killakee Grn 124 B2
Killakee Gro 124 B2
Killakee Lawns 124 B2
Killakee Pk 124 B2
Killakee Ri 124 B2
Killakee Vw 124 B2
Killakee Wk 124 B2
Killakee Way 124 B2
Killala Rd 76 B2
Killan Rd 91 C1
Killarney Av 78 B3
Killarney Par 78 A2
Killarney St 78 B3
Killarney Vil **5** 142 A2
Killary Gro
　off Ardara Av 56 A1
Kill Av 132 B1
Killeen 19 C2
Killeen Av 19 C2
Killeen Ct **2** 19 C2
Killeen Cres 19 C2
Killeen Ms 20 A2
Killeen Pk 19 C2
Killeen Rd *Dublin 6* 102 A2
Killeen Rd *Dublin 10* 98 A1
Killeen Rd *Dublin 12* 98 A1
Killeen Ter 20 A2
Killegland Ct 10 B2
Killegland Pk 10 B2
Killegland Ri 11 C3
Killegland Rd 11 C3
Killester Av 80 B1
Killester Ct 54 B3
Killester Pk 54 B3
Killester Sta 80 B1
Killinarden Est 122 B2
Killinarden Hts 123 C2
Killinarden Rd 122 B3
Killinardin Enterprise Pk 123 C2
Killincarrick Rd 143 C2
Killincarrig Manor 143 C2
Killiney Av 139 C2
Killiney Cen 133 C3
Killiney Ct **5** 139 C2
Killiney Gate 139 C2
Killiney Gro 134 A3
Killiney Heath 139 C2
Killiney Hill Pk 134 B3
Killiney Hill Rd 139 C1
Killiney Oaks **6** 139 C3
Killiney Rd 134 A2
Killiney Sta 139 D2
Killiney Ter **2** 134 B1
Killiney Twrs **8** 134 A2
Killiney Vw 134 A1
Killininy Cotts 124 B2
Killininy Ct Apts **1** 124 B2
Killininy Rd 124 B2
Kill La 132 A2
Kilmacud Av 130 A1
Kilmacud Rd 116 A3
Kilmacud Rd Upr
　Dublin 14 115 D3
Kilmacud Rd Upr *Still.* 130 A1
Kilmacud Sta 129 D1
Kilmahuddrick Av 95 C1
Kilmahuddrick Cl 95 C1
Kilmahuddrick Cres 95 C1
Kilmahuddrick Dr 95 C1

Kilmahuddrick Grn 95 C1
Kilmahuddrick Gro 95 C1
Kilmahuddrick Lawn 95 C1
Kilmahuddrick Pl 95 C1
Kilmahuddrick Rd 95 C1
Kilmahuddrick Wk 95 C1
Kilmahuddrick Way 95 C1
Kilmainham Br 88 A2
Kilmainham La 88 A2
Kilmantain Pl 6 142 A2
Kilmartin Av 108 A3
Kilmartin Cres 108 B3
Kilmartin Dr 108 A3
Kilmartin Gdns 108 A3
Kilmartin Pk 108 A3
Kilmashogue Br 127 D3
Kilmashogue Cl
  off Kilmashogue Dr 110 B1
Kilmashogue Dr 110 B1
Kilmashogue Gro 110 B1
Kilmore Av Dublin 5 54 A1
Kilmore Av Kill. 139 C2
Kilmore Cl 54 A1
Kilmore Cres 54 A1
Kilmore Dr 54 A1
Kilmore Rd 54 A2
Kilmorony Cl 56 A1
Kilnamanagh Rd 99 C2
Kilnamarragh
  Shop Cen 110 A2
Kilohan Gro 111 C1
Kilrock Rd 61 C2
Kilshane Rd Dublin 11 49 D2
Kilshane Rd Kilsh. 34 B1
Kiltalown Av 122 A2
Kiltalown Cl 122 A2
Kiltalown Ct 122 A2
Kiltalown Cres 122 A2
Kiltalown Dr 122 A2
Kiltalown Grn 122 A2
Kiltalown Gro 122 A2
Kiltalown Hts 122 A2
Kiltalown Pk 122 A2
Kiltalown Rd 122 A2
Kiltalown Vw 122 A2
Kiltalown Wk 122 A2
Kiltalown Way 122 A2
Kilteragh Dr 136 B1
Kilteragh Pines 3 131 D3
Kilteragh Rd 137 C1
Kiltipper Av 124 A2
Kiltipper Cl 124 A2
Kiltipper Dr 124 A2
Kiltipper Gate 3 123 D3
Kiltipper Ri 1 123 D3
Kiltipper Rd 123 D3
Kiltipper Vw 2 123 D3
Kiltipper Way 123 D2
Kiltuck Pk 2 141 C3
Kilvere 112 B2
Kilworth Rd 87 D3
Kimberley Rd 143 D1
Kimmage Ct 100 B3
Kimmage Gro 101 C3
Kimmage Manor Way 112 A1
Kimmage Rd Lwr 101 C2
Kimmage Rd W 100 A3
Kinahan St 88 B1
Kincora Av 80 A2
Kincora Ct 81 C2
Kincora Dr 80 B2
Kincora Gro 80 B2
Kincora Pk 80 B2
Kincora Rd 80 B2
Kindlestown Lwr 143 C1
Kindlestown Pk 143 C1
King Edward Ct 7 142 A2
Kingram La 90 B3
Kings Av 79 C3
Kingsbury 64 B3
Kings Hall Dublin 20 86 B1
Kings Hall 2 Swords 18 A2
Kings Inns St 144 C1
Kingsland Par 102 A1
Kingsland Pk Av 90 A3
Kingsmill Rd 142 B1

Kingston 128 B3
Kingston Av 128 B3
Kingston Cl 128 B3
Kingston Ct 127 C1
Kingston Cres 128 B3
Kingston Dr 128 B3
Kingston Grn 128 B3
Kingston Gro 128 B3
Kingston Hall 128 B3
Kingston Hts 128 B3
Kingston Lawn 128 B3
Kingston Pk 128 B3
Kingston Ri 128 B3
Kingston Vw 128 B3
Kingston Wk 128 B3
King St N 144 B1
King St S 145 D4
Kingswood Av
  Dublin 24 109 D1
Kingswood Av City W 107 C3
Kingswood Castle 97 D3
Kingswood Dr
  Dublin 24 109 D1
Kingswood Dr Kings. 107 D3
Kingswood Rd 107 D3
Kingswood Sta 110 A1
Kingswood Vw 109 C1
Kinlen Rd 143 D2
Kinsaley Br 25 D2
Kinsaley Business Pk 25 D2
Kinsaley La 25 D2
Kinsaley Research Cen 25 C3
Kinsealy Ct 18 B2
Kinsealy Downs 18 A3
Kinvara Av 75 D1
Kinvara Dr 75 D1
Kinvara Gro 75 D1
Kinvara Pk 75 D1
Kinvara Rd 75 D1
Kippure Av 110 B1
Kippure Pk 50 A3
Kirkfield 1 46 A2
Kirkpatrick Av 46 B3
Kirkpatrick Dr 46 B3
Kirkwood 104 A1
Kirwan St 89 C1
Kirwan St Cotts
  off Kirwan St 77 C3
Kitestown Rd 61 C3
Knapton Cl
  off Vesey Pl 119 C3
Knapton Lawn 119 C3
Knapton Rd 119 C3
Knights Br 80 B2
Knights Wd 39 C2
Knockaire 126 A1
Knockaulin 68 A2
Knockcullen 112 A3
Knockcullen Dr 112 A3
Knockcullen Lawn 112 A3
Knockcullen Pk 112 A3
Knockcullen Ri 126 A1
Knockdara 20 B3
Knockfield Grn 125 D1
Knockfield Manor 125 D1
Knocklyon Av 111 D3
Knocklyon Cl 125 D1
Knocklyon Ct 125 D1
Knocklyon Cres 125 C2
Knocklyon Dr 112 A3
Knocklyon Gate Apts 1 125 C2
Knocklyon Grn 125 D1
Knocklyon Gro 125 D1
Knocklyon Hts 125 D1
Knocklyon Hill 125 C2
Knocklyon Ms 111 D3
Knocklyon Pk 125 D1
Knocklyon Rd 126 A1
Knockmaroon Hill 74 A3
Knockmaroon Rd 74 A3
Knockmeenagh La 97 C3
Knockmeenagh Rd 96 B3
Knockmitten Cl 97 D1
Knockmitten La 97 D1
Knockmitten La N 97 D1
Knockmore Av 122 B2
Knockmore Cres 122 B2
Knockmore Dr 122 B2
Knockmore Gdns 122 B2
Knockmore Grn 122 B2
Knockmore Gro 122 B2
Knockmore Pk 122 B2

Knock-na-Cree Gro 135 C3
Knock-na-Cree Pk 134 B2
Knock-na-Cree Rd 134 B3
Knocknarea Av 100 A1
Knocknarea Rd 99 D1
Knocknashee 115 D3
Knock Riada 86 B1
Knocksinna 131 D2
Knocksinna Ct 8 131 D2
Knocksinna Cres 131 D2
Knocksinna Gro 4 131 D2
Knocksinna Pk 131 D2
Knowth Ct 37 D3
Kor Dev Pk 98 B1
Kyber Rd 75 D3
Kyle-Clare Rd 92 A2
Kylemore Av 86 A3
Kylemore Dr 86 B3
Kylemore Pk Ind Est 86 B3
Kylemore Pk N 86 A3
Kylemore Pk S 86 B3
Kylemore Pk W 86 B3
Kylemore Rd Dublin 10 86 B2
Kylemore Rd Dublin 12 86 B2
Kylemore Rd Dublin 20 86 A1
Kylemore Sta 98 B1

L

Labre Pk 86 B3
Laburnum Rd 103 C3
Laburnum Wk 73 C3
Lad La 90 B3
Lady's Well Rd 32 B2
Lagan Rd 50 B3
Lake Dr 107 D3
Lakelands, The 113 C2
Lakelands Av 130 A1
Lakelands Cl 130 A1
Lakelands Cres 130 A1
Lakelands Gro 130 A1
Lakelands Lawn 130 A1
Lakelands Pk 113 C1
Lakelands Rd 130 A1
Lakeshore Dr 17 D2
Lakeview Dr 17 D2
Lally Rd 87 C2
Lambay Cl 139 C3
Lambay Ct 21 C2
Lambay Dr 139 C3
Lambay Rd 52 A3
Lambourne Av 45 D2
Lambourne Ct 45 D2
Lambourne Dr 45 D2
Lambourne Pk Clons. 45 D2
Lambourne Pk D'bate 13 D1
Lambourne Rd 45 D2
Lambourne Village 80 B2
Lambourne Wd 137 D2
Lambs Ct
  off James's St 88 B2
Landen Rd 86 B3
Landscape Av 114 A2
Landscape Cres 114 A2
Landscape Gdns 114 A2
Landscape Pk 114 A2
Landscape Rd 114 A2
Landys Ind Est 112 A3
Lanesborough Av 36 B2
Lanesborough Ct 37 C2
Lanesborough Gdns 36 B2
Lanesborough Gro 37 C2
Lanesborough Pk 36 B3
Lanesborough Rd 36 B2
Lanesborough Ter 36 B2
Lanesborough Vw 36 B3
Lanesville 132 B1
Langrishe Pl
  off Summerhill 78 B3
Lanndale Lawns 109 C3
Lansdowne Gdns
  off Shelbourne Rd 91 D3
Lansdowne Hall
  off Tritonville Rd 91 D3
Lansdowne La 91 D3
Lansdowne Pk
  Dublin 4 91 C3
Lansdowne Pk
  Dublin 16 112 A3
Lansdowne Rd 91 C3
Lansdowne Rd Stadium 91 D3
Lansdowne Rd Sta 91 D3

Lansdowne Ter
  off Shelbourne Rd 91 D3
Lansdowne Valley Apts 99 C1
Lansdowne Valley Cres
  off Kilworth Rd 99 D1
Lansdowne Village 87 D3
Lansdown Valley Pk 87 D3
Laracor Gdns 56 A1
Laragh 139 C2
Laragh Cl 56 A1
Laraghcon 70 A2
Laragh Gro
  off Laragh Cl 56 A1
Larch Dr 4 126 B2
Larchfield Dublin 14 114 B2
Larchfield Dunb. 29 C3
Larchfield Pk 115 C2
Larchfield Rd 115 C2
Larch Gro 102 B2
Larkfield 71 D3
Larkfield Av Dublin 6W 101 C3
Larkfield Av Lucan 83 D1
Larkfield Cl 71 D3
Larkfield Ct 83 D1
Larkfield Gdns 101 C2
Larkfield Grn 71 D3
Larkfield Gro
  Dublin 6W 101 C3
Larkfield Gro (Ballyowen)
  Lucan 71 D3
Larkfield Ms 66 B2
Larkfield Pk 101 C2
Larkfield Pl 83 D1
Larkfield Ri 83 D1
Larkfield Vw 83 D1
Larkfield Way 71 D3
Larkhill Rd 52 A2
Latchford Cl 30 B3
Latchford Grn 31 C3
Latchford Pk 31 C3
Latchford Sq 31 C3
Latchford Ter 31 C3
La Touche Av 143 D1
La Touche Ct 128 A2
La Touche Dr 87 C3
La Touche Pk 143 C1
La Touche Pl 143 D1
La Touche Rd Dublin 12 99 C1
La Touche Rd Grey. 143 D1
Lauderdale Est 142 A3
Lauderdale Ter 3 142 A3
Lauders La 58 B1
Laundry La 101 C2
Laurel Av Dublin 14 114 B3
Laurel Av Lough. 138 B3
Laurel Ct 47 C3
Laurel Dr 114 B3
Laurel Hill 133 D1
Laurel Lo Rd 47 D3
Laurel Pk 96 B2
Laurel Rd 114 B3
Laurels, The Dublin 6W 101 C3
Laurels, The Dublin 14 114 B3
Laurelton Dublin 6 113 D1
Laurelton Swords 14 B2
Laurence Brook 86 B1
Laurleen 131 C2
Lavarna Gro 112 B1
Lavarna Rd 100 B3
Laverna Av 47 C3
Laverna Dale 47 C3
Laverna Gro 47 C3
Laverna Way 73 C1
Lavery Av 85 D3
Lavista Av (Killester)
  Dublin 5 80 B1
La Vista Av Dublin 13 59 C3
Lawn, The Dublin 11 50 B1
Lawn, The (Ballinteer)
  Dublin 16 128 B2
Lawn, The (Ballyboden)
  Dublin 16 126 A1
Lawn, The (Cookstown)
  Dublin 24 109 C2
Lawn, The Celbr. 66 A2
Lawn, The Dunb. 28 A1
Lawn, The Kins. 18 A2
Lawn, The Mayn. 64 A1
Lawns, The
  (Abbeyfarm) 66 A3
Lawnswood Pk 131 C1
Lawrence's Av 65 C3

Name	Page	Grid
Lawson Spinney	19	C2
Lawson Ter **18**	134	A1
Lea Cres	104	A1
Leahys Ter	92	A3
Lealand Av	95	D2
Lealand Cl	95	D2
Lealand Cres	95	D2
Lealand Dr	95	D2
Lealand Gdns	95	D2
Lealand Gro	95	D2
Lealand Rd	95	D1
Lealand Wk	95	D2
Lea Rd	104	A1
Le Bas Ter		
off Leinster Rd W	101	D2
Le Broquay Av	86	A3
Lee Rd	77	C1
Leeson Cl	90	B3
Leeson La	90	B3
Leeson Pk	102	B1
Leeson Pk Av	102	B1
Leeson Pl	90	B3
Leeson St Br	90	B3
Leeson St Lwr	90	B3
Leeson St Upr	90	B3
Leeson Village	102	B1
Le Fanu Av	86	A3
Le Fanu Rd	86	A2
Lehaunstown Rd	137	D3
Leicester Av	101	D2
Leighlin Rd	100	B2
Lein Gdns		
(Gardini Lein)	55	D3
Lein Pk	55	C2
Lein Rd	55	C2
Leinster Av	79	C3
Leinster Ct	65	C1
Leinster La		
off Leinster St S	145	E4
Leinster Lawn	115	C1
Leinster Lo Apts **1**	65	C1
Leinster Mkt		
off D'Olier St	145	D2
Leinster Pk	65	C2
Leinster Pl	101	D2
Leinster Rd	101	D2
Leinster Rd W	101	D2
Leinster Sq	102	A2
Leinster St	64	B2
Leinster St E	79	C3
Leinster St N	77	D2
Leinster St S	145	E4
Leinster Ter **2**	96	B2
Leitrim Pl off Grand		
Canal St Upr	91	C3
Leixlip Br	68	B2
Leixlip Pk	68	A2
Leixlip Rd	69	D3
Leix Rd	77	C2
Leland Pl	91	C1
Lemon St	145	D4
Lennox Pl	102	A1
Lennox St	102	A1
Lentisk Lawn	56	A1
Leo Av off Leo St	78	A3
Leopardstown Av	131	C2
Leopardstown		
Business Cen	136	A1
Leopardstown **2**	130	B2
Leopardstown Dr	131	C2
Leopardstown Gro	131	C2
Leopardstown Hts	130	A3
Leopardstown Lawn **2**	131	C2
Leopardstown Oaks	131	C2
Leopardstown		
Office Pk	130	B2
Leopardstown Pk	131	C2
Leopardstown		
Retail Pk	130	B3
Leopardstown Ri	130	A3
Leopardstown Rd	130	B3
Leopardstown Valley	136	A1
Leo St	78	A3
Leslie Av	135	C2
Leslies Bldgs	77	D3
Leukos Rd	92	A2
Le Vere Ter	101	D1
Liberty La	90	A3
Library Rd D.L.	119	C3
Library Rd Shank.	140	B2
Liffey Cl	83	D1
Liffey Ct	83	D1
Liffey Cres	83	D1
Liffey Dale	83	D1
Liffey Dockyard	91	D1
Liffey Downs **1**	71	D3
Liffey Dr	83	D1
Liffey Gdns	83	D1
Liffey Glen **2**	83	D1
Liffey Grn	83	D1
Liffey Hall	83	D1
Liffey Lawn	84	A1
Liffey Pk	83	D1
Liffey Pl **3**	83	D1
Liffey Ri	83	D1
Liffey Rd	83	D1
Liffey Row	71	D3
Liffey St	87	C2
Liffey St Lwr	144	C2
Liffey St Upr	144	C2
Liffey St W		
off Benburb St	89	C1
Liffey Vale	83	D1
Liffey Valley Av	83	D1
Liffey Valley Pk	83	D1
Liffey Vw	83	D1
Liffey Vw Apts **2**	68	B2
Liffey Wk	84	A1
Liffey Way	83	D1
Liffey Wd	83	D1
Lilys Rd	30	B3
Limekiln Av	111	C1
Limekiln Cl	111	D1
Limekiln Dr	111	D1
Limekiln Gro	99	D3
Limekiln La	111	D1
Limekiln Pk	111	D1
Limekiln Rd	111	C1
Limelawn Pk	46	A2
Limelawn Pk Ct	46	A2
Limelawn Pk Glade	46	A2
Limelawn Pk Grn	46	A2
Limelawn Pk Hill	46	A2
Limelawn Pk Ri	46	A2
Limelawn Pk Wd	46	A2
Limes Rd	129	D2
Lime St	91	C2
Limetree Av	27	C1
Limewood Av	55	D1
Limewood Pk	55	D1
Limewood Rd	55	D1
Lincoln Hall	15	C1
Lincoln La	144	A2
Lincoln Pl	145	E4
Linden	117	C3
Linden Gro	117	C3
Linden Lea Pk	130	B1
Linden Vale	117	D3
Lindisfarne Av	95	D1
Lindisfarne Dr	95	D1
Lindisfarne Grn	95	D1
Lindisfarne Gro	95	D1
Lindisfarne Lawns	95	D1
Lindisfarne Pk	95	D1
Lindisfarne Vale	95	D1
Lindisfarne Wk	95	D1
Lindsay Ms	11	C3
Lindsay Rd	77	D2
Linenhall Par	144	B1
Linenhall Ter	144	B1
Link Rd	134	A1
Links, The D'bate	13	D1
Links, The Port.	26	B3
Linnetfields	30	B3
Linnetfields Av	30	B3
Linnetfields Cl	31	C3
Linnetfields Ct	30	B3
Linnetfields Dr	30	B3
Linnetfields Pk	30	B3
Linnetfields Ri	30	B3
Linnetfields Sq	30	B3
Linnetfields Vw	30	B3
Linnetfields Wk	30	B3
Lios Cian	14	B3
Lios Na Sidhe	123	D2
Lisburn St	144	B1
Liscannor Rd	76	B1
Liscanor **1**	135	C1
Liscarne Ct	84	B2
Liscarne Gdns	84	B2
Lisle Rd	99	D2
Lismore Rd	100	B2
Lissadel Av	88	A3
Lissadel Ct	100	A1
Lissadel Cres	18	B1
Lissadel Dr	100	A1
Lissadel Gro	18	B2
Lissadel Pk	18	B2
Lissadel Rd	100	A1
Lissadel Wd	18	B2
Lissenfield	102	A1
Lissen Hall Av	15	D3
Lissenhall Br Swords	15	D3
Lissen Hall Br (bridge)		
Swords	15	D2
Lissen Hall Ct	15	D3
Litten La	145	D2
Little Britain St	144	B1
Little Gro, The	66	B3
Little Meadow **5**	132	B3
Littlepace	31	C2
Littlepace Cl	31	C2
Littlepace Ct	31	C2
Littlepace Cres	31	C2
Littlepace Dr	31	C2
Littlepace Gallops	31	C2
Littlepace Meadow	31	C2
Littlepace Pk	31	C2
Littlepace Rd	31	C2
Littlepace Vw	31	C2
Littlepace Wk	31	C2
Littlepace Way	31	C2
Littlepace Wds	31	C2
Little Strand St	144	B2
Llewellyn Av	128	A1
Llewellyn Cl	128	A1
Llewellyn Ct	128	A1
Llewellyn Gro	128	A1
Llewellyn Lawn	128	A1
Llewellyn Pk	128	A1
Llewellyn Way	128	A1
Lockkeepers Wk	50	A3
Lock Rd	82	A2
Lodge, The	133	D1
Loftus La	144	C1
Lohunda Cres	46	A2
Lohunda Dale	46	A2
Lohunda Downs	46	A2
Lohunda Dr	46	A2
Lohunda Gro	46	A2
Lohunda Pk	45	D1
Lohunda Rd	46	A2
Lombard Ct	145	F2
Lombard St E	145	F2
Lombard St W	89	D3
Lomond Av	79	C2
London Br	91	D3
Londonbridge Dr		
off Londonbridge Rd	91	D3
Londonbridge Rd	91	D3
Longdale Ter	52	A1
Longfield Rd	43	C3
Longford La		
off Longford St Gt	144	C4
Longford Pl	119	C3
Longford St Gt	144	C4
Longford St Little	144	C4
Longford Ter	118	B3
Longlands	17	D1
Long La Dublin 7	78	A3
Long La (Tenter Flds)		
Dublin 8	89	D3
Long La Gro	89	D3
Longmeadow	137	D3
Longmeadow Gro	133	C3
Long Mile Rd	98	B2
Longs Pl	89	C2
Longwood Av	89	D3
Longwood Pk	113	D3
Lorcan Av	53	C1
Lorcan Cres	53	C1
Lorcan Dr	53	C1
Lorcan Grn	53	D1
Lorcan Gro	53	C1
Lorcan O'Toole Pk	100	A3
Lorcan Pk	53	C1
Lorcan Rd	53	C1
Lorcan Vil	53	D1
Lord Edward St	144	B3
Lordello Rd	140	B3
Lord's Wk	76	A3
Loreto Av Dublin 14	113	D3
Loreto Av Dalkey	135	C2
Loreto Ct	113	D3
Loreto Cres	113	D3
Loreto Gra	142	A3
Loreto Pk	113	D3
Loreto Rd	89	C3
Loreto Row	113	D3
Loreto Ter	113	D3
Loretto Av **2**	142	B2
Loretto Ter **3**	142	B2
Loretto Vil **4**	142	B2
Lorne Ter		
off Brookfield Rd	88	B2
Lotts	145	D2
Lough Conn Av	86	A1
Lough Conn Dr	86	A1
Lough Conn Rd		
(Bothar Loch Con)	86	A1
Lough Conn Ter	86	A1
Lough Derg Rd	55	D2
Loughlinstown Dr	138	B3
Loughlinstown Ind Est	138	B3
Loughlinstown Pk	138	B3
Loughlinstown Wd	138	B3
Loughsallagh Br	30	A1
Lourdes Rd	89	C3
Louvain	115	D2
Louvain Glade	115	D2
Love La E	91	C3
Lower Dodder Rd	113	D1
Lower Glen Rd	74	A3
Lower Kilmacud Rd		
Dublin 14	115	D3
Lower Kilmacud Rd		
Still.	116	A3
Lower Lucan Rd	71	D1
Lower Rd Dublin 20	73	D2
Lower Rd Shank.	141	C3
Luby Rd	88	A2
Lucan	70	B3
Lucan Br	70	B3
Lucan Bypass	82	B1
Lucan Hts	70	B3
Lucan Rd Dublin 20	74	A3
Lucan Rd Lucan	71	D3
Lucan Rd Palm.	73	C3
Lucan Shop Cen	82	A1
Ludford Dr	128	B1
Ludford Pk	128	B2
Ludford Rd	128	B1
Lugaquilla Av	110	B1
Lugmore La	121	D3
Luke St	145	E2
Lullymore Ter	89	C3
Lurgan St	144	B1
Lutterell Hall	28	B1
Luttrell Pk	46	B3
Luttrell Pk Cl	46	B3
Luttrell Pk Ct	46	B3
Luttrell Pk Cres	72	B1
Luttrell Pk Dr	46	B3
Luttrell Pk Grn	46	B3
Luttrell Pk Gro	46	B3
Luttrell Pk La	46	B3
Luttrell Pk Vw	46	B3
Luttrellstown Av	72	B1
Luttrellstown Beeches	72	B1
Luttrellstown Chase	72	A1
Luttrellstown Cl	72	B1
Luttrellstown Ct	72	A1
Luttrellstown Dale	72	B1
Luttrellstown Dr	72	B1
Luttrellstown Glade	72	B1
Luttrellstown Grn	72	B1
Luttrellstown Gro	72	B1
Luttrellstown Heath	72	B1
Luttrellstown Hts	72	B1
Luttrellstown Lawn	72	B1
Luttrellstown Oaks	72	B1
Luttrellstown Pk	72	B1
Luttrellstown Pl	72	B1
Luttrellstown Ri	72	B1
Luttrellstown Thicket	72	B1
Luttrellstown Vw	72	B1
Luttrellstown Wk	72	B1
Luttrellstown Way	72	B1
Luttrellstown Wd	72	B1
Lymewood Ms	38	A2
Lynchs La	86	B2
Lynchs Pl	77	D3

Lyndon Gate 76 A2
Lynwood 129 C1
Lyreen Ct **5** 65 C2
Lyreen Pk 65 C1

M
M50 Business Pk 110 A1
Mabbot La 145 E1
Mabel St 78 B2
Macartney Br 90 B3
McAuley Av 55 C2
McAuley Dr 55 C2
McAuley Pk 55 C2
McAuley Rd 55 C2
McCabe Vil 116 B1
McCarthy's Bldgs
  off Cabra Rd 77 D2
McCreadie's La 19 D2
McDowell Av 88 B3
McGrane Ct **3** 129 C1
McKee Av 36 B3
McKee Barracks 76 B3
McKee Dr 76 B3
McKee Pk 76 B3
McKee Rd 50 B1
McKelvey Av 36 A3
McKelvey Rd 36 B3
Macken St 91 C2
Macken Vil 91 C2
Mackies Pl 90 B3
Mackintosh Pk 132 B3
McMahon St 89 D3
McMorrough Rd 101 C3
Macroom Av 40 B3
Macroom Rd 40 B3
Mac Uilliam Av 121 D1
Mac Uilliam Cl **11** 121 D1
Mac Uilliam Ct **1** 121 D1
Mac Uilliam Cres 121 D1
Mac Uilliam Dale **3** 121 D1
Mac Uilliam Dr **10** 121 D1
Mac Uilliam Grn **8** 121 D1
Mac Uilliam Gro **7** 121 D1
Mac Uilliam Lawns **4** 121 D1
Mac Uilliam Ms **2** 121 D1
Mac Uilliam Par **5** 121 D1
Mac Uilliam Rd 121 D1
Mac Uilliam Wk **6** 121 D1
Mac Uilliam Way **9** 121 D1
Madden's La 138 B2
Madeleine St 87 D2
Madison Rd 88 B3
Magennis Pl 145 F3
Magennis Sq
  off Magennis Pl 145 F3
Magenta Cres 39 C3
Magenta Hall 53 C1
Magenta Pl 133 D1
Mageough Home 102 A3
Magna Business Pk 121 D1
Magna Dr 121 D2
Mahers Pl
  off Macken St 91 C2
Maiden Row 86 B1
Main Rd 110 A3
Main Rd Tallaght 110 B3
Main St (Raheny)
  Dublin 5 55 D3
Main St (Ballymun)
  Dublin 9 38 A3
Main St (Finglas)
  Dublin 11 50 B1
Main St (Baldoyle)
  Dublin 13 43 D3
Main St (Clongriffin)
  Dublin 13 42 B2
Main St (Howth)
  Dublin 13 61 C2
Main St (Dundrum)
  Dublin 14 114 B3
Main St (Rathfarnham)
  Dublin 14 113 C2
Main St Dublin 20 86 B1
Main St Dublin 24 110 A3
Main St Black. 117 D2
Main St Bray 142 A2

Main St Celbr. 66 B3
Main St Clond. 96 B2
Main St D'bate 13 D2
Main St Dunb. 28 B2
Main St Leix. 68 B2
Main St Lucan 70 A3
Main St Mala. 20 A3
Main St Mayn. 64 B2
Main St Swords 17 C1
Malachi Rd 89 C3
Malahide Rd Dublin 3 79 D2
Malahide Rd Dublin 5 54 A3
Malahide Rd Dublin 17 55 C1
Malahide Rd Balg. 41 D1
Malahide Rd Swords 17 D1
Malahide Rbt 17 C1
Malahide Sta 20 A2
Malborough Ct **9** 134 A2
Mall, The Dublin 15 46 B2
Mall, The Leix. 68 B2
Mall, The Lucan 70 A3
Mall, The Mala. 20 A2
Mallin Av 89 C3
Malone Gdns 91 D2
Malpas Pl
  off Malpas St 89 D3
Malpas St 89 D3
Malpas Ter
  off Malpas St 89 D3
Maltings, The 142 A1
Mander's Ter
  off Ranelagh Rd 102 B1
Mangerton Rd 99 C1
Mannix Rd 78 A1
Manor Av Dublin 6W 112 B1
Manor Av Grey. 143 D2
Manor Cl 128 A2
Manor Ct 65 C2
Manor Cres 31 C3
Manor Dr 42 A3
Manorfields 31 C3
Manorfields Pk 31 C3
Manorfields Ter 31 C3
Manor Grn 127 D2
Manor Heath 128 A1
Manor Pk (Ballinteer)
  Dublin 16 127 D2
Manor Pk Dublin 20 85 D1
Manor Pl Dublin 7 89 C1
Manor Pl Clons. 30 B3
Manor Ri 128 A2
Manor Rd 85 D1
Manor Sq 30 B3
Manor St 77 D2
Mansion Ho 145 D4
Mantua Pk 15 D3
Mapas Av 134 A2
Mapas Rd 134 B2
Maple Av Castle. 47 C3
Maple Av Still. 130 A1
Maple Cl 47 C3
Maple Dr Dublin 6W 101 C3
Maple Dr Castle. 47 C3
Maple Dr Dunb. 29 C2
Maple Glen 47 C3
Maple Grn 47 C3
Maple Gro Ashb. 11 C2
Maple Gro Castle. 47 C3
Maple Lawn 47 C3
Maple Manor 138 A1
Maple Rd 103 C3
Maples, The Dublin 14 115 C1
Maples, The D.L. 118 A3
Maples Rd 129 D2
Maplewood Av 123 C1
Maplewood Cl 123 C1
Maplewood Ct 123 C1
Maplewood Dr 123 C1
Maplewood Grn 123 C1
Maplewood Lawn 123 C1
Maplewood Pk 123 C1
Maplewood Rd 122 C1
Maplewood Way 123 C1
Maquay Br 91 C3
Maretimo Gdns E 118 A2
Maretimo Gdns W
  off Newtown Av 118 A2
Maretimo Pl
  off Newtown Av 118 A2
Maretimo Rd
  off Newtown Av 118 A2

Maretimo Vil
  off Newtown Av 117 D2
Marewood Cres 37 D3
Marewood Dr
  off Belclare Cres 37 D3
Marfield Cl **5** 123 D3
Marfield Ct **6** 123 D3
Marfield Cres **8** 123 D3
Marfield Grn 123 D3
Marfield Gro **7** 123 D3
Marfield Lawn **4** 123 D3
Marfield Pl 123 D3
Margaret Pl 91 D2
Marguerite Rd 78 A1
Marian Cres 112 B3
Marian Dr 112 B2
Marian Gro 112 B3
Marian Pk Dublin 13 57 C1
Marian Pk (Rathfarnham)
  Dublin 14 112 B3
Marian Pk Black. 131 D1
Marian Rd 112 B3
Marie Vil **5** 142 B2
Marigold Av 41 C3
Marigold Ct **4** 41 C3
Marigold Cres **5** 41 C3
Marigold Gro **6** 41 C3
Marigold Pk **7** 41 C3
Marina Village 20 A1
Marine Av 134 A1
Marine Ct 134 A1
Marine Dr 92 A3
Marine Par 134 A1
Mariners Cove 61 C3
Mariner's Port 91 C1
Marine Ter **9** Bray 142 B1
Marine Ter D.L. 119 D3
Marine Ter Grey. 143 D1
Marino Av 79 D1
Marino Av E 139 D2
Marino Av W 139 C2
Marino Grn 79 D1
Marino Inst of Ed 79 C1
Marino Mart 79 D2
Marino Pk 79 C2
Marino Pk Av 79 C2
Marion Vil 89 C2
Market Sq **8** 142 A2
Market St S 89 C2
Marks All W 144 B4
Marks La 145 F3
Mark St 145 F3
Marlay Vw 128 A3
Marlborough Ms 76 B3
Marlborough Pk **2** 133 D2
Marlborough Pl 145 D1
Marlborough Rd (Donnybrook)
  Dublin 4 102 B2
Marlborough Rd
  Dublin 7 76 B3
Marlborough Rd
  G'geary 134 A2
Marlborough St 145 D1
Marlborough Ter **10** 142 B1
Marley Av 127 D1
Marley Cl 128 A1
Marley Ct N 128 A1
Marley Ct S 128 A1
Marley Dr 127 D1
Marley Gro 127 D1
Marley Lawn 127 D1
Marley Ri 127 D1
Marley Vil **1** 127 D1
Marley Wk 127 D1
Marlfield 137 D1
Marne Vil 77 C3
Marrowbone La 89 C3
Marrowbone La Cl 89 C2
Marshal La 89 C2
Marsham Ct 130 A1
Martello Av 119 D3
Martello Ct 27 C1
Martello Ms 104 B2
Martello Ter Boot. 117 C1
Martello Ter **1** Bray 142 B1
Martello Vw 104 A1
Martello Wd 104 B1
Martin Savage Pk 49 C3
Martin Savage Rd 75 D2
Martins Row 86 B1
Martin St 102 A1

Mart La 132 A3
Maryfield Av 54 A2
Maryfield Coll 53 C3
Maryfield Cres 54 A2
Maryfield Dr 54 A2
Maryland **3** 141 C2
Mary's Abbey 144 B2
Mary's La 144 B2
Mary St 144 C2
Mary St Little 144 B2
Maryville Rd 55 C3
Mask Av (Ascal Measc) 54 B2
Mask Cres 54 B2
Mask Dr 54 B2
Mask Grn 54 B2
Mask Rd 54 B2
Mastersons La
  off Charlemont St 90 A3
Mather Rd N 116 A2
Mather Rd S 116 A2
Maunsell Pl
  off Mountjoy St 78 A3
Maxwell Rd 102 A2
Maxwell St 89 C3
Mayberry Pk 109 D2
Mayberry Rd 109 D2
Mayeston Boul 37 C2
Mayeston Cl 37 C2
Mayeston Ct 37 C2
Mayeston Cres 37 C2
Mayeston Downs 37 C2
Mayeston Dr 37 C2
Mayeston Lawn 37 C2
Mayeston Ri 37 C2
Mayeston Sq 37 C2
Mayeston Wk 37 C2
Mayfair 20 B2
Mayfield 113 D1
Mayfield Rd (Terenure)
  Dublin 6W 101 C3
Mayfield Rd (Kilmainham)
  Dublin 8 88 B3
Mayfield Ter Dublin 16 128 B2
Mayfield Ter **4** Bray 142 A3
May La 144 A2
Mayne Br 43 D2
Mayne River Av 41 D2
Mayne Rd 42 B1
Maynooth Rd 65 C3
Maynooth Rd 28 A3
Maynooth Sta 65 C2
Mayola Ct 114 B2
Mayor St Lwr 91 C1
Mayor St Upr 91 C1
May St 78 B2
Mayville Ter **1** 135 C2
Maywood Av 56 A3
Maywood Cl 56 A3
Maywood Cres 56 A3
Maywood Dr 56 A3
Maywood Gro 56 A3
Maywood La 56 A3
Maywood Pk 56 A3
Maywood Rd 56 A3
Meades Ter 91 C2
Meadow, The
  Dublin 16 128 B2
Meadow, The Mala. 21 C3
Meadow Av **2** 128 B1
Meadowbank 113 D1
Meadowbrook 64 B3
Meadowbrook Av
  Dublin 13 57 C1
Meadowbrook Av
  Mayn. 64 B3
Meadowbrook Cl 64 B3
Meadow Brook Ct Ashb. 11 C3
Meadowbrook Ct Mayn. 64 B3
Meadowbrook Cres 64 B3
Meadowbrook Dr 64 B3
Meadowbrook Lawn 57 D1
Meadowbrook Lawns 64 B3
Meadowbrook Pk 57 D1
Meadowbrook Rd 64 B3
Meadow Cl Dublin 16 128 A1
Meadow Cl Black. 131 D1
Meadow Copse 31 D3
Meadow Ct **1** 138 B3
Meadow Dale **1** 31 D3
Meadow Downs 45 D1
Meadow Dr 31 D3
Meadow Grn 45 D1

Name	Page	Grid
Meadow Gro	128	A1
Meadow Mt	128	A1
Meadow Pk	128	A1
Meadow Pk Av	114	A3
Meadows, The *Dublin 5*	55	C3
Meadows, The *Celbr.*	66	A1
Meadows, The *Dunb.*	28	B2
Meadows E, The	109	C2
Meadows W, The	109	C2
Meadow Vale	132	B3
Meadow Vw *Dublin 14*	128	A1
Meadow Vw *Dunb.*	28	B2
Meadow Vil 1	128	A1
Meadow Way	31	D3
Meakstown Cotts	36	B2
Meath Pl *Dublin 8*	144	A4
Meath Pl *Bray*	142	B2
Meath Rd	142	B2
Meath Sq *off Gray St*	144	A4
Meath St	144	A3
Meehan Sq	116	A1
Meetinghouse La		
off Mary's Abbey	144	C2
Méile An Rí Cres	83	D2
Méile An Rí Dr	83	D2
Méile An Rí Grn	83	D2
Méile An Rí Pk	83	D2
Méile An Rí Rd	83	D3
Mellifont Av	119	D3
Mellowes Av	50	A1
Mellowes Ct	50	B1
Mellowes Cres	50	B1
Mellowes Pk	50	A1
Mellowes Rd	50	A1
Mellows Br	89	C1
Melrose Av *Dublin 3*	79	C2
Melrose Av *Clond.*	95	D1
Melrose Cres	95	D1
Melrose Grn	95	D1
Melrose Gro	95	D1
Melrose Lawn	95	D1
Melrose Pk *Clond.*	95	D1
Melrose Pk *Swords*	18	A3
Melrose Rd	95	D1
Melville Cl	37	C3
Melville Ct	36	B3
Melville Cres	36	B3
Melville Dr	36	B3
Melville Grn	36	B3
Melville Gro	37	C3
Melville Pk	36	B3
Melville Ter	36	B3
Melville Vw	36	B3
Melville Way	36	B3
Melvin Rd	101	C3
Memorial Rd	145	E2
Mercer St Lwr	144	C4
Mercer St Upr	90	A3
Merchamp	81	C2
Merchants Quay	144	A3
Merchants Rd	91	D1
Meretimo Vil 26	142	B2
Meridianpoint	143	D2
Merlyn Dr	104	A2
Merlyn Pk	104	A2
Merlyn Rd	104	A2
Merrion Cres	104	B3
Merrion Gro	116	B1
Merrion Pk	116	B2
Merrion Pl	145	E4
Merrion Rd	103	D1
Merrion Row	90	B3
Merrion Shop Cen	104	A2
Merrion Sq E	90	B3
Merrion Sq N	145	F4
Merrion Sq S	145	F4
Merrion Sq W	145	E4
Merrion Strand	104	B2
Merrion St Lwr		
off Lincoln Pl	145	F4
Merrion St Upr	90	B3
Merrion Vw Av	104	A2
Merrion Village	104	A2
Merrywell Business Pk	98	A3
Merryvell Ind Est	98	A3
Merton Av	89	C3
Merton Cres	102	B3
Merton Dr	102	B2
Merton Rd	102	B3
Merton Wk	102	B3
Merville Av *Dublin 3*	79	C2
Merville Av *Still.*	130	B1
Merville Rd	130	B1
Mespil Rd	90	B3
Mews, The *Dublin 3*	80	B2
Mews, The (Dollymount)		
Dublin 3	81	D2
Mews, The 6 *Mala.*	21	C3
Mews, The *Sally.*	133	C3
Michael Collins Pk	96	A1
Middle Ill	80	B1
Milesian Av	18	A2
Milesian Ct	18	A2
Milesian Gro	18	A2
Milesian Lawn	18	A2
Milford	19	C1
Military Cem	76	A2
Military Rd (Rathmines)		
Dublin 6	102	A1
Military Rd (Kilmainham)		
Dublin 8	88	B2
Military Rd (Phoenix Pk) *Dublin 8*		
87		C1
Military Rd *Kill.*	139	C2
Millbank	26	B3
Millbourne Av	78	A1
Millbrook Av	55	D1
Millbrook Ct	88	B2
Millbrook Dr	56	A1
Millbrook Gro	55	D1
Millbrook Lawns	124	A1
Millbrook Rd	55	D1
Millbrook Village		
off Prospect La	103	C3
Mill Cen	96	B1
Mill Ct Av	95	D2
Mill Ct Dr	95	D2
Mill Ct Way	95	D2
Millennium Br	144	C2
Millennium Business Pk	34	B2
Millfarm	29	C2
Millfield	26	B3
Millgate Dr	111	D1
Mill Gro	143	C3
Mill La *Dublin 8*	89	D3
Mill La *Dublin 15*	49	C3
Mill La *Dublin 20*	73	C3
Mill La *Leix.*	68	B2
Mill La *Lough.*	141	C1
Mill La Business Pk	69	C2
Millmount Av	78	A1
Millmount Gro	114	B1
Millmount Pl	78	B1
Millmount Ter (Drumcondra)		
Dublin 9		
off Millmount Av	78	B1
Millmount Ter (Dundrum)		
Dublin 14		
off Millmount Gro	114	B2
Millmount Vil	78	A1
Mill Pk	96	A2
Mill Pond Apts, The 4	96	B2
Mill Race Av	120	A2
Millrace Cl	75	C1
Mill Race Ct	120	A2
Mill Race Cres	120	A2
Mill Race Dr	120	A2
Mill Race Gdn	120	A2
Mill Race Grn	120	B2
Mill Race Pk	120	A2
Millrace Rd	75	C1
Mill Race Vw	120	A2
Mill Race Wk	120	A2
Mill Rd *Dublin 15*	47	D2
Mill Rd *Grey.*	143	C3
Mill Rd *Sagg.*	120	A2
Millstead	47	D2
Millstream	26	B3
Millstream Rd	69	D3
Mill St	89	D3
Milltown Av	102	B3
Milltown Br	11	D3
Milltown Br Rd	102	B3
Milltown Dr	114	A2
Milltown Est	11	C3
Milltown Gro	114	A2
Milltown Hill		
off Milltown Rd	102	B3
Milltown Path	102	B3
Milltown Rd *Dublin 6*	102	B3
Milltown Rd *Ashb.*	11	D3
Milltown Sta	102	B3
Millview Cl 1	19	C2
Millview Ct	19	C2
Millview Lawns	19	C2
Millview Rd	19	C2
Millwood Pk	55	D1
Millwood Vil	55	D1
Milners Sq	52	B1
Milton Ter 14	142	A1
Milward Ter 16	142	B2
Misery Hill	91	C1
Moatfield Av	55	C1
Moatfield Pk	55	C1
Moatfield Rd	55	C1
Moatview Av	40	B3
Moatview Ct	40	B2
Moatview Dr	40	B2
Moatview Gdns	40	B3
Moeran Rd	99	D2
Moira Rd	89	C1
Moland Pl		
off Talbot St	145	E1
Molesworth Pl		
off Schoolhouse La	145	E4
Molesworth St	145	D4
Molyneux Yd	144	A3
Monalea Dr	125	C1
Monalea Gro	125	C1
Monalea Pk	125	C1
Monalea Wd	125	C1
Monaloe Av	137	D1
Monaloe Ct 1	137	D1
Monaloe Cres 2	132	B3
Monaloe Dr	132	B3
Monaloe Pk	132	B3
Monaloe Pk Rd	132	B3
Monaloe Way	132	B3
Monarch Ind Est	109	D3
Monasterboice Rd	100	A1
Monastery Cres	97	C2
Monastery Dr	97	C2
Monastery Gate	97	D2
Monastery Gate Av	97	C2
Monastery Gate Cl	97	C2
Monastery Gate Copse	97	C2
Monastery Gate Grn	97	C2
Monastery Gate Lawns	97	D2
Monastery Gate Vil	97	C2
Monastery Heath	97	C2
Monastery Heath Av	97	C2
Monastery Heath Ct	97	C2
Monastery Heath Grn	97	C2
Monastery Heath Sq	97	C2
Monastery Hts 1	97	C2
Monastery Rd	96	B2
Monastery Ri	96	B2
Monastery Rd	96	B2
Monastery Shop Cen	97	C2
Monastery Wk	97	C2
Monck Pl	77	D3
Monksfield Ct	97	C2
Monksfield Downs	97	C1
Monksfield Gro	97	C2
Monksfield Hts	97	C2
Monksfield Lawn	97	C1
Monksfield Meadows	97	C2
Monksfield Wk	97	C2
Monks Meadow	21	D3
Monkstown Av	132	B3
Monkstown Cres	118	B3
Monkstown Fm	132	B1
Monkstown Gate	119	C3
Monkstown Gro	132	B1
Monkstown Rd	118	A2
Monkstown Sq 4	132	B1
Monkstown Valley	118	B3
Montague Ct		
off Protestant Row	90	A3
Montague La	90	A3
Montague Pl		
off Montague La	90	A3
Montague St	90	A3
Montebello Ter 17	142	B2
Monte Vella 4	134	B2
Montgommery Vw	18	A1
Montone Business Pk	97	D1
Montpelier Dr	88	B1
Montpelier Gdns	88	B1
Montpelier Hill	88	B1
Montpelier Par	118	A3
Montpelier Pk	89	C1
Montpelier Pl	118	A2
Montpelier Vw	122	A2
Montrose Av	53	D2
Montrose Cl	53	D2
Montrose Ct	53	D2
Montrose Cres	54	A1
Montrose Dr	53	D1
Montrose Gro	53	D2
Montrose Pk	53	D2
Moorefield	138	B2
Moore La	145	D1
Moore's Cotts 4	131	D1
Moore St	145	D1
Mooretown Av	15	C3
Mooretown Gro	15	C3
Mooretown Pk	14	B3
Mooretown Rd	15	C3
Moorfield	84	A3
Moorfield Av	84	B3
Moorfield Cl 2	84	B3
Moorfield Dr	84	B3
Moorfield Grn	84	B3
Moorfield Gro	84	A3
Moorfield Lawns	84	B3
Moorfield Par	84	B3
Moorfield Wk	84	A3
Moorings, The	20	B2
Moreen Av	129	D2
Moreen Cl	129	D3
Moreen Lawn 3	129	D3
Moreen Pk	129	D3
Moreen Rd	129	D3
Moreen Wk	129	D3
Morehampton La	103	C1
Morehampton Rd	103	C1
Morehampton Sq	102	B1
Morehampton Ter	103	C1
Morgan Pl		
off Inns Quay	144	B2
Morgan's Pl	48	B3
Morning Star Av	144	A1
Morning Star Rd	89	C3
Mornington Av	134	B1
Mornington Gro	54	B2
Mornington Rd	102	B2
Morrogh Ter	79	C1
Moss St	145	E2
Mountain Pk	124	A1
Mountain Vw	140	B3
Mountain Vw Apts 5	142	A3
Mountain Vw Av		
off Shamrock Vil	101	D2
Mountain Vw Cotts		
Dublin 6	102	B2
Mountain Vw Cotts		
Castle.	72	B1
Mountain Vw Dr	114	A3
Mountain Vw Pk		
Dublin 14	114	A3
Mountainview Pk *Grey.*	143	C1
Mountain Vw Rd		
Dublin 6	102	B2
Mountain Vw Rd 1 *Kill.*	139	C2
Mountain Vil 2	139	C2
Mount Albany	131	D1
Mount Albion Rd	114	A3
Mount Albion Ter 1	114	A3
Mount Alton	125	D1
Mount Alton Ct	125	D1
Mount Andrew	71	D3
Mount Andrew Av	72	A3
Mount Andrew Cl	71	D3
Mount Andrew Ct	71	D3
Mount Andrew Dale	72	A3
Mount Andrew Gro	72	A3
Mount Andrew Ri	72	A3
Mount Annville	116	A3
Mount Annville Conv	115	D3
Mount Annville Lawn	115	D3
Mount Annville Pk	116	A3
Mount Annville Rd	116	A3
Mount Annville Wd	116	A3
Mount Argus Cl	101	C2
Mount Argus Ct	101	C2
Mount Argus Cres	101	C2
Mount Argus Grn	101	C2
Mount Argus Gro	101	C2
Mount Argus Pk	101	C2
Mount Argus Rd	101	C2

Mount Argus Ter	101	C2
Mount Argus Vw	101	C2
Mount Argus Way	101	C2
Mount Auburn **1**	134	A3
Mount Bellew Cres **1**	83	B1
Mount Bellew Grn **2**	83	C1
Mount Bellew Ri **1**	83	C1
Mount Bellew Way	83	C1
Mount Brown	88	B2
Mount Carmel Av	115	C2
Mount Carmel Pk	125	C2
Mount Carmel Rd	115	C2
Mount Dillon Ct	54	B2
Mountdown Dr	111	D1
Mountdown Pk	111	D1
Mountdown Rd	111	D1
Mount Drinan Av	18	A3
Mount Drinan Cres	18	A3
Mount Drinan Gro **5**	18	A3
Mount Drinan Lawn **1**	18	B3
Mount Drinan Pk	18	A3
Mount Drinan Wk	18	A3
Mount Drummond Av	101	D1
Mount Drummond Sq	101	D1
Mount Eagle Dr	130	A3
Mount Eagle Grn	130	A3
Mount Eagle Gro	130	A3
Mount Eagle Lawn	130	A3
Mount Eagle Ri	130	A3
Mount Eagle Vw	130	A3
Mount Eden Rd	103	C2
Mountfield	20	A3
Mount Gandon	70	A3
Mount Harold Ter	101	D2
Mount Jerome Cem	101	C1
Mountjoy Cotts	78	A2
Mountjoy Par		
off North Circular Rd	78	B3
Mountjoy Pl	78	B3
Mountjoy Prison	78	A2
Mountjoy Prison Cotts		
off Cowley Pl	78	A2
Mountjoy Sq E	78	B3
Mountjoy Sq N	78	A3
Mountjoy Sq S	78	A3
Mountjoy Sq W	78	A3
Mountjoy St	77	D3
Mountjoy St Mid	77	D3
Mount Merrion Av	116	B2
Mount Norris Vil **18**	142	B2
Mount Olive Gro	56	A1
Mount Olive Pk	56	A1
Mount Olive Rd	56	A1
Mountpleasant Av Lwr	102	A1
Mountpleasant Av Upr	102	A1
Mountpleasant Par		
off Prices La	102	A1
Mountpleasant Pl	102	A1
Mountpleasant Sq	102	A1
Mount Prospect Av	81	C2
Mount Prospect Dr	81	C1
Mount Prospect Gro	81	D1
Mount Prospect Lawns	81	C2
Mount Prospect Pk	81	C2
Mount Sackville Conv	74	A2
Mount Salus Rd	135	C3
Mountsandel	137	C2
Mount Sandford	103	C2
Mount Shannon Rd	88	B3
Mount St Cres	91	C3
Mount St Lwr	91	C2
Mount St Upr	90	B3
Mount Symon	45	C1
Mount Symon Av	45	D2
Mount Symon Cl	45	D1
Mount Symon Cres	45	C1
Mount Symon Dale	45	C1
Mount Symon Dr	45	D1
Mount Symon Grn	45	C2
Mount Symon Lawn	45	D2
Mount Symon Pk	45	D2
Mount Symon Ri	45	D1
Mount Tallant Av	101	C3
Mount Tallant Ter		
off Harolds Cross Rd	101	D1
Mount Temple Rd	89	C1
Mount Town Lwr	133	C1
Mounttown Pk **4**	133	C1
Mount Town Rd Upr	118	B3
Mount Vw Rd	46	A1
Mount Wd	133	C1
Mourne Rd	88	B3
Moyclare Av	57	D1
Moyclare Cl	57	D1
Moyclare Gdns	58	A1
Moyclare Pk	57	D1
Moyclare Rd	57	D1
Moycullen Rd	85	D2
Moy Elta Rd	79	C3
Moyglare Abbey	64	A1
Moyglare Meadows	64	B1
Moyglare Rd	64	B1
Moyglare Village	64	B1
Moy Glas Av	83	C2
Moy Glas Chase	83	C2
Moy Glas Cl	83	C2
Moy Glas Ct	83	C2
Moy Glas Dale	83	C2
Moy Glas Dene	83	C2
Moy Glas Glen	83	C2
Moy Glas Grn	83	C2
Moy Glas Gro	83	C2
Moy Glas Lawn	83	C2
Moy Glas Rd	83	C2
Moy Glas Vale	83	C2
Moy Glas Vw	83	C2
Moy Glas Way	83	C2
Moy Glas Wd	83	C2
Moyle Cres	96	B2
Moyle Rd	76	B1
Moyne Pk	43	C2
Moyne Rd	102	B2
Moynihan Ct	110	B3
Moyville	126	B2
Moyville Lawns	126	B1
Muckross Av	99	D3
Muckross Cres	99	D3
Muckross Dr	100	A3
Muckross Grn	100	A3
Muckross Gro	99	D3
Muckross Par		
off Killarney Par	78	A2
Muckross Pk	99	D3
Muirfield Dr	99	C1
Mulberry Cres	73	C1
Mulberry Dr	73	C1
Mulberry Pk	73	C1
Mulcahy Keane Est	99	C3
Muldowney Ct	20	A1
Mulgrave St	119	D3
Mulgrave Ter	133	D1
Mulhuddart Wd	32	A2
Mullinastill Rd	140	A1
Mulroy Rd	77	C1
Mulvey Rd	115	C2
Munster St	77	D2
Munster Ter **3**	134	B1
Murphystown Rd	130	A3
Murray's Cotts		
off Sarsfield Rd	87	D2
Murtagh Rd	89	C1
Museum of Modern Art		
(Royal Hospital)	88	A2
Museum Sta	89	C1
Muskerry Rd	86	B2
Mygan Business Pk	36	B3
Mygan Pk Ind Est	36	B3
Myra Cotts	88	A2
Myra Manor	25	D1
Myrtle Av Dublin 13	43	C3
Myrtle Av **16** D.L.	133	D1
Myrtle Ct	43	C3
Myrtle Dr	43	C3
Myrtle Gro	130	B1
Myrtle Pk	133	D1
Myrtle Sq	43	C3
Myrtle St	77	D3
N		
Naas Rd Dublin 12	98	A2
Naas Rd Dublin 22	97	D2
Naas Rd Sagg.	106	B3
Naas Rd Business Pk	99	C1
Naas Rd Ind Pk	99	C1
Nangor Cres **1**	96	A1
Nangor Pl **2**	95	D2
Nangor Rd Dublin 12	97	C1
Nangor Rd Clond.	96	A2
Nangor Rd		
Business Cen	97	D1
Nanikin Av	55	D3
Nash St	87	C3
Nashville Pk	61	C2
Nashville Rd	61	C2
Nassau Pl	145	E4
Nassau St	145	D3
National Mus Dublin 2	145	E4
National Mus		
(Collins Barracks)		
Dublin 7	89	C1
National Transport Mus	59	D2
National Uni Ireland		
Maynooth	64	A1
Naul Rd	22	B1
Navan Rd Dublin 7	75	D1
Navan Rd Dublin 15	48	A3
Navan Rd (Blanchardstown)		
Dublin 15	32	B3
Navan Rd Clonee	31	C2
Navan Rd Dunb.	28	B2
Navan Rd Mulh.	31	D2
Neagh Rd	101	C3
Neillstown Av	84	B3
Neillstown Cres	84	B3
Neillstown Dr	84	B2
Neillstown Gdns	84	B3
Neillstown Pk	84	B3
Neilstown Cotts **2**	96	B1
Neilstown Rd	84	B2
Neilstown Shop Cen	84	A3
Neilstown Village Ct **1**	84	B3
Nelson St	78	A3
Nephin Rd	76	A2
Neptune Ter **4**	134	B1
Nerano Rd	135	C3
Nerneys Ct	78	A3
Neville Rd	102	A3
Nevinston La	17	C3
New Bawn Dr	124	A1
New Bawn Pk	124	A1
New Bride St	90	A3
Newbridge Av Dublin 4	91	C3
Newbridge Av D'bate	13	C2
Newbridge Dr	91	D3
New Brighton Ter **9**	142	A2
Newbrook Av	56	B1
Newbrook Rd	56	B1
Newbury Av	40	A3
Newbury Dr	40	A3
Newbury Gro	40	A3
Newbury Lawns	40	A3
Newbury Pk	40	A3
Newbury Ter **1**	40	A3
Newcastle Rd	82	A1
New Ch St	144	A2
Newcomen Av	79	C3
Newcomen Br	79	C3
Newcomen Ct		
off Newcomen Av	79	C3
Newcourt	15	D3
Newcourt Av	142	B3
Newcourt Business Pk	36	A1
Newcourt Ms	15	D3
Newcourt Rd	142	B3
Newcourt Vil **6**	142	A3
New Gra Rd Dublin 7	77	C2
New Gra Rd Black.	131	C1
Newgrove Av	92	A3
New Gro Est	42	B3
Newhall Ct	122	A2
New Ireland Rd	88	B3
Newlands Av	97	C3
Newlands		
Business Cen	96	B3
Newlands Dr	96	B3
Newlands Manor	108	A1
Newlands Manor Ct	108	A1
Newlands Manor Dr	108	A1
Newlands Manor		
Fairway	108	A1
Newlands Manor Grn	108	A1
Newlands Manor Pk	108	A1
Newlands Pk	96	B3
Newlands Retail Cen	96	B3
Newlands Rd Clond.	96	B3
Newlands Rd Lucan	70	B3
Newlands Rd Ronan.	83	D2
New Lisburn St		
off Coleraine St	144	B1
New Lucan Rd	72	B3
Newman Pl	65	C2
Newmarket	89	D3
Newmarket St	89	D3
New Nangor Rd	96	A1
New Pk Lo **7**	131	D2
New Pk Rd	131	D1
Newport St	89	C2
New Rd (Inchicore)		
Dublin 8	87	C3
New Rd Dublin 13	61	C3
New Rd Clond.	96	B2
New Rd (Killincarrig)		
Grey.	143	C3
New Rd **1** Swords	17	C1
New Rd, The Dublin 11	34	B3
New Row S	89	D3
New Row Sq	144	B4
New St	20	A2
New St Gdns	89	D3
New St S	89	D3
Newtown	28	A2
Newtown Av Dublin 17	41	C3
Newtown Av Black.	118	A2
Newtown Br	15	D2
Newtown Cotts		
Dublin 17	55	C1
Newtown Cotts Swords	15	C1
Newtown Ct	64	A3
Newtown Dr	55	C1
Newtown Glendale	68	B1
Newtown Gro	64	B2
Newtown Ind Est	41	C3
Newtown Pk Dublin 17	41	C3
Newtown Pk Dublin 24	110	B3
Newtown Pk Black.	131	D1
Newtownpark Av	117	D3
Newtown Pk Ct **5**	131	D1
Newtown Rd Dublin 17	41	C3
Newtown Rd Celbr.	66	B3
Newtown Rd Mayn.	64	A3
Newtown Vil	118	A2
New Vale	140	B2
New Vale Cotts	140	B3
New Vale Cres	140	B2
New Wapping St	91	C1
Niall St	77	C3
Nicholas Av		
off Church St	144	B1
Nicholas Pl		
off Patrick St	144	B4
Nicholas St	144	B4
Ninth Lock Rd	96	B2
Nore Rd	76	B1
Norfolk Mkt		
off Parnell St	78	A3
Norfolk Rd	77	D2
Norseman Pl	89	C1
North Av	116	A2
Northbrook Av	102	B1
Northbrook Av Lwr		
off North Strand Rd	79	C3
Northbrook Av Upr	79	C3
Northbrook La	102	B1
Northbrook Rd	102	A1
Northbrook Ter	79	C3
Northbrook Vil		
off Northbrook Rd	102	A1
Northbrook Wk	102	B1
North Circular Rd		
Dublin 1	78	A3
North Circular Rd		
Dublin 7	78	A2
Northcote Av	119	C3
Northcote Pl	119	C3
North Dublin		
Docklands	92	A1
Northern Cl	40	B2
Northern Cross		
Business Pk	36	A3
North Gt Clarence St	78	B3
North Gt Georges St	78	A3
Northland Dr	51	C3
Northland Gro	51	C3
North Pk Business &		
Office Pk	36	A3
North Quay Ext	91	D1
North Rd Dublin 8	75	C1
North Rd Dublin 11	36	A3

Name	Grid	
Northside Shop Cen	40	A3
North Strand Rd		
Dublin 1	78	B3
North Strand Rd		
Dublin 3	78	B3
North St	15	D3
North St Business Pk	15	D3
Northumberland Av	119	D3
Northumberland Pk	119	D3
Northumberland Pl *off*		
Northumberland Av	119	D3
Northumberland Rd	91	C3
North Wall Quay	91	C1
Northway Est	36	A3
North W Business Pk	34	A1
Nortons Av	77	D3
Norwood	139	C3
Norwood Pk	102	B2
Nottingham St	79	C3
Novara Av	142	A1
Novara Ms **15**	142	A1
Novara Pk **10**	142	A2
Novara Ter **11**	142	A2
Nugent Rd	114	A3
Nurney Lawn	42	A3
Nurseries, The **4**		
B'brack	139	C2
Nurseries, The *Mulh.*	32	B2
Nurseries, The *Swords*	16	B2
Nutgrove Av (Ascal An		
Charrain Chno)	113	D3
Nutgrove Cres	114	A3
Nutgrove Enterprise Pk	114	A3
Nutgrove Office Pk	114	A3
Nutgrove Pk	115	C1
Nutgrove Shop Cen	114	A3
Nutgrove Way	114	A3
Nutley Av	103	D2
Nutley La	104	A3
Nutley Pk	104	A3
Nutley Rd	103	D2
Nutley Sq	103	D3

O

Name	Grid	
Oak Apple Grn	101	D3
Oak Av	39	C3
Oak Cl	97	D1
Oak Ct	39	C3
Oakcourt Av	85	D1
Oakcourt Cl	85	D1
Oakcourt Dr	85	D1
Oakcourt Gro	85	D1
Oakcourt Lawn	85	D1
Oakcourt Lawns	85	D1
Oakcourt Pk	85	D1
Oak Cres	39	C2
Oakdale Cl	125	C3
Oakdale Cres	124	B3
Oakdale Dr *Dublin 24*	125	C3
Oakdale Dr *Corn.*	133	C3
Oakdale Gro	125	C3
Oakdale Pk	124	B3
Oakdale Rd	124	B3
Oak Dene	134	A3
Oakdown Rd	114	A3
Oak Downs	96	A3
Oak Dr *Dublin 9*	39	C3
Oak Dr *Dublin 12*	97	D2
Oakfield	96	B1
Oakfield Ind Est	96	B1
Oakfield Pl	89	D3
Oak Grn	39	C3
Oak Gro	39	C3
Oaklands	143	C1
Oaklands Av	17	C1
Oaklands Cres	102	A3
Oaklands Dr *Dublin 6*	102	A3
Oaklands Pk *Dublin 4*	103	D1
Oaklands Pk *Swords*	17	D1
Oaklands Ter *Dublin 4*		
off Serpentine Av	103	D2
Oaklands Ter *Dublin 6*	101	D3
Oak Lawn *Dublin 9*	39	C3
Oak Lawn *Dublin 15*	47	D3
Oak Lawn *Castle.*	48	A3
Oaklawn *Leix.*	68	A2
Oaklawn Cl	68	A2
Oaklawn W	68	A1
Oakleigh	66	A3
Oakley Gro	117	D3
Oakley Pk *Dublin 3*	81	C2

Name	Grid	
Oakley Pk *Black.*	117	D3
Oakley Rd	102	B1
Oak Lo	74	A1
Oak Pk Av	53	C1
Oak Pk Cl	53	C1
Oak Pk Dr	39	C3
Oak Pk Gro	39	C3
Oak Ri *Dublin 9*	39	C3
Oak Ri *Clond.*	96	A3
Oak Rd *Dublin 9*	79	D1
Oak Rd *Dublin 12*	97	D2
Oak Rd Business Pk	97	D1
Oaks, The *Dublin 3*	81	D2
Oaks, The *Dublin 14*	114	B3
Oaks, The *Dublin 16*	128	B2
Oaks, The (Cookstown)		
Dublin 24	109	C2
Oaks, The **16** *Abb.*	139	C3
Oaks, The *Celbr.*	66	B2
Oaks, The **5** *Lough.*	138	B3
Oaks, The (Hilltown)		
Swords	16	B2
Oakton Ct	138	B2
Oakton Dr	138	B2
Oakton Grn **2**	138	B2
Oakton Pk	138	B2
Oaktree Av	47	C3
Oaktree Dr	47	C3
Oaktree Grn	47	C3
Oaktree Gro	47	C3
Oaktree Lawn	47	C3
Oaktree Rd	130	B2
Oak Vw	39	C3
Oakview Av	45	D1
Oakview Cl	45	D1
Oakview Ct	45	D1
Oakview Dr	45	D1
Oakview Gro **1**	45	D1
Oakview Lawn	45	D1
Oakview Pk	45	D1
Oakview Ri	45	D1
Oakview Wk	45	D1
Oakview Way	45	D1
Oak Way	96	A3
Oakwood Av *Dublin 11*	51	C1
Oakwood Av *Swords*	17	C1
Oakwood Cl	37	C3
Oakwood Gro Est	96	A1
Oakwood Pk	37	C3
Oakwood Rd	37	C3
Oatfield Av	84	B2
Oatfield Cl	84	B2
Oatfield Cres	84	B2
Oatfield Dr	84	B2
Oatfield Gro	84	B2
Oatfield Lawn	84	B2
Oatfield Pk	84	B2
Obelisk Ct **6**	131	D1
Obelisk Gro	117	D3
Obelisk Ri	131	D1
Obelisk Vw	131	C1
Obelisk Wk	117	D3
O'Brien Rd	99	D2
O'Brien's Inst	79	D1
O'Brien's Pl N	78	A1
O'Brien's Ter		
off Prospect Rd	77	D2
Observatory La	102	A1
O'Byrne Rd	142	A3
O'Byrne Vd **7**	142	A3
O'Carolan Rd	89	D3
Ocean Pier	92	A1
O'Connell Av	77	D3
O'Connell Br	145	D2
O'Connell Gdns	91	D3
O'Connell St Lwr	145	D1
O'Connell St Upr	145	D1
O'Curry Av	89	D3
O'Curry Rd	89	D3
O'Daly Rd	52	B2
Odd Lamp Rd	75	D2
O'Devaney Gdns	88	B1
O'Donnell Gdns **9**	133	D1
O'Donoghue St	87	C3
O'Donovan Rd	89	D3
O'Donovan Rossa Br	144	B3
O'Dwyer Rd	99	D2
Offaly Rd	77	C2
Offington Av	59	C1
Offington Ct	59	C2
Offington Dr	59	C1
Offington Lawn	59	C2

Name	Grid	
Offington Pk	59	C1
O'Hanlon's La	20	A2
O'Hogan Rd	87	C2
Olaf Rd	89	C1
Olcovar	140	B3
Old Ballycullen Rd	125	C1
Old Bawn Av	123	D1
Old Bawn Cl	124	A2
Old Bawn Ct	124	A1
Old Bawn Dr	124	A2
Old Bawn Pk	123	D2
Old Bawn Rd	124	A1
Old Bawn Ter **1**	124	A2
Old Bawn Way	123	D1
Old Belgard Rd	109	C2
Old Belgard Rd		
Business Pk	109	C2
Oldbridge	83	C3
Oldbridge Cl	83	C2
Oldbridge Ct	82	B3
Oldbridge Glen	83	C3
Oldbridge Grn	83	C3
Oldbridge Gro	83	C3
Oldbridge Pk	82	B3
Old Br Rd	112	A2
Oldbridge Vw	83	C3
Oldbridge Wk	83	C3
Oldbridge Way	82	B3
Old Brighton Ter **12**	142	A2
Old Cabra Rd	76	B2
Old Camden St		
off Harcourt Rd	90	A3
Old Castle Av	59	C3
Oldcastle Dr	95	C2
Oldcastlepark	95	C2
Oldcastlepark Cl	95	C2
Oldcastlepark Grn	95	C2
Oldcastlepark Gro	95	C2
Oldcastlepark Lawn	95	C2
Oldcastlepark Vw	95	C2
Oldchurch Av	95	D2
Oldchurch Cl	95	D2
Oldchurch Ct	95	D2
Oldchurch Cres	95	D2
Oldchurch Dr	95	D2
Oldchurch Gro	95	D2
Oldchurch Lawn	95	D2
Oldchurch Pk	95	D2
Oldchurch Way	95	D2
Old Corduff Rd	47	C1
Old Cornmill Rd	69	D3
Old Co Glen	100	B1
Old Co Rd	100	A1
Oldcourt Av	124	B3
Oldcourt Cl	124	B3
Oldcourt Cotts	124	B3
Oldcourt Fm	124	B3
Oldcourt Lawn	124	A2
Oldcourt Lo	124	B2
Oldcourt Manor	124	B3
Oldcourt Rd	125	C3
Oldcourt Ter **8**	142	A3
Oldcourt Vw	124	B2
Old Dublin Rd	116	B3
Old Dunleary	119	C3
Old Fairgreen	28	B2
Old Fm, The	115	D3
Old Forge, The	82	B3
Old Golf Links, The	20	B2
Old Greenfield	64	B2
Old Hill *Leix.*	68	A2
Old Hill, The *Lucan*	70	B3
Old Kilmainham	88	A2
Old Kilmainham Village	88	B2
Old Malahide Rd	54	B1
Old Mill Ct	89	D3
Old Mountpleasant		
off Ranelagh Rd	102	B1
Old Naas Rd *Dublin 12*	98	B1
Old Naas Rd *Kings.*	107	C1
Old Orchard	112	A3
Old Quarry	134	B2
Old Rathmichael	140	A3
Old Rectory	70	B3
Old Rectory Pk	115	C3
Old Rd	26	A3
Old Sawmills Ind Est	99	C3
Old St	20	A2
Oldtower Cres	84	A1
Oldtown Av	52	A1
Oldtown Cotts	66	A2
Oldtown Mill	66	A2

Name	Grid	
Oldtown Mill Rd	66	A2
Oldtown Pk	52	A1
Oldtown Rd	52	A1
Old Yellow Walls Rd	19	C1
O'Leary Rd	88	A3
Olivemount Gro	115	C1
Olivemount Rd	115	C1
Oliver Bond St	144	A3
Oliver Plunkett Av		
(Irishtown) *Dublin 4*	91	D2
Oliver Plunkett Av *D.L.*	132	B1
Oliver Plunkett Rd	132	B1
Oliver Plunkett Sq **9**	132	B1
Oliver Plunkett Ter **10**	132	B1
Oliver Plunkett Vil **5**	132	B1
Olney Cres	113	C3
Omac Business Cen	96	B2
Omni Pk	52	B2
Omni Pk Shop Cen	52	B2
O'Moore Rd	87	C2
O'Neachtain Rd	78	A1
O'Neill Pk	65	C1
O'Neill's Bldgs	90	A3
Ongar Chase	30	A3
Ongar Grn	44	B1
Ongar Pk	45	C1
Ongar Village	44	B1
Ontario Ter	102	A1
Onward Cl	27	C1
Onward Wk	27	C1
Ophaly Ct	115	C2
O'Quinn Av	88	B2
O'Rahilly Par		
off Moore St	145	D1
Oranmore Rd	85	D2
Orchard, The *Dublin 3*	79	C3
Orchard, The *Dublin 5*	54	B3
Orchard, The *Dublin 6W*	100	B3
Orchard, The **3**		
Dublin 13	41	D3
Orchard, The *Black.*	131	D1
Orchard, The **3** *Cool.*	46	B3
Orchard, The *Palm.*	73	C3
Orchard Av *City W*	107	C3
Orchard Av *Clons.*	46	A2
Orchard Cl (Blanchardstown)		
Dublin 15	46	B2
Orchard Cl *D'bate*	13	D1
Orchard Cotts **2**	117	D3
Orchard Ct	46	B2
Orchard Grn	46	B2
Orchard Gro		
(Blanchardstown)	46	B2
Orchard La *Dublin 6*	102	A1
Orchard La *Black.*	131	D1
Orchard Lawns	85	D2
Orchard Pk	37	D3
Orchard Rd *Dublin 3*	79	C2
Orchard Rd *Dublin 5*	56	B3
Orchard Rd *Dublin 6*	102	A3
Orchard Rd *Clond.*	96	B2
Orchardston	112	B3
Orchardstown Av	112	B3
Orchardstown Dr	112	A3
Orchardstown Pk	112	B3
Orchardstown Vil	112	B3
Orchard Ter **9**	142	A3
Orchardton **1**	126	B1
Ordnance Survey Office	74	B2
Ordnance Survey Rd	74	B2
O'Reilly's Av	88	B2
Oriel Pl	79	C3
Oriel St Lwr	91	C1
Oriel St Upr	91	C1
Orlagh Av	125	D2
Orlagh Cl	126	A2
Orlagh Ct	125	D2
Orlagh Cres	125	D2
Orlagh Downs	126	A2
Orlagh Gra	126	A2
Orlagh Grn	125	D2
Orlagh Gro	125	D2
Orlagh Lawn	125	D2
Orlagh Lo	126	A2
Orlagh Meadows	126	A2
Orlagh Pk	125	D2

Orlagh Pines	125	D2
Orlagh Ri	125	D2
Orlagh Vw	126	A2
Orlagh Way	125	D2
Orlagh Wd	126	A2
Ormeau Dr	134	B2
Ormeau St		
off Gordon St	91	C2
Ormond Av	14	A3
Ormond Cl	14	A3
Ormond Cres	14	A3
Ormond Dr	14	A3
Ormond Gro	14	A3
Ormond Lawn	14	A3
Ormond Mkt Sq off		
Ormond Quay Upr	144	B2
Ormond Quay Lwr	144	C2
Ormond Quay Upr	144	B3
Ormond Rd N	78	B1
Ormond Rd S		
(Rathmines)	102	A2
Ormond Sq	144	B2
Ormond St	89	C3
Ormond Vw	14	A3
Ormond Way	14	A3
O'Rourke Pk	133	C2
Orpen Cl	117	C3
Orpen Dale	117	C3
Orpen Grn	131	C1
Orpen Hill	131	C1
Orpen Ri	131	C1
Orwell Gdns	114	A1
Orwell Pk	114	A1
Orwell Pk Av	111	D2
Orwell Pk Cl	111	D2
Orwell Pk Cres	111	D2
Orwell Pk Dale	111	D2
Orwell Pk Dr	111	D2
Orwell Pk Glade	111	D2
Orwell Pk Glen	111	D2
Orwell Pk Grn	111	D2
Orwell Pk Gro	111	D2
Orwell Pk Hts	111	D2
Orwell Pk Lawns	111	D2
Orwell Pk Ri	111	D2
Orwell Pk Vw	111	D2
Orwell Pk Way	111	D2
Orwell Rd Dublin 6	101	D3
Orwell Rd Dublin 6W	111	D2
Orwell Rd Dublin 14	114	A1
Orwell Shop Cen	111	D2
Orwell Wk	114	A1
Orwell Wds	114	A1
Oscar Sq	89	D3
Oscar Traynor Rd	40	A3
O'Shea's Cotts 3	137	D1
Osprey Av	111	C1
Osprey Dr	111	D2
Osprey Lawn	111	D1
Osprey Pk	111	C1
Osprey Rd	111	D2
Ossory Rd	79	C3
Ossory Sq	89	D3
Ostman Pl	77	C3
O'Sullivan Av	78	B2
Oswald Rd	92	A3
Otranto Pl	134	A1
Otterbrook	113	C3
Oulart	17	C2
Oulton Rd	80	B2
Our Ladys Cl	89	C2
Our Lady's Hospice	101	C1
Our Lady's Rd	89	C3
Oval, The	73	D3
Ovoca Rd	89	D3
Owendoher Haven	126	B1
Owendoher La	126	B1
Owendore Av	113	C2
Owendore Cres	113	C2
Owens Av	88	B2
Owenstown Pk	116	A2
Oxford Rd	102	A1
Oxford Ter Dublin 3		
off Church Rd	91	C1
Oxford Ter Dublin 6		
off Oxford Rd	102	A1
Oxmantown La		
off Blackhall Pl	89	C1
Oxmantown Rd	77	C3
Oxmantown Rd Lwr		
off Arbour Hill	89	C1

P

Pace Av	31	C2
Pace Cres	31	C2
Pacelli Av	57	C2
Pace Rd	31	C2
Pace Vw	31	C2
Packenham	119	C3
Paddock, The Dublin 7	75	C1
Paddock, The Celbr.	66	A1
Paddocks, The 4 Clons.	30	B3
Paddocks, The Dalkey	134	B1
Paddocks, The Dunb.	28	B2
Pairc Baile Munna	51	D1
Pairc Clearmont		
(Claremont Pk)	92	A3
Pairc Gleannaluinn		
(Glenaulin Pk)	74	A3
Pairc Gleann Trasna	123	D2
Pairc Mhuire	120	B2
Pairc Na Cuilenn	51	D1
Pakenham Br	44	B2
Pakenham Rd	118	B3
Palace St		
off Dame St	144	C3
Palmer Pk	127	C1
Palmers Av	85	C1
Palmers Cl	85	C1
Palmers Copse	85	C1
Palmers Ct	85	C1
Palmers Cres	85	C1
Palmers Dr	85	C1
Palmers Glade	85	C1
Palmers Gro	85	C1
Palmers Lawn	85	C1
Palmers Pk	85	C1
Palmers Rd	85	C1
Palmerston Av	85	D1
Palmerston Dr	73	D3
Palmerston Gdns	102	A3
Palmerston Gro	103	C3
Palmerston La	102	A3
Palmerston Pk		
Dublin 6	102	A3
Palmerston Pk Palm.	85	C1
Palmerston Pl	77	D3
Palmerston Rd	102	A2
Palmerston Vil	102	A3
Palmerstown Av	85	C1
Palmerstown Cl	85	C1
Palmerstown Ct	85	C1
Palmerstown Dr	73	D3
Palmerstown Grn	85	C1
Palmerstown Hts	85	C1
Palmerstown Lawn	85	C1
Palmerstown Manor	85	C1
Palmers Wk	85	C1
Palms, The	115	D2
Paradise Pl	78	A3
Parc Na Silla Av	140	B1
Parc Na Silla Cl	140	B1
Parc Na Silla La	140	B1
Parc Na Silla Ri	140	B1
Park, The Dublin 9	53	D2
Park, The Dublin 17	39	D2
Park, The Dublin 24	124	B1
Park, The (Greenhills)		
Dublin 24	109	D1
Park, The (Oldtown Mill Rd)		
Celbr.	66	A2
Park, The (Wolstan Haven Av)		
Celbr.	66	A2
Park, The (Dunboyne Castle)		
Dunb.	28	B3
Park, The (Lutterell Hall)		
Dunb.	28	B1
Park, The (Plunkett Hall)		
Dunb.	28	A1
Park, The Gra M.	82	B2
Park, The Kins.	16	A2
Park, The Lou.V.	68	A1
Park, The Mala.	21	C3
Park Av Dublin 4	104	A1
Park Av (Willbrook)		
Dublin 14	127	C1
Park Av Dublin 15	73	D1
Park Av Deans Gra	132	A2
Park Av (Hilltown)		
Swords	16	B1
Park Cl	133	D2
Park Ct	133	D2
Park Cres Dublin 8	76	A2
Park Cres Dublin 10	100	A3
Park Dr Dublin 6	102	B2
Park Dr Dublin.	137	C1
Park Dr Av	47	D3
Park Dr Cl	47	D3
Park Dr Ct	47	D3
Park Dr Cres	47	D3
Park Dr Grn	73	D1
Park Dr Gro	47	D3
Park Dr Lawn	47	D3
Parker Hill	102	A1
Parkgate Pl		
Business Cen	88	B1
Parkgate St	88	B1
Parkhill Av	109	D2
Parkhill Cl		
off Parkhill Ri	109	D2
Parkhill Ct	109	D2
Parkhill Dr	109	D2
Parkhill Grn	109	D2
Parkhill Lawn	109	D2
Parkhill Ri	109	D2
Parkhill Rd	109	D2
Parkhill Way	109	D2
Parklands Castle.	47	D3
Parklands Mayn.	65	D2
Parklands, The		
Dublin 14	113	C2
Parklands Av	124	B2
Parklands Cl	65	C2
Parklands Ct		
Dublin 24	124	B2
Parklands Ct Mayn.	65	C2
Parklands Cres	65	C2
Parklands Dr	124	B3
Parklands Gro	65	D2
Parklands Lawns	65	C2
Parklands Ri	65	C2
Parklands Sq	65	C2
Parklands Vw	124	B2
Parklands Way	65	C2
Park La Dublin 4	104	A1
Park La Dublin 20	86	B1
Park La E	145	E3
Park Lawn	81	D1
Park Lo	47	D3
Park Manor	73	C1
Parkmore	48	A3
Parkmore Dr	112	B1
Parkmore Ind Est	98	B2
Park Pl		
off South Circular Rd	88	A1
Park Rd Dublin 7	75	D1
Park Rd D.L.	119	D3
Park Rd Sally.	133	D3
Park Shop Cen	77	C3
Park St	87	C2
Park Ter	144	A4
Parkvale Dublin 13	57	D1
Parkvale Dublin 16	129	C2
Parkview Dublin 7	76	B3
Park Vw Dublin 15	74	B1
Park Vw Clons.	46	A2
Park Vw Mala.	21	C3
Parkview Port.	27	C1
Parkview Swords	16	A1
Parkview Av (Haroldscross)		
Dublin 6	101	D2
Park Vw Av (Rathmines)		
Dublin 6	102	A2
Park Vw Lawns	96	A3
Park Vil Dublin 15	48	A3
Park Vil Black.	117	C3
Parkway Business Cen	98	A3
Park W Av Dublin 10	97	D1
Park W Av Dublin 22	97	D1
Park W Business Pk	85	D3
Park W Ind Pk	86	A3
Park W Rd	85	D3
Parkwood Av	124	A2
Parkwood Gro	124	A2
Parkwood Lawn	124	A2
Parkwood Rd 2	124	A2
Parliament Row		
off Fleet St	145	D2
Parliament St	144	C3
Parnell Av		
off Parnell Rd	101	D1
Parnell Cotts	20	A3
Parnell Ct	101	D1
Parnell Pl	78	A3
Parnell Rd Dublin 12	89	C3
Parnell Rd Bray	142	A1
Parnell Sq E	78	A3
Parnell Sq N	78	A3
Parnell Sq W	78	A3
Parnell St Dublin 1	144	C1
Parnell St Sally.	133	D2
Parochial Av 2	43	D3
Parslickstown Av	32	B2
Parslickstown Cl	32	B2
Parslickstown Ct	32	B2
Parslickstown Dr	32	B2
Parslickstown Gdns	32	A2
Parslickstown Grn	32	B2
Parson Ct	64	B2
Parson Lo	64	B2
Parsons Hall	64	A2
Parson St	64	B2
Partridge Ter	87	C3
Patrician Pk 5	133	C1
Patrician Vil	117	C3
Patrick Doyle Rd	114	B1
Patrick's Row		
off Carysfort Av	117	D2
Patrick St Dublin 8	144	B4
Patrick St D.L.	119	D3
Patrickswell Pl	50	B2
Patriotic Ter		
off Brookfield Rd	88	B2
Paul St	144	A2
Pavilion Rd	143	D2
Pavilions Shop Cen, The	17	C1
Pavillion Gate 1	137	C2
Pea Fld	117	C2
Pearse Av	133	C3
Pearse Brothers Pk	127	C1
Pearse Cl 9	133	C2
Pearse Dr	133	C2
Pearse Gdns	133	C2
Pearse Grn 10	133	C2
Pearse Gro		
off Great Clarence Pl	91	C2
Pearse Ho	145	F3
Pearse Pk	133	C2
Pearse Rd	133	C2
Pearse Sq	91	C2
Pearse Sta	145	F3
Pearse St Dublin 2	145	E3
Pearse St Sally.	133	C3
Pearse Vil	133	C3
Pear Tree Fld 3	131	C1
Pebble Hill	65	C1
Pecks La	48	A3
Pelletstown Av	49	D3
Pembroke Cotts (Donnybrook)		
Dublin 4	103	C2
Pembroke Cotts (Ringsend)		
Dublin 4	91	D2
Pembroke Cotts (Dundrum)		
Dublin 14	115	C3
Pembroke Cotts Boot.	116	B1
Pembroke Gdns	91	C3
Pembroke La Dublin 2	90	B3
Pembroke La Dublin 4	91	C3
Pembroke Pk	103	C1
Pembroke Pl		
off Pembroke St Upr	90	B3
Pembroke Rd	90	B3
Pembroke Row	90	B3
Pembroke St	91	D2
Pembroke St Lwr	90	B3
Pembroke St Upr	90	B3
Penrose St	91	C2
Percy French Rd	99	D2
Percy La	91	C3
Percy Pl	91	C3
Peter Row	144	C4
Petersons Ct	145	F2
Peters Pl	90	A3
Peter St	144	C4
Petrie Rd	89	D3
Pheasant Av	50	A3
Pheasant Run The Dr	31	D2
Pheasant Run The Grn	31	D2
Pheasant Run The Gro	31	D2
Pheasant Run The Pk	31	D2
Phelan Av	50	A3

Name	Page	Grid
Phibsborough	77	D2
Phibsborough Av	77	D3
Phibsborough Pl	77	D3
Phibsborough Rd	77	D3
Philipsburgh Av	79	C2
Philipsburgh Ter	79	C1
Philomena Ter	91	D2
Phoenix Av	48	A3
Phoenix Ct *Dublin 7*		
off Slade Row	89	C1
Phoenix Ct *Dublin 15*	48	A3
Phoenix Dr	48	A3
Phoenix Gdns	48	A3
Phoenix Manor	76	B3
Phoenix Pk Av	75	C1
Phoenix Pk Way	75	C1
Phoenix Pl	48	A3
Phoenix St *Dublin 7*	144	A2
Phoenix St *Dublin 10*	87	C2
Phoenix Ter	117	C1
Pigeon Ho Rd	91	D2
Pig La	78	B3
Piles Bldgs		
off Golden La	144	B4
Piles Ter		
off Sandwith St Upr	145	F3
Pilot Vw	134	B1
Pimlico	144	A4
Pimlico Sq		
off The Coombe	144	A4
Pim St	89	C2
Pine Av	131	D3
Pinebrook	31	D3
Pinebrook Av	54	A3
Pinebrook Cl	31	D3
Pinebrook Cres		
off Pinebrook Av	54	A2
Pinebrook Downs	31	D3
Pinebrook Glen	31	D3
Pinebrook Gro		
off Pinebrook Rd	54	A3
Pinebrook Hts	31	D3
Pinebrook Lawn	32	A3
Pinebrook Ri	54	A3
Pinebrook Rd	54	A3
Pinebrook Vale	31	D3
Pinebrook Vw	31	D3
Pinebrook Way	32	A3
Pine Copse Rd	128	B1
Pine Ct *Black.*	131	D1
Pine Ct *Port.*	27	C2
Pine Gro	112	A3
Pine Gro Pk	14	B3
Pine Gro Rd	14	B3
Pine Haven	117	C1
Pine Hurst	76	B2
Pine Lawn *Dublin 24*	124	A1
Pine Lawn *Black.*	131	D1
Pine Rd	92	A2
Pines, The *Dublin 5*	54	B3
Pines, The *2 Dublin 14*	129	D1
Pines, The *Dublin 15*	48	A3
Pines, The *Dublin 16*	128	A3
Pinetree Cres	109	D2
Pinetree Gro	109	D2
Pine Valley Av	128	A3
Pine Valley Dr	128	A3
Pine Valley Gro	128	A3
Pine Valley Pk	128	A3
Pine Valley Way	128	A3
Pineview Av	123	D2
Pineview Dr	123	D2
Pineview Gro	123	D2
Pineview Lawn	123	D2
Pineview Pk	124	A2
Pineview Ri	124	A2
Pineview Rd	123	D2
Pinewood	138	B2
Pinewood Av	51	D1
Pinewood Cl	142	A3
Pinewood Ct *Ashb.*	11	C3
Pinewood Ct *Mulh.*	32	A3
Pinewood Cres	51	D1
Pinewood Dr	51	D1
Pinewood Grn	51	D1
Pinewood Gro	51	D1
Pinewood Pk	112	B3
Pinewoods	96	A3
Pinewood Vil	51	D1
Pinnockhill Rbt	17	C2
Place, The *Carrick.*	136	B3
Place, The *Dunb.*	28	B3
Plato Business Pk	32	A1
Plaza Shop Cen, The	17	D1
Pleasants La	90	A3
Pleasants Pl	90	A3
Pleasants St	90	A3
Plums Rd	129	D2
Plunkett Av *Dublin 11*	36	A3
Plunkett Av *Fox.*	131	D3
Plunkett Cres	36	A3
Plunkett Dr	36	A3
Plunkett Grn	36	A3
Plunkett Gro	36	A3
Plunkett Hall	28	A1
Plunkett Rd	50	A1
Poddle Pk	100	B3
Polo Rd	76	A3
Poolbeg St	145	E2
Poole St	89	C2
Poplar Row	79	C2
Poplars, The	118	A3
Poppintree Ind Est	37	C3
Poppintree Pk La W	37	C3
Porters Av	46	B2
Portersfield	46	B2
Porters Gate	45	C2
Porters Gate Av	45	D2
Porters Gate Cl	45	C2
Porters Gate Ct	45	C2
Porters Gate Cres	45	C2
Porters Gate Dr	45	C2
Porters Gate Grn	45	D2
Porters Gate Gro	45	D2
Porters Gate Hts	45	D2
Porters Gate Ri	45	D2
Porters Gate Vw	45	C2
Porters Gate Way	45	D2
Porters Rd	46	A2
Porterstown Rd	46	A2
Portland Cl	78	B3
Portland Pl	78	A2
Portland Rd	143	D2
Portland Rd N	143	D2
Portland Row	78	B3
Portland St N	78	B3
Portmahon Dr	88	B3
Portmarnock Av *2*	27	C1
Portmarnock Br	26	B3
Portmarnock Cres	27	C1
Portmarnock Dr	27	C1
Portmarnock Gro	27	C1
Portmarnock Pk	27	C1
Portmarnock Ri	27	C2
Portmarnock Sta	26	A3
Portmarnock Wk	27	C1
Portobello Harbour	102	A1
Portobello Pl	102	A1
Portobello Rd	101	D1
Portobello Sq		
off Clanbrassil St Upr	101	D1
Portraine Rd	13	D1
Portside Business Cen	79	D3
Port Side Ct	79	C3
Potato Mkt		
off Green St Little	144	B2
Pottery Rd	132	B3
Pound La	64	B2
Pound Pk	64	B1
Pound St	68	B2
Powers Ct		
off Warrington Pl	91	C3
Powers Sq		
off John Dillon St	144	B4
Prebend St	144	B1
Preston St	78	B3
Price's La *Dublin 2*	145	D2
Prices La *Dublin 6*	102	A1
Priestfield Cotts	89	C3
Priestfield Dr		
off Dolphin Av	89	C3
Priestfield Ter		
off South Circular Rd	89	C3
Primrose Av	77	D3
Primrose Gro	41	C3
Primrose Hill *Celbr.*	66	B3
Primrose Hill *D.L.*	119	C3
Primrose La	70	A3
Primrose St	77	D3
Prince Arthur Ter	102	A2
Prince of Wales Ter		
Dublin 4	103	D1
Prince Of Wales Ter *16*		
Bray	142	A1
Princes St N	145	D2
Princes St S	145	F2
Princeton	115	D2
Priorswood Rd	40	B3
Priory, The *Dublin 7*	76	A1
Priory, The *Dublin 16*	127	D1
Priory, The *4 Mala.*	20	A2
Priory Av	117	C2
Priory Chase	66	A3
Priory Cl	66	A3
Priory Ct *1 Dublin 16*	127	D2
Priory Ct *Celbr.*	66	A3
Priory Cres	66	A3
Priory Dr *Black.*	116	B3
Priory Dr *Celbr.*	66	A3
Priory E	76	A1
Priory Grn	66	A3
Priory Gro *Black.*	116	B3
Priory Gro *Celbr.*	66	A3
Priory Hall *Dublin 12*	112	A1
Priory Hall *Black.*	116	B3
Priory Lo	66	A3
Priory N	76	A1
Priory Rd	101	C2
Priory Vw	66	A3
Priory Wk *Dublin 12*	100	A3
Priory Wk *Celbr.*	66	A3
Priory Way *Dublin 12*	112	A1
Priory Way *Celbr.*	66	A2
Priory W	76	A1
Proby Pk	134	A2
Probys La	144	C2
Proby Sq	117	C2
Promenade Rd	80	A3
Prospect Av *Dublin 9*	77	D1
Prospect Av *Dublin 16*	126	B2
Prospect Cem	77	D1
Prospect Ct	126	B3
Prospect Dr	126	B2
Prospect Glen	126	B3
Prospect Gro	126	B2
Prospect Heath	126	B2
Prospect Hts	126	B3
Prospect Hill	13	C2
Prospect La	103	C3
Prospect Lawn	137	D1
Prospect Meadows	126	B2
Prospect Rd	77	D2
Prospect Sq	77	D1
Prospect Ter (Sandymount)		
off Beach Rd	92	A3
Prospect Vw	126	B2
Prospect Way	77	D1
Protestant Row	90	A3
Prouds La	145	D4
Prussia St	77	C3
Purley Pk	27	C1
Purser Gdns	102	A2
Putland Rd	142	A3
Putland Vil *10*	142	A3
Q		
Quarry Dr	99	D3
Quarryfield Ct	97	C3
Quarry Rd (Cabra)		
Dublin 7	77	C2
Quarry Rd *Grey.*	143	D2
Queens Pk	118	A3
Queens Rd	119	D3
Queen St	144	A2
Quinns La	90	B3
Quinn's Rd	141	C3
Quinsborough Rd	142	A1
R		
Racecourse Shop Cen	43	C3
Race Hill Cl	10	B1
Race Hill Cres	11	C2
Race Hill La	10	B1
Race Hill Lo	10	B1
Race Hill Manor	11	C1
Race Hill Pk	10	B1
Race Hill Rd	10	B2
Race Hill Vw	10	B1
Radlett Gro	27	C1
Rafters Av	100	A1
Rafters La	100	A1
Rafters Rd	100	A1
Raglan La	103	C1
Raglan Rd	103	C1
Raheen Av	122	B1
Raheen Cl	122	B1
Raheen Ct	122	B1
Raheen Cres	122	B1
Raheen Dr *Dublin 10*	86	A3
Raheen Dr *Dublin 24*	122	B1
Raheen Lawn	142	B3
Raheen Pk *Dublin 10*	86	A3
Raheen Pk *Dublin 24*	122	B1
Raheen Pk *Bray*	142	B3
Raheen Rd	122	B1
Raheny Pk	56	A3
Raheny Rd	55	D2
Raheny Sta	55	D3
Rail Pk	65	C3
Railway Av *Dublin 8*		
off Tyrconnell Rd	87	D3
Railway Av (Inchicore)		
Dublin 8	87	C3
Railway Av *Dublin 13*	58	A1
Railway Av *3 Mala.*	20	A2
Railway Cotts		
off Serpentine Av	103	D1
Railway Ct *2*	20	A2
Railway Ms	42	B3
Railway Rd *Dublin 13*	43	C3
Railway Rd *5 Dalkey*	134	B2
Railway St	145	E1
Railway Ter		
off Grattan St	91	C2
Rainsford Av	89	C2
Rainsford La *3*	139	C2
Rainsford St	89	C2
Ralahine	138	B2
Raleigh Sq	100	A1
Ralph Sq *1*	68	B2
Ramillies Rd	86	B2
Ramleh Cl	103	C3
Ramleh Pk	103	C3
Ramleh Vil	102	B3
Ramor Pk	47	C2
Ranelagh Av	102	A1
Ranelagh Rd	102	A1
Ranelagh Sta	102	B1
Raphoe Rd	100	A1
Rathbeale Ct	15	C3
Rathbeale Cres	15	C3
Rathbeale Ri	17	C1
Rathbeale Rd	14	B2
Rathbone Av	49	D3
Rathbone Cl	49	D3
Rathbone Dr	49	D3
Rathbone Pl	49	D3
Rathbone Way	49	D3
Rath Cross Rds	10	B1
Rathdown Av	113	C1
Rathdown Cl	143	C1
Rathdown Ct		
Dublin 6W	101	C3
Rathdown Ct *Grey.*	143	C1
Rathdown Cres	113	C1
Rathdown Dr	113	C1
Rathdown Gro *6*	129	D2
Rathdown Pk		
Dublin 6W	113	C1
Rathdown Pk *Grey.*	143	C1
Rathdown Rd *Dublin 7*	77	D3
Rathdown Rd *Grey.*	143	C1
Rathdown Sq	77	C3
Rathdown Ter *7*	129	D2
Rathdown Vil	113	C1
Rathdrum Rd	101	C1
Rathfarnham Gate	113	C1
Rathfarnham Castle	113	C2
Rathfarnham Mill	113	C2
Rathfarnham Pk	113	C1
Rathfarnham Rd		
Dublin 6W	113	C1
Rathfarnham Rd		
Dublin 14	113	C1
Rathfarnham		
Shop Cen	112	B2
Rathfarnham Wd	113	D2
Rathgar Av	101	C2
Rathgar Pk	101	D3
Rathgar Rd	101	D3
Rathgar Vil	101	D3
Rathingle Rd	16	B2

Rathland Rd			Redwood Lawn	109 D2		Rise, The *Manor.*	31 D3
(Bothar Raitleann)	100 B3		Redwood Pk	110 A2		Rise, The *Still.*	116 B2
Rathlin Rd	52 A3		Redwood Ri			Riverbank Hall	51 D3
Rath Lo	10 B1		*off Redwood Pk*	110 A2		River Cl **2**	141 C1
Rathlyon	125 C2		Redwood Vw			River Ct **1**	29 C3
Rathlyon Pk	125 C2		*off Redwood Av*	110 A2		Riverdale	68 B2
Rathmichael Dales	140 A2		Redwood Wk	109 D2		River Forest	68 B1
Rathmichael Haven	140 A2		Reginald Sq			River Gdns	52 A3
Rathmichael Hill	140 A2		*off Gray St*	144 A4		River La	141 C1
Rathmichael La	140 A2		Reginald St	144 A4		River Rd *Dublin 11*	49 D3
Rathmichael Manor	140 B1		Rehoboth Av	89 C3		River Rd *Dublin 15*	48 A2
Rathmichael Pk	141 C2		Rehoboth Pl	89 C3		Riversdale	73 C3
Rathmichael Wds	141 C2		Reillys Av			Riversdale Av *Dublin 6*	113 D1
Rathmines Av	102 A2		*off Dolphin's Barn St*	89 C3		Riversdale Av *Clond.*	96 B1
Rathmines Cl	102 A3		Reuben Av	88 B3		Riversdale Av *Palm.*	73 C3
Rathmines Pk	102 A2		Reuben St	89 C3		Riversdale Ct	73 C3
Rathmines Rd Lwr	102 A1		Rialto Br	88 B3		Riversdale Cres	96 B1
Rathmines Rd Upr	102 A2		Rialto Bldgs			Riversdale Dr	96 B1
Rathmintan Cl **3**	122 A2		*off Rialto Cotts*	88 B3		Riversdale Grn	96 B1
Rathmintan Ct	122 A2		Rialto Cotts	88 B3		Riversdale Gro	
Rathmintan Cres	122 A2		Rialto Dr	88 B3		*Dublin 6w*	100 B3
Rathmintan Dr	122 A2		Rialto Sta	88 B3		Riversdale Gro *Palm.*	73 C3
Rathmore	26 B3		Rialto St	88 B3		Riversdale Ind Est	98 B1
Rathmore Av	130 A1		Ribh Av	55 C3		Riversdale Pk *Clond.*	96 B1
Rathmore Pk	56 A3		Ribh Rd	55 C3		Riversdale Pk *Palm.*	73 C3
Rathmore Vil	101 C3		Richelieu Pk	104 A2		Riversdale Rd	96 B1
Rath Row	145 E2		Richmond	131 D1		Riverside **3**	96 B1
Rathsallagh Av	141 C1		Richmond Av	118 B3		Riverside Av	40 A3
Rathsallagh Br	141 C1		Richmond Av N	79 C2		Riverside Cotts	112 B2
Rathsallagh Dr	141 C2		Richmond Av S	102 B3		Riverside Cres	40 A3
Rathsallagh Gro	141 C1		Richmond Cotts			Riverside Dr *Dublin 14*	113 D2
Rathsallagh Pk	141 C1		*Dublin 1*	78 B3		Riverside Dr *Dublin 17*	40 A3
Rathvale Av	55 C1		Richmond Cotts (Inchicore)			Riverside Dr *Palm.*	73 C3
Rathvale Dr	55 C1		*Dublin 8*	88 A2		Riverside Gro	40 A3
Rathvale Gro			Richmond Cotts N			Riverside Pk	40 A3
off Rathvale Av	55 C1		*off Richmond Cotts*	78 B3		Riverside Rd	40 A3
Rathvale Pk	55 C1		Richmond Ct	114 B1		Riverside Wk	103 C3
Rathvilly Dr	50 A2		Richmond Cres	78 B3		Riverston Abbey	76 A1
Rathvilly Pk	50 A2		Richmond Est	79 C2		River Valley Av	17 C1
Rathvilly Rd	50 A2		Richmond Grn	118 B3		River Valley Cl	16 B1
Ratoath Av			Richmond Gro	118 B3		River Valley Ct	16 B1
(Ascal Ratabhachta)	49 D2		Richmond Hill *Dublin 6*	102 A1		River Valley Dr	16 B1
Ratoath Dr	49 D1		Richmond Hill *Black.*	118 B3		River Valley Gro	16 B2
Ratoath Est	76 A1		Richmond La			River Valley Hts	17 C2
Ratoath Rd *Dublin 7*	76 B2		*off Russell St*	78 B3		River Valley Lawn	16 B1
Ratoath Rd *Dublin 11*	49 D2		Richmond Ms	102 A1		River Valley Pk	16 B2
Ratra Rd	75 D1		Richmond Par	78 B3		River Valley Ri	16 B2
Ravens Ct	50 A1		Richmond Pk	118 B3		River Valley Rd	16 B1
Ravensdale Cl	100 B3		Richmond Pl	102 A1		River Valley Vw	16 B1
Ravensdale Pk	100 B3		Richmond Pl S			River Valley Way	16 B1
Ravensdale Rd	79 D3		*off Richmond St S*	102 A1		Riverview *Dublin 24*	124 A2
Ravens Rock Rd	130 A2		Richmond Rd	78 B1		Riverview *Palm.*	73 D3
Ravenswell Rd	142 A1		Richmond Row	102 A1		Riverview Business Cen	97 D1
Ravenswood	31 C3		Richmond Row S			Riverview Ct	86 B1
Ravenswood Av	45 C1		*off Richmond St S*	90 A3		Riverwood Chase	46 A3
Ravenswood Cres	45 C1		Richmond St N	78 B3		Riverwood Cl	46 B3
Ravenswood Dr	45 C1		Richmond St S	90 A3		Riverwood Copse	46 A3
Ravenswood Grn	45 C1		Richmond Ter **19**	142 B2		Riverwood Ct	46 B3
Ravenswood Lawn	45 C1		Richview Office Pk	103 C3		Riverwood Cres	72 B1
Ravenswood Ri	31 C3		Richview Pk	102 B3		Riverwood Dale	46 B3
Ravenswood Rd	45 C1		Ridge Hill	139 C3		Riverwood Dene	46 A3
Ravenswood Vw	45 C1		Ridgewood Av	16 A2		Riverwood Dr	46 B3
Raymond St	89 D3		Ridgewood Cl	16 A2		Riverwood Gdns	72 B1
Red Arches Av	43 C3		Ridgewood Ct	16 A2		Riverwood Glebe	72 A1
Red Arches Dr	43 C3		Ridgewood Grn	16 A3		Riverwood Glen	46 B3
Redberry	82 A2		Ridgewood Gro	16 B3		Riverwood Grn	46 B3
Red Brick Ter **3**	117 D3		Ridgewood Pk	16 A2		Riverwood Gro	46 B3
Redcourt Oaks	81 D2		Ridgewood Pl	16 A2		Riverwood Heath	46 A3
Red Cow Business Pk	98 A2		Ridgewood Sq	16 A2		Riverwood Lawn	46 B3
Red Cow Cotts **3**	73 D3		Rinawade Lawns	67 D2		Riverwood Pk	46 B3
Red Cow La	144 A1		Ringsend Br	91 D2		Riverwood Pl	72 A1
Red Cow Sta	97 D3		Ringsend Pk	91 D2		Riverwood Rd	46 B3
Redesdale Cres	116 A3		Ringsend Rd	91 C2		Riverwood Ter	46 A3
Redesdale Rd	116 A3		Ring St	87 D3		Riverwood Vale	46 B3
Redfern Av	27 C1		Ring Ter	87 D3		Riverwood Vw	46 B3
Redmonds Hill	90 A3		Rise, The (Drumcondra)			Riverwood Way	46 B3
Redwood Av	110 A2		*Dublin 9*	52 A3		Road, The	31 C3
Redwood Cl			Rise, The (Ballinteer)			Robert Emmet Br	101 D1
off Redwood Av	110 A2		*Dublin 16*	128 B3		Robert Pl	
Redwood Ct *Dublin 14*	114 A2		Rise, The (Ballyboden)			*off Clonliffe Rd*	78 B2
Redwood Ct *Dublin 24*			*Dublin 16*	126 B2		Robert St *Dublin 3*	
off Parkhill Rd	109 D2		Rise, The (Cookstown)			*off Clonliffe Rd*	78 B2
Redwood Dr	109 D2		*Dublin 24*	109 C2		Robert St *Dublin 8*	89 C2
Redwood Gro	117 C2		Rise, The (Kilnamanagh)			Robinhood Business Pk	98 A2
Redwood Hts			*Dublin 24*	109 D1		Robinhood Ind Est	98 B2
off Redwood Pk	110 A2		Rise, The *Carrick.*	136 B3		Robinhood Rd	98 B2
			Rise, The *Dalkey*	134 B2		Robinsons Ct	144 A4
			Rise, The *Kins.*	18 A2		Robin Vil	73 D3
			Rise, The *Leix.*	68 A1		Robswall	21 C3
			Rise, The *Mala.*	20 A2		Rochestown Av	133 C3
			Rise, The (Robswall) **3**			Rochestown Pk	133 C3
			Mala.	21 C3		Rochfort Av	83 D1

Rochfort Cl	83 D1
Rochfort Cres	83 D2
Rochfort Downs	83 D1
Rochfort Grn	83 D1
Rochfort Pk	83 D1
Rochfort Way	83 D2
Rock Br	66 A3
Rock Enterprise Cen	106 B2
Rockfield *Dublin 14*	129 C1
Rockfield *Lucan*	82 A2
Rockfield *Mayn.*	65 C3
Rockfield Av *Dublin 12*	111 D1
Rockfield Av *Mayn.*	65 C3
Rockfield Cl	46 B3
Rockfield Dr *Dublin 12*	100 A3
Rockfield Dr *Clond.*	96 B3
Rockfield Dr *Cool.*	46 B3
Rockfield Gdns	65 C2
Rockfield Grn	65 C2
Rockfield Lo	65 C3
Rockfield Manor	65 C3
Rockfield Pk *Clons.*	46 B3
Rockfield Pk *Mayn.*	65 C3
Rockfield Ri	65 C3
Rockfield Sq	65 C2
Rockfield Wk	65 C2
Rockford Pk	118 A3
Rockfort Av	135 C2
Rock Hill	117 D2
Rockingham Av	68 A1
Rockingham Grn	68 A1
Rockingham Gro	68 A1
Rockingham Pk	68 A1
Rocklands **2**	135 C1
Rock Lo	134 A3
Rock Rd	104 B3
Rockview	129 C3
Rockville Cres	118 A3
Rockville Dr	118 A3
Rockville Pk	118 A3
Rockville Rd	118 A3
Rockwood	82 A2
Rocwood	131 C2
Roebuck Av	116 B2
Roebuck Castle	115 D1
Roebuck Downs	115 C2
Roebuck Dr	99 D3
Roebuck Hall	115 D2
Roebuck Rd	115 C1
Roe La	89 C2
Roger's La	90 B3
Rollins Ct **7**	133 C2
Rollins Vil	133 C2
Roncalli Rd	57 C2
Rookery, The	126 A1
Roosevelt Cotts	76 A2
Rooske Ct	28 B3
Rooske Rd	28 B3
Rope Wk Pl	91 D2
Rory O'Connor Pk	132 B1
Rory O'More Br	89 C1
Rosapenna Dr	42 A3
Rosary Gdns E	119 C3
Rosary Gdns W	119 C3
Rosary Rd	89 C3
Rosary Ter	91 D2
Rosbeg Ct	57 C2
Rosberry	82 B3
Rosberry Av	82 B3
Rosberry Ct	82 B3
Rosberry La	82 B3
Rosberry Pk	82 B3
Rosberry Pl	82 B3
Rosebank (Hartstown)	
Clons.	30 B3
Rosedale *Dunb.*	28 B3
Rosedale Dr	30 B3
Rose Glen Av	56 B2
Rose Glen Rd	56 A2
Rosehaven **1**	46 B3
Rosehill **7**	131 D1
Roselawn	71 C3
Roselawn Av	47 C2
Roselawn Cl	47 D2
Roselawn Ct	47 D2
Roselawn Cres	47 C2
Roselawn Dr *Bray*	142 A3
Roselawn Dr *Castle.*	47 C2
Roselawn Glade	47 C2
Roselawn Gro	47 C2
Roselawn Pk	142 A3

Name	Page	Grid
Roselawn Rd	47	D2
Roselawn Shop Cen	47	C2
Roselawn Vw	47	C2
Roselawn Wk	47	C2
Roselawn Way	47	D2
Rosemount	114	B2
Rosemount Av	54	B3
Rosemount Business Pk	34	B3
Rosemount Ct *Dublin 14*	115	C3
Rosemount Ct *Boot.*	116	B1
Rosemount Cres	115	C1
Rosemount Pk	115	C2
Rosemount Pk Rd	34	A3
Rosemount Rd	77	D3
Rosemount Ter	116	B1
Rose Pk	132	B1
Rosevale Ct *off Brookwood Glen*	55	C3
Rosevale Mans	55	C3
Rosewood Gro	83	D2
Rosmeen Gdns	119	D3
Rosmeen Pk	133	D1
Rossecourt Av **2**	83	D2
Rossecourt Grn **6**	83	D2
Rossecourt Gro **1**	83	D2
Rossecourt La **5**	83	D2
Rossecourt Ri **8**	83	D2
Rossecourt Sq **4**	83	D2
Rossecourt Ter **7**	83	D2
Rossecourt Way **3**	83	D2
Rossfield Av	108	A3
Rossfield Cres	122	A1
Rossfield Dr	108	A3
Rossfield Gdns	122	A1
Rossfield Grn	122	A1
Rossfield Gro	122	A1
Rossfield Pk	108	A3
Rossfield Way	122	A1
Rosslyn **13**	142	A2
Rosslyn Ct	142	A2
Rosslyn Gro **14**	142	A2
Rossmore Av *Dublin 6W*	111	D2
Rossmore Av *Dublin 10*	86	A2
Rossmore Cl	111	D3
Rossmore Cres	111	D2
Rossmore Dr *Dublin 6W*	111	D2
Rossmore Dr *Dublin 10*	86	A1
Rossmore Gro	111	D3
Rossmore Lawns	111	D2
Rossmore Pk	111	D3
Rossmore Rd *Dublin 6W*	111	D2
Rossmore Rd *Dublin 10*	86	A1
Ross Rd	144	B4
Ross St	76	B3
Ross Vw	73	D3
Rostrevor Rd	113	D1
Rostrevor Ter	113	D1
Rothe Abbey	88	A3
Rowan Av	130	A2
Rowanbyrn	118	A3
Rowan Cl	66	B2
Rowan Hall *off Prospect La*	103	C3
Rowan Pk Av	118	A3
Rowans, The **17**	139	C3
Rowans Rd	129	D2
Rowlagh Av	84	A2
Rowlagh Cres	84	A2
Rowlagh Gdns	84	A2
Rowlagh Grn	84	A2
Rowlagh Pk	84	A2
Roxboro Cl	134	A3
Royal Canal Av	49	D3
Royal Canal Bk	77	D3
Royal Canal Ter	77	D3
Royal Liver Retail Pk	98	B1
Royal Marine Ter **3**	142	B1
Royal Oak	39	C3
Royal Ter *off Inverness Rd*	79	C2
Royal Ter E	133	D1
Royal Ter La **9**	133	C1
Royal Ter N **10**	133	D1
Royal Ter W	133	D1

Name	Page	Grid
Rouse Rd	77	D2
Royston	100	A3
Ruby Hall	132	B2
Rugby Rd	102	A1
Rugby Vil *off Rugby Rd*	102	A1
Rugged La	72	A1
Rushbrook	47	C2
Rushbrook Av	111	C2
Rushbrook Ct	111	D2
Rushbrook Dr	111	D2
Rushbrooke Cres	111	C2
Rushbrooke Rd	111	C2
Rushbrook Gro	111	D2
Rushbrook Pk	111	D2
Rushbrook Vw	111	C2
Rushbrook Way	111	D2
Rusheeney Av	31	C3
Rusheeney Cl	31	D3
Rusheeney Ct	31	D3
Rusheeney Cres	31	C3
Rusheeney Gdns	31	D3
Rusheeney Gro	31	D3
Rusheeney Manor	31	C3
Rusheeney Pk	31	C3
Rusheeney Vw	31	D3
Rusheeney Way	31	D3
Rus-in-Urbe Ter **11**	133	D1
Russell Av *Dublin 3*	78	A2
Russell Av E.	79	C3
Russell Cl	122	A1
Russell Ct	122	A1
Russell Cres	122	A1
Russell Downs	122	A1
Russell Dr	122	A1
Russell Grn	122	A1
Russell Gro	122	A1
Russell La	122	A1
Russell Lawns	122	A1
Russell Meadows	122	A1
Russell Pl	122	A1
Russell Ri	122	A1
Russell St	78	B3
Russell Vw	122	A1
Russell Wk	122	A1
Rutland Av	101	C1
Rutland Gro	101	C1
Rutland Pl *off Clontarf Rd*	80	B3
Rutland Pl N	78	B3
Rutland Pl W	78	A3
Rutland St Lwr	78	B3
Rutledges Ter	89	C3
Ryders Row *off Parnell St*	144	C1
Rye Br	68	B2
Ryecroft	142	A2
Ryemont Abbey	68	A1
Rye River	68	B1
Rye River Av	68	B1
Rye River Cl	68	B2
Rye River Ct	68	B2
Rye River Cres	68	B2
Rye River Gdns	68	B2
Rye River Gro	68	B2
Rye River Mall	68	B2
Rye River Pk	68	B2
Ryevale Lawns	68	B1

S

Name	Page	Grid
Sackville Av	78	B3
Sackville Gdns	78	B3
Sackville La *off O'Connell St Lwr*	145	D1
Sackville Pl	145	D2
Saddlers Av	32	B3
Saddlers Cl	32	B3
Saddlers Cres	32	B3
Saddlers Dr **1**	32	B3
Saddlers Glade	32	B3
Saddlers Gro	32	B3
Saddlers Lawn	32	B3
Sadleir Hall	28	A2
Saggart Abbey	121	C2
St. Agnes Pk	100	A2
St. Agnes Rd	100	A2
St. Aidan's Dr	115	D2
St. Aidan's Pk	79	D2
St. Aidan's Pk Av	79	D2
St. Aidan's Pk Rd	79	D2

Name	Page	Grid
St. Aidan's Ter **20**	142	A1
St. Alban's Pk	104	B2
St. Alban's Rd	89	D3
St. Alphonsus Av	78	B2
St. Alphonsus Rd	78	A2
St. Andoens Ter *off Cook St*	144	A3
St. Andrews	71	C3
St. Andrews Dr	71	D3
St. Andrews Fairway	83	D1
St. Andrews Grn	71	D3
St. Andrew's Gro	20	A2
St. Andrew's La *off Trinity St*	145	D3
St. Andrews Pk	14	B3
St. Andrew's St	145	D3
St. Andrews Wd	71	C3
St. Annes	100	A3
St. Anne's Av	55	D3
St. Anne's Dr	55	D3
St. Anne's Pk	141	C3
St. Annes Rd	89	C3
St. Anne's Rd N	78	A2
St. Anne's Sq	117	D2
St. Anne's Ter	55	D3
St. Ann's Sq **5**	26	B3
St. Ann's Sq Lwr **4**	26	B3
St. Anthony's Av	96	B3
St. Anthony's Business Pk	97	D2
St. Anthony's Cres	99	C3
St. Anthony's Pl *off Temple St N*	78	A3
St. Anthony's Rd	88	B3
St. Aongus Cres	110	B2
St. Aongus Grn	110	B2
St. Aongus Gro	110	B2
St. Aongus Lawn	110	B2
St. Aongus Rd	110	B2
St. Assam's Av	56	A3
St. Assam's Dr	56	A3
St. Assam's Pk	56	A3
St. Assam's Rd E	56	A3
St. Assam's Rd W	56	A3
St. Attracta Rd	77	C2
St. Aubyn's Ct **9**	139	C3
St. Audoens Ter *off School Ho La W*	144	B3
St. Augustine's Pk	131	D1
St. Augustine St	144	A3
St. Barnabas Gdns	79	C3
St. Begnet's Vil	134	B2
St. Brendan's Av	54	B2
St. Brendan's Cotts	91	D2
St. Brendan's Cres	111	C1
St. Brendan's Dr	54	B2
St. Brendan's Pk	55	C2
St. Brendan's Ter *Dublin 5*	54	B1
St. Brendan's Ter *D.L.* *off St. Mary's St*	119	C3
St. Bricin's Pk	89	C1
St. Bridget's Av	79	C3
St. Bridget's Dr	99	C3
St. Bridget's Pk	143	C1
St. Brigid's Av **3**	26	B3
St. Brigids Ch Rd	131	C1
St. Brigid's Cotts (Blanchardstown) *Dublin 15*	47	D2
St. Brigids Cotts *Clond.*	97	C3
St. Brigid's Ct *off St. Brigid's Dr*	54	B3
St. Brigid's Cres	54	B2
St. Brigid's Dr *Dublin 5*	54	B3
St. Brigid's Dr *Clond.*	96	B3
St. Brigids Flats	103	C3
St. Brigids Gdns	91	C1
St. Brigids Grn	54	B3
St. Brigids Gro	54	B3
St. Brigids Lawn	54	B3
St. Brigid's Pk (Blanchardstown) *Dublin 15*	47	D2
St. Brigid's Pk **1** *Clond.*	96	B3
St. Brigid's Pk *Corn.*	132	A3
St. Brigid's Rd *Dublin 5*	54	B2
St. Brigid's Rd *Clond.*	96	B3
St. Brigid's Rd Lwr	78	A2
St. Brigid's Rd Upr	78	A2
St. Brigids Shop Mall	54	B3
St. Brigid's Ter **21**	142	A1

Name	Page	Grid
St. Broc's Cotts	103	C2
Saintbury Av	139	C2
St. Canice's Pk	51	D2
St. Canice's Rd	51	D2
St. Catherine's Av	89	C3
St. Catherines Gro **3**	95	D2
St. Catherine's La W	144	A3
St. Catherine's Pk *Dalkey*	134	A2
St. Catherine's Rd *D.L.*	134	A1
St. Catherine's Rd	134	A2
St. Catherine's Vw	69	C1
St. Clare's Av *off Harolds Cross Rd*	101	D1
St. Clare's Home	51	D2
St. Clare's Ter *off Mount Drummond Av*	101	D1
St. Clement's Rd	78	A2
St. Colmcilles Ct **1**	17	C1
St. Colmcille's Way	125	C2
St. Columbanus Av	114	B1
St. Columbanus Pl	114	B1
St. Columbanus Rd	114	B1
St. Columbas Hts	17	C1
St. Columbas Ri	17	C1
St. Columba's Rd	99	C3
St. Columba's Rd Lwr	78	A2
St. Columba's Rd Upr	78	A2
St. Columcille's Cres **2**	17	C1
St. Columcille's Dr	17	D1
St. Columcille's Ter **22**	142	A1
St. Columcills Pk	17	D1
St. Conleth's Rd	99	C3
St. Cronan's Av	14	B3
St. Cronan's Cl **1**	16	B1
St. Cronan's Ct	14	B3
St. Cronan's Gro	14	B3
St. Cronan's Lawn	14	B3
St. Cronan's Rd **23**	142	A1
St. Cronan's Vw **2**	16	B1
St. Cronan's Way **3**	16	B1
St. Davids	54	A3
St. Davids Pk	54	A3
St. David's Ter *Dublin 7* *off Blackhorse Av*	76	B3
St. David's Ter (Glasnevin) *Dublin 9*	52	A3
St. Davids Wd	52	A3
St. Declan Rd	79	C1
St. Declan Ter	79	D1
St. Dominic's Av	124	A1
St. Dominic's Cen	124	A1
St. Dominic's Ct **3**	124	A1
St. Dominic's Rd	124	A1
St. Dominic's Ter	124	A1
St. Donagh's Cres	56	A1
St. Donagh's Pk	56	B1
St. Donagh's Rd	56	A1
St. Edmunds	72	A3
St. Eithne Rd	77	C2
St. Elizabeth's Ct *off North Circular Rd*	77	C3
St. Enda's Dr	113	C3
St. Enda's Pk	113	C3
St. Enda's Rd	101	C3
St. Finbar's Cl	111	C1
St. Finbar's Rd	76	B1
St. Finian's	82	B1
St. Finian's Av	82	B1
St. Finian's Cl	82	B1
St. Finian's Cres	82	B1
St. Finian's Gro	82	B1
St. Fintan Rd	77	C2
St. Fintan's Cres	59	C3
St. Fintan's Gro	59	C3
St. Fintan's Pk *Dublin 13*	59	C3
St. Fintan's Pk *Black.*	132	A1
St. Fintan's Rd	59	C3
St. Fintan's Ter **4**	73	D3
St. Fintan's Vil	132	A1
St. Fintan Ter	77	C1
St. Gabriel's	137	D1
St. Gabriels Ct	81	D2
St. Gabriel's Rd	81	D2
St. Gall Gdns N	114	B1

St. Gall Gdns S 114 B3
St. Gatien Ct 127 C1
St. Gatien Rd **2** 127 C1
St. George's Av
  Dublin 3 78 B2
St. George's Av *Kill.* 139 C1
St. Gerard's Rd 99 C3
St. Helena's Dr 50 B2
St. Helena's Rd 50 B2
St. Helen's 134 A1
St. Helen's Rd 116 B1
St. Helens Wd 116 B2
St. Ignatius Av 78 A2
St. Ignatius Rd 78 A2
St. Ita's Rd 78 A1
St. Ive's 20 A2
St. James PI 87 D2
St. James's Av *Dublin 3* 78 B2
St. James's Av *Dublin 8* 89 C2
St. James's PI
  off Tyrconnell Rd 87 D3
St. James's Rd 99 C3
St. James's Ter 89 C3
St. James's Wk 88 B3
St. Jarlath Rd 77 C2
St. Johns 104 A2
St. John's Av *Dublin 8*
  off John St S 144 A4
St. John's Av *Clond.* 96 A3
St. John's Cl 96 A3
St. John's Ct *Dublin 3* 80 A1
St. Johns Ct *Dublin 5* 54 A1
St. John's Ct *Clond.* 96 A3
St. John's Cres 96 A3
St. John's Dr 96 A3
St. John's Grn 96 A3
St. John's Lawn 96 A3
St. John's Pk *Clond.* 96 A3
St. John's Pk *D.L.* 119 C3
St. John's Pk W 96 A3
St. John's Rd *Dublin 4* 104 A1
St. John's Rd *Clond.* 96 A3
St. John's Rd W 88 A2
St. John St
  off Blackpitts 89 D3
St. Johns Wd *Dublin 3* 80 B2
St. Johns Wd *Clond.* 96 A2
St. John's Wd Ct 10 B2
St. John's Wd Dr 10 B2
St. Johns Wd Pk 10 B2
St. John's Wd W 96 A2
St. Joseph's 49 D2
St. Joseph's Av
  Dublin 3 78 B2
St. Joseph's Av
  Dublin 9 78 A2
St. Joseph's Conv 101 C3
St. Josephs Ct 77 C3
St. Josephs Gro 115 C3
St. Joseph's Par 78 A3
St. Joseph's PI
  off St. Joseph's Par 78 A3
St. Joseph's Rd
  Dublin 7 77 C3
St. Joseph's Rd
  Dublin 12 99 C3
St. Joseph's Sq
  off Vernon Av 81 C2
St. Joseph's St
  off Synnott PI 78 A3
St. Joseph's Ter *Dublin 1*
  off North Circular Rd 78 B3
St. Joseph's Ter
  Dublin 3 79 C2
St. Kevins Ct 102 A3
St. Kevins Gdns 102 A3
St. Kevin's Par 89 D3
St. Kevins Pk *(Rathgar)*
  Dublin 6 102 A3
St. Kevin's Pk *Still.* 130 A1
St. Kevin's Rd 101 D1
St. Kevin's Sq 142 A1
St. Kevin's Ter **15** 142 A2
St. Kevin's Vil 133 C1
St. Killian's Av 98 B3
St. Killian's Pk **1** 96 B2

St. Laurence Gro 86 B1
St. Laurence Rd 86 B1
St. Laurence's Mans 91 C1
St. Laurences Pk 116 B3
St. Laurence's Ter **24** 142 A1
St. Laurence St N
  off Sheriff St Lwr 145 F1
St. Laurence Gro 80 A2
St. Laurence
  O'toole Av **1** 26 B3
St. Laurence PI
  off Sheriff St Lwr 145 F1
St. Laurence Rd (Clontarf)
  Dublin 3 80 A2
St. Laurence Rd (Howth)
  Dublin 13 60 B2
St. Lawrences Ct 80 A2
St. Lawrence St
  off Sheriff St Lwr 145 F1
St. Lawrence Ter 61 C2
St. Lomans Rd 71 D3
St. Luke's Av 144 A4
St. Luke's Cres 114 B1
St. Maelruans Pk 124 A1
St. Magdalene Ter 91 D2
St. Malachy's Dr 99 C3
St. Malachy's Rd 78 A1
St. Margaret's Av
  Dublin 5 56 B2
St. Margaret's Av *Mala.* 20 A2
St. Margaret's Av N
  off North Circular Rd 78 B3
St. Margaret's
  Business Pk 36 A3
St. Margaret's Cl **5** 134 B1
St. Margaret's Cl **1** 36 B3
St. Margaret's
  Halting Site 37 D2
St. Margaret's Pk 20 A2
St. Margaret's Rd
  Dublin 11 36 B3
St. Margaret's Rd *Mala.* 20 A2
St. Margaret's Ter 89 C3
St. Mark's Av 84 A1
St. Mark's Cres 84 A2
St. Mark's Dr 84 B2
St. Mark's Gdns 84 A2
St. Mark's Grn 84 A2
St. Mark's Gro 84 A2
St. Marnock's Av 26 B3
St. Martin's Dr 100 B3
St. Martin's Pk 100 B2
St. Mary's Av
  (Rathfarnham) 113 C2
St. Mary's Av N 78 A3
St. Mary's Av W 87 D2
St. Mary's Coll 102 A1
St. Mary's Cres 99 D1
St. Mary's Dr 99 D1
St. Mary's La 91 C3
St. Mary's Pk *Dublin 12* 99 D2
St. Mary's Pk *Dublin 15* 49 D2
St. Mary's Pk *Leix.* 68 A1
St. Mary's PI
  off Main St 61 C2
St. Mary's PI N **1** 78 A3
St. Mary's Rd *Dublin 3* 79 C3
St. Mary's Rd *Dublin 12* 99 D2
St. Mary's Rd *Dublin 13*
  off Main St 61 C2
St. Mary's Rd N 79 C3
St. Mary's Rd S 91 C3
St. Mary's St 119 C3
St. Mary's Ter *Dublin 7* 78 A3
St. Marys Ter **22** *Bray* 142 B2
St. Mary's Ter **1** *Dunb.* 28 B2
St. Mel's Av 111 C1
St. Michael's Est 88 A3
St. Michael's Hill 144 B3
St. Michael's La
  off High St 144 B3
St. Michael's Rd 78 A1
St. Michael's Ter 89 D3
St. Michan's St 144 B2
St. Mobhi Boithrin 52 A3
St. Mobhi Ct 52 A3
St. Mobhi Dr 78 A1
St. Mobhi Gro 78 A1
St. Mobhi Rd 78 A1
St. Mobhis Br 78 A1
St. Mochtas 46 B3
St. Mochtas Av 46 B2

St. Mochtas Chase 46 B2
St. Mochtas Dr 46 A3
St. Mochtas Grn 46 B3
St. Mochtas Gro 46 B3
St. Mochtas Lawn 46 A2
St. Mochtas Rd 46 A3
St. Mochtas Vale 46 B2
St. Nessan's Ter
  off Tuckett's La 60 B2
St. Nicholas PI 144 B4
St. Oliver's Pk 85 C3
St. Pappin Grn 51 D2
St. Pappin Rd 51 D2
St. Patrick Av
  off Annesley Av 79 C3
St. Patrick's Av **1**
  Clond. 96 A1
St. Patrick's Av **6**
  Dalkey 134 B2
St. Patrick's Av *Port.* 26 B3
St. Patrick's Cath 144 B4
St. Patrick's Cl *Dublin 8* 144 B4
St. Patrick's Cl **11** *D.L.* 132 B1
St. Patrick's Coll
  Maynooth 64 B2
St. Patrick's Cotts 113 C3
St. Patrick's Cres 132 B1
St. Patrick's Nat Sch 78 B1
St. Patrick's Par 78 A2
St. Patrick's Pk
  (Blanchardstown)
  Dublin 15 47 C2
St. Patrick's Pk *Celbr.* 66 B2
St. Patrick's Pk *Clond.* 96 A1
St. Patricks Pk *D'bate* 13 D2
St. Patrick's Pk *Dunb.* 28 B2
St. Patrick's Rd
  Dublin 9 78 A2
St. Patrick's Rd
  Dublin 12 99 C3
St. Patrick's Rd *Clond.* 96 A1
St. Patrick's Rd *Dalkey* 134 B2
St. Patrick's Sq **1** *Bray* 142 A1
St. Patrick's Sq **7**
  Dalkey 134 B2
St. Patrick's Ter *Dublin 1*
  off Russell St 78 B3
St. Patrick's Ter *Dublin 3*
  off North Strand Rd 79 C3
St. Patrick's Ter
  Dublin 8 87 D2
St. Patricks Ter *D'bate* 13 D2
St. Patrick's Ter **6** *D.L.* 133 C1
St. Patrick's Vil 91 D2
St. Paul's Dr 99 D3
St. Paul's Ter **21** 134 A1
St. Peters Av 77 D3
St. Peters Cl 77 D3
St. Peter's Cres 99 D3
St. Peter's Dr 99 D3
St. Peter's Pk 28 B2
St. Peter's Rd *Dublin 7* 77 D3
St. Peter's Rd *Dublin 12* 99 C3
St. Peter's Ter *Dublin 13* 60 B2
St. Peter's Ter **6** *D.L.* 134 A1
St. Philomena's Rd 77 D2
St. Raphaels Av 66 A3
St. Ronans Av 84 A3
St. Ronan's Cl 84 A2
St. Ronan's Cres 84 A2
St. Ronan's Dr 84 A2
St. Ronan's Gdns 84 A2
St. Ronan's Grn 84 A2
St. Ronan's Gro 84 A2
St. Ronan's Pk 84 A2
St. Ronan's Way 84 A3
St. Samson Cl 41 D2
St. Samson Sq 41 D2
St. Stephen's Grn 90 B3
St. Stephen's Grn N 145 D4
St. Stephen's Grn Pk 90 A3
St. Stephen's Grn
  Shop Cen 145 D4
St. Stephen's Grn S 90 A3
St. Stephen's Grn Sta 145 D4
St. Stephen's Grn W 90 A3
St. Stephen's Pl 90 B3
St. Sylvester Vil 20 A3
St. Teresa's La 100 A3
St. Teresa's PI
  off Prospect Av 77 D1
St. Teresa's Rd *Dublin 9* 77 D1

St. Teresa's Rd (Crumlin)
  Dublin 12 100 A3
St. Theresa Gdns 89 C3
St. Thomas' Mead 116 B2
St. Thomas' Rd (Tenter Flds)
  Dublin 8 89 D3
St. Thomas' Rd *Still.* 116 A2
St. Thomas's Av
  off Constitution Hill 144 B1
St. Vincent's Home 75 D1
St. Vincent's Pk 118 A3
St. Vincents Rd 143 D2
St. Vincent St N 77 D3
St. Vincent St S
  (Tenter Flds) 89 D3
St. Vincent St W 87 D2
St. Werburghs 18 A1
St. Wolstan's Abbey 66 B3
Salamanca 115 D2
Sallowood Vw 38 B3
Sallyglen Rd 133 D2
Sallymount Av 102 B1
Sallymount Gdns 102 B1
Sallynoggin Pk 133 C2
Sallynoggin Rd 133 C2
Sally Pk 125 C1
Sally Pk Cl 125 C1
Sally's Br 101 C1
Salthill &
  Monkstown Sta 118 B2
Salzburg 115 D2
Sampsons La 144 C1
Sandford Av (Donnybrook)
  Dublin 4 103 C2
Sandford Av *Dublin 8* 89 C3
Sandford Cl 102 B2
Sandford Gdns *Dublin 4* 103 C2
Sandford Gdns *Dublin 8*
  off Donore Av 89 C3
Sandford Rd 102 B2
Sandford Ter 102 B2
Sandford Wd 14 B2
Sand Holes, The 73 D1
Sandon Cove 80 B2
Sandwith Pl 145 F3
Sandwith St Lwr 145 F3
Sandwith St Upr 145 F3
Sandycove Av E 134 B1
Sandycove Av W 134 A1
Sandycove E La 134 B1
Sandycove Glastule Sta 133 D1
Sandycove Rd 134 A1
Sandyford
  Business Cen 130 A2
Sandyford Downs 129 D3
Sandyford Ind Est 130 B2
Sandyford Office Pk 130 B2
Sandyford Pk
  Dublin 16 129 D3
Sandyford Pk *Leo.* 130 B2
Sandyford Rd 129 C1
Sandyford Sta 130 B2
Sandyford Vw 129 C3
Sandyford Village 129 D3
Sandyhill Ct 37 D3
Sandyhill Gdns 37 D3
Sandymount Av 103 D1
Sandymount Castle Dr 104 A1
Sandymount Castle Rd 104 A1
Sandymount Grn 92 A3
Sandymount Rd 92 A3
Sandymount Sta 104 A1
Sans Souci Pk 116 B1
Sans Souci Wd 142 A2
Santa Sabina Manor 59 C2
Santry Av 38 A3
Santry Av Ind Est 38 B3
Santry Business Pk 39 C2
Santry Cl 39 C3
Santry Ct 39 C3
Santry Hall Ind Est 52 B1
Santry Vil 39 C3
Santry Way 38 B3
Sarah Curran Av 127 C1
Sarah Curran Rd **1** 127 C1
Sarah PI 88 A1
Sarsfield Ct 70 A3
Sarsfield Pk 70 B3
Sarsfield Quay 88 A2
Sarsfield Rd *Dublin 8* 87 D2
Sarsfield Rd *Dublin 10* 87 C2
Sarsfield St *Dublin 7* 77 D3

Sarsfield St *Sally.*	133	C2
Sarsfield Ter **4**	70	A3
Sarto Lawn	57	C1
Sarto Pk	57	C1
Sarto Ri	57	C2
Sarto Rd	57	C2
Saul Rd	100	B1
Saval Gro	134	A3
Saval Pk Cres	134	A3
Saval Pk Gdns	134	A2
Saval Pk Rd	134	A2
Scholarstown Pk	126	A2
Scholarstown Rd	126	A2
School Av	54	B3
Schoolhouse La	145	D4
School Ho La W	144	B3
School St	89	C2
Scotchstone Br	15	D3
Scott Pk	142	B3
Scribblestown	49	D3
Scribblestown Rd	49	C3
Seabank Ct	134	A1
Seabrook Manor	26	A3
Seabury	104	B2
Seabury Av	19	C1
Seabury Cl	19	C1
Seabury Ct **5**	19	C2
Seabury Cres	19	C2
Seabury Dale **3**	19	C1
Seabury Downs	19	C2
Seabury Dr	19	C1
Seabury Gdns	18	B1
Seabury Glen	19	C1
Seabury Grn	19	C1
Seabury Gro **4**	19	C2
Seabury Hts	18	B1
Seabury La	19	C2
Seabury Lawns **1**	18	B1
Seabury Meadows	18	B1
Seabury Orchard	19	C1
Seabury Par	19	C1
Seabury Pk	18	B1
Seabury Pl	19	C2
Seabury Rd	19	C1
Seabury Vale	19	C1
Seabury Vw	18	B1
Seabury Wk	19	C2
Seabury Wd	18	B1
Seacliff Av	57	D1
Seacliff Dr	57	C1
Seacliff Rd	57	C1
Seacourt	81	C2
Seacrest	142	B2
Seafield	141	D1
Seafield Av *Dublin 3*	81	C2
Seafield Av *Black.*	118	B3
Seafield Cl	116	A1
Seafield Ct *Dublin 13*	58	A1
Seafield Ct *Kill.*	139	C3
Seafield Ct *Mala.*	20	A2
Seafield Cres	116	B1
Seafield Down	81	D2
Seafield Dr	116	A1
Seafield Gro	81	D2
Seafield Pk	116	B1
Seafield Rd *Boot.*	116	A1
Seafield Rd *Kill.*	139	C3
Seafield Rd E	81	C2
Seafield Rd W	80	B2
Seafield Ter **6**	135	C2
Seafort Av	92	A3
Seafort Cotts		
off Seafort Av	92	A3
Seafort Gdns	92	A3
Seafort Vil		
off Seafort Av	92	A3
Seagrange Av	43	C3
Seagrange Dr	57	D1
Seagrange Rd	57	C1
Seagrave	26	B3
Seagrave Cl	37	C2
Seagrave Ct	36	B2
Seagrave Dr	36	B2
Seagrave Ri	37	C2
Seagrave Ter	37	C2
Seagrave Way	36	B2
Seamount Dr	20	B3
Seamount Gro	20	B3
Seamount Hts	20	B3
Seamount Pk	20	B3
Seamount Rd	20	B3
Seamount Vw	18	A1
Seamus Ennis Rd	50	B1
Sean Heuston Br	88	B1
Sean McDermott St Lwr	78	B3
Sean McDermott St Upr	145	D1
Sean More Rd	92	A3
Sean O'Casey La	78	B3
Seapark *Dublin 3*	81	C2
Seapark *Mala.*	20	B2
Seapark Dr	81	C2
Seapark Hill	20	B3
Seapark Rd	81	C2
Seapoint Av **1**		
Dublin 13	43	D3
Seapoint Av *Black.*	118	A2
Seapoint Ct **5**		
Dublin 13	43	D3
Seapoint Ct *Bray*	142	A1
Seapoint Rd	142	A1
Seapoint Sta	118	A2
Seapoint Ter **17**	142	A1
Seapoint Vil **18**	142	A1
Sea Rd	19	D1
Seatown Pk	15	D3
Seatown Rd	15	D3
Seatown Rbt	15	D3
Seatown Ter	17	D1
Seatown Vil	15	D3
Seatown Wk	17	D1
Seatown W	15	D3
Seaview Av	79	C3
Seaview Av N	80	A2
Seaview Lawn	140	B1
Seaview Pk	140	B1
Sea Vw Ter *Dublin 4*	103	D2
Seaview Ter *Dublin 13*	61	C2
Seaview Wd	140	B1
Second Av *Dublin 1*	91	C1
Second Av (Cookstown)		
Dublin 24	109	C2
Sefton Grn	132	B2
Selskar Ter	102	A1
Serpentine Av	103	D1
Serpentine Pk	91	D3
Serpentine Rd	91	D3
Serpentine Ter	103	D1
Seskin Vw Av	124	A1
Seskin Vw Dr	124	A1
Seskin Vw Pk	124	A2
Seskin Vw Rd	124	A1
Seven Hos **12**	133	D1
Seven Oaks	52	B3
Seville Pl	79	C3
Seville Ter	78	B3
Seymour Rd	142	A1
Shamrock Cotts		
off Shamrock Pl	79	C3
Shamrock Pl	79	C3
Shamrock St		
off Primrose St	77	D3
Shamrock Ter	79	C3
Shamrock Vil	101	D2
Shanard Av	52	A1
Shanard Rd	52	A1
Shanboley Rd	53	C1
Shancastle Av	84	A1
Shancastle Cl	84	A1
Shancastle Cres	84	A1
Shancastle Dr	84	A1
Shancastle Lawns	84	A1
Shancastle Pk	84	A1
Shandon Cres	77	D2
Shandon Dr	77	D2
Shandon Gdns	77	C1
Shandon Pk *Dublin 7*	77	C2
Shandon Pk *Black.*	118	A2
Shandon Rd	77	D2
Shanganagh Cliffs	141	C1
Shanganagh Gro	141	C3
Shanganagh Rd	139	C3
Shanganagh Ter	139	C2
Shanganagh Vale	138	A2
Shanganagh Wd	141	C2
Shangan Av	52	B1
Shangan Cres	38	B3
Shangan Gdns	52	B1
Shangagh Rd	78	A2
Shangan Grn	52	B1
Shangan Pk	52	B1
Shangan Rd	52	A1
Shanglas Rd	53	C1
Shanid Rd	101	C3
Shankill Business Cen	141	C2
Shankill Shop Cen	141	C2
Shankill Sta	141	C2
Shankill Vw **19**	142	A1
Shanliss Av	52	B1
Shanliss Dr	52	B1
Shanliss Gro	52	B1
Shanliss Pk	52	B1
Shanliss Rd	52	A1
Shanliss Wk	52	B1
Shanliss Way	52	B1
Shannon Ter	88	B2
Shanowen Av	52	A2
Shanowen Cres	52	B1
Shanowen Dr	52	B1
Shanowen Gro	52	A1
Shanowen Pk	52	A1
Shanowen Rd	52	A1
Shanowen Rd Ind Est	52	B2
Shanrath Rd	53	C1
Shantalla Av	53	C2
Shantalla Dr	53	C2
Shantalla Pk	53	C2
Shantalla Rd	53	C2
Shanvarna Rd	53	C1
Sharavogue	134	A2
Shaws La	91	D3
Shaw St	145	E3
Sheelin Av	139	C3
Sheelin Dr	139	C3
Sheelin Gro	139	C3
Sheelin Hill **8**	139	C3
Sheelin Wk	139	C3
Sheephill Av	33	D3
Sheephill Grn	33	D3
Sheephill Pk	33	D3
Sheepmoor Av	46	A1
Sheepmoor Cl	46	A1
Sheepmoor Cres	46	A1
Sheepmoor Gdns	46	A1
Sheepmoor Grn	46	A1
Sheepmoor Gro	46	A1
Sheepmoor Lawn	46	A1
Sheepmoor Way	46	A1
Shelbourne Av	91	D3
Shelbourne La	91	C3
Shelbourne Pk		
Greyhound Stadium	91	D2
Shelbourne Rd	91	D3
Shelerin Rd	46	A2
Shellysbanks Rd	92	B3
Shelmalier Rd	79	C2
Shelmartin Av	79	C2
Shelmartin Ter	79	C1
Shelton Dr	100	A3
Shelton Gdns	100	A3
Shelton Gro	100	A3
Shelton Pk	100	A3
Sheriff St Lwr	145	F1
Sheriff St Upr	91	C1
Sherkin Gdns	52	B3
Sherrard Av	78	A2
Sherrard St Lwr	78	A3
Sherrard St Upr	78	A3
Shielmartin Dr	59	C3
Shielmartin Pk	62	A2
Shielmartin Rd	62	A2
Ship St Gt	144	C3
Ship St Little	144	B3
Shrewsbury	104	A1
Shrewsbury Hall	141	C3
Shrewsbury Lawn	138	A1
Shrewsbury Pk	104	A1
Shrewsbury Rd		
Dublin 4	103	D2
Shrewsbury Rd *Shank.*	141	C3
Shrewsbury Wd	138	A1
Sibthorpe La	102	B1
Sidbury Ct **20**	142	B2
Sidmonton Av	142	B2
Sidmonton Ct	142	B2
Sidmonton Gdns	142	A2
Sidmonton Pk	142	B2
Sidmonton Pl **6**	142	B2
Sidmonton Rd *Bray*	142	B2
Sidmonton Rd *Grey.*	143	D1
Sidmonton Sq **7**	142	B2
Sigurd Rd	77	C3
Silchester Ct	133	D1
Silchester Cres	133	D1
Silchester Pk	133	D1
Silchester Rd	133	D1
Silchester Wd **3**	133	D2
Silken Vale	64	B2
Silleachain La	69	C1
Silloge Av	51	D1
Silloge Gdns	52	A1
Silloge Rd	37	D3
Silverberry	82	B2
Silver Birches *Dublin 14*	115	C3
Silver Birches *Dunb.*	29	C2
Silver Birches Cl	29	C2
Silver Birches Cres	29	C2
Silverdale	82	A2
Silver Pines **3**	130	B2
Silverwood	82	B2
Silverwood Dr *Dublin 6W*		
off Templeville Dr	112	A2
Silverwood Dr *Dublin 14*	112	B3
Silverwood Rd	112	B3
Simmon's Ct *off*		
Simmonscourt Castle	103	D2
Simmonscourt Av	103	D2
Simmonscourt Castle	103	D1
Simmonscourt Rd	103	D1
Simmonscourt Ter	103	D2
Simmonstown Manor	66	B3
Simmonstown Pk	66	B3
Simonscourt Sq	103	D1
Simonscourt Vw	103	D1
Simons Ridge	129	C3
Sion Hill	117	C1
Sion Hill Av	101	C2
Sion Hill Ct	53	C3
Sion Hill Rd	53	C3
Sion Rd	133	D3
Sir Ivor Mall **1**	131	C3
Sir John Rogersons		
Quay	91	C1
Sitric Rd	89	C1
Skelligs Ct	33	D3
Skellys La	53	D2
Skippers All	144	B3
Skreen Rd	76	A2
Slade Av	120	B2
Slade Castle	120	B2
Slade Cl	120	B2
Slade Hts	120	B2
Slademore Av	41	C3
Slademore Cl	55	D1
Slademore Ct	41	C3
Slademore Dr	55	D1
Slade Row	89	C1
Slane Rd	100	B1
Slaney Cl	77	C1
Slaney Rd	77	C1
Slemish Rd	76	A2
Slieve Bloom Pk	99	D1
Slieve Bloom Rd	99	D1
Slievemore Rd	100	A1
Slievenamon Rd	88	A3
Slieve Rua Dr	116	A3
Sloan Ter **21**	142	B2
Sloperton	119	C3
Slopes, The	119	C3
Smithfield	144	A2
Smithfield Sta	144	A2
Smiths Vil	119	C3
Snowdrop Wk	41	C3
Snugborough Rd	33	D3
Snugborough Rd		
(extension)	46	B2
Somerby Rd	143	D2
Somerset St		
off Dennis St	91	D2
Somerton *D'bate*	13	D1
Somerton *Sally.*	133	C2
Somerville Av	99	D2
Somerville Grn	99	D2
Somerville Pk	99	D2
Sommerton La	72	B2
Sommerville	114	B2
Sonesta	19	D1
Sorbonne	115	D2
Sorrel Dale	46	A2
Sorrel Dr	46	A2
Sorrel Heath	46	A2
Sorrento Cl **7**	135	C2
Sorrento Ct **8**	135	C2

Sorrento Dr 134 B2
Sorrento Hts **1** 135 C3
Sorrento Lawn **9** 135 C2
Sorrento Ms **2** 135 C3
Sorrento Rd 134 B2
South Av 116 A3
South Bk Rd 92 A2
South Circular Rd 88 A1
South Co Business Pk 130 B3
Southdene 118 B3
South Docks Rd 91 D2
Southern Cross Av 88 A2
Southern Cross Route 128 A3
South Esplanade 142 B2
South Gt Georges St 144 C4
South Hill *Dublin 6* 102 A3
South Hill *Dublin 13* 59 C3
South Hill Av 116 B2
South Hill Pk 116 B2
South Lotts Rd 91 D3
South Pk *Corn.* 132 A3
South Pk *Swords* 15 C2
South Pk Dr 132 A3
South Winds **11** 134 B1
Southwood Pk 117 C2
Spade Enterprise Cen 89 C1
Spafield Ter 103 D1
Spa Rd (Kilmainham)
  Dublin 8 87 D2
Spa Rd (Phoenix Pk)
  Dublin 8 76 A3
Spawell Br 112 A3
Spencer Dock 91 C1
Spencer St
  off South Circular Rd 89 C3
Spencer St N 79 C3
Spencer Vil 134 A1
Sperrin Rd 87 D3
Spiddal Pk 85 D2
Spiddal Rd 85 D2
Spires, The 13 D2
Spire Vw Ct 101 D2
Spire Vw La 101 D2
Spitalfields 144 A4
Spring Bk Cotts 120 A1
Springdale Rd 55 C1
Springfield *Dublin 7* 76 A2
Springfield *Dublin 24* 109 C3
Springfield Av 112 B2
Springfield Cl 66 A3
Springfield Cres 112 B2
Springfield Dr 112 B2
Springfield La 136 B3
Springfield Pk
  Dublin 6W 112 B2
Springfield Pk
  Deans Gra 131 D3
Springfield Rd 112 B2
Spring Gdn La 145 E3
Spring Gdn St 79 C3
Springhill Av 132 A1
Springhill Cotts **3** 132 A1
Springhill Pk *Dalkey* 134 A2
Springhill Pk *Deans Gra* 132 A1
Springlawn 47 C1
Springlawn Cl 47 C1
Springlawn Ct 47 C1
Springlawn Dr 47 C1
Springlawn Hts 47 C1
Springlawn Rd 47 C1
Springvale 126 B2
Spruce Av 130 A2
Square, The *Dublin 4* 91 D2
Square, The *Dublin 6W* 101 C2
Square, The *Dublin 13* 39 D3
Square, The *Dublin 24* 123 D1
Square, The **3** *Lucan* 70 A3
Square Ind Complex,
  The 109 D3
Square Shop &
  Leisure Cen, The 123 D1
Stable La *Dublin 2* 90 A3
Stable La *Dublin 4*
  off Londonbridge Rd 91 D3
Stables, The 116 B1
Stadium Business Pk 35 C3

Stamer St 90 A3
Stanford Grn 99 D2
Stanhope Cen 77 D3
Stanhope Grn 89 C1
Stannaway Av 100 A2
Stannaway Dr 100 B2
Stannaway Rd 100 A2
Stapolin Av 43 C3
Stapolin Lawns 43 C3
Station Cl 96 B1
Stationcourt *Cool.* 46 B3
Station Ct *D'bate* 13 C2
Stationcourt Pk 46 B3
Stationcourt Vw 46 B3
Stationcourt Way 46 B3
Station Rd *Dublin 5* 55 D2
Station Rd *Dublin 13* 58 A1
Station Rd *Clond.* 96 B1
Station Rd *Dunb.* 29 C2
Station Rd *D.L.* 134 A1
Station Rd *Kill.* 139 D2
Station Rd *Lou.V.* 68 A3
Station Rd *Port.* 26 A3
Station Rd **4** *Shank.* 141 D2
Station Rd Business Pk 84 B3
Station Vw **2** 46 B3
Station Way 42 B3
Steeple, The 64 A1
Steeples, The 87 C2
Steevens La 89 C2
Stella Av 52 A3
Stephens La 91 C3
Stephens Pl
  off Merrion Sq E 145 F4
Stephens Rd 88 A3
Stephen St 144 C4
Stephen St Upr 144 C4
Stiles Ct, The
  off The Stiles Rd 80 A2
Stiles Rd, The 80 A2
Stillorgan Ct **2** 130 B3
Stillorgan Gro 131 C1
Stillorgan Heath 130 B1
Stillorgan Ind Est 129 D2
Stillorgan Pk 117 C3
Stillorgan Pk Av 117 C3
Stillorgan Rd *Dublin 4* 103 D2
Stillorgan Rd *Still.* 116 B2
Stillorgan Shop Cen 116 B3
Stillorgan Sta 130 A2
Stillorgan Wd 130 A1
Stirling Pk 114 A1
Stirrup La
  off Beresford St 144 B1
Stockhole La 23 C1
Stocking Av 126 A3
Stocking La 126 A3
Stocking Wd 125 D3
Stockton Ct 48 A3
Stockton Dr 74 A1
Stockton Grn 74 A1
Stockton Gro 74 A1
Stockton Lawn 48 A3
Stockton Pk 74 A1
Stonebridge Av 45 C1
Stonebridge Cl **1** 141 C3
Stonebridge Dr 45 C1
Stonebridge La **1** 140 B2
Stonebridge Rd *Clons.* 45 C1
Stonebridge Rd *Shank.* 140 B2
Stonemasons Grn **2** 128 A2
Stonemasons Way 128 A2
Stonepark Abbey 113 D3
Stonepark Ct 113 D3
Stonepark Dr 113 D3
Stonepark Grn 113 D3
Stonepark Orchard 113 D3
Stoneview Pl 119 D3
Stoneybatter 89 C1
Stoneylea Ter **11** 142 A3
Stoney Rd *Dublin 3 off*
  Northbrook Av Upr 79 C3
Stoney Rd (Dundrum)
  Dublin 14 115 C3
Store St 145 E1
Stormanstown Rd 51 D2
Stradbrook Cl 132 A1
Stradbrook Gdns 118 A3
Stradbrook Hill **4** 132 A1
Stradbrook Lawn 118 A3
Stradbrook Pk 118 A3

Stradbrook Rd 118 A3
Straffan Av 64 B3
Straffan Cl 64 B3
Straffan Ct 64 B3
Straffan Cres 64 B3
Straffan Dr 64 B3
Straffan Grn 64 B3
Straffan Gro 64 B3
Straffan Lawn 64 B3
Straffan Way 65 C3
Stralem Ct 45 C1
Stralem Gro 45 C1
Stralem Ms 45 C1
Stralem Ter 45 C1
Strand, The 13 D2
Strandmill Av 27 C3
Strandmill Pk **1** 27 C3
Strandmill Rd 27 C3
Strand Rd (Sandymount)
  Dublin 4 92 A3
Strand Rd *Dublin 13* 59 C2
Strand Rd *Bray* 142 B1
Strand Rd *Kill.* 139 D2
Strand Rd *Mala.* 19 D1
Strand Rd *Port.* 26 B3
Strand St *Dublin 4* 91 D2
Strand St *Mala.* 20 A2
Strand St Gt 144 C2
Strandville Av E 80 A2
Strandville Av N 79 C3
Strandville Ho 80 A2
Strangford Gdns 79 C3
Strangford Rd E 79 C3
Strathmore Rd 139 C1
Streamstown La 19 C3
Streamville Ct **10** 139 C3
Streamville Rd 56 A1
Suffolk St 145 D3
Sugarloaf Cres 142 A3
Sugarloaf Ter **12** 142 A3
Suir Rd 88 A2
Suir Rd Sta 88 A3
Sullivan St 88 B1
Summerfield
  (Blanchardstown)
  Dublin 15 47 C2
Summerfield **2**
  Dublin 24 124 A1
Summerfield Av 47 C2
Summerfield Cl
  (Blanchardstown)
  Dublin 15 47 C2
Summerfield Cl **8**
  Dalkey 134 B2
Summerfield Grn 47 C2
Summerfield Lawns 47 C2
Summerfield Meadows 47 C2
Summerfield Pk 47 C2
Summerfield Ri 47 C1
Summerhill 78 B3
Summerhill Par
  Dublin 1 78 B3
Summerhill Par *D.L.* 119 D3
Summerhill Pl 78 B3
Summerhill Rd *Dunb.* 28 A1
Summerhill Rd *D.L.* 119 D3
Summer Pl 78 B3
Summerseat Ct 30 B2
Summer St N 78 B3
Summer St S 89 C2
Summerville 80 B2
Summerville Pk 102 A2
Sunbury Gdns 102 A3
Suncroft Av **2** 27 C3
Suncroft Dr 122 A1
Suncroft Pk 122 A1
Sundale Av 122 A2
Sundale Cl 122 A2
Sundale Cres 122 A1
Sundale Grn 122 A1
Sundale Gro 122 A1
Sundale Hts 122 A1
Sundale Lawn 121 D1
Sundale Meadows **12** 121 D1
Sundale Par 121 D1
Sundale Pk 122 A1
Sundale Rd 122 A2
Sundale Vil 122 A1
Sundale Wk 122 A1
Sunday Well Br 15 D1
Sundrive Pk 101 C2
Sundrive Rd 100 B1

Sundrive Shop Cen 101 C2
Sunnybank Ter 114 B3
Sunshine Ind Est 100 A1
Superquinn Shop Cen
  Dublin 12 99 C2
Superquinn Shop Cen
  Dublin 16 126 A1
Susan Ter 89 C3
Susanville Rd 78 B2
Sussex Rd 102 B1
Sussex St 119 D3
Sussex Ter Lwr
  off Mespil Rd 90 B3
Sussex Ter Upr
  off Sussex Rd 90 B3
Sutton Ct 57 D1
Sutton Cross Shop Cen 58 B1
Sutton Downs 57 D2
Sutton Gro 57 D1
Sutton Lawns 57 D1
Sutton Pk 57 D1
Sutton Sta 58 A1
Swallowbrook 31 D2
Swallowbrook Cres 31 D2
Swallowbrook Pk 31 D2
Swallowbrook Vw 31 D2
Swan Pl
  off Morehampton Rd 103 C1
Swan Shop Cen 102 A2
Swans Nest Av 56 B1
Swans Nest Ct 56 B1
Swans Nest Rd 56 A1
Swanville Pl 102 A2
Swanward
  Business Cen 98 A3
Swanward Ct 101 C1
Swan Yd
  off Harry St 145 D4
Sweeneys Ter
  off Mill St 89 D3
Sweetbriar La 130 A1
Sweetmans Av 117 D2
Sweetmount Av 114 B3
Sweetmount Dr 114 B3
Sweetmount Pk 114 B3
Swiftbrook 122 A1
Swiftbrook Av 122 A1
Swiftbrook Cl 122 A1
Swiftbrook Dr 122 A1
Swiftbrook Pk 122 A1
Swifts All 144 A4
Swift's Gro 40 A2
Swifts Row *off Ormond*
  Quay Upr 144 B2
Swiftwood 120 B1
Swilly Rd 76 B2
Swords
  Business Campus 15 D2
Swords Business Pk 15 D3
Swords Manor Av 14 B3
Swords Manor Ct 14 B3
Swords Manor Cres 14 B3
Swords Manor Dr 14 B3
Swords Manor Gro 14 B3
Swords Manor Vw 14 B3
Swords Manor Way 14 B3
Swords Rd *Dublin 9* 52 B3
Swords Rd *Collins.* 22 B3
Swords Rd *Mala.* 19 C2
Swords St 77 C3
Sybil Hill Av 55 C3
Sybil Hill Rd 55 C3
Sycamore Av *Dublin 24* 109 D1
Sycamore Av *Cabin.* 137 C1
Sycamore Av *Castle.* 47 C3
Sycamore Cl *Dublin 24* 109 D1
Sycamore Cl *Cabin.* 137 C1
Sycamore Ct **6** 133 C2
Sycamore Cres *Cabin.* 137 C1
Sycamore Cres *Still.* 116 B2
Sycamore Dr **1**
  Dublin 16 128 B1
Sycamore Dr *Dublin 24* 110 A1
Sycamore Dr *Cabin.* 137 C1
Sycamore Dr *Castle.* 47 C3
Sycamore Grn 137 C1
Sycamore Gro *Cabin.* 137 C1
Sycamore Gro **3** *Fox.* 131 D2
Sycamore Lawn *Cabin.* 137 C1
Sycamore Lawn *Castle.* 47 C3
Sycamore Pk *Dublin 11* 37 C3
Sycamore Pk *Dublin 24* 110 A1

Sycamore Pk *Castle.*	47	C3
Sycamore Rd (Finglas)		
Dublin 11	37	C3
Sycamore Rd *Dublin 12*	98	A2
Sycamore Rd *Dublin 16*	128	B1
Sycamore Rd *Still.*	116	B2
Sycamores, The **18** *Abb.*	139	C3
Sycamores, The *Mala.*	20	B2
Sycamore St	144	C3
Sycamore Vw	47	C3
Sycamore Wk	137	C1
Sydenham Ms *Bray*	142	B2
Sydenham Ms *D.L.*	119	D3
Sydenham Rd (Sandymount)		
Dublin 4	103	D1
Sydenham Rd (Dundrum)		
Dublin 14	115	C3
Sydenham Vil		
Dublin 14	115	C3
Sydenham Vil **27** *Bray*	142	B2
Sydney Av	117	D2
Sydney Par Av	104	A2
Sydney Par Sta	104	A2
Sydney Ter	117	D2
Sykes La	101	D3
Sylvan Av	109	D1
Sylvan Cl	109	D1
Sylvan Dr	109	D1
Synge La	90	A3
Synge Pl	90	A3
Synge St	90	A3
Synge Way	97	C1
Synnott Pl	78	A3
Synnott Row	78	A2

T

Tailor's Mkt	144	B3
Talbot Av	19	C2
Talbot Ct *Dublin 15*	47	D2
Talbot Ct **6** *Mala.*	19	C2
Talbot Downs	47	D2
Talbot Hall	14	B1
Talbot La *Dublin 1*		
off Talbot St	145	D1
Talbot La *Kill.*	134	A3
Talbot Lo	117	C3
Talbot Mem Br	145	E2
Talbot Pk	19	C2
Talbot Pl	145	E1
Talbot Rd **2** *Kill.*	139	C1
Talbot Rd *Mala.*	19	C2
Talbot St	145	D1
Tallaght Business Pk	123	C1
Tallaght Bypass	124	A1
Tallaght Enterprise Cen	110	A3
Tallaght Retail Cen	109	D3
Tallaght Rd	111	C3
Tallaght Sta	109	C3
Tallaght Rd	111	D3
Tamarisk Av	110	A1
Tamarisk Cl		
off Tamarisk Way	110	A1
Tamarisk Ct	110	A2
Tamarisk Dale		
off Tamarisk Dr	110	A1
Tamarisk Dr	110	A1
Tamarisk Gro		
off Tamarisk Pk	110	A2
Tamarisk Hts	110	A2
Tamarisk Lawn	110	A2
Tamarisk Pk	110	A2
Tamarisk Vw		
off Tamarisk Pk	110	A2
Tamarisk Wk		
off Tamarisk Dr	110	A1
Tamarisk Way	110	A1
Tandys La	82	A2
Taney Av	115	C3
Taney Ct	115	C3
Taney Cres	115	C3
Taney Dr	115	C3
Taney Gro	115	D3
Taney Lawn	115	C3
Taney Manor	115	C3
Taney Pk	115	C3
Taney Ri	115	C3
Taney Rd	115	C3
Tara Hill Cres	113	C3
Tara Hill Gro	113	C3
Tara Hill Rd	113	C3
Tara Lawn	56	A1
Tara St	145	E2

Tara St Sta	145	E2
Tassagard Grns	120	B2
Tassagart Dr	120	B2
Taylor's Hill	128	A3
Taylors La *Dublin 8*	89	C2
Taylor's La *Dublin 16*	126	B1
Temple Bar	144	C3
Temple Cotts	77	D3
Temple Ct *Dublin 7*	89	C1
Temple Ct *Dublin 9*	38	B2
Temple Cres	118	A2
Temple Gdns *Dublin 6*	102	A3
Temple Gdns *Dublin 9*	38	B2
Temple Hill	118	A2
Temple La N	78	A3
Temple La S	144	C3
Temple Lawns *Dublin 9*	38	B2
Temple Lawns *Celbr.*	66	B3
Temple Manor	29	C1
Temple Manor Av	111	C1
Temple Manor Cl	111	C1
Temple Manor Ct	111	C1
Temple Manor Dr	111	C1
Temple Manor Gro	111	C1
Temple Manor Way	111	C1
Templemore Av	101	D3
Templeogue Lo	111	D2
Templeogue Rd	112	B2
Templeogue Wd	112	A2
Temple Pk	102	B3
Temple Pk Av	118	A2
Temple Pl	102	B1
Temple Rd *Dublin 6*	102	A3
Temple Rd *Black.*	117	D2
Templeroan	126	A1
Templeroan Av	126	A1
Templeroan Cl	126	A1
Templeroan Ct	126	A1
Templeroan Cres	126	A1
Templeroan Downs	126	B1
Templeroan Dr	126	A1
Templeroan Grn	126	A2
Templeroan Gro	126	A1
Templeroan Lo		
off Ballyboden Way	126	A2
Templeroan Meadows	126	B1
Templeroan Ms	126	A1
Templeroan Pk	126	A1
Templeroan Vw	126	A1
Templeroan Way	126	A1
Temple Sq	102	A3
Temple St N	78	A3
Temple St W	89	C1
Temple Ter **10**	135	C2
Templeview Av	41	D3
Templeview Cl	41	D3
Templeview Copse	41	D3
Templeview Ct	41	D3
Templeview Cres	41	D3
Templeview Downs	41	D3
Templeview Dr	42	A3
Templeview Grn	41	D3
Templeview Gro	41	D3
Templeview Lawn	41	D3
Templeview Pk	41	D3
Templeview Pl	41	D3
Templeview Ri	41	D3
Templeview Row	41	D3
Templeview Sq	41	D3
Templeview Vale **1**	41	D3
Templeview Wk	42	A3
Templeview Way	42	A3
Temple Vil		
off Palmerston Rd	102	A2
Templeville Av	112	A2
Templeville Dr	112	A2
Templeville Pk	112	B2
Templeville Rd	111	D1
Terenure Coll	112	B1
Terenure Pk	101	C3
Terenure Pl	113	C1
Terenure Rd E	101	C3
Terenure Rd N	101	C3
Terenure Rd W	100	B3
Terminal Rd N	93	C1
Terminal Rd S	93	C1
Termon Ct **1**	37	D3
Terrace, The	136	B3
Tetrarch Gro	29	C1
Texas La	19	D2
Thatch Rd, The	53	C2
Thicket, The	136	B1

Third Av *Dublin 1*	91	C1
Third Av *Dublin 8*		
off Dolphin's Barn	89	C3
Third Av (Cookstown)		
Dublin 24	109	C3
Thomas Ct	89	C2
Thomas Davis St S	144	B4
Thomas Davis St W	87	D3
Thomas La		
off Cathedral St	145	D1
Thomas Moore Rd	99	C2
Thomas St E	91	C2
Thomas St W	89	C2
Thomastown Cres **11**	133	C2
Thomastown Rd	133	D3
Thomond **5**	141	C2
Thomond Rd	86	B2
Thormanby Lawns	61	C2
Thormanby Lo	61	D3
Thormanby Rd	61	C2
Thormanby Wds	61	C3
Thornbury Apts	32	A2
Thorncastle St	91	D2
Thorncliffe	114	B1
Thorncliffe Pk	114	A1
Thorndale Av		
off Elm Mt Rd	54	A3
Thorndale Ct	53	C2
Thorndale Cres		
off Elm Mt Rd	54	A3
Thorndale Dr	52	A3
Thorndale Gro	52	A3
Thorndale Lawns		
off Elm Mt Rd	54	A3
Thorndale Pk		
off Elm Mt Rd	54	A3
Thornhill Gdns	66	A1
Thornhill Hts	66	A1
Thornhill Meadows	66	A1
Thornhill Rd	116	A3
Thornleigh	15	C2
Thornleigh Av	15	C2
Thornleigh Grn	14	B2
Thornleigh La	15	C2
Thornleigh Pl	15	C2
Thornleigh Rd	15	C2
Thornleigh Row	15	C2
Thornleigh Sq	14	B2
Thornville Av	56	B2
Thornville Dr	56	B2
Thornville Pk	56	B2
Thornville Rd	56	B2
Thor Pl	89	C1
Three Rock Cl	110	B1
Three Rock Rd	130	A2
Thundercut All		
off Smithfield	144	A1
Tibradden Cl		
off Tibradden Dr	110	B1
Tibradden Dr	110	B1
Tibradden Gro		
off Tibradden Dr	110	B1
Ticknock Av	129	C3
Ticknock Dale	129	C3
Ticknock Gro	128	B3
Ticknock Hill	128	B3
Ticknock Way	129	C3
Timber Quay	92	A1
Tinkler's Path	74	B2
Tionscail Ind Est	17	D1
Tivoli Av	101	D2
Tivoli Cl	133	C1
Tivoli Rd	119	C3
Tivoli Ter E	119	C3
Tivoli Ter N	119	C3
Tivoli Ter S	119	C3
Tolka Cotts	51	C3
Tolka Est Rd	51	C3
Tolka Quay Rd	91	D1
Tolka Rd	78	B2
Tolka Vale	51	C3
Tolka Valley		
Business Pk	50	B3
Tolka Valley Grn	50	B3
Tolka Valley Ind Est	50	B3
Tolka Valley Rd	50	A3
Tom Clarke Ho	79	C2
Tom Kelly Rd	102	A1
Tonduff Cl		
off Lugaquilla Av	110	B1
Tonguefield Rd	100	B2
Tonlegee Av	55	D1

Tonlegee Dr	55	C1
Tonlegee Rd	55	C1
Torca	135	C3
Torlogh Gdns	79	C2
Torlogh Par	79	C1
Torquay Rd	131	C2
Torquay Wd	131	C2
Tory Sq	47	C1
Tourmakeady Rd	52	B2
Tower Av	101	D3
Tower Rd *Dublin 15*	74	A2
Tower Rd *Clond.*	96	B2
Tower Shop Cen	96	B2
Tower Vw Cotts	77	D1
Townsend St	145	E2
Townyard La	20	A2
Trafalgar La	118	A2
Trafalgar Rd	143	D1
Trafalgar Ter *Black.*	118	A2
Trafalgar Ter **4** *Bray*	142	B1
Tram Ter	81	C3
Tramway Cotts	77	D2
Tramway Ct		
off Station Rd	58	A1
Tramway Ter	104	A1
Tranquility Gro	54	A1
Treepark Av	110	A2
Treepark Cl	110	A2
Treepark Dr	110	A2
Treepark Rd	110	A2
Trees Av	116	B3
Trees Rd Lwr	116	B3
Trees Rd Upr	116	A3
Tresilian	136	B1
Trevor Ter		
off Grattan St	91	C2
Trimbleston	115	D2
Trimleston Av	104	B3
Trimleston Dr	104	B3
Trimleston Gdns	104	B3
Trimleston Pk	104	B3
Trimleston Rd	116	B1
Trim Rd	53	D1
Trinity Coll	145	D3
Trinity Coll		
Enterprise Cen	91	C2
Trinity St	145	D3
Trinity Ter	79	C2
Tritonville Av	92	A3
Tritonville Ct	91	C3
Tritonville Cres	92	A3
Tritonville Rd	91	C3
Trosyrafon Ter **23**	142	B2
Tryconnell Pk	87	D2
Tubbermore Av **11**	135	C2
Tubbermore Rd	134	B2
Tuckett's La	60	B2
Tudor Ct **2**	19	C1
Tudor Cres	10	B2
Tudor Gro	10	B2
Tudor Hts	10	B2
Tudor Lawns	131	C3
Tudor Rd	102	B3
Tulip Ct	41	C3
Tullyhall	82	B3
Tullyhall Av	82	B3
Tullyhall Cl	82	B3
Tullyhall Ct	82	B3
Tullyhall Cres	82	B3
Tullyhall Dr	82	B3
Tullyhall Grn	82	B3
Tullyhall Pk	82	B3
Tullyhall Ri	82	B3
Tullyhall Way	82	B3
Tullyvale	138	A3
Turnapin Cotts	39	D2
Turnapin Grn	39	C2
Turnapin Gro	39	D2
Turnapin La	39	C2
Turnberry	57	D1
Turnpike Rd	97	D2
Turret Rd	85	D1
Turrets, The	91	D3
Turrets Flats		
off Rathmines Rd Upr	102	A2
Turvey Av	12	A1

198

Turvey Cl 13 C1
Turvey Cres 13 C2
Turvey Dr 13 C2
Turvey Gdn 13 C2
Turvey Gro 13 C2
Turvey Pk 13 C2
Turvey Wds 13 C1
Tuscany Downs 55 D2
Tuscany Pk 57 D1
Tymon Cl 123 D2
Tymon Cres 123 D1
Tymon Gro 123 D1
Tymon Hts 124 B2
Tymon La 111 C2
Tymon Lawn 123 D2
Tymon N Av 110 B2
Tymon N Gdns 110 B3
Tymon N Grn 110 B2
Tymon N Gro 110 B2
Tymon N Lawn 110 B2
Tymon N Pk 110 B3
Tymon N Rd 110 B2
Tymonville Av 110 B2
Tymonville Ct 110 A2
Tymonville Cres 110 A2
Tymonville Dr 110 B2
Tymonville Gro 110 B2
Tymonville Pk 110 B2
Tymonville Rd 110 B2
Tynan Hall 109 D1
Tynan Hall Av 109 D1
Tynan Hall Gro 109 C1
Tynan Hall Pk 109 C1
Tyrconnell Rd 87 D3
Tyrconnell St 87 D3
Tyrconnell Vil
  off Grattan Cres 87 D2
Tyrone Pl 87 D3

U
Ullardmor 9 134 B2
Ulster St 77 D2
Ulster Ter 1 117 C3
Ulverton Cl 134 B1
Ulverton Ct 12 134 B1
Ulverton Rd 134 B1
University Coll Dublin 2 90 A3
University Coll Dublin 4 115 D1
University Coll
  (Sch of Nursing &
  Midwifery) Dublin 4 91 D3
Upper Cliff Rd 61 C2
Uppercross 71 D3
Uppercross Rd 88 B3
Upper Glen Rd 74 B3
Upper Portraine Rd 13 D1
Urney Gro 134 A3
U.S.A. Embassy
  (Residence) 75 C3
Ushers Island 89 C1
Ushers Quay 144 A2
Usher St 144 A3

V
Vale, The Celbr. 66 A2
Vale, The Palm. 73 C3
Valentia Par 78 A2
Valentia Rd 52 A3
Vale Vw Av 137 C1
Vale Vw Cl 137 C1
Valeview Cres 50 A2
Valeview Dr 50 A2
Valeview Gdns 50 A2
Vale Vw Lough. 137 C1
Vale Vw Lawn 137 C1
Valley Av 138 A3
Valley Cl 138 A3
Valley Dr 138 A3
Valley Pk Av 49 D2
Valley Pk Dr 49 D3
Valley Pk Rd 49 D3
Valley Vw Lough. 138 A3
Valley Vw Swords 14 B3
Valley Wk 138 A3
Vanessa Cl 66 A2
Vanessa Lawns 66 A2

Vauxhall Av 89 C3
Vavasour Sq 91 D3
Venetian Hall 54 B3
Ventry Dr 76 B1
Ventry Pk 76 B1
Ventry Rd 76 B1
Verbena Av Dublin 13 57 C3
Verbena Av Fox. 131 D3
Verbena Gro 57 C1
Verbena Lawns 57 C1
Verbena Pk 57 C1
Verdemont 46 B2
Vergemount
  off Clonskeagh Rd 103 C3
Vergemount Hall 103 C3
Vergemount Pk 103 C2
Vernon Av (Clontarf)
  Dublin 3 81 C2
Vernon Av Dublin 6
  off Frankfort Av 101 D2
Vernon Ct 81 C3
Vernon Dr 81 C1
Vernon Gdn 81 C3
Vernon Gro Dublin 3 81 C2
Vernon Gro (Rathgar)
  Dublin 6 102 A3
Vernon Heath 81 C1
Vernon Par
  off Clontarf Rd 80 A2
Vernon Pk 81 C2
Vernon Ri 81 C1
Vernon St 89 D3
Vernon Ter
  off Frankfort Av 102 A3
Veronica Ter 91 D2
Verschoyle Av 121 C2
Verschoyle Cl 121 D2
Verschoyle Ct
  off Verschoyle Pl 91 C3
Verschoyle Cres 121 D2
Verschoyle Glen 121 D2
Verschoyle Grn 121 C2
Verschoyle Hts 121 C2
Verschoyle Pk 121 D2
Verschoyle Pl 91 C3
Verschoyle Ri 121 C2
Verschoyle Vale 121 C2
Vesey Ms 119 C3
Vesey Pk 82 A1
Vesey Pl 119 C3
Vevay Cres 16 142 A3
Vevay Rd 142 A3
Vevay Vil 13 142 A3
Vicar St 144 A3
Vico Rd 139 D1
Victoria Av Dublin 4 103 C2
Victoria Av Bray 142 B2
Victoria Br 91 C1
Victoria Quay 89 C1
Victoria Rd (Clontarf)
  Dublin 3 80 A2
Victoria Rd (Terenure)
  Dublin 6 113 D1
Victoria Rd Dalkey 135 C2
Victoria Rd Grey. 143 C1
Victoria Rd Kill. 139 D1
Victoria St 89 D3
Victoria Ter Dublin 3
  off Clontarf Rd 81 C3
Victoria Ter Dublin 6 114 B3
Victoria Ter 1 Dalkey 134 B2
Victoria Vil Dublin 3 79 D2
Victoria Vil (Rathgar)
  Dublin 6 101 D3
View, The Dublin 16 128 B3
View, The Dublin 17 39 D3
View, The Dublin 24 124 B1
View, The (Cookstown)
  Dublin 24 109 C2
View, The (Oldtown Mill)
  Celbr. 66 A2
View, The
  (St. Wolstan's Abbey)
  Celbr. 66 B3
View, The Dunb. 28 A3
View, The Mala. 21 C3
View, The Manor. 31 C3
Viking Pl off Viking Rd 89 C1
Viking Rd 89 C1
Villa, The 18 A2
Villa Blanchard 47 D2

Village, The Dublin 9 52 B3
Village, The Clons. 45 D2
Village Cen Clond. 96 B2
Village Cen, The 5
  Lucan 70 A3
Village Ct Dublin 14 113 C2
Village Ct, The 6 Lucan 70 A3
Village Gate, The 134 B2
Village Grn 110 A3
Village Hts 32 B3
Village Sq 124 A1
Villa Pk Av (Ascal Pairc
  An Bhailtini) 76 A2
Villa Pk Dr (Ceide Pairc
  An Bhailtini) 76 A2
Villa Pk Gdns (Gardini Pairc
  An Bhailtini) 76 A2
Villa Pk Rd (Bothar Pairc
  An Bhailtini) 76 A2
Villarea Pk 134 A1
Villiers Rd 102 A3
Vincent Ter 78 A1
Violet Hill Dr 51 C3
Violet Hill Pk 51 C3
Violet Hill Rd 51 C3
Virginia Dr
  off Virginia Pk 50 A2
Virginia Hts 109 C3
Virginia Pk 50 A2
Viscount Av 39 C2

W
Wad Br 52 A2
Wadelai Grn 52 A2
Wadelai Rd 51 D2
Wade's Av 55 D3
Wainsfort Av 112 A1
Wainsfort Cres 112 A1
Wainsfort Dr 100 A3
Wainsfort Gdns
  off Wainsfort Cres 112 A1
Wainsfort Gro 112 B1
Wainsfort Manor Cres 112 A1
Wainsfort Manor Dr 112 A1
Wainsfort Manor Grn 112 A1
Wainsfort Manor Gro 112 A1
Wainsfort Pk 112 A1
Wainsfort Rd 112 A1
Waldemar Ter 114 B3
Waldrons Br 114 A1
Walk, The Dublin 6W 112 A1
Walk, The Dublin 16 128 B3
Walk, The Dublin 24 124 A1
Walk, The Carrick. 136 B3
Walk, The Celbr. 66 A2
Walk, The Dunb. 28 B3
Walk, The Kins. 18 A3
Walk, The Lou.V. 68 A1
Walk, The Mala. 21 C3
Walk, The Manor. 31 C3
Walkinstown Av 99 C2
Walkinstown Cl 99 C2
Walkinstown Cres 99 C2
Walkinstown Cross 99 C2
Walkinstown Dr 99 C2
Walkinstown Grn 99 C2
Walkinstown Mall 99 C2
Walkinstown Par 99 C2
Walkinstown Pk 99 C2
Walkinstown Rd (Bothar
  Chille Na Manac) 99 C2
Wallace Rd 99 D2
Walled Gdns, The 66 B1
Walnut Av Dublin 9 52 B3
Walnut Av 1 Dublin 24 109 D1
Walnut Cl 109 D1
Walnut Ct 52 B3
Walnut Dr 2 109 D1
Walnut Lawn 52 B3
Walnut Pk 52 B3
Walnut Ri 52 B3
Walnut Vw 5 126 B2
Walsh Rd 52 A3
Waltersland Rd 130 B1
Waltham Ter 117 C2
Walton Hall 15 C1
Walworth Rd
  off Victoria St 101 D1
Warburton Ter 24 142 B2
Wards Hill 89 D3
Warners La 90 B3
Warren, The 19 C2

Warren Av 72 B1
Warren Cl 72 B1
Warren Cres 72 B1
Warren Grn Dublin 13 58 A1
Warren Grn Carp. 72 B1
Warrenmount 89 D3
Warrenmount Pl 89 D3
Warren Pk 72 B1
Warrenpoint 80 A2
Warrenstown 33 C3
Warrenstown Cl 33 C3
Warrenstown Ct 33 C3
Warrenstown Downs 33 C3
Warrenstown Dr 33 C2
Warrenstown Garth 32 B3
Warrenstown Grn 33 C3
Warrenstown Gro 33 C3
Warrenstown Lawn 33 C3
Warrenstown Pk 33 C3
Warrenstown Pl 32 B3
Warrenstown Ri 33 C3
Warrenstown Row 33 C3
Warrenstown Vale 33 C3
Warrenstown Vw 32 B3
Warrenstown Wk 33 C3
Warrenstown Way 33 C3
Warren St 102 A1
Warrington La
  off Warrington Pl 91 C3
Warrington Pl 91 C3
Warwick Ter
  off Sallymount Av 102 B1
Wasdale Gro 113 D1
Wasdale Pk 113 C1
Washington La 112 B3
Washington Pk 112 B2
Washington St 89 D3
Watercourse 111 D2
Waterfall Av 78 B2
Waterfall Rd 55 D3
Watergate Est 123 D1
Waterloo Av 79 C3
Waterloo La 102 B1
Waterloo Rd 103 C1
Watermeadow Dr 123 D1
Watermeadow Pk 123 D1
Watermill Av 55 D3
Watermill Cl 124 A2
Watermill Dr 55 D3
Watermill Gro 124 A2
Watermill Lawn
  Dublin 5 56 A3
Watermill Lawn
  Dublin 24 124 A2
Watermill Pk 55 D3
Watermill Rd
  (Bothar An Easa) 55 D3
Waterside Av 18 A2
Waterside Cl 18 A2
Waterside Ct 18 A2
Waterside Cres Port. 27 C1
Waterside Cres Swords 18 B2
Waterside Dr 18 A2
Waterside Grn 18 A2
Waterside Lawn 18 A2
Waterside Pk 18 A2
Waterside Ri 1 18 A2
Waterside Rd 1 18 A2
Waterside Wk 18 A2
Waterside Way 3 18 A2
Waterstown Av 73 D3
Waterville Rd 33 D3
Waterville Row 47 C1
Waterville Ter 47 D1
Watery La Clond. 96 B1
Watery La Swords 15 C3
Watling St 89 C2
Watson Av 138 B1
Watson Dr 138 B1
Watson Pk 138 B1
Watson Rd 138 B1
Watson's Est 138 B1
Waverley Av 79 C2
Waverley Business Pk 98 B1
Waverley Ter Dublin 6
  off Kenilworth Rd 101 D2
Waverley Ter 5 Bray 142 B1
Way, The 28 B3
Weatherwell Ind Est 84 B3
Weaver La
  off Phibsborough Rd 77 D3
Weaver's Row 45 D2

Name	Page	Grid
Weavers Sq	89	C3
Weaver's St	144	A4
Wedgewood Est	129	D2
Weirview	70	A2
Weirview Dr	130	B1
Weldon's La **8**	43	D3
Wellesley Pl		
off Russell St	78	B3
Wellfield Br	42	A2
Wellington Ct **17**	142	A2
Wellington La *Dublin 4*	103	C1
Wellington La *Dublin 6W*	111	D2
Wellington Monument	88	B1
Wellington Pk	111	D1
Wellington Pl (Donnybrook)	103	C1
Wellington Pl N	77	D3
Wellington Quay	144	C3
Wellington Rd *Dublin 4*	103	C1
Wellington Rd *Dublin 6W*	111	D2
Wellington Rd *Dublin 8*	88	A1
Wellington St	119	C3
Wellington St Lwr	78	A3
Wellington St Upr	77	D3
Wellmount Av	50	A2
Wellmount Ct	50	A2
Wellmount Cres	50	A2
Wellmount Dr	50	A2
Wellmount Grn	50	A2
Wellmount Par	50	A2
Wellmount Pk	50	A2
Wellmount Rd	50	A2
Wellpark Av	52	B3
Well Rd **2**	17	C1
Wellview Av	32	B2
Wellview Cres	32	B2
Wellview Grn	32	B1
Wellview Lawn	32	B1
Wellview Pk	32	B2
Wendell Av	27	C1
Wentworth Ter		
off Hogan Pl	91	C2
Werburgh St	144	B3
Wesbury	130	B1
Wesley Hts	129	C2
Wesley Lawns	129	C2
Wesley Pl	89	D3
Wesley Rd	101	D3
Westbourne Av	95	D2
Westbourne Cl	95	D2
Westbourne Dr	95	D2
Westbourne Gro	95	D2
Westbourne Lo	125	D1
Westbourne Ri	95	D2
Westbourne Rd	113	C1
Westbourne Ter **25**	142	A1
Westbourne Vw	95	D2
Westbrook	100	A3
Westbrook Lawns	121	D2
Westbrook Rd	114	B2
Westbury	82	A1
Westbury Av	82	A1
Westbury Cl	82	A1
Westbury Dr	82	A1
Westbury Pk	82	A2
Westcourt		
off Basin St Upr	89	C2
Westcourt La	89	C2
Westend Village	46	B1
Western Ind Est	98	A2
Western Parkway *Dublin 15*	73	C1
Western Parkway *Dublin 20*	85	C1
Western Parkway *Dublin 22*	97	D3
Western Parkway *Dublin 24*	97	D3
Western Parkway Business Cen	98	B3
Western Parkway Business Pk	98	B3
Western Rd	89	C3
Western Way	77	D3
Westerton Ri **5**	128	B1
Westfield Av	69	C3
Westfield Grn	10	B2
Westfield Pk	142	B2
Westfield Rd	101	C2
Westfield Vw	10	B2
Westgate Business Pk	98	A3
Westhampton Pl	101	C3
Westhaven	31	D3
Westland Ct		
off Cumberland St S	145	F4
Westland Row	145	F3
Westlink Ind Est	86	B3
Westminster Ct **4**	136	B1
Westminster Lawns	131	C2
Westminster Pk	131	D2
Westminster Rd	131	D3
Westmoreland Pk	102	B1
Westmoreland St	145	D3
West Oil Jetty	92	B2
Weston Av	114	B3
Weston Cl *Dublin 14*	114	B3
Weston Cl *Lucan*	69	D3
Weston Ct	69	C3
Weston Cres	69	C3
Weston Dr	69	C3
Weston Grn	69	C3
Weston Gro	114	B3
Weston Hts	69	C3
Weston La	69	C3
Weston Lawn	69	C3
Weston Meadow	69	C3
Weston Pk *Dublin 14*	114	B3
Weston Pk *Lucan*	69	D3
Weston Rd	114	B3
Weston Ter	114	B3
Weston Way	69	C3
West Pk *Dublin 5*	55	C2
Westpark *Dublin 24*	124	A1
West Pk Dr	51	D3
Westpoint Business Pk	31	D2
Westpoint Ct Business Pk	98	B1
West Rd	79	C3
West Row	144	C1
West Ter	87	D2
Westview	10	B3
Westview Ter **6**	142	B1
Westway	33	D3
Westway Cl	33	D3
Westway Gro	33	D3
Westway Lawns		
off Westway Gro	33	D3
Westway Pk	33	D3
Westway Ri	33	D3
Westway Vw	33	D3
Westwood Av	49	D2
Westwood Rd	49	D2
Wexford St	90	A3
Wharton Ter		
off Harolds Cross Rd	101	D1
Whately Pl	130	A1
Wheatfield Gro	27	C1
Wheatfield Rd *Dublin 20*	85	D1
Wheatfield Rd *Port.*	27	C1
Wheatfields Av	84	B2
Wheatfields Cl	84	B2
Wheatfields Ct	84	B2
Wheatfields Cres	84	B2
Wheatfields Dr	84	B2
Wheatfields Gro	84	B2
Wheatfields Pk	84	B2
Whiteacre Ct	52	B1
Whiteacre Cres	52	B1
Whitebank Rd	92	B2
Whitebarn Rd	114	A2
Whitebeam Av	103	C3
Whitebeam Rd	103	C3
Whitebeams Rd	129	D2
Whitebrook Pk	122	B1
Whitechapel Av	46	A1
Whitechapel Ct	46	A1
Whitechapel Cres	46	A1
Whitechapel Grn	46	A1
Whitechapel Gro	46	A1
Whitechapel Lawn	46	A1
Whitechapel Pk	46	A1
Whitechapel Rd	46	A1
Whitechurch	127	C2
Whitechurch Abbey **7**	113	C3
Whitechurch Av	127	C2
Whitechurch Cl	127	C2
Whitechurch Ct	127	C2
Whitechurch Cres	127	C2
Whitechurch Dr	127	C2
Whitechurch Grn	127	C2
Whitechurch Gro	127	C2
Whitechurch Hill	127	C3
Whitechurch Lawn	127	C2
Whitechurch Pk	127	C2
Whitechurch Pines	113	C3
Whitechurch Pl	127	C2
Whitechurch Rd *Dublin 14*	113	C3
Whitechurch Rd *Dublin 16*	113	C3
Whitechurch Stream **5**	113	C3
Whitechurch Vw	127	C2
Whitechurch Wk	127	C2
Whitechurch Way	127	C2
Whitecliff	127	C1
Whitefriar Pl		
off Peter Row	144	C4
Whitefriar St	144	C4
White Hall	109	C1
Whitehall Cl	111	D1
Whitehall Gdns	100	A3
Whitehall Ms	131	D3
Whitehall Rd (Rathfarnham)	114	A3
Whitehall Rd E	111	D1
Whitehall Rd W	111	D1
White Oak	115	C1
Whites La N	77	D3
Whites Rd	74	A2
Whitestown	32	B3
Whitestown Av	32	B3
Whitestown Business Pk	123	C2
Whitestown Cres	32	B3
Whitestown Dr *Dublin 24*	123	C1
Whitestown Dr *Mulh.*	32	A3
Whitestown Gdns	46	B1
Whitestown Grn	32	B3
Whitestown Gro	32	B3
Whitestown Pk	32	B3
Whitestown Rd	123	C2
Whitestown Wk	46	B1
Whitestown Way	123	D1
White's Vil	134	B2
Whitethorn	85	C2
Whitethorn Av	54	A2
Whitethorn Cl	53	D2
Whitethorn Cres *Dublin 5*	54	A2
Whitethorn Cres *Dublin 10*	85	C2
Whitethorn Dr	85	C2
Whitethorn Gdns	85	C2
Whitethorn Gro	54	A2
Whitethorn La		
off Thorncastle St	91	D2
Whitethorn Pk *Dublin 5*	54	A2
Whitethorn Pk *Dublin 10*	85	C2
Whitethorn Ri	54	A2
Whitethorn Rd *Dublin 5*	53	D2
Whitethorn Rd *Dublin 14*	103	C3
Whitethorn Wk **1** *D.L.*	132	B2
Whitethorn Wk **2** *Fox.*	131	D3
Whitethorn Way	85	C2
Whitshed Rd	143	C2
Whitton Rd	101	C3
Whitworth Av		
off Whitworth Pl	78	A2
Whitworth Pl	78	A2
Whitworth Rd *Dublin 1*		
off Seville Pl	79	C3
Whitworth Rd *Dublin 9*	77	D2
Whyteleaf Gro	42	A3
Wicklow La		
off Wicklow St	145	D3
Wicklow St	145	D3
Wigan Rd	78	A2
Wikeford Hall	15	C1
Wilderwood Gro	111	D2
Wilfield	104	A1
Wilfield Rd	104	A1
Wilfrid Rd	101	C2
Willans Av	44	B1
Willans Dr	44	B1
Willans Grn	44	B1
Willans Ri	44	B1
Willans Row	44	B1
Willans Way	44	B1
Willbrook	127	C1
Willbrook Downs	127	C1
Willbrook Gro	113	C3
Willbrook Lawn	113	C3
Willbrook Pk	113	C3
Willbrook Rd	113	C3
Willbrook St	113	C3
Willfield Pk	104	A1
William's La		
off Princes St N	145	D2
William's Pk	102	A1
William's Pl S	89	D3
William's Pl Upr	78	A2
William's Row		
off Abbey St Mid	145	D2
William St N	78	B3
William St S	145	D4
Willie Nolan Rd	43	D3
Willington Av	111	D2
Willington Ct	111	D1
Willington Cres	111	D2
Willington Dr	111	D2
Willington Grn	111	D1
Willington Gro	111	D2
Willington Pk		
off Willington Gro	111	D2
Willmont Av	134	A1
Willow Av *Clond.*	96	A3
Willow Av *Lough.*	138	A3
Willowbank *Dublin 16*	129	C3
Willowbank *D.L.*	119	C3
Willowbank Dr	127	C1
Willowbank Pk	112	B3
Willowbrook	13	D1
Willowbrook Gro	66	A2
Willowbrook Lawns	66	A2
Willowbrook Lo	66	A1
Willowbrook Pk	66	A1
Willow Business Pk	98	A1
Willow Ct *Clond.*	96	A3
Willow Ct *Lough.*	138	A3
Willow Cres	138	A3
Willow Dr	96	A3
Willowfield	104	A1
Willowfield Av	115	D2
Willowfield Pk	115	D2
Willow Gate	128	B1
Willow Gro *Clond.*	96	A3
Willow Gro *Corn.*	132	A3
Willow Gro **4** *D.L.*	133	C2
Willow Ms	104	B2
Willow Pk *Dunb.*	29	C2
Willow Pk **5** *Fox.*	131	D2
Willow Pk *Lough.*	138	A3
Willow Pk Av	51	D1
Willow Pk Cl	51	D1
Willow Pk Cres	51	C1
Willow Pk Dr	51	D1
Willow Pk Gro	51	D1
Willow Pk Lawn	51	D1
Willow Pk Rd	51	D1
Willow Pl *Boot.*	117	C1
Willow Pl *Lough.*	138	A3
Willow Rd *Dublin 12*	97	D1
Willow Rd *Dublin 16*	128	B1
Willows, The *Dublin 11*	77	C1
Willows, The **19** *Abb.*	129	C3
Willows, The *Celbr.*	66	B2
Willows, The *D.L.*	118	A3
Willows Ct	45	D1
Willows Dr	45	D1
Willows Grn	45	D1
Willows Rd	45	D1
Willow Ter		
off Rock Rd	117	C1
Willow Vale	138	B2
Willow Wd Cl	45	D1
Willow Wd Downs	45	D1
Willow Wd Grn	45	D1
Willow Wd Gro	45	D1
Willow Wd Lawn	45	D1
Willow Wd Pk	45	D1

Willow Wd Ri	45	D1
Willow Wd Vw	45	D1
Willow Wd Wk	45	D1
Willsborough Ind Est	39	D2
Willsbrook Av	71	C3
Willsbrook Cres	71	D3
Willsbrook Dr	71	C3
Willsbrook Gdns	71	C3
Willsbrook Grn	71	C3
Willsbrook Gro	71	C3
Willsbrook Pk	71	C3
Willsbrook Pl	71	C3
Willsbrook Rd	83	C1
Willsbrook Vw	71	C3
Willsbrook Way	71	C3
Wilson Cres	116	A2
Wilson Rd	116	A2
Wilsons Pl		
off Grants Row	91	C2
Wilton Pl	90	B3
Wilton Ter	90	B3
Windele Rd	78	A1
Windermere	45	C1
Windgate Ri	63	D2
Windgate Rd	61	C3
Windmill Av Dublin 12	100	A2
Windmill Av Swords	17	C1
Windmill Cres	100	A1
Windmill La	145	F2
Windmill Pk	100	A2
Windmill Ri	17	C1
Windmill Rd	100	A2
Windrush	141	C2
Windsor Av	79	C2
Windsor Ct 12	132	B1
Windsor Dr	132	B1
Windsor Ms 5	20	A2
Windsor Pk	132	B1
Windsor Pl	90	B3
Windsor Rd	102	A2
Windsor Ter Dublin 8	101	D1
Windsor Ter D.L.	119	D3
Windsor Ter Mala.	20	A2
Windsor Vil	79	C2
Windy Arbour Sta	114	B2
Winetavern St	144	B3
Winton Av	101	D3
Winton Rd	102	B1
Wogans Fld	68	A2
Wolfe Tone Av	119	C3
Wolfe Tone Quay	89	C1
Wolfe Tone Sq E	142	A3
Wolfe Tone Sq Mid	142	A3
Wolfe Tone Sq N	142	A3
Wolfe Tone Sq S	142	A3
Wolfe Tone Sq W	142	A3
Wolfe Tone St	144	C2
Wolseley St	89	D3
Wolstan Haven Av	66	A2
Wolstan Haven Rd	66	A2
Wolverton Glen	134	A2
Wood, The Dublin 24	124	A1
Wood, The Carrick.	136	B3
Wood, The Shank.	140	B3
Wood Avens	84	A3
Woodbank Av	49	D2
Woodbank Dr	49	D2
Woodberry Castle.	73	C1
Woodberry Lucan	82	A2
Woodbine Av	104	A3
Woodbine Cl	55	D1
Woodbine Dr	55	D2
Woodbine Pk Dublin 5	55	D2
Woodbine Pk Boot.	104	B3
Woodbine Rd Dublin 5	56	A1
Woodbine Rd Boot.	104	A3
Woodbrook Ct	46	A3
Woodbrook Cres	46	A3
Woodbrook Hall	46	A3
Woodbrook Lawn	142	A3
Woodbrook Pk Dublin 16	112	A3
Woodbrook Pk Carp.	46	A3
Woodbrook Sq	46	A3
Woodcliff Hts	61	C3
Wood Dale Cl	125	C3
Wood Dale Cres	125	C2
Wood Dale Dr	125	C2
Wood Dale Grn	125	C2
Wood Dale Gro	125	C2
Wood Dale Oak 2	125	C2
Wood Dale Vw	125	C2
Woodfarm Av	85	D1
Woodfarm Dr	85	D1
Woodfield	126	A2
Woodfield Av	87	D2
Woodfield Pl		
off Woodfield Av	87	D2
Woodford	130	B2
Woodford Av	97	C2
Woodford Business Pk	39	C2
Woodford Cl	97	C2
Woodford Ct	97	C2
Woodford Cres	97	C1
Woodford Downs	97	C2
Woodford Dr	97	C2
Woodford Garth	97	C2
Woodford Grn	97	C2
Woodford Gro	97	C2
Woodford Hts	97	C2
Woodford Hill	97	C2
Woodford Lawn	97	C2
Woodford Meadows	97	C1
Woodford Par	97	C1
Woodford Pk	97	C1
Woodford Pk Rd	97	C2
Woodford Ri	97	C2
Woodford Rd	97	C2
Woodford Ter	97	C2
Woodford Vw	97	C2
Woodford Vil	97	C2
Woodford Wk	97	C2
Woodford Way	97	C1
Woodhaven	102	B3
Woodhazel Cl	38	A3
Woodhazel Ter	38	A3
Woodhazel Way	38	A3
Woodlands Dublin 6	113	D1
Woodlands Grey.	143	D3
Woodlands Mayn.	64	A2
Woodlands 5 Mulh.	32	A3
Woodlands Port.	27	C2
Woodlands, The Dublin 14	113	D2
Woodlands, The Celbr.	66	B2
Woodlands Av Corn.	138	A1
Woodlands Av Still.	116	B3
Woodlands Ct	27	C2
Woodlands Dr Corn.	138	A1
Woodlands Dr Still.	116	B3
Woodlands Pk Black.	116	B2
Woodlands Pk Corn.	138	A1
Woodlands Rd	138	A1
Woodland Vil	102	B1
Woodlawn	39	C3
Woodlawn Av	39	D3
Woodlawn Cl	39	D3
Woodlawn Ct	39	D3
Woodlawn Cres Dublin 14	114	B2
Woodlawn Cres Dublin 17	39	D3
Woodlawn Dr	39	D3
Woodlawn Grn	39	D3
Woodlawn Gro Dublin 14	114	B2
Woodlawn Gro Dublin 17	39	D3
Woodlawn Ind Est	39	C1
Woodlawn Pk Dublin 14	114	B2
Woodlawn Pk Dublin 17	39	D3
Woodlawn Pk Dublin 24	125	C2
Woodlawn Pk 7 D.L.	125	C2
Woodlawn Pk Av	124	B1
Woodlawn Pk Dr	125	C1
Woodlawn Pk Gro	125	C1
Woodlawn Ri	39	D3
Woodlawn Ter	114	B3
Woodlawn Vw	39	D3
Woodlawn Wk	39	D3
Woodlawn Way	39	D3
Woodley Pk	129	D1
Woodley Rd	138	A1
Woodpark Dublin 15	47	D2
Woodpark Dublin 16	128	B2
Wood Quay	144	B3
Woodscape	82	A2
Woodside Dublin 3	81	C1
Woodside Dublin 14	113	D2
Woodside Leix.	68	A1
Woodside Dr	113	D2
Woodside Gro	113	D2
Woodstock Gdns	102	B2
Woodstock Pk	126	A1
Woodstown	125	C2
Woodstown Abbey	125	D2
Woodstown Av	125	C2
Woodstown Cl	125	C2
Woodstown Ct 3	125	C2
Woodstown Dale	125	C2
Woodstown Dr	125	D2
Woodstown Gdns	125	C2
Woodstown Grn	125	D2
Woodstown Heath	125	C2
Woodstown Height	125	D3
Woodstown La	125	C2
Woodstown Lawn	125	C2
Woodstown Meadow	125	D2
Woodstown Par	125	D2
Woodstown Pk	125	C2
Woodstown Pl	125	D3
Woodstown Ri	125	D2
Woodstown Rd 2	125	D2
Woodstown Vale	125	D3
Woodstown Village Cen	125	C2
Woodstown Wk 1	125	D2
Woodstown Way	125	D3
Wood St	144	C4
Woodthorpe 4	130	B1
Woodtown Pk	126	A3
Woodvale Av	46	A1
Woodvale Cres	46	A1
Woodvale Dr	46	A1
Woodvale Garth	46	A1
Woodvale Grn	32	A3
Woodvale Gro	46	A1
Woodvale Pk	32	A3
Woodvale Way	32	A3
Woodview Black.	117	C2
Woodview Celbr.	66	B1
Woodview Lucan	69	D3
Woodview Cl	56	A1
Woodview Cotts	113	C2
Woodview Ct 4	131	C1
Woodview Dr 14	142	A3
Woodview Gro	47	C2
Woodview Hts	28	B3
Woodview Pk Dublin 13	56	A1
Woodview Pk Dublin 15	48	A3
Woodville Av	71	C3
Woodville Cl	71	C3
Woodville Ct	54	A1
Woodville Grn	71	C3
Woodville Gro	71	C3
Woodville Lawn	71	C3
Woodville Rd		
off Botanic Av	78	A1
Woodville Wk	71	C3
Wyattville Cl	138	B3
Wyattville Hill	138	B3
Wyattville Pk	138	B3
Wyattville Rd	138	B3
Wyckham Pk Rd	128	B1
Wyckham Pl	129	C1
Wyckham Pt	129	C1
Wyckham Way	129	C2
Wynberg Pk	118	A3
Wyndham Pk	142	A1
Wynnefield Rd	102	A2
Wynnsward Dr	115	C1
Wynnsward Pk	115	C1
Wyvern Est	134	A3

X

Xavier Av	79	C3

Y

Yale	115	D2
Yankee Ter	117	D3
Yeates Way	85	D3
Yellow Meadows Av	97	C1
Yellow Meadows Dr	97	C1
Yellow Meadows Est	97	C1
Yellow Meadows Gro	97	C1
Yellow Meadows Lawn	97	C1
Yellow Meadows Pk	97	C1
Yellow Meadows Vale	97	C1
Yellow Rd	53	C2
Yellow Walls Rd	19	D1
Yewland Ter	101	C3
York Av	102	A2
York Rd Dublin 4	91	D2
York Rd Dublin 6	102	A2
York Rd D.L.	119	C3
York St	144	C4
York Ter	119	C3

Z

Zion Rd	113	D1
Zoo Rd	88	B1